Teachers as Learners

WITHDRAWN

WITHDRAWN

TEACHERS AS LEARNERS

TOURO COLLEGE LIBRARY
Kings Hwy

SHARON FEIMAN-NEMSER

HARVARD EDUCATION PRESS

CAMBRIDGE, MASSACHUSETTS

KH

Copyright © 2012 by the President and Fellows of Harvard College

All rights reserved. No part of this publication may be reproduced or transmitted in any form or by any means, electronic or mechanical, including photocopy, recording, or any information storage and retrieval systems, without permission in writing from the publisher.

Library of Congress Control Number 2011945498

Paperback ISBN 978-1-61250-113-0
Library Edition ISBN 978-1-61250-114-7

Published by Harvard Education Press,
an imprint of the Harvard Education Publishing Group

Harvard Education Press
8 Story Street
Cambridge, MA 02138

Cover Design: Sarah Henderson

The typefaces used in this book are Sabon for text and Myriad Pro for display.

4/15/13

Much have I learned from my teachers,
more from my colleagues,
and from my students,
most of all.

Babylonian Talmud, Ta'anit 7a

Contents

T eaching is the most prevalent occupation in the United States. Whereas other professions and skilled trades—from nursing to airplane piloting—have developed systems for preparing people for responsible practice, learning how to teach has remained a variable and unsettled enterprise. Widely considered a skill learned primarily "on the job," teaching seems to be something almost anyone can do. Beginning with her own journey into the work as an English major at the University of Michigan, and continuing over the last forty years, Sharon Feiman-Nemser has challenged common-sense conceptions of teaching and what it takes to learn to do it. Through her writing and practice, she has framed the questions and defined the problems central to making teaching learnable.

In 1982, as a first-year doctoral student at Michigan State University, I wrote a "pedagogical autobiography" that Sharon Feiman-Nemser assigned to our class. Spurred by her questions and comments, I revised it several times as I began to appreciate the wild territory that I had been traversing as a new teacher. Under her guidance, I first encountered the problems that would fascinate me for the next several decades. I was fortunate to be nearby as Feiman-Nemser redefined the boundaries and opened new vistas onto the world of teacher learning. Like many others, I was changed and shaped by her imagination and fresh thought.

As a young teacher and scholar, Feiman-Nemser's attention was captured by others who had, by identifying key issues, broken new ground. Her study of their work helped to crystallize her own. In 1975, sociologist Dan Lortie published a landmark study of the occupation of teaching that revealed its pervasive and structural individualism. Based on historical analyses of teaching in the United States and interviews with teachers, Lortie noted that teachers' learning is characterized more by idiosyncratic experience than by professional socialization. The work of teaching becomes familiar as people sit in classrooms as children, and because teaching is an everyday human activity, teachers enter their profession having completed an "apprenticeship of observation" that makes the work seem natural.

Over three-quarters of a century earlier, philosopher and education reformer John Dewey had written about learning to teach as a problem of learning to attend to the minds of learners. Highlighting teaching as intellectual work, he argued for a "laboratory approach" wherein beginning teachers were helped to focus on inquiry into how children think, instead of on the imitation fostered through apprenticeship, in which teaching's surface features dominated beginning teachers' attention.

Dewey also highlighted the special forms of attention to subject matter entailed by teaching, in order to know and use both the psychological and logical aspects of the material to be taught. Still, the teacher knowing the content well enough to teach it was broadly taken for granted. What educated adult couldn't do second-grade arithmetic, discuss *Romeo and Juliet*, or name the causes of the Civil War? It was something of a surprise to many when, in the mid-1980s, educational psychologist Lee Shulman and his colleagues pointed to subject-matter knowledge as the "missing paradigm" in teaching and teacher education, and peeled back the complex and distinctive understanding required to help others learn.

Feiman-Nemser was influenced and impressed by these and other thinkers. She was also not satisfied with the common ways of thinking about training or preparing teachers. Deeply curious, she began to question that which was often taken for granted. She knew that teaching was complex work. She knew it was far from natural. From this standpoint, Feiman-Nemser began to write about "learning to teach" and "teachers as learners." If, as Lortie showed, teachers entered the work impressed with the power of their apprenticeships of observation, then those prior experiences would require challenge and change.

Feiman-Nemser was puzzling over these problems of learning as scholars in many other fields—from reading to science to mathematics—were developing new thinking about cognition. That learners' prior experiences and ideas were profoundly influential on their learning, and sometimes not positively so, was increasingly recognized. These shifts supported Feiman-Nemser's ideas about learning teaching. If teacher students already "knew" what teaching was and what good teachers did, how could their preconceptions and habits be both used and challenged? Teacher education was broadly cited as weak. Teacher educators cited the overwhelmingly conservative influence of school contexts on beginning teachers' practice, a phenomenon that "washed out" the effects of professional preparation. But others placed blame on the curriculum and disconnection of teacher education itself. Feiman-Nemser resisted simple characterizations of the "problem" and instead probed the complex interactions among learners, settings, and programs.

This book gathers in one place the remarkable body of writing that Feiman-Nemser produced, changing the questions, interrogating unexamined assumptions, and providing the tools for changing practice. In a field under siege from many directions, this work is as useful now as it was when she first developed it. By reconceptualizing the terms of reference as she mapped the field, Feiman-Nemser's work is distinctive for its close attention to concepts and language. Why might *structures* of teacher education not be the most important defining features? What is more worthy of attention than the amount or length of *field experience*? What is *student teaching*, and why is not necessarily educative?

Feiman-Nemser continued closely engaging with the basic enterprise of teacher preparation through her studies of the "cross-purposes" embedded in student teachers' school-based practice, her examination of learning in and from formal and informal experience. Central to her ideas is the sheer complexity of harnessing experience and making it educative. This continues into the work on mentoring and induction, two ideas that, like so many others in the field, gained popularity and support without careful unpacking and specification.

This compendium of Sharon Feiman-Nemser's groundbreaking scholarship comprises a conceptual and practical handbook for the study and improvement of teachers' learning, the professional practice of teaching, and the enterprise of teacher education. It provides tools for combating the urge to reduce teaching to a matter of being smart, caring about kids, and getting experience. It offers an antidote to the tendency toward shortsightedness and a set of ideas for building a profession of teaching and its support.

Because the problems on which Feiman-Nemser focuses are endemic to learning teaching, her book is as timely now as ever, providing a foundation for the development of more responsible and responsive approaches to teacher education and support.

Deborah Loewenberg Ball
William H. Payne Collegiate Professor in Education
Arthur F. Thurnau Professor
School of Education
University of Michigan

Investigating Teacher Learning
Framing an Inquiry

Be patient toward all that is unsolved in your heart
and try to love the questions themselves.
—*Rainer Maria Rilke*

In their review of the history of teacher education research over the past hundred years, Marilyn Cochran-Smith and Kim Fries (2005) identify four overlapping periods. In each period, they argue, researchers framed the "problem" of teacher education in different ways, and that framing shaped the researchers' questions, methods, and findings. From the 1920s to the 1950s, researchers construed teacher education as a *curricular* problem, studying where and how teachers should be prepared and what they should know and be able to do. From the late 1950s through the 1970s, researchers treated teacher education as a *training* problem, identifying specific teacher behaviors that correlated with student achievement and treating those behaviors as dependent variables in research on teacher training. Beginning in the 1980s, the language of *teacher learning* replaced the language of teacher training as researchers studied teacher thinking and investigated the impact of teacher education on teachers' knowledge, attitudes, and beliefs. Since the 1990s, researchers have framed teacher education as a *policy* problem, studying aspects of teacher education policy such as certification requirements, academic majors, teacher testing, and alternate routes to teaching that are likely to affect teacher quality.

My own engagement with questions about teacher learning began in the mid-1960s, when I became a high school English teacher and found myself completely absorbed in the process of learning to teach. It continued through the 1970s, during my doctoral studies and early years as a teacher educator/scholar, as I sought ways to study and nurture teacher learning outside the dominant behaviorist training paradigm. It blossomed in the 1980s and 1990s at Michigan State University, where my colleagues and I pioneered research on teacher thinking and teacher learning and experimented with new models of teacher education. And it continues today in my studies of new teacher induction and my work with beginning teachers and teacher educators.

This book has grown out of my fascination with how people learn to teach and improve at teaching over time within an evolving body of scholarship on teaching, teacher education, and teacher learning. The essays collected in this volume document and reflect a lifetime of engagement with a changing field—one that continues to be the focal point of fundamental questions about the purposes of education and the quality of teaching and learning. In this introduction, I describe the insights, experiences, theories, and research models that formed and sustained that engagement over more than three decades. Three overarching themes emerge and run through the essays that follow: teacher learning as a continuum, rather than a finite event; the necessary—but problematic—role of experience in learning to teach; and teacher learning as a result of the interaction of person, program, and setting.

I recently heard a commencement speaker advise graduating seniors to treat the next decade of their lives as a time to search for enduring commitments. "Find a problem that you can wrap yourself around," he urged. Listening to him, I thought to myself that, in my twenties, I had indeed found such a problem, one that held my abiding interest as a scholar and teacher educator and one that has evolved into an important focus of research with significant implications for educational policy and practice. I hope this book and the essays in it will spark the interest of a new generation of young teachers, teacher educators, and scholars.

FINDING THE QUESTIONS

I began my teaching career with a teaching certificate but virtually no formal preparation. As an undergraduate at the University of Michigan, I majored in English while sampling a rich array of courses, mainly in the humanities. I also completed the minimum requirements for a teaching certificate by spending a semester in Sheffield, England, where I student taught in a primary school and a secondary modern school. As a young American with a midwestern accent, I was an object of interest and, when President Kennedy was assassinated, of genuine sympathy. It amused me to see my young pupils jump to their feet and call out in unison, "Good morning, Mrs. Jones; good morning, Miss Feiman," when the teacher and I entered the classroom. My most vivid memories of the secondary school experience are the tea cart that appeared every day at 11:00 a.m. and the yellow custard poured over dessert at lunch.

After traveling in Europe "on five dollars a day," I returned to the U.S. to complete my undergraduate studies, which included writing an honors thesis on Thomas Hardy and taking a required course in the history of American education. The latter did nothing to alter my low opinion of education courses. I also did a stint of student teaching at University High School, where I invited folk singer Ed McCurty, who was performing at the Golden Vanity in downtown Ann Arbor, to come and sing English and Scottish ballads for my classes.

After graduation, I decided to pursue an MA in English literature at the University of Chicago rather than a Master of Arts in Teaching (MAT) degree at Harvard.[1] I welcomed the heady atmosphere of the University of Chicago and relished my graduate studies, which included a heavy dose of *new criticism*, a form of literary study that emphasizes the close reading of texts without reference to outside influences such as the reader's response, the author's intentions, or the intellectual and historical context of the work. [2] I wrote a major paper on a poem by Marianne Moore, studied Mark Twain and his writings with Walter Blair, and took a fascinating course in linguistics. One winter day, I saw a notice for a part-time job teaching English at the University of Chicago Laboratory High School. I applied and got the job, filling in for a teacher on leave while completing my master's degree. In the spring, the principal offered me a full-time position teaching tenth-grade English, which I accepted.

Of the career options open to women of my generation, teaching met the requirements for socially useful, personally meaningful work. I loved learning, enjoyed working with young people, and wanted to share my enthusiasm for literature. My limited qualifications included strong subject-matter knowledge and some positive experiences working with children as a Sunday school teacher, camp counselor, social work intern, and student teacher. I muddled through my first year of teaching, relying on materials and advice supplied by the department chair. Then an opportunity came my way that had a lasting effect on my ideas about teaching and teacher learning.

Jim McCampbell and Darlene Friedman, two talented English teachers, invited me to work with them on a new curriculum. The Lab School had received funding from the State of Illinois to support teacher-initiated curriculum projects in the disciplines, part of the curriculum reforms of the 1960s.[3] I spent the next two summers and the intervening school year working closely with Jim and Darlene as we designed, piloted, and evaluated a unit on the relationship between writer, reader, and text.

In our early conversations, Jim and Darlene discussed their philosophy of teaching English and some of the pedagogical challenges they faced. Many of our students resisted the close reading of literature. They also treated writing as a school assignment, not a search for effective ways to communicate important ideas or represent their experiences. Gradually, we began to visualize a way to help students get inside the art and science of reading and writing by exploring firsthand the role of writer and reader. Our curriculum, "Literary Man: Writer and Reader" (Feiman, Friedman, & McCampbell, 1968), began with a series of exercises that spanned three weeks and resulted in students producing a piece of imaginative writing based on a persistent memory. Next, the student writers handed their pieces to a student reader, who wrote a review of the work. Then the student writers wrote back, responding to the appropriateness of the reader's interpretation in light of their intentions. The unit was built around cycles of writing, reading, and responding, as students produced poems, short stories, and other artistic creations. Along the way, we read professional writers' accounts of writing, comparing their insights and experiences with our own.

Jim wrote up the unit, lesson by lesson, using a format I had not encountered before. Each lesson had an objective, learning activity, and assessment. I still remember my "aha" feeling—here was a new kind of strategic ends/ means thinking. Until then, most of my planning had consisted of figuring out what my students or I would be doing in class. I did not clarify what I wanted students to learn, consider what sort of task or activity would promote that learning, or reflect on how I could determine whether it was happening. This was my introduction to a systematic approach to planning (what today might be called *backward mapping*), and it changed how I thought about planning and helped me internalize the purpose of teaching— ensuring that students learn. Later, in studies of preservice teachers, I characterized this conceptual change as a "transition to pedagogical thinking."[4]

The next year, each of us piloted the unit in our ninth-, tenth-, and eleventh-grade classes. I watched Jim and Darlene teach, and they, in turn, observed me. Seeing two excellent teachers teaching the same curriculum to students of different ages was a rich learning experience. I saw how different classes responded to the same activities and how Jim and Darlene adapted and extended our plans in new ways based upon their students' reactions.

Because I knew where they were headed, I could appreciate the decisions they made on their feet as well as the long-term adaptations and extensions. By the time I taught the unit, I had concrete models for how to enact the goals and activities we had designed. The second summer, I was assigned the task of writing up the results of our pilot tests—drawing on lesson plans, observers' field notes, and student work.

Over the years, this experience has been an important touchstone for me, embodying vital lessons about teaching and laying a foundation for my thinking about teacher education and learning to teach. Working with Jim and Darlene helped me crystallize the kind of teacher I wanted to be and eventually help others become. It gave me vivid examples of content-rich, learner-centered teaching. It taught me that, with clear purposes, a teacher can adjust her plans in the moment and take advantage of the unexpected. Before I ever read John Dewey, encountered the notion of pedagogical content knowledge, or studied constructivist learning theories, I had a powerful object lesson in how to transform disciplinary concepts into learning activities and use students' experiences to teach the curriculum. I also experienced the power of trusting students.

I learned all this not through formal study or deliberate mentoring, but by doing the work of teaching in the company of more experienced practitioners. Through our conversations, observations, reflections, and writing, I gained access to Jim's and Darlene's teaching practices, knowledge, and ways of thinking. In the process of developing the unit, I learned what they thought high school students should be learning in English, and I was inducted into a new way of thinking about planning and teaching. When observing them, I studied how they set up their classrooms and interacted with students as well as how they pulled off the different activities we had designed. Watching them teach our unit deepened my understanding of how teachers can respect content knowledge and student thinking at the same time. My learning was a product of my participation, as a novice, in the work of curriculum development and teaching with two outstanding teachers. As the experienced members of the group, Jim and Darlene clearly had more to contribute. Understandably, I did a lot more watching and listening, but I always felt that my questions and ideas were respected and my participation valued.[5]

Imagine my disequilibrium when, some years later, I entered a doctoral program in curriculum and instruction and found myself in a department closely associated with *competency-based teacher education* (CBTE). Having experienced teaching as an intellectual practice and learning to teach as an experimental, collaborative adventure, I was allergic to the behavioral studies of teaching and teacher training that dominated the discourse. I looked for research that captured the complexities and uncertainties of life in classrooms and models of teacher education that respected the intellectual, relational, and practical demands of teaching. I often felt buffeted between what Merle Borrowman (1965) called "the liberal and the technical" in teacher education. Over time, I began to forge an integrated position based on disparate strands of scholarship, formative experiences as a beginning teacher educator, and the wisdom of practice.

THE LIBERAL VERSUS THE TECHNICAL

As a doctoral student in the late 1960s and early 1970s, I lived in what often felt like two cultures—the humanistic culture of educational history and philosophy, and the scientific or pseudoscientific culture of research on teaching and teacher education. For the first time, I took education courses worth their salt, courses that gave me conceptual tools for understanding teaching and teacher education in the context of public schooling.[6] These liberal learning opportunities did what Israel Scheffler (1989) says foundations courses are supposed to do: "continually raise the sorts of questions that concern the larger goals, setting and meaning of educational practice" (pp. 92–93). I learned how teaching became "women's true profession" (Hoffman, 2003), why teacher education has such a bad reputation, what aspirations and tensions shape the U.S. vision of public education, and how progressive education got derailed. Studying ways of knowing and the work of analytic philosophers helped me think about disciplinary knowledge for teaching; spot educational slogans; and unpack basic concepts like learning, teaching, education, training, play, and competence. My work in the philosophy of education formed a lifelong habit of collaborating with philosophers, shaped my interest in the epistemology of teaching and teacher education, and sensitized me to issues of language and meaning.[7]

My studies of teaching and teacher education offered a different kind of intellectual fare. The empirical study of teaching was still in its infancy, and researchers had only recently begun to investigate classroom teaching directly. Some researchers focused on describing "the way teaching is" (Jackson, 1966); others sought to relate teaching behaviors (*process* variables) to learning outcomes (*product* variables). Early reviews of this work reflect a cautious optimism, noting the immature state of the field but expressing faith in the prospect of empirical knowledge that could be useful to teachers and teacher educators (Dunkin & Biddle, 1974; Rosenshine & Furst, 1973). I doubted the possibility of discovering lawful relationships between teaching and learning independent of content, context, and purpose.

The thin knowledge base did not prevent teacher educators from embracing competency-based teacher education (alternatively, *performance-based teacher education*, or PBTE), which presumes that teachers can and should be trained in "validated" skills needed to perform core tasks of teaching (Smith, 1969). In 1968, the year I began my doctoral program, the American Association of Colleges of Teacher Education (1968) issued performance-based standards for teacher education programs, the U.S. Office of Education funded the design of ten model CBTE programs (Clarke, 1971), and the field was caught up in the short-lived CBTE/PBTE movement. I recognized that good teaching involves skilled performance and even saw the merits of some training as part of a larger conception of teacher education. However, I questioned the elevation of research knowledge over other sources of knowledge and warrants for action in teaching, and I identified more with the critics than the proponents of CBTE (Broudy, 1972).

My humanistic orientation and recent teaching experience drew me to a different research tradition, represented by two groundbreaking ethnographic studies, *Life in Classrooms* (Jackson, 1968) and *Complexities of an Urban Classroom* (Smith & Geoffrey, 1968). Both books documented the complexities and uncertainties of classroom teaching. They resonated with the work I knew firsthand and captured what was missing from efforts to link teaching behaviors to student learning. Philip Jackson's image of teaching and learning contrasted sharply with the linear, deterministic view that informed the dominant research paradigm, as the following passage from *Life in Classrooms* illustrates.[8]

> Teaching is an opportunistic process. Neither the teacher nor the students can predict with any certainty exactly what will happen next. Plans are forever going awry and unexpected opportunities for the attainment of educational goals are constantly emerging . . . Although most teachers make plans in advance, they are aware as they make them of the likelihood of change . . . They know, or come to know, that the path of educational progress more closely resembles the *flight of a butterfly than the flight of a bullet*. (emphasis added, p. 167)

The idea of teaching as the skillful chasing of butterflies did not figure into discussions about a science of teaching or even "a scientific basis for the art of teaching" (Gage, 1977).[9] Although some scholars rejected the possibility of applying the aims and methods of science to teaching (Highet, 1955; Stephens, 1967), others maintained that "although teaching requires artistry, it can be subjected to scientific scrutiny" (Gage, 1972, p. 58). This was not a new theme. Since the 1890s, scholars had been pursuing and debating the possibility of a science of education (Lagemann, 2000), and critics and supporters of teacher education had cited the lack of such knowledge as a major weakness. But things heated up in the 1960s and early 1970s, when federal funding became available and research on teaching and teacher effectiveness made it possible to imagine a performance-based education for teachers.

Of the myriad studies on teaching at the time, two programs of research—one focused on classroom management and the other on classroom interaction—spoke to my teacher sensibilities, although I wondered whether prospective or beginning teachers would find this research useful.[10] I will briefly summarize this research as examples of the kind of scholarship that intrigued and troubled me.

In the late 1950s, Jacob Kounin and his colleagues at Wayne State University began a program of research on how teachers deal with *pupil deviancy* (whispering, talking out of turn, inattention—behaviors familiar to many teachers). This research evolved into studies of classroom management, which generated a set of variables that correlated strongly with pupils' behavior (Kounin, 1970). For example, Kounin found that good classroom managers are alert monitors, aware of what is going on at all times. They demonstrate this quality of "withitness" (eyes in the back of the head) by disciplining the "deviant" student, not an innocent bystander, and by not ignoring major problems to deal with minor ones. Kounin also found that successful managers could sustain one activity while doing something else at the same time ("overlappingness"); they maintain the continuity of their lessons without unnecessary interruptions or confusion ("smoothness"); and they pace their lessons appropriately ("momentum"). While some of these findings seem self-evident, I liked the idea of developing a distinctive vocabulary for talking about classroom management and appreciated the shift away from a focus on pupil deviancy. Still, I doubted whether learning about such research would do much to promote these qualities in new teachers.[11]

A second program of research on teaching, conducted by Ned Flanders, was very popular with teacher educators. Flanders posited the *law of two-thirds*, which says that two-thirds of classroom time is devoted to talk, and two-thirds of the talking is done by the teacher.[12] Flanders developed the most widely used instrument for observing classroom behavior, the Flanders Interaction Analysis Category system (FIAC), which consists of seven categories of teacher verbal behavior and two categories of pupil verbal behavior. Designed for live observation, the instrument requires the observer to categorize classroom verbal behavior at three-second intervals and then calculate an I/D (indirect/direct) ratio for the teacher. Flanders's (1970) research provided evidence that *indirect* teaching (questioning and discussion vs. lecturing and demonstration; frequent pupil-to-pupil interaction; frequent praise and infrequent criticism) is associated with improved student learning and/or more positive student attitudes toward teachers and school. This fed the inference, not supported by the data, that indirect teaching was better than direct teaching.[13]

Despite this misrepresentation, teacher educators adopted the FIAC as a tool for promoting indirect teaching, perhaps because it fit their teaching philosophy or because they assumed its effectiveness had been established. I learned about Flanders's interaction analysis in a course on clinical supervision, where it was presented as a basis for giving student teachers objective feedback on their teaching and fostering the behaviors associated with indirect teaching. My penchant for progressive pedagogy, my lack of sophistication as a researcher, and my inexperience as a student-teaching supervisor led me to experiment with the instrument when I supervised student teachers in the South Bronx.[14] I discovered that its simplicity was both a strength and a weakness. Interaction analysis allowed me to document how frequently a student teacher asked questions or presented information, but it revealed nothing about the nature or appropriateness of the questions or the presentation.

The direct study of teaching challenged the long-standing view that guidance in how to teach could be derived from what philosophers and, more recently, psychologists had to say about thinking and learning. Historically, these academic disciplines were considered the main sources of knowledge about teaching and learning. For generations, teachers-in-training encountered a mixture of learning theories, philosophical principles, and practical prescriptions, which they were somehow supposed to put into practice. With the prospect of scientific knowledge of teaching in sight, teacher educators could move beyond "romanticized lectures, on the one hand, and fuzzy or unplanned practical experience, on the other," and give teachers solid training in how to teach, as the authors of a major review of research at the time proclaimed:

> We are genuinely in sight of the theoretical principles, the operational measures, and even the developmental technology for moving onto a per-

formance-based method of appraising teaching . . . it is no longer wishful thinking to foresee a performance-based system for the certification of teachers. (Peck & Tucker, 1973, p. 171)

In his two-year study of teacher education, James Conant (1963), former president of Harvard University, had characterized educational psychology as "common sense" and criticized "those terrible methods courses" for wasting students' time (p. 137). Conant eschewed general methods courses because "there is no agreement on a common body of knowledge that all teachers should have before taking their first teaching job" (p. 141). Such knowledge, he argued, should be based on empirically verified findings, not personal preference. That left practice teaching, which Conant viewed as "the one indisputably essential element of teacher education" (p. 142). But Dewey (1904) had detailed the limitations of an apprenticeship model of learning to teach, and researchers had recently documented the undesirable effects of student teaching on student teachers' attitudes and behaviors (Hoy, 1968; Iannaconne, 1963).[15] Moreover, studies of teacher training were showing that technical skills could be taught, and such training was more effective in changing teachers' behavior than traditional methods courses (Rosenshine & Furst, 1973). The stage was set for a radical reform of traditional teacher education—or so the leaders of competency-based teacher education believed.

Advanced by the U.S. Office of Education, the American Association of Colleges of Teacher Education, and a group of reform-minded universities and educational researchers, CBTE stimulated considerable interest at the time. The logic of designing teacher education programs around the competencies needed to carry out the tasks of teaching was compelling, and the possibility of assessing teacher candidates' progress on the basis of performance appealing, especially at a time of great concern about equity and accountability. But what were those core competencies that beginning teachers needed to master? How could they be identified, developed, and assessed? The very concept of teaching competencies proved elusive. How big or small should they be? Were they generic or subject specific? The behaviors validated in studies of teaching (e.g., clarity, enthusiasm, a business-like demeanor, "withitness") hardly added up to a comprehensive view of teaching; nor did they address the normative question of what constitutes "good" teaching.

Designers of CBTE programs had replaced the typical structures of courses, credits, and time with small curricular units called *modules*, each of which specified objectives, learning experiences, and assessments.[16] Michigan State University had the most developed design, with more than two thousand seven hundred modules (Houston, 1968)! The sheer number of individual competencies, ridiculous on the face of it, called into question the possibility of tracking each student's progress toward mastery. A quality of unreality permeated the whole enterprise and its rhetoric.

The signature pedagogy of CBTE was *microteaching*, a system of training in the skills of teaching built around cycles of practice with feedback in controlled situations (Allen & Ryan, 1969). Developed at Stanford in the early 1960s, microteaching combined new video technology with the "technical skills" approach to teaching. In the microteaching clinic, teacher candidates planned and taught a short (five to ten minutes) lesson to a small group of students. The lesson was recorded for immediate viewing by the candidate, who also received a critique and advice from trained supervisors. Then the candidate retaught the lesson to a new group of students in an effort to improve his performance of the specified skill. The subject of numerous field studies, microteaching provided the foundation for the design of training materials called Mini-Courses, each organized around a different teaching skill (Borg, Kelly, Langer, & Gall, 1964).[17]

Considered a major breakthrough, microteaching offered teacher candidates a chance to acquire skills and develop confidence in a scaled-down teaching context before facing all the complexities of classroom teaching. Such training was contrasted with student teaching, where supervision was uneven, critic teachers rarely modeled exemplary practice, and candidates mainly learned through trial and error. Some leaders even proposed that student teaching should be replaced with systematic training in teaching skills followed by a genuine internship (Smith, 1969).

The idea of practicing complex skills in a simplified setting foreshadows contemporary calls for a return to *practice-centered teacher education* (Ball & Cohen, 1999; Ball & Forzani, 2009; Grossman & McDonald, 2009). Still, it leaves open the question of what the core skills consist of and how to help beginning teachers transfer those skills to the classroom, integrate them into a coherent performance, and develop the professional judgment to decide what to do when. Furthermore, despite their structural differences, skills training and practice teaching often share the same overarching purpose—developing technical proficiency. In an essay on the relationship of theory and practice in education, Dewey (1904) argues for an alternative approach, the "laboratory view," directed toward a different overarching purpose. His essay gave me a way of thinking about the development of practical skills that emphasized their principled use.

Dewey acknowledges that teachers need management and instructional skills, but he distinguishes routine behavior from intelligent conduct, mechanical performance from actions governed by purpose and the awareness of meaning. Instead of turning out "masters of the craft," a goal associated with the technical tradition of the normal school, teacher education should develop "the intellectual methods required for personal and independent mastery of practical skills" (p. 144). According to Dewey, the supreme mark of a teacher is the ability to interpret and activate students' motivational and intellectual processes. This means seeing what is going on in students' minds and figuring out how to engage them in worthwhile learning. To develop teachers' mental habits and help them bring subject matter and educational principles to bear in decisions about what and how to teach, Dewey outlines a sequence of "laboratory" experiences. These include classroom observation of students' "mind activity"; curriculum study to see what it means for students of different ages to learn mathematics, geography, and science; and finally, designing and teaching sequences of lessons to particular groups of students. Even at this stage of practical work, Dewey cautions against too close supervision and critique, lest it undermine the student teacher's developing sense of independence and intellectual authority.

For me, Dewey's essay was a raft in the sea of CBTE. It offered a view of teachers as practical intellectuals, students of subject matter and children's thinking who learn from experience, including their own experience as learners. It underscored the place of dispositions—habits of mind and heart—in teaching and learning to teach. It offered a vision of liberal/professional teacher education that contrasted sharply with the narrow, technical views of teaching and teacher training associated with CBTE. To be fair, thoughtful advocates like my advisor, Margaret Lindsey, never claimed that all teaching could be broken down into trainable elements or that the job of teacher preparation consisted solely of skills training. She believed that effective teachers exhibit knowledge and skills that can be identified and taught, and the job of teacher preparation is to teach that as part of the foundation for developing a mature practice (Lindsey, 1973).

But who should decide what knowledge and skills were foundational? How did one's vision of good teaching enter into that formulation? If research on teaching could not provide a coherent knowledge base, where would such knowledge come from? How could university-based teacher educators find appropriate schools and teachers to partner with? Would preparing "thoughtful and alert students of teaching" ready beginning teachers for the challenges and responsibilities they would face in the classroom? My doctoral studies had taught me more about what *not* to do in teacher preparation than what to do, and I brought many questions to my first academic position in teacher education.

CREATING A LIBERAL/PROFESSIONAL SYNTHESIS

With doctorate in hand, I returned to the University of Chicago, this time as director of the Master of Science in Teaching (MST) program, the elementary equivalent of the well-established secondary MAT program. Here was my first opportunity to work on the question of how to nurture a reflective stance while developing the practical know-how needed for beginning teaching. Dewey's influence was evident in the program's embrace of a laboratory approach, the emphasis on reflective thinking, and the underlying view of teaching as a form of situated inquiry. My exposure to CBTE was visible in several experiments with microteaching. To help students get inside the intellectual and practical demands of teaching, we depended on experienced (cooperating) teachers and on a local teacher center.

Alongside my preservice experiment in inquiry-oriented teacher preparation, I got involved in the teacher center movement, a national, grassroots effort to support the growth and learning of teachers interested in open education.[18] In joining this community of progressive educators, I tapped into a rich vein of thought about teachers as learners and the conditions that support their learning. The developmental approach of teacher centers, with its faith in teachers' capacity for self-directed learning, contrasted sharply with conventional inservice training, which treated teachers as lacking in professional skills.

The MST program involved a year of graduate study made up of foundations and methods courses following by student teaching. I kept the basic program structure intact but added a yearlong clinical component to serve as an integrating core. Designed to help students connect theory and practice, the practicum had three components, each combining university study with work in schools. In the fall, students took a seminar, "Conceptions of Education and Schooling," and did a month of participant/observation in an elementary classroom.[19] In the winter, they participated in a curriculum and instruction lab and spent three mornings a week in the same classroom, tutoring individual children and teaching small groups. In the spring, they student taught and participated in a seminar on the problems of teaching.

We introduced Dewey's concept of reflective thinking by having students investigate a question or problem that stood out to them as they observed the opening weeks of school. We helped them identify something that troubled or surprised them and turn it into a question that could be investigated through more focused observations. For example, if a student marveled at how smoothly the classroom was running, she could try to figure out what the teacher was doing to create and maintain a smoothly running classroom. If a student felt the teacher was ignoring a "needy" child, he could document the interactions the child had with peers and the teacher, and try to learn more about that child. The main point was to investigate a matter of genuine concern and gather some data to shed light on the situation. After collecting and analyzing their data, students wrote up their inquiries, tracing the evolution of their thinking about the initial problem or situation.

At this point, we read Dewey's (1933) account of reflective thinking, a kind of thinking that begins in "a state of doubt, perplexity or mental difficulty" and involves "an act of searching, hunting, inquiring to find material that will resolve the doubt, settle and dispose of the perplexity" (p. 12). As students recognized parallels between Dewey's formulation and their own inquiry, the idea of reflective thinking took on meaning, and their experiences provided a basis for identifying conditions that support meaningful learning for teachers and their pupils.

To help students develop a beginning instructional repertoire, I tried introducing them to three models of teaching drawn from a larger collection of instructional models developed by Bruce Joyce and Marsha Weil (1972).[20] The models represent conceptual and practical maps for creating different kinds of learning environments. Each one is framed around a set of operational principles that specify what the teacher and students must do to enact the model and link these interactions to particular learning outcomes. I demonstrated each model, and we studied the underlying theories. Then students built lessons around the models, which they taught to their peers, refined based on group feedback, and tried out with small groups of children.

Instead of adapting their actions to children's responses, guided by an understanding of the model's intent, students concentrated on making the model work (e.g., "doing a Taba lesson"). I realized that until students clarified their own instructional purposes and developed their own hypotheses about the relationship between ends and means, they could not treat the models as suggestions to adapt rather than ready-made solutions. So I altered the approach, focusing on the intellectual demands of instructional activities as a basis for structuring and understanding pupils' responses. Students designed learning tasks and activities, which they tried out on their peers. Feedback generally led to a clarification of the activity's purpose, a refinement of the verbal instructions or materials, and a consideration of alternative approaches. The shared planning, peer teaching, and reflection enabled my students to concentrate more on the reactions of their pupils during interactive teaching and reinforced the need for clarity of purpose and continuity in learning.[21]

Adjusting their teaching to pupils' responses and taking responsibility for their own learning were key themes during student teaching. Student teachers were expected to "(a) plan and implement learning activities appropriate to [their] goals and the developmental needs of [their] students; (b) develop meaningful activities in several curricular areas that reflect an understanding of what it means to make progress in these subjects; (c) take charge of instructional and non-instructional situations; (d) modify and adjust [their] plans on the spot and in further planning on the basis of formal and informal feedback about children's learning; (e) take an active responsibility for improving [their] competence as a teacher by careful reflection and specific actions" (Feiman, 1979, p. 76). Using this framework, students outlined the specific responsibilities they wished to undertake and identified aspects of teaching they needed to work on. In the weekly "problems of teaching" seminar, they took turns presenting written accounts of problematic situations and leading the discussions. These meetings offered additional practice in reflective thinking—locating and describing problems, imagining alternative solutions, rehearsing consequences, and choosing appropriate courses of action.

The student-teaching framework, with its emphasis on intellectual responsibility and personal initiative, recalled Dewey's (1904) recommendation that during the apprenticeship phase, "the student (teacher) should be given as much responsibility and initiative as he is capable of taking" (p. 270). It also reflected Dewey's (1933) stress on cultivating the attitudes that make up a reflective disposition, such as open-mindedness and intellectual responsibility. In this spirit, I was looking for a readiness on the student teachers' part to consider thoughtfully whatever came up in their experience.

A general framework of expectations and responsibilities could work as a meaningful basis for student-teacher learning only in a community of practice where people shared a common language and vision of the work. We built such a community with the help of methods instructors, cooperating teachers, and the Teacher Curriculum Work Center, a local teacher center that had recently opened in the neighborhood YMCA. MST students studied learner-centered approaches to subject-matter teaching and learning in their methods courses, and then worked out the practical implications with their cooperating teachers and the teacher center staff.

Cooperating teachers were chosen for their interest in open education and their desire to serve as teachers of teaching. A few taught at the University of Chicago Laboratory School or at a local Montessori school, but most taught in public schools on the south side of Chicago that were participating in a community-initiated project to bring open education to public schools. We met regularly with cooperating teachers to discuss our joint work with student teachers. I still recall one meeting in which Vivian Paley, a kindergarten teacher at the University of Chicago Laboratory School, explained her approach to working with student teachers: "I simply say out loud all the things that are going through my head. That way, my student teachers can see how I think about teaching—how I interpret what children do, make on-the-spot decisions, plan, connect what goes on in my classroom with larger issues and concerns."[22]

The idea that student teaching could open a window on teacher thinking was revolutionary at the time. Even a sympathetic scholar like Philip Jackson (1968) had described the "conceptual simplicity" of teacher thinking, and teachers' practical knowledge and understanding had not yet become a legitimate focus of research. Paley's practice provoked my thinking about the role of experienced teachers in novices' learning and influenced later research on student teaching and mentoring.

Another critical resource in helping MST students to develop an understanding of active, content-rich teaching and learning, and to acquire some curricular and instructional tools to enact that vision, was our local teacher center. The Teacher Curriculum Work Center provided a supportive environment where teachers could get help tailoring curriculum for their classrooms. Many of the cooperating teachers were regular visitors, and they and their student teachers often met there to plan lessons, explore curriculum materials, attend a workshop, and interact with other teachers.

The Teacher Curriculum Work Center was part of a national network of centers that had sprung up since the early 1970s. Many were inspired by curriculum projects of the 1960s that emphasized active learning and efforts by American educators to learn more informal, inquiry-oriented ways of working with children associated with English primary schools.[23] Kathleen Devaney (1978), director of the Teachers' Centers Exchange, dubbed them "teachers' centers" because they "accept teachers' own definitions of their learning needs and rely on their intrinsic motivation for collegiality and professionalism as incentives to participate" (p. 15).[24] Some centers included a staff of advisors composed of former teachers who worked with current teachers in their classrooms, solving problems, bringing new ideas, demonstrating alternative ways of working with children and materials, and provoking thinking.[25]

Some observers criticized teachers' centers as make-and-take operations; others countered that, at their best, teachers' centers were minds-on as well as hands-on. This was more often the case in centers that combined curriculum workshops with advisory services. In an interview study of sixty teachers working with advisors to implement more open approaches to instruction, researchers from Educational Testing Services found that teachers' confidence and competence in using informal curriculum depended on their ability to articulate clear connections between the surface curriculum of their classrooms and their purposes and priorities for children's learning (Bussis, Chittenden, & Amarel, 1976).

I was inspired by teacher centers' respect for the complexity and seriousness of teachers' work and by their faith in teachers' potential for professional growth. I thought of my own experience of learning to teach, in which curriculum development and collegial exchange played such a formative role. I saw the Teacher Curriculum Work Center as an open classroom for teachers, and wondered whether providing an environment where teachers could express their own learning needs and get help working on them would lead teachers to create classrooms where students could in turn reveal *their* learning needs so that teachers could support them. The teacher center literature was full of ideas and claims about teacher learning that raised many questions and called out for conceptual clarification and empirical study. These questions led me to study the Teacher Curriculum Work Center and undertake conceptual research on *development* as a metaphor for *teacher learning*.[26]

The term *staff development* had come into vogue, reflecting a new appreciation for the learning needs of practicing teachers in the context of school change. It also signaled a rejection, at least in some quarters, of inservice training, with its deficit view of teachers, reliance on outside experts, and disregard for the "social realities of teaching" (Lieberman & Miller, 1978). Curriculum development projects in the 1960s and change-agent projects in the 1970s had shown that teachers need time and help to work out the practical implications of reforms, and that without teachers' active and willing participation, not much changes (McLaughlin & Marsh, 1978). These ideas were common sense to teachers' center leaders.

When Congress passed a national teacher center bill as part of the 1976 Education Amendments, my teacher center colleagues and I felt a mixture of hope and skepticism—hope for the possibility of funding, skepticism because of the likely co-opting of the teachers' center vision. [27] The teacher center federal legislation combined aspects of grassroots teachers' centers with the experience of federally funded training complexes and educational renewal centers. These competing images rested on different assumptions about what teachers need, how they learn, and who should control their education and training. Watching the teachers' center concept get swallowed up by the federal program reinforced my preference for close-to-the-ground research and practice over policy as means of improving teaching and learning to teach.

Directing the MST program at the University of Chicago and participating in the teacher center movement had given me a chance to consolidate a stance on teacher preparation and begin thinking about teacher learning in more systematic ways. Working closely with MST students and cooperating teachers piqued my curiosity about how intending teachers transform professional knowledge into practice and how experienced teachers contribute to that learning process. I also wondered how teacher education at an elite university in a small program with top-notch students and thoughtful teacher colleagues compared with teacher education in more mainstream settings. When Lee Shulman and Judy Lanier invited me to join the Institute for Research on Teaching at Michigan State University, I was drawn by the prospect of working in a community of researchers interested in the mental life of teachers. I knew that I could find thoughtful teacher collaborators wherever I went, but finding a critical mass of research colleagues interested in teacher thinking and teacher learning was unheard of in 1978.

FINDING AN INTELLECTUAL HOME

The 1980s and 1990s were heady times at Michigan State University.[28] During these decades, the fields of research on teaching and teacher education came into their own, spurred by programs of research at MSU, Stanford, and the University of Wisconsin, and by the work of individual scholars in other institutions.[29] While researchers pursued a knowledge base for teaching and learning to teach for understanding, MSU, along with other research universities affiliated with the Holmes Group based there, undertook a major reform of teacher education that called for high entry standards, graduate-level professional preparation, extended internships, and the creation of professional development schools.[30] These research and reform initiatives took place within a broad national debate about how to improve the quality of teaching.

During my twenty years on the faculty, Michigan State University was home to a series of national research centers, starting with the Institute for Research on Teaching (IRT), established in 1976; followed by the National Center for Research on Teacher Education (NCRTE), launched in 1985; and finally the National Center for Research on Teacher Learning (NCRTL), which followed in 1991. MSU also participated in the National Partnership for Excellence and Accountability in Teaching (NPEAT), which supported research on promising policies and practices for improving teaching. Under the auspices of these centers, I was involved in a set of research projects that redefined the challenge of teacher education from one of training to one of learning (Cochran-Smith & Fries, 2005). These projects advanced a larger conversation about what teachers need to know, care about, and be able to do, and what and how teacher education contributes to that learning. They also served as training and dissertation research sites for doctoral students in teacher education.

All along, I was deeply involved in the work of teacher education. During the 1980s, with a team of faculty colleagues and doctoral students, I led the redesign of a required introductory education course offered in multiple sections each term, year after year, until it was phased out by the new five-year, field-based teacher education program (Feiman & Featherstone, 1992).[31] In the 1990s, I codirected one of four teams offering a version of that program and worked in a professional development school that played a leading role in developing the yearlong internship component (Carroll, Featherstone, Featherstone, Feiman-Nemser, & Roosevelt, 2007). These practical experiments were sites for self-study by participating faculty, doctoral students, and collaborating teachers as well as opportunities to test and extend our thinking on teacher learning.

In keeping with the cognitive turn in psychology, the Institute for Research on Teaching embraced a view of teaching as clinical work dependent on diagnosis, judgment, and decision making. This was partly a reaction to the behavioral emphasis of competency-based teacher education and process-product research. IRT researchers pioneered the study of teacher thinking, planning, and decision making, opening the field to new research perspectives from cognitive science, anthropology, and other interpretive traditions, and to new areas of investigation. At first, people seemed to believe that if researchers discovered how good teachers think and plan, teacher educators could teach those ways of thinking and planning to prospective teachers. Few asked how teachers *learned* to think or plan like that, which was my starting point.

My IRT project, Knowledge Use in Learning to Teach (KULT), focused on how prospective teachers construct knowledge about teaching during preservice preparation. Between 1982 and 1984, we followed six elementary-education students through two years of undergraduate teacher education, documenting courses and field experiences and interviewing students about what they were learning and how it would help them in teaching. We selected students enrolled in two contracting programs because we thought the programs' structural and ideological differences might help explain differences in student teachers' thinking and learning.[32] The project sought to describe and analyze what students learned in relation to what they were taught at the university and in the field, and to appraise that learning in terms of a conception of the central tasks of teaching and teacher preparation (Feiman-Nemser & Buchmann, 1989).

The National Center for Research on Teacher Education took research on teacher education and teacher learning to a new level by conducting one large, coordinated study. The TELT (Teacher Education and Learning to Teach) study combined case studies of eleven teacher education programs (six preservice, two induction, two inservice, and one alternate route) with longitudinal studies of what teachers in these programs learned about teaching mathematics and writing to diverse learners (NCRTE, 1988). Instrument development was a major undertaking and contribution to the field, especially the design of survey and interview questions that tapped teachers' subject-matter and pedagogical-content knowledge and reasoning, and their dispositions toward diverse learners (Kennedy, Ball, & McDiarmid, 1993). According to Mary Kennedy (1998), who directed the NCRTE, the "single most important finding" was that program substance—not structure—had the biggest impact on teacher learning, particularly the program's subject specific vision of good teaching (p. 21).

Through the TELT study, I began to investigate the induction phase of learning to teach in the context of two beginning-teacher assistance programs in our sample—a graduate intern program cosponsored by the University of New Mexico and the Albuquerque school district, and an alternative training and certification program sponsored by the Los Angeles school district. Interest in programs for beginning teachers was on the rise, and many proponents saw mentoring as an ideal way to address the needs of new teachers while rewarding outstanding experienced teachers. Through observing and interviewing mentor teachers in these two programs, we uncovered strik-ing differences in how they defined and enacted their roles.[33] As we learned more about the overall programs, including how mentors were selected and prepared in each setting, we saw how the contexts of mentoring shaped the practices of mentors (Feiman-Nemser & Parker, 1993).

Through the National Center for Research on Teacher Learning, I con-tinued my study of mentors and novice teachers in a cross-cultural, compar-ative study of *mentored learning to teach*, a phrase we coined to emphasize the necessary link between mentoring and teacher learning.[34] In keeping with the NCRTL focus on teaching for understanding,[35] we chose reform-oriented programs in Shanghai, China; Oxford, England; and several pre-service and induction programs in the U.S. to study what reform-minded mentors do, what novices learn as a result, and how the multiple con-texts of mentoring shape mentors' practice and novices' learning (Wang, 2001).[36]

The U.S. sites included two professional development schools affiliated with MSU's new teacher education program. We found that teachers who practice ambitious teaching do not automatically help novices learn it. If, however, they get help conceptualizing their practice and what it entails, they can use this knowledge to figure out what novices need to learn and how to help them learn ambitious teaching.[37] The comparative, cross-cul-tural research design helped us refine the concept of educative mentoring and deepen our understanding of the nested contexts of mentoring.

Policy as context figured prominently in my NPEAT-sponsored study of three well-established induction programs situated in states or districts with strong induction policies. With extensive firsthand knowledge of men-toring and induction, I felt ready to consider how induction policy helped or hindered thoughtful mentoring in the service of standards-based teach-ing and learning (Carver & Feiman-Nemser, 2010). One powerful finding concerned the relationship between new teacher assistance and assessment. Contrary to conventional thinking, we found that it was possible (and pow-erful), under the right conditions, for mentors to combine these two func-tions in responsible and productive ways (Yusko & Feiman-Nemser, 2008).

Informed by my ongoing involvement in the work of teacher education, the research I did at Michigan State University combined in-depth case studies with new conceptual frameworks. Given the immature state of our knowledge, there was a pressing need for analytic perspectives to illumi-nate the conceptual, empirical, and normative issues covered by the phrase *learning to teach*. There was an equally pressing need to get close to the phenomena in order to describe and analyze what was going on and probe the relationship between teacher education and teacher learning.

In the beginning, both teacher education and teacher learning were unstudied problems, and ideas that seem commonplace today were not self-evident then. There was limited research on the attitudes and beliefs that preservice teachers bring to teacher preparation and the difficulties of changing them. While it was widely recognized that beginning teachers had a lot to learn, the assumption was that they would somehow learn *from experience*. No one had really conceptualized the kind of help needed at this stage of the game. Presumably, experienced teachers had finished learning to teach—for better or worse.

Evolving conceptions of learning informed my thinking about teacher learning as psychologists moved from behavioral theories of skills acquisition, to cognitive theories of conceptual change and the construction of meaning, to sociocultural theories concerned with the contexts and conditions of learning. So did advances in our understanding of teaching, especially the requirements of what was variously called *standards-based*, *reform-minded*, *ambitious* teaching for understanding. And all of this took place in a dynamic political and economic context, in which teachers and teacher education were viewed as both the problem and solution to national and global concerns.

This book offers a sample of scholarship produced over a quarter-century and unified by a view of teachers as learners. It represents the fruits of my journey from teacher to teacher educator and scholar of teacher education and teacher learning. It reflects the impact of the many colleagues, teachers, and students who advanced my thinking about learning to teach and contributed to a growing body of knowledge and a new field of research.

The book is organized into three sections. The four chapters that make up the first section present arguments about—and conceptual maps of—learning to teach, teacher preparation, the teacher learning continuum, and new teacher induction. The section includes the first piece I wrote on *learning to teach* and the most recent, written twenty years later. Comparing the two, the reader can gauge how much progress has been made in the field. The second section focuses on teacher learning during teacher preparation. Its three chapters examine how the learning of intending teachers is shaped by their personal biography combined with the learning opportunities offered at the university and in the field. The third section focuses on the role of mentoring in fostering new teacher learning. The emphasis on educative mentoring connects with work on the pitfalls of experience in learning to teach, and highlights the pervasive influence of Dewey throughout. At a time when many of the premises and institutions that support teacher learning are under fire, I hope these essays will serve as a guide and witness to the progress we have made in the field over the past thirty years, and will offer a foundation for its further growth and development. In particular, I hope that teacher learning along the continuum from initial preparation to new teacher induction and ongoing professional development will be recognized as a critical link between effective teaching practices and successful student development and learning.

REFERENCES

Allen, D., & Ryan, K. (1969). *Microteaching*. Reading, MA: Addison-Wesley.

American Association of Colleges of Teacher Education (1968). Standards and evaluative criteria for the accreditation of teacher education. Washington, DC: AACTE.

Amidon, E., & Hough, J. (Eds.). (1967). *Interaction analysis: Theory, research and application*. Reading, MA: Addison-Wesley.

Ball, D. L., & Cohen, D. K. (1999). Developing practice, developing practitioners: Toward a practice-based theory of professional education. In G. Sykes & L. Darling-Hammond (Eds.), *Teaching as the learning profession: Handbook of policy and practice* (pp. 3–32). San Francisco: Jossey-Bass.

Ball, D. L., & Forzani, F. (2009). The work of teaching and the challenge for teacher education. *Journal of Teacher Education*, 60(5). 497–511.

Borrowman, M. (1965). *Teacher education in America*. New York: Teachers College Press.

Borg, W.R., Kelly, M., Langer, P., & Gall, M. (1964). *The mini-course: A micro-teaching approach to teacher education*. Beverly Hills, CA: Macmillan Educational Services.

Broudy, H. (1972). A critique of performance-based teacher education. *PBTE Series*, No. 4. Washington, DC: American Association of Colleges of Teacher Education.

Bussis, A., Chittenden, E., & Amarel, M. (1976). *Beyond surface curriculum: An interview study of teachers' understanding*. Boulder, CO: Westview Press.

Carroll, D., Featherstone, H., Featherstone, J., Feiman-Nemser, S., & Roosevelt, D. (2007). *Transforming teacher education: Reflections from the field*. Cambridge, MA: Harvard Education Press.

Carver, C., & Feiman-Nemser, S. (2010). Policy lessons for new teacher induction: Critical elements and missing pieces. *Educational Policy*, 23(2), 295-328.

Clarke, S. (1971). Designs for programs of teacher education. In B.O. Smith, *Research in teacher education* (pp. 119–157). Englewood Cliffs, NJ: Prentice Hall.

Cochran-Smith, M., & Fries, K. (2005). Researching teacher education in changing times. In M. Cochran-Smith and K. Zeichner (Eds.), *Studying teacher education: The report of the AERA panel on research and teacher education* (pp. 69–109). Mahwah, NJ: Lawrence Erlbaum.

Conant, J. (1963). *The education of American teachers*. New York: McGraw Hill.

Cuban, L. (1984). *How teachers taught: Constancy and change in American classrooms, 1880–1990*. New York: Teachers College Press.

Devaney, K. (1978). Warmth, concreteness, time and thought in teachers' learning. In K. Devaney (Ed.), *Essays on teachers' centers* (pp. 13–27). San Francisco: Far West Laboratory for Educational Research and Development.

Dewey, J. (1904). On the relation of theory and practice. In J. Boydston (Ed.), *The middle works of John Dewey, 1899–1924* (pp. 249–272). Carbondale, IL: Southern Illinois University Press.

Dewey, J. (1933). *How we think*. Boston: Houghton Mifflin.

Dunkin, M., & Biddle, B. (1974). *The study of teaching*. New York: Holt, Rinehart and Winston.

Feiman, S. (1979). Technique and inquiry in teacher education: A curricular case study. *Curriculum Inquiry*, 9:1, 63–79.

Feiman, S., & Featherstone, H. (1992). *Exploring teaching: Reinventing an introductory course*. New York: Teachers College Press.

Feiman, S., Friedman, D., & McCampbell, J. (1967). Literary man: Writer and reader. State of Illinois Independent Learning Project, 65 pgs. (excerpted in H. Robinson (Ed.), *Fusing Reading Skills and Content*. Newark, DE: IRA.

Feiman, S. (1975a). *The teacher curriculum work center: A descriptive study*. Grand Forks, ND: North Dakota Study Group on Evaluation.

Feiman, S. (1975b). Patterns of teacher behavior in a teacher center. *Interchange*, 6(2), 6–62.

Feiman-Nemser, S., & Beasley, K. (1997). Mentoring as assisted performance: The case of co-planning. In V. Richardson (Ed.), *Constructivist teacher education* (pp. 108–126). London: Falmer Press.

Feiman-Nemser, S., & Buchmann, M. (1986). The first year of teacher preparation: Transition to pedagogical thinking. *Journal of Curriculum Studies*, 18(3), 239–256.

Feiman-Nemser, S., & Buchmann, M. (1989). Describing teacher education: A framework and illustrative findings from a longitudinal study of six students. *Elementary School Journal*, 89(3), 365–377.

Feiman-Nemser, S., & Floden, R. (1980). A consumer's guide to teacher development. *Journal of Staff Development*, 126–147.

Feiman-Nemser, S., & Parker, M. (1993). Mentoring in context: A comparison of two U.S. programs for beginning teachers. *International Journal of Educational Research*, 699–718.

Flanders, N. (1970). *Analyzing teacher behavior*. Reading, MA: Addison-Wesley.

Floden, R., & Feiman, S. (1980). *What's all this talk about teacher development?* East Lansing, MI: Institute for Research on Teaching.

Gage, N. (1972). *Teacher effectiveness and teacher education: The search for a scientific basis*. Palo Alto, CA: Pacific Books.

Gage, N. (1977). *The scientific basis of the art of teaching*. New York: Teachers College Press.

Gage, N. (1985). *Hard gains in the soft sciences: The case of pedagogy*. Bloomington, IL: Phil Delta Kappa, Center on Evaluation, Development, and Research.

Grossman P., & McDonald, M. (2008). Back to the future: Directions for research in teaching and teacher education. *American Educational Research Journal, 45*, 184–205.

Hansen, D., Driscoll, M., & Arcilla, R. (2007). *A life in classrooms: Philip W. Jackson and the practice of education*. New York: Teachers College Press.

Highet, G. (1955). *The art of teaching*. New York: Vintage Books.

Hoffman, N. (2003). *Woman's "true" profession: Voices from the history of teaching*. New York: McGraw Hill.

Houston, R. (1974). *Exploring competency-based teacher education*. Berkeley, CA: McCutchan Publishing Co.

Houston, W. (1968). *Behavioral science elementary teacher education program*. Washington, DC: USOE Bureau of Research, U.S. Government Printing Office.

Hoy, W. (1968). The influence of experience on the beginning teacher. *School Review*, 76, 312–323.

Iannaconne, L. (1963). Student teaching: A transitional stage in the making of a teacher. *Theory into Practice*, 2, 73–80.

Jackson, P. (1966). The way teaching is. *Report of the seminar on teaching*. Washington, DC: National Education Association, Association for Supervision and Curriculum Development and the Center for the Study of Instruction, 7–27.

Jackson, P. (1968). *Life in classrooms*. New York: Holt, Rinehart and Winston.

Joyce, B. (1968). *The teacher innovator: A program to prepare teachers*. Washington, DC: USOE Bureau of Research, U.S. Government Printing Office.

Joyce, B., & Weil, M. (1972). *Models of teaching*. Needham Heights, MA: Allyn & Bacon.

Kennedy, M. (1998). *Learning to teach writing: Does teacher education make a difference?* New York: Teachers College Press.

Kennedy, M., Ball, D., & McDiarmid, W. (1993). *A study package for examining and tracking changes in teachers' knowledge*. East Lansing, MI: National Center for Research in Teacher Education.

Kounin, J. (1970). *Discipline and group management in classrooms*. New York: Holt.

Lagemann, E. (2000). *An elusive science: The troubling history of education research*. Chicago: University of Chicago Press.

Lieberman, A., & Miller, L. (1978). The social realities of teaching. *Teachers College Record*. vol. 80. No. 1, 54–78.

Lindsey, M. (1973). Performance-based teacher education: Examination of a slogan. *Journal of Teacher Education*, 24(3), 180–186.

McLaughlin, M., & Marsh, D. (1978). Staff development and school change. *Teachers College Record*, vol. 80, No. 1, 69–94.

National Center for Research on Teacher Education (1988). Teacher education and learning to teach: A research agenda. *Journal of Teacher Education*, 39(6), 27–32.

Peck, R., & Tucker, J. (1973). Research on teacher education. In R. Travers (Ed.), *Handbook of research on teaching* (2nd ed.) (pp. 940–978). Chicago: Rand McNally.

Public Law 94-482, Amendment. Part B: *Teacher Training Programs*, Sec. 632, Teacher Centers (1976).

Rosenshine, B., & Furst, N. (1973). The use of direct observation to study teaching. In R.M. Travers (Ed.), *Second handbook of research on teaching* (pp. 122-183). Chicago: Rand McNally.

Saphier, J., Haley-Speca, M., & Gower, R. (2008). *The skillful teachers: Building your teaching skills*. Acton, MA: Research for Better Schools.

Sarason, S., Davidson, K., & Blatt, B. (1962). *The preparation of teachers: An unstudied problem.* New York: Wiley.

Scheffler, I. (1989). University scholarship and the education of teachers. In I. Scheffler, *Reason and teaching* (pp. 92–94). Indianapolis: Hackett Publishing Co.

Smith, B.O. (1969). *Teachers for the real world.* Washington, DC: American Association of College of Teacher Education.

Smith. B.O. (Ed.) (1971). *Research in teacher education: A symposium.* Englewood Cliffs, NJ: Prentice-Hall.

Smith, L., & Geoffrey, W. (1968). *Complexities of an urban classroom.* New York: Holt, Rinehart and Winston.

Stephens, J. (1967). *The Process of Schooling.* New York: Holt, Rinehart and Winston.

Wang, J. (2001). Contexts of mentoring and opportunities for learning to teach: A comparative study of mentoring practice. *Teaching and Teacher Education,* 17(1), 51–73.

Wang, J., & Paine, L. (2001). Mentoring as assisted performance: A pair of Chinese teachers work together. *Elementary School Journal,* 102(2), 157–181.

Weber, L., & Dropkin, R. (1973). The City College Workshop Center for Open Education. *Ideas.* No. 26. London: University of London Goldsmiths' College.

Yusko, B., & Feiman-Nemser, S. (2008). Embracing contraries: Assistance and assessment in new teacher induction. *Teachers College Record,* 110(5), 923–953.

CHAPTER 1

Learning to Teach

In an essay on what it means to teach, David Hawkins (1973) tells of an exchange between a veteran teacher of thirty-five years and a student teacher. The veteran commented that what held her to teaching after all these years was that there was still so much to be learned. The student teacher responded in amazement that she thought it could all be learned in two or three years. Hawkins observes: "It may be possible to learn in two or three years the kind of practice which then leads to another twenty years of learning. Whether many of our colleges get many of their students on to that fascinating track or whether the schools are geared to a thoughtful support of such learning by their teachers is another matter" (p. 7)

The two teachers in Hawkins' story represent competing views of teaching and learning to teach. The student teacher believes that learning to teach is the special province of the beginner. Once a certain level of mastery is achieved, the necessity for further learning on the teacher's part is basically over. Since teaching can be mastered in a relatively short time (two or three years), it must be rather predictable and routine work. By contrast, the veteran teacher believes that the work of teaching cannot be based entirely on past knowledge and experience. It must be informed by knowledge derived from studying the particular students and classroom situation. Moreover, this teacher recognizes that the classroom is not only a place to teach children, but a place to learn more about teaching and learning. For her, learning is part of the job of teaching.

Hawkins clearly admires the veteran teacher who, after thirty-five years, continues to learn from teaching. Perhaps she is one of those exceptional persons whose zest for learning and dedication to teaching keep them going year after year. And yet, Hawkins does not focus on this teacher's individual qualities, qualities that no doubt characterized her before she became a teacher. Rather, he directs our attention to the institutional settings where teachers study and work. He asks whether the colleges that prepare teachers and schools that employ them cultivate and support their capacity to learn from their teaching and to grow in their work. His observation implies that becoming a learning teacher is not only a matter of individual disposition, it also depends on how teachers are prepared and the conditions under which they carry out their work.

Hawkins's story introduces the main argument of this chapter which looks at how teachers learn to teach in relation to how they are taught. The argument has three premises: (1) that formal arrangements for teaching teachers and helping them to improve do not fit with what we know about how teachers learn to teach and get better at teaching over time; (2) that informal influences are far more salient in learning to teach, but have often miseducative effects; (3) that creating appropriate arrangements to support teachers' learning involves changing not only what we *do*, but also how we *think* about learning to teach throughout the teacher's career.

Formal and Informal Influence on Learning to Teach

Teacher educators are fond of talking about the preservice-inservice continuum as a way of expressing their view that professional education should be a continuous process, starting with preservice preparation, moving on to induction and continuing through the teacher's years of service. In fact, formal teacher education is quite discontinuous. There are no structural or conceptual links between preservice preparation and inservice education and training.

Nor is learning to teach synonymous with teacher education. In fact, when teachers talk about their professional learning they rarely mention formal preservice or inservice courses. Instead, they talk about the experience of teaching itself, and the chance to observe and talk with other teachers. A comprehensive look at learning to teach must take into account what we know about formal and informal sources.

The State of the Art of Learning to Teach

In order to find out what is known about learning to teach, one must first decide what the phrase stands for. Does "learning to teach" mean developing a personal style or mastering the content to be taught or completing a certification program? All these interpretations have been linked with the notion of learning to teach and each points to a different body of research.

There are studies of teacher socialization and teacher development. There is research on teacher education and teacher training at both the preservice and inservice levels. There is a body of literature on staff development and school improvement. There are autobiographies and descriptive accounts by teachers about their teaching experiences over time. From all these sources together, one can begin to construct a general picture of how someone learns to teach and improves at teaching over time. Rarely is this topic addressed directly, however, and what we know is far from adequate. The following conclusion about the research on student teaching, the most highly valued and widely studied aspect of preservice preparation, also describes the state of the art in these other areas. "A review of the research leaves one with a great feeling of urgency to expedite the study of student teaching; given its ascribed importance in teacher education, it is alarming to find so little systematic research related to it. Discussions and descriptive reports are plentiful but comprehensive basic study of the processes involved is lacking" (Davies & Amershek, 1969, p. 1384).

With few exceptions, the existing research tells us very little about the actual conduct of teacher preparation and inservice training. Nor does it say much about on the job learning.

This chapter offers a more comprehensive way of putting together a data base on learning to teach. It is organized chronologically around the four phases of a learning-to-teach. The first section focuses on the pretraining phase before prospective teachers even realize that they are learning things that will shape their future teaching. The second section looks at the preservice phase when future teachers undertake their formal preparation. The third section examines the induction phase which coincides with the first year of teaching, while the fourth section examines the inservice phase which covers the rest of the teacher's career. In each phase we are particularly concerned with the relative contributions of formal and informal influences on the teacher's capacity for continued learning.

This broad perspective has important implications for all who view the quality of teaching as a key to the quality of schooling. Effective schools have been defined as places where students learn. It is time to include in our definition a requirement about teachers' learning as well.

THE PRETRAINING PHASE: EARLY INFLUENCES ON LEARNING TO TEACH

Before teachers start their formal pedagogical work, they have already had considerable informal preparation for teaching. From infancy onward, they have been taught many things by other people, most prominently their parents and teachers. They have also been exposed to patterns and ideas of teaching and schooling that pervade the culture. Teacher educators tend to underestimate the pervasive effects of these formative experiences. There is little empirical research on the role of early experiences on learning to teach. Still, some researchers have argued that formal teacher preparation is not powerful enough to overcome the impact of early experiences. At least three different explanations have been offered.

An Evolutionary Account

Stephens (1969) proposes an "evolutionary" theory to account for basic pedagogical tendencies in teachers. Human beings have survived because of their deeply ingrained habits of correcting one another, telling each other what they know, pointing out the moral, supplying the answer. These tendencies have been acquired over the centuries and are lived out in families and classrooms. Thus children not only learn what they are told by parents and teachers, they also learn to be teachers. Just listen to the imitative play of young children and you will hear them instruct one another as their parents and teachers do. Prospective teachers have their share of these spontaneous pedagogical tendencies, but they also have a sense of mission. According to Stephens, this combination is far more powerful than our current teacher training efforts.

A Psychoanalytic Account

Wright and Tuska (1968) look to psychoanalytic theory for an explanation of how childhood makes a teacher. Their research focuses on the influence of important adults (mother, father, teacher) on the decision to teach and on subsequent teaching. Becoming a teacher is viewed as a way of becoming like the significant others in a person's childhood. Some elementary teachers may unconsciously become like the interfering teachers who once frightened them, with the consequence that their pupils, in turn, become the victims they once were. Wright (1959) has also collected anecdotes, written by teachers, which illustrate that, for many, a conscious identification with a teacher during childhood is important. The following is a typical example, "One of the nicest parts of the day was when my teacher told a story. I watched very carefully how she looked, and listened to the way her voice sounded as she talked. At home, I would play school and talk to my imaginary children in exactly the same way that she had talked, retelling exactly the same stories . . . It all happened a long time ago, but it is still easy to remember how much this teacher meant to me" (p. 362).

A Socialization Account

Lortie (1966, 1975) emphasizes the powerful role that being a student plays in becoming a teacher. "Teachers start their professional preparation early in life, their entire school experience contributes to their work socialization" (1966, p. 56). From more than 10,000 hours of exposure to teachers, prospective teachers have stored up countless impressions of life in classrooms. Since "psyching out the teacher" may be crucial to a student's survival, it is often undertaken with considerable intensity. From this "apprenticeship of observation," students internalize models of teaching which are activated when they become teachers.

Lortie supports this theory of teacher socialization with interview data in which teachers acknowledge the influence of former teachers and the tangential role of their former training. While some teachers recognize this influence of the past, Lortie suggests that many are probably influenced in ways they do not perceive. In the press of classroom interaction, teachers end up imitating internalized models of past practice, e.g., doing what their second grade teacher did when the children got restless.

The tendency of teachers to maintain their early preconceptions supports the argument that formal preparation does not challenge early informal influences. When teachers describe former teachers, for example, they rarely alter the assessments they made when they were younger. Their favorite teacher still represents good teaching. Formal training does not mark a separation between the perceptions of naive laypersons and the informed judgments of professionals.

It is clear that students remember their teachers, but there is little basis for assuming that they can place teachers' actions within a pedagogical framework. As Lortie writes (1975), "What students learn about teaching is intuitive and imitative, rather than explicit and analytical; it is based on individual personalities rather than 'pedagogical principles' " (p. 62).

The Influence of Biography on Learning to Teach

Clearly biography is a power influence on learning to teach. Wright and Lortie stress the need for teachers to be freed from the "hand of the past," the influence of parents, teachers, and the culture at large. What Wright has in mind sounds closer to psychotherapy than education. What Lortie recommends is that future teachers be helped to examine their past, to see how it shapes their beliefs about the way schools ought to be. Unless future teachers get some cognitive control over prior school experience, it may influence their teaching unconsciously and contribute to the perpetuation of conservative school practices. On the other hand, Stephens has more faith in the adaptive pedagogical tendencies that have evolved over time and that make people capable of undertaking at least some aspects of teaching.

It is fruitful to look at these claims about the influence of the past in relation to significant qualities that future teachers believe they bring to their professional preparation, and to their hopes and expectations about what they will learn. Typically elementary education students cite warmth, patience, and empathy as qualities that they possess that will make them effective teachers. Rarely do they mention intellectual strengths or subject matter knowledge. What they most hope to learn through their professional studies are instructional techniques, ways of diagnosing learning problems, methods of classroom control (O'Shea, 1981).

Many judge the adequacy of their formal preparation by the extent to which it gives them technical knowledge. Unless formal training can modify pre-existent images of teachers and teaching, future teachers will practice what their teachers did. Skills have a place, but they cannot replace ideas. The likelihood that professional study will affect what powerful early experiences have inscribed on the mind and emotions will depend on its power to cultivate images of the possible and desirable and to forge commitments to make those images a reality.

THE PRESERVICE PHASE OF LEARNING TO TEACH

Most people think that when students enter college with the intention of becoming teachers, they spend most of their four years preparing for that role. Actually, as Howey, Yarger and Joyce (1978) point out, "the majority of degree requirements met by teacher education students are not related to learning about teaching, learning how to teach or demonstrating the ability to teach" (p. 25). Elementary education students spend 25 percent of their academic career in education courses and another 13 percent in some form of supervised practice. Secondary education majors spend less.

Still, many teacher educators and students attach considerable hope to what professional education ought to and can achieve. Actually education courses and field experience offer distinct occasions for learning to teach. They represent commitments to ways of knowing and coming to know—

formal knowledge and firsthand experience—that are typically not articulated and often compete with each other.

Formal Knowledge and Learning to Teach

Education courses are the most formal and systematic part of learning to teach. They offer an opportunity to expose future teachers to the knowledge base of the profession. What this knowledge base consists of is unclear. Some are confident about its value and promise; others point out the limitations of theory and research as a bases for educational practice.

The prevailing view, modeled after the natural sciences, is that general principles about good teaching can be derived from social science theory and research and applied in the classroom. This view is institutionalized in the structure of the standard preservice curriculum—separate courses in educational foundations (psychology, philosophy, sociology) and methods of teaching followed by practice teaching.

Increasingly field experiences are being attached to education courses. This may be an attempt to help students "see" the relevance of formal coursework to classroom problems and make connections they might not otherwise make. On the other hand, it may reflect a stronger faith in the experiential side of learning to teach. There is some evidence for this interpretation. In a survey of 270 institutions preparing teachers, 99 percent indicated that they offered early (pre-student teaching) field experiences such as observation, tutoring, working with small groups, assisting with non-instructional tasks. Significantly, a quarter reported that they had no stated objectives for the experience (Webb, 1981).

The list of courses that education students take gives some indication of the knowledge presumed to be relevant to teaching. Unfortunately, we know very little about what these courses are like and how future teachers make sense of them. There is a general impression that teachers think their education courses are too theoretical and not sufficiently practical. Lortie (1975) interprets this to mean that the courses hold out unrealistic goals and high expectations without providing the practical know-how to make things happen.

Lortie's interpretation may be persuasive; it is also problematic. It implies that teacher educators could give teachers the practical know-how to realize their ideals. It ignores the power of ideals to challenge the taken-for-granted in prior experience and current models and to hold out high standards of effective practice. For example, without a view of more equitable and responsive classrooms, future teachers are more susceptible to what Katz

(1974) calls "excessive realism," accepting the kind of teaching they observe as the upper and outer limits of the possible.

How future teachers encounter formal knowledge may influence what they think about the contributions of theory and research to teaching. If education courses nourish the belief that theory and research can give teachers rules to follow, they undermine the teacher's own problem-solving capacity and convey a false security about the authority of science. Formal knowledge can provide ways of thinking and alternative solutions, but the teacher must decide what the specific situation requires. Most preservice students want recipes. They rarely see a place for foundational knowledge except perhaps psychology. Even here they may often assume that psychology can provide prescriptions for classroom practice. William James' (1904/1958) message to teachers bears repeating not only in relation to educational psychology, but also in relation to research on teaching, a relatively new source of content for education courses, "You make a great, a very great mistake if you think that psychology, being the science of the mind's laws, is something from which you can deduce definite programs and schemes and methods of instruction for immediate classroom use. Psychology is a science, and teaching is an art; and sciences never generate arts directly out of themselves. An intermediary inventive mind must make the application by using its originality" (p. 23–24).

There is a prevailing myth that the university has a liberalizing influence on future teachers which is dissipated by the conservative influence of the schools during field experiences. Recent research on student teaching challenges this myth by showing how university seminars and supervisory conferences also encourage acquiescence and conformity to existing school practice (Tabachnick, Popkewitz and Zeichner, 1980). Education courses socialize future teachers too, but we know less about their message and its impact.

Student Teaching: Learning by Doing

Student teaching is generally viewed as a necessary and useful part of teacher preparation. Teachers typically regard it as the most valuable part of their preservice work. Even a critic like James Conant (1963) called it "the one indisputably essential element in professional education."

Student teaching is also the most widely studied aspect of learning to teach at the preservice level. Most of the empirical research focuses on changes in the attitudes and behavior of student teachers as a result of their student teaching experience and demonstrates Becker's (1964) assertion that people take on the characteristics required by the situations in which they participate. Some studies show how students become like their cooperating teachers, the professionals whom student teachers encounter most directly (Friebus, 1970). Some studies show that student teachers take on the attitudes and beliefs associated with the school bureaucracy. For example, a series of studies by Hoy (1967, 1968, 1969) and Hoy and Rees (1977) finds student teachers becoming more bureaucratic (e.g., more conforming and impersonal) and more custodial in their orientation by the end of their student teaching.

These findings are confirmed by a handful of field studies which describe how student teaching contributes to a utilitarian perspective that conflicts with the expressed purposes of teacher education programs (Iannaccone, 1963; Fox, Grant, Popkewitz, Romberg, Tabachnick and Wehlage, 1976; Tabachnick, Popkewitz and Zeichner, 1979–80). A summary of findings from one of these studies illustrates the dominant patterns (Tabachnick, Popkewitz and Zeichner, 1978):

1. Student teaching involved a very limited range of activities and interactions. When teaching occurred, it was typically concerned with short-term skills or routine testing and management procedures.
2. Student teachers had little control over their classroom activities. Why something taught was taken for granted and not questioned.
3. The student teachers defined the most significant problem of teaching as discipline. Keeping children busy and doing things that would ensure that children moved through the lesson on time and in a quiet and orderly fashion became ends in themselves rather than means toward some specific educational purpose.
4. The student teachers seemed to develop a high degree of technical proficiency; however, they applied criteria of pupil success which were almost entirely utilitarian, separating their everyday activities from their ideas by maintaining a distance between theory and practice.

This research challenges the widespread belief that practical school experience necessarily helps people become good teachers. Long ago Dewey (1904/1965) warned against an early and exclusive focus on technique in field experiences because the prospective teacher would adjust his methods of teaching "not to the principles he is acquiring but to what he sees succeed and fail in an empirical way from moment to moment; to what he sees other teachers doing who are more experienced and successful in keeping order than he is; and to the injunctions and directions given him by others" (p. 14). While it may give future teachers a taste of reality, student teaching can also foster bad habits and narrow vision. What helps to solve an immediate problem may not be good teaching. A deceptive sense of success, equated with keeping order and discipline, is liable to close off avenues for further learning.

The Impact of Formal Preparation

It is impossible to understand the impact of preservice preparation without knowing more about what it is like. Sarason (1962) characterized the preparation of teachers as "an unstudied problem" and called for "detailed descriptions of how teachers are actually trained." We begin to know more, though, about student teaching. Research suggests that student teaching leaves future teachers with a utilitarian perspective in which getting through the day, keeping children busy, maintaining order are the main priorities. When preservice training gives students technical knowledge, they feel prepared for teaching and satisfied with their program. Good teaching appears to be a matter of using the right technique; learning to teach requires being there.

Schools alone are not responsible for bringing about these changes; despite a rhetoric of reflection and experimentation, universities also contribute to them. Or are they changes?

Some researchers found that student teachers did not change their perspectives during student teaching. Rather, student teachers became more articulate about stating and more skillful about implementing the perspectives they came with (Tabachnick, Zeichner, Densmore, Adler and Egan, 1982). This confirms the powerful influences of early models and preconceptions that remain unchallenged by preserve preparation. Changes are continuous, not discontinuous. This research supports Lortie's thesis about the continuity of influence from generation to generation in teaching.

Many people, including future teachers, expect that preservice training is a preparation for teaching. That seems unrealistic on several counts. Informal influences are too strong, the time is short, and preparing for teaching inevitably continues on the job. It would be far more realistic to think about preparing people to begin a new phase of learning to teach. That would orient formal preparation more toward developing *beginning* competence and laying a foundation for learning and teaching.

THE INDUCTION PHASE OF LEARNING TO TEACH

Under the best of circumstances, preservice teacher education can only provide a beginning. Whatever beginning teachers bring to their first teaching situation, that situation will have a powerful effect on them, shaping them to fit the requirements of the role and place. Waller (1935) framed the issue almost fifty years ago when he wrote that those who enter the ranks of teachers, "do not know how to teach, although they may know everything that is in the innumerable books telling them how to teach. They will not know how to teach until they have got the knack of certain personal adjustments which adapt them to their profession, and the period of learning may be long or short. These recruits that face teaching as a life work are ready to learn to teach, and they are ready, though they know it not, to be formed by teaching" (p. 380).

At the same time, the first encounter with "real" (as opposed to student) teaching enables beginners to start seeking answers to their own questions. As Herbert Kohl (1976) puts it, "the essentials of learning to teach begin when one has the responsibility for a class or group of young people. At that point, it begins to be possible to know what resources are needed, what questions need to be answered by more experienced teachers, and what skills one needs" (p. 11). Thus the workplace is a setting for adaptation *and* inquiry during the first year of teaching.

Various labels (induction phase or transition phase) have been used to signal the fact that the first year of teaching has a character of its own, that it is different from what has gone before and likely to influence what is to come. Some go so far as to argue that what happens during the first year of teaching determines not only whether someone remains in teaching but also what kind of teacher they become. This assumes that the first year is *the* critical year in learning to teach. A recent request for proposals from the National Institute of Education (1978) asserted this position, "The conditions under which a person carries out the first year of teaching have a strong influence on the level of effectiveness which that teacher is able to achieve and sustain over the years; on the attitudes which govern teacher behavior over even a forty year career; and indeed, on the decision whether or not to continue in the teaching profession" (p. 3).

We have no longitudinal data to test these assumptions about the relationship between the induction period and the teacher's long term development. Much of what we know about the first year of teaching comes from the firsthand accounts by beginning teachers who recall the year as an intense and stressful period of learning. Understandably, these accounts are subject to some limitations of perspective and colored by affect.

The Shock of Reality and Learning to Teach

Often beginning teachers approach their first assignments with idealistic and unrealistic expectations. After watching teachers for many years and participating in the routines and rituals of school life, beginning teachers may think they know what they are getting into. When they actually move to the other side of the teacher's desk, however, the once familiar scene looks strangely unfamiliar. In a chapter entitled "X is for the Unknown" in a book appropriately titled *Don't Smile Until Christmas*, Gail Richardson (1970) describes the combinations of hopes and fears that she brought to her first job as a high school math teacher:

> I was going to be a good teacher—interesting and fair and encountering my students as people . . . I would regard each student as an individual, having dignity and worth. I would create a class atmosphere that was friendly and encouraging, in which a person could make a mistake without being made to feel he was an idiot. I would communicate enthusiasm for my subject.
>
> These imprecise, flattering notions of myself as a teacher were the thoughts that brought me to Belden High School. I knew little of the school, other than it was in a changing neighborhood. . . .
>
> Despite my optimistic self-concept, my expectations for the year did not reflect complete confidence for I was uncertain of grading, discipline and parental contact. . . . I also had preconceived notions of classroom mechanics. I anticipated three classes with no more than thirty-five students each. I hoped to receive copies of my text before school began so that I could begin planning. I was worried about what I would do on the first day. *From that first day, all my optimistic visions were gradually but steadily eclipsed by the reality which confronted me* (p. 61; emphasis added).

Sometimes the first day of school proceeds smoothly as teachers and students size each other up, but the "honeymoon period" quickly ends and an sense of panic develops as beginning teachers realize how ill prepared they are for their teaching responsibilities. These responsibilities do not differ in any way from the responsibilities which an experienced teacher must handle (Lortie, 1975). Like everyone else, the beginning teacher must ready the room, organize the curriculum for the year, plan activities for the opening day.

The need to act, the pressure to respond, launches the beginning teacher on a period of trial and error learning. Lortie (1967) compares the beginner's entrance into the profession to Robinson Crusoe's struggle for survival, "As for Defoe's hero, the beginning teacher may find that prior experience supplied him with some alternatives for action, but his crucial learning comes from his personal errors; he fits together solutions and specific problems into some kind of whole and at times finds leeway for the expression of personal tastes. Working largely alone, he cannot make the specifics of his working knowledge base explicit, nor need he, as his victories are private" (p. 59).

Basically, beginners work things out on their own. This leaves room for self expression. But it also narrows the range of alternatives that will be tried and increases the likelihood that the novice will misinterpret successes and failures; this may help in the short run, but may not be educative in the long run. Nor need "what works" build and sustain a teacher's capacity to learn from teaching and to keep asking questions.

Beginning teachers may come to believe that good teaching is something you figure out on your own by trying out one technique after another. Differences among teachers appear to be simply matters of personal style. Such beliefs work against a commitment to keep on learning and to hold high standards of effective practice that make such learning possible.

Beginners' Problems and Where They Come From

A recurrent theme in accounts by beginning teachers is their attempt to establish a level of classroom control that allows them to teach (Fuchs, 1969; Ryan, 1970). Many first year teachers are reluctant to assume the role of classroom leader. They are unsure about what to teach and how. They have little feel for students and insufficient experience to predict student response. They are also unclear about how to evaluate students and communicate with parents.

These problems are often linked with inadequate preparation at the preservice level; however, as McDonald (1982) hypothesizes, contextual and personality factors also play a part, "Certainly some of the beginning teachers' floundering . . . is due to lack of adequate preparation in the fundamentals of instruction. Some of it is due to a lack of proper organization so that beginning teachers are prepared for the subjects they are to teach. Some is due to a lack of adequate support at the time that they are teaching—support in the form of prescriptive advice about how to cope with certain kinds of problems. An unknown portion derives from the characteristics of the life and personality of the individuals who are beginning teachers" (p. 203).

These four claims deserve some attention since they have implications for what might be done to prevent or ameliorate at least some of the problems of beginning teachers. In regard to the first claim, it is not clear whether a grounding in (assumed) generic principles of teaching would help beginning teachers cope with the specific problems they may face. In fact, the extent to which a preservice program can do something about most of the problems of beginning teachers is altogether unclear.

The second claim is more straightforward. If proper organization means getting textbooks to beginning teachers before school opens and assigning them to teach subjects for which they have some preparation, then there is no reason why new teachers should have to cope with such problems. There are institutional solutions for some of the problems of the beginning teacher.

What constitutes, thirdly, adequate support and appropriate advice for a beginning teacher is tricky. Newberry (1977) found, for example, that beginning teachers were quite selective about whom to turn to. They relied almost entirely on teachers at their grade level whose "teaching ideologies" seemed compatible with their own and who "taught the way they wanted to."

Asking for help in order to get advice sets up a pattern for collegial interaction which depends on someone having a difficulty. Given this pattern, questions about teaching unrelated to problems will seem out of place (Little, 1981). Under such circumstances it is hard to separate judgments of competence from discussions of practice.

Finally the claim that some of the problems beginning teachers experience stem from their own personalities or life situation implies that some of their problems are not amenable to solution. If preservice programs are not selective, then the first year of teaching will become a point where some selection occurs. Not every problem of the beginning teacher can or should be resolved.

Should Support Be Provided?

Since the publication of the Conant Report (1963), which contained several specific recommendations about the support of beginning teachers, there have been repeated calls for the development of programs to assist beginning teachers (Ryan, 1970; Howey and Bents, 1979). Some experimental programs have been implemented with federal or foundation support, but most beginning teachers receive little help over and above what is available to all teachers (Grant and Zeichner, 1981). Two approaches to induction highlight some of the issues regarding support for beginning teachers.

The British have experimented with induction programs for beginning teachers for the past five years. Although there is some variation among the pilot programs, most share the following characteristics (Bolam 1973, 1979):

1. Beginning teachers have a teaching load reduced by up to 25 percent.
2. An experienced teacher is appointed to help a group of not more than ten beginning teachers and is given released time to do so.
3. Special college courses are offered during the school year. These vary in length and do not carry credit or a tuition charge.

Whereas the British induction schemes are outside the assessment process, the state of Georgia has tied induction to the evaluation and permanent certification of beginning teachers. Each beginning teacher is regularly evaluated during the first year on the basis of fourteen competencies which were identified through an extensive program of research and development funded by the state. Beginning teachers are also evaluated by their school administrators and by a master teacher certified in the same area. All three determine when competence is achieved and what remediation is necessary (e.g., work with a master teacher or formal course work).

The assumption that beginning teachers should be "competent" or else get remediation ignores the fact that important aspects of learning to teach are associated with teaching experience over time. It also reinforces the view that teaching is relatively easy to master in a brief period of time. Furthermore, connecting induction with formal evaluation may legitimize a tendency already strong among beginners: to value technique that gets results over understanding that grows slowly.

Survival and Development

While survival may be the paramount goal of beginning teachers, how they survive will have consequences for the kind of teacher they will become. McDonald (1980) argues that the strategies a teacher uses to cope with first-year problems become the basis for a style that endures.

> The beginning teacher focuses on what is necessary to 'get the job done'—manage the class, prepare lessons, grade papers, teach each lesson. Effectiveness means doing these things reasonably well, without getting into trouble; it means being accepted, even liked by the students. The teaching practices which seem to produce these ends merge into a style, which—whatever its other merits—works for the beginner. This is his style, and he will rationalize it and ignore its limitations (p. 44).

Future professional growth can be limited by teachers' reluctance to give up the very practices which helped them get through.

Of course, it is possible that the exhilaration of surviving the first year of teaching provides the necessary confidence to continue searching for better ways of teaching. It is unlikely that teachers with one year of experience will feel completely satisfied with their performance.

This interpretation highlights the tension between efforts to eliminate the problems of beginning teachers and efforts to support and sustain them in on-the-job learning. The view that problems should be prevented or eliminated overshadows the fact that problems often alert one to things that need work. If one has solutions in hand, why go on searching? Unnecessary trauma during the first year of teaching should certainly be avoided. But it is useful to subsume some of the problems of the beginning teacher under a perspective that looks at learning to teach in general and at learning from teaching over time.

ON-THE-JOB LEARNING: THE INSERVICE PHASE

Researchers and teacher educators have put forward a variety of descriptions of the "stages" teachers go through as they gain experience in teaching. Most of these descriptions posit three stages: a beginning stage of survival, a middle stage of consolidation, and a final stage of mastery. The stages are loosely tied to the amounts of teaching experience, even though there is a recognition of the fact that teachers change at different rates. As one teacher put it: "I was a beginning teacher for three years."

The first stage is generally associated with the first year of teaching. Burden (1981) provides a useful summary of the characteristics of "first-stage" teachers:

1. limited knowledge of teaching activities;
2. limited knowledge about the teaching environment;
3. conformity to an image of the teacher as authority;
4. subject-centered approach to curriculum and teaching;
5. limited professional insights and perceptions;
6. feelings of uncertainty, confusion and insecurity;
7. unwillingness to try new teaching methods. (p. 7)

The second stage generally extends through the third or fourth year of teaching. Growing confidence and mastery of basic teaching tasks enables teachers to concentrate less on themselves and more on their teaching. Concerns about "Can I?" change to questions about "How to." Increased self-confidence encourages feelings of worth, and success provides some appropriate and reliable solutions to problems. "Stage two" teachers have extended planning from one day at a time to weeks. They have a better grasp of long term goals, are more comfortable with the teacher's role, and their understanding of the problematics of teaching begins to grow.

The third stage is characterized by a sense of confidence and ease. The mechanics of teaching and classroom management are well under control. Teacher concerns center on whether pupils are learning what the teacher is teaching and whether the instructional content is appropriate for students. Whereas the beginning teacher focuses on the immediate problem—today, this child, that lesson—mature teachers are interested in the overall pattern. They can take in the whole room at once and have some sense of the relationship between their classroom and the rest of the school. Some teachers begin to think about the role of the teacher and the school in society.

First year teachers are confused and uncertain about many aspects of teaching. About five years later, if they are still teaching, most teachers feel confident, secure and professionally competent. They know how things are done in their school and they can function smoothly in the classroom. They have discovered that students are people and let students see their own personal side as well. They do not necessarily think that they know all the answers, but they feel more secure in what they are trying to do. The extent of these changes come through in the following retrospective observations about the first and fifth year of teaching taken from Burden's (1979) interviews with experienced teachers.

> [My first year] was frightening. It was all of a sudden the feeling of bringing everything I was supposed to know altogether and really doing something with it. I had a great feeling of responsibility and a feeling of maybe not being able to handle it. It was a lot of apprehension and a lot of wanting to do well. I think there was a feeling that I couldn't measure up (p. 122).

But over time, the picture changes.

> I'm really feeling like I know what's going on and I feel that I am able to look more objectively at school and say this is where I want to go this year and with these kids. I'm able to do that now ahead of time a little more than before. And I'm able to 'read' my class a little more quickly and know what they're going to need. I feel like I have more resources to draw from in handling situations and knowing what to teach and how to deal with people. So I do feel kind of like a mature teacher (p. 124).

The stage descriptions suggest that a major part of learning to teach occurs on the job, in the first five to seven years. During this segment of the inservice phase, teachers master the craft of teaching in one form or another and learn to live the life of a teacher. Missing from the formulations, however, is an understanding of how such changes come about and what happens once mastery is achieved. There is a notion that with time, experience and a little help, a natural process of improvement will occur. Actually, the stage descriptions reflect someone's view of an ideal path of professional growth, a path that some teachers may have taken. Characteristics associated with the "third stage" may be attainable, but their specification is conventional and their attainment not automatic (Floden and Feiman, 1981).

Basically two pictures have been painted of what happens to teachers once they master the tasks of teaching. According to one view, teachers stabilize their basic teaching style, setting into workable routines and resist efforts to change. According to a second view, teachers continue to change not only because they want to be more effective with students, but also because they need to have challenge and intellectual stimulation in their work. How can the latter view be fostered? What do we know about the conditions and strategies that promote teachers' continued learning and openness to new ideas?

There are basically two perspectives on how to support and stimulate professional development of teachers. One perspective focuses on the individual teacher. The underlying assumption is that teachers have the potential to achieve a professional level of practice if they have access to appropriate support and service. Teacher centers represent this perspective with their emphasis on work with individual teachers over time.

The second perspective looks at schools as a context for teachers' learning. The underlying assumption is that prevailing norms and patterns of interaction in schools can limit or promote opportunities for professional development. Recent research on successful schools and staff development suggests the kinds of expectations and practices that can promote on-the-job learning.

In combination, these perspectives blend formal and informal approaches to teacher development. They suggest that the alternatives of boredom and burnout or growth in effectiveness are less a function of individual characteristics and more a reflection of the opportunities and expectations that surround teachers in their work.

Inservice Programs Ignore Teacher Development

Schools have no well defined structures for helping teachers learn from the everyday experience of teaching, nor have they given priority to what teachers feel are their job-related needs. Most inservice programs are designed to help teachers meet certification requirements or comply with district objectives. Colleges and universities offer courses and schools support this form of continuing education by granting salary increases for advanced degrees. If teachers find intellectual stimulation in formal study, they often have trouble seeing the connection with their daily classroom work. Districts mount inservice training to put new curriculum or management systems into operation. Too often the training is perfunctory with no follow up help. As a result teachers do not adapt new approaches to their own teaching situation and school practices do not change. In short, improving the practice of experienced teachers has not been taken seriously as a legitimate inservice priority.

A Teacher Centered Approach to Teacher Development

What distinguishes teacher centers from most school district and university inservice programs is their responsiveness to teachers' self-defined needs and their faith in teachers' potential for professional growth. Devaney and Thorn (1975) summarize the basic premises that make teacher centers a genuine alternative to conventional forms of inservice education:

> Teachers must be more than technicians, must continue to be learners. Long lasting improvements in education will occur through inservice programs that identify individual starting points for learning, build on teachers' motivation to take more not less responsibility for curriculum and instruction decisions in the school and classroom, and welcome teachers to participate in the design of professional development programs (p. 7).

Warmth, concreteness, time and thought—these are the enabling conditions that centers believe teachers need on order to develop (Devaney, 1977). Teaching has been called a lonely profession. Often teachers feel unsupported and ill-prepared to do the job expected of them. Teacher centers provide a responsive, nonjudgmental setting that promotes collegial sharing and provides support for the risks of change. "Concrete" refers to the hands-on curricular materials that teachers explore and construct in center workshops. From the center perspective, teachers must continuously create, adapt and collect curriculum materials to meet the diverse and changing needs of their students. "Concrete" also refers to a focus on the specific and particular in teaching. Many centers have advisory services, master teachers who consult on classroom problems either in the center or in the teacher's classroom. It takes time to learn new things. Genuine change comes from an awareness of needs that evolves over time. Centers structure activities to give teachers time to discover their needs and those of their students. Increased responsibility for curricular and instructional designs require increased understanding. Centers try to engage teachers in serious study of subject matter and students.

Centers with a clear commitment to teacher development try to respond to immediate needs without losing sight of long-term goals. The strategy that typifies this developmental style is advisory work. Unlike inservice coordinators, the advisor is not responsible for implementing official policy. Unlike curriculum specialists and principals, the role carries no supervisory or evaluative functions. The focus is on concentrated work in the teacher's own situation with the purpose of helping teachers improve their practice. The long-term goal is to stimulate teachers' critical thinking about their work (Bussis, Chittenden, & Amarel, 1976).

This individualized form of inservice has something to offer teachers at every stage of development. Beginning teachers need support and advice from someone they trust as a mentor. Middle stage teachers want practical assistance, but they also need the encouragement to look closely at what they are doing and why. Watts (1980) observes that the most important role for advisors working with middle stage teachers is "to keep alive a vision of what education might become, far beyond what it is, and to insist on an attitude of inquiry, even when it is uncomfortable" (p. 8). Finally, the advisory role offers master teachers a chance to share their expertise with less experienced colleagues, which can also be a powerful form of professional development.

The teacher center concept represents a serious effort to identify conditions that support teachers' learning. Still, centers have been criticized for emphasizing individual work and paying less attention to the effects of schools on individuals. It appears that patterns of participation in center activities and teachers' latitude to experiment in their classrooms are influenced by expectations in the schools where they work. There is no getting around the fact that it is easier to be a learning teacher in some schools than others.

The School as a Setting for On-the-Job Learning

The daily work of teaching shapes teachers' notions about how one becomes a good teacher. It would not be surprising, for example, if many teachers believed that learning to teach was a matter of independent trial and error with occasional assistance from others. This view is built into the typical conditions of the first years of teaching and reflected in the norms that govern both asking and offering help. Many teachers are cautious about revealing problems and reticent to enter the private domain of another teacher's classroom. Thus, the chance to see advice played out or get feedback on one's own progress is limited. The isolation of teachers in their classrooms also makes it easier to stick to comfortable practices without having to justify them in terms of students' learning.

Despite these dominant patterns, schools differ. Little (1981) has identified two powerful norms that appear to characterize schools where teachers view their own continued learning as part of the job of teaching. The "norm of collegiality" refers to the expectation that improving one's own teaching is a collective undertaking. The "norm of continuous improvement" refers to expectations that analysis, evaluation and experimentation are tools of the profession that can help teachers be more effective. Both norms are shaped by the kinds of interactions that teachers have in the normal course of their work. These include:

1. Frequent talk among teachers about the practice of teaching
2. Frequent opportunities to observe and evaluate one another's teaching
3. Regular opportunities to design and evaluate teaching materials
4. Regular opportunities to teach and learn from one another

These interactions occur in various locations—training sessions, faculty meetings, teachers' lounges, hallways, and classrooms. They focus on specific practices as distinct from teachers, which helps to preserve self-respect and minimize barriers to discussion. They tend to involve a large portion of the faculty. In short, collegial experimentation is a way of life in these schools.

Little calls these "the critical practices of adaptability" because they enable schools to respond to changing social conditions, including changes in student populations. Not surprisingly, they coincide with the enabling conditions associated with teacher centers. What unifies these efforts at school improvement and teacher development is a shared perspective on teachers and how they can be helped to improve in their work. This perspective is relevant to various activities—curriculum development, inservice education, and innovation adoption.

A Point of View About Teacher/Staff Development

In studying effective inservice programs, researchers from the Rand Corporation discovered that successful districts did not have a *program* per se but a *point of view* which explicitly acknowledged teachers as professionals and visibly supported their efforts to grow and learn. One tangible sign of this point of view was the existence of a teacher center which provided a context for "useful peer interaction, for cross-fertilization, and for peer evaluation." The researchers judged these informal activities as more important than any new technologies or formal center programs (McLaughlin, 1977, p. 80). In an earlier study of federally initiated change efforts, the same researchers found that successful projects emphasized local invention rather than the implementation of "validated products." From the start, teachers were involved in the planning, and local leaders were utilized more than outside experts. Frequent project meetings gave teachers a forum to relate the project to their own situation and to get support for trying new ideas. Classroom advising provided timely assistance. In short, the most successful projects were not "projects" at all, but an integral part of an ongoing process of problem solving and school improvement (McLaughlin & Marsh, 1978).

Successful change efforts like effective inservice education reflect an expectation that teachers can grow and improve in their work. They set into motion a process of professional learning that is adaptive, concrete, tied to ongoing activities. They give teachers the skills to identify and solve problems themselves.

Traditional approaches to inservice training and school reform reflect different expectations and practices. They try to eliminate the process of professional learning with teacher-proof packages and one-shot training by outside experts. They convey a message that teachers are deficient and that other (researchers, administrators, legislators) know better what teachers need to improve.

There is growing evidence that an approach which views teachers as professionals and visibly supports their efforts to learn is more effective and enduring. The capacities that enable teachers to make something work are not unique to a given program or innovation. They are the same capacities that teachers use when they develop and evaluate materials, adapt their instruction to fit the needs of individual students, monitor their teaching and make necessary changes. If schools were organized so that teachers engaged in these activities as part of their work, we would not have to mount special training efforts in response to every new social mandate. The structures to deal with social change would already be in place.

CONCLUSIONS

This journey along the learning to teach continuum lends support to the arguments advanced at the beginning of the chapter about the relationship between how teachers learn to teach and how they are taught. Despite the limitations of the knowledge-base, a broad perspective enables us to assess the relative contribution of formal and informal sources of teachers' learning and to see the mismatch between formal arrangements for teacher education and the actual processes of teacher learning. Adjusting this mismatch involves more than filling in the gaps or responding to immediate needs.

Learning to teach begins long before formal programs of teacher preparation. Its roots are personal experiences with parents and teachers and images and patterns of teaching shaped by the culture. Most preservice programs do not challenge these early influences which provide unexamined models of practice.

We know very little about what prospective teachers actually learn during the preservice phase of learning to teach, but what we know indicates that preservice programs are not very powerful interventions. If schools were organized to support on-the-job learning, perhaps expectations for preservice teacher education could be adjusted to fit more realistic and appropriate goals.

Whatever preservice preparation is or could be, a major part of learning to teach inevitably occurs on the job. Some have called the first year of teaching *the* formative phase in the teacher's career. Moreover, studies of teacher development suggest that teachers only *begin* to concentrate on the relation between what they do as teachers and what students learn *after* they master the basic tasks of teaching somewhere around their fifth year.

Despite the centrality of learning on the job, helping teachers study their practice and make appropriate changes has not been considered a legitimate priority for inservice programming. Even the current interest in induction programs for beginning teachers is short-sighted if the primary intent is to ease the trauma of the first year of teaching rather than to help teachers learn from their classroom behavior and its consequences.

Given the relative impotence of formal programs at both the preservice and inservice levels, learning to teach is mostly influenced by informal sources, especially the experience of teaching itself. Experience is not always a good or effective teacher, however, and the problematic role of firsthand experience is apparent at every phase of the learning-to-teach continuum.

In the pretraining phase, prospective teachers store up countless impressions of teaching from more than 10,000 hours of teacher watching. Formal preparation does not offset these early experiences which contribute to the perpetuation of conservative school practice.

Teachers rate student teaching as the most valuable part of their preservice preparation. Research on student teaching suggests that the experience fosters a utilitarian perspective and a view of good teaching as a matter of maintaining order and keeping kids busy.

The first year of teaching is generally considered a critical time in learning to teach, but most beginning teachers have to flounder on their own. This strengthens their attachment to practices that helped them survive and reinforces a belief that learning to teach is a matter of independent trial and error.

In general, the isolation of teachers in their classrooms makes it easier to stick to comfortable practices without having to justify them. School norms often limit collegial interaction to giving advice and keep teachers from scrutinizing their own and each other's practice. Improvements in teaching are linked to ideas imported from the outside not to the ongoing responsibilities of teachers themselves.

Simple adjustments such as giving more time for classroom experience at the preservice level, providing support to beginning teachers, placing more importance on teachers' sharing their experiences with one another may appear to realign formal teacher education and actual processes of learning to teach. They are not likely to improve teaching or teacher education, however, unless we pay close attention to the content and context of these experiences. Furthermore without appropriate structures in formal teacher preparation and a school culture that supports learning from teaching, we cannot take advantage of the educative potential of teaching experience nor guard against its miseducative tendencies.

Learning to teach is a bigger job than universities, schools, experience or personal disposition alone can accomplish. Recognizing that fact, we can begin to develop a concept of learning to teach that fits the reality and fosters a vision of the possible.

REFERENCES

Becker, H. Personal change in adult life. *Sociometry*, 1964, 27, 40–53.

Berman, P. and McLaughlin, M. *Federal programs supporting educational changes*, (Vol. IV). *The findings in review.* Santa Monica, CA: The Rand Corp., 1975.

Bolam, R. *Introduction programmes for probationary teachers.* Bristol, England: University of Bristol, 1973.

Bolam, R., Baker, K. and McMahon, A. *The T.I.P.S. project national evaluation report.* Bristol, England: University of Bristol, School of Education, 1979.

Burden, P. *Teachers' perceptions of the characteristics and influences on their personal and professional development* (Doctoral dissertation, The Ohio State University, 1979). University Microfilms International, 1979, No. 8008776.

Conant, J. *The education of American teachers.* New York: McGraw Hill, 1963.

Davies, D., and Amershek, K. Student teaching. In R. Ebel (Ed.), *The encyclopedia of educational research.* New York: Macmillan, 1969.

Devaney, K. Warmth, concreteness, time, and thought in teachers' learning. In K. Devaney (Ed.) *Essays on teachers' centers*. San Francisco, CA: Far West Laboratory for Educational Research and Development, 1977.

Dewey, J. The relation of theory to practice in education. In M. Borrowman (Ed.), *Teacher education in America: A documentary history*. New York: Teachers College Press, 1904/1965.

Feiman, S. Technique and inquiry in teacher education: A curricular case study. *Curriculum Inquiry*, 9(1), 1979.

Feiman, S. Evaluating teacher centers. *School Review*, 85(3), May 1977, 395–411.

Field, K. *Teacher development: A study of the stages in the development of teachers*. Brookline, MA: Brookline Teacher Center, 1979.

Floden, R., and Feiman, S. *A developmental approach to the study of teacher change: What's to be gained?* (Research Series No. 93). East Lansing: Michigan State University, Institute for Research on Teaching, Feb. 1981.

Fox, T., Grant, C., Popkewitz, T., Rombert, T., Tabachnick, B. and, Wehlage, G. *The CMTI impact study*. Technical Reports No's. 1–21, Madison, WI: USOE Teacher Corps., 1976.

Friebus, R. Agents of socialization involved in student teaching. *The Journal of Educational Research*, 70, 1977.

Fuchs, E. *Teacher talk: View from inside city schools*. New York: Anchor Books, 1969.

Fuller, F., and Bown, O. On becoming a teacher. In K. Ryan (Ed.), *Teacher education* (The 74th National Society for the Study of Education yearbook). Chicago: University of Chicago Press, 1975.

Grant, C., and Zeichner, K. Inservice support for first year teachers: The state of the scene. *Journal of Research and Development in Education*, 1981, *14*, 99–111.

Hawkins, D. What it means to teach. *Teachers College Record*, 1973, 75(1), 7–16.

Howey, K. *School focused inservice education, clarification of a new concept and strategy: Synthesis report center for educational research and development*. OECP, Paris, France, 1980.

Howey, K., and Bents, R. *Toward meeting the needs of the beginning teacher: Initial training/induction/inservice*. Minneapolis, MN, 1979.

Howey, K., Yarger, S., and Joyce, B. *Improving teacher education*. Washington, D.C.: Association of Teacher Educators, 1978.

Hoy, W., Organizational socialization: The student teacher and pupil control ideology. *Journal of Educational Research*, 1967, 61, 153–155.

Hoy, W. The influence of experience on the beginning teacher. *School Review*, 1968, 76, 312–323.

Hoy, W. Pupil ideology and organizational socialization: A further examination of the influence of experience on the beginning teacher. *School Review*, 1969, 77, 257–265.

Hoy, W., and Rees, R. The bureaucratic socialization of student teachers. *Journal of Teacher Education*, 31(1), 1977.

Iannaccone, L. Student teaching: A transitional stage in the making of a teacher. *Theory into Practice*, 1963, 2, 73–80.

James, W. *Talks to teachers*. New York: Norton, 1958. (Originally published, 1904).

Katz, L. Issues and problems in teacher education. In B. Spodek (Ed.), *Teacher Education: Of the teacher, by the teacher, for the child*. Washington, D.C.: NAEYC, 1974.

Kohl, H. *On teaching.* New York Schocken Books, 1976.

Little, J. *School success and staff development: The role of staff development in urban desegregated schools* (Contract No. 400-79-0049). Boulder, CO: Center or Action Research, Inc., January 1981.

Lortie, D. Teacher socialization: The Robinson Crusoe model. *The real world of the beginning teacher.* Washington, D.C.: National Commission on Teacher Education and Professional Standards, 1966.

Lortie, D. *School teacher: A sociological study.* Chicago: The University of Chicago Press, 1975.

McDonald, F. The problems of beginning teachers: A crisis in training (Vol. 1). *Study of induction programs for beginning teachers.* Princeton, N.J.: Educational Testing Service, 1980.

McLaughlin, M. Pygmalion in the school district. In K. Devaney (ed.), *Essays on teachers' centers.* San Francisco, CA: Far West Laboratory for Educational Research and Development, 1977.

McLaughlin, M., and Marsh, D. Staff development and school change. In A. Lieberman and L. Miller (Eds.), *Staff development: New demands, new realities, new perspectives.* New York: Teachers College Press, 1979.

National Institute of Education. *Beginning teachers and internship programs* (R.F.P. No. 78-0014) Washington, D.C.: NIE, 1978.

Newberry, J. *The first year of experience: Influences on the beginning teacher.* Paper presented at the annual meeting of the American Educational Research Association, New York, 1977.

O'Shea, D. *The experience of teacher training: A case study.* Paper presented at the annual meeting of the American Educational Research Association, Los Angeles, 1981.

Richardson, G. X is for the unknown: Accounts of the first year of teaching. In K. Ryan (Ed.), *Don't smile until Christmas.* Chicago: The University of Chicago Press, 1970.

Ryan, K. *Don't smile until Christmas: Accounts of the first year of teaching.* Chicago: The University of Chicago Press, 1970.

Sarason, S. *The culture of the school and the problem of change.* Boston, MA: Allyn and Bacon, Inc., 1977.

Sarason, S., Davidson, K., and Blatt, B. *The preparation of teachers: An unstudied problem in education.* New York: John Wiley and Sons, Inc., 1962.

Stephens, J. Research in the preparation of teachers: Background factors that must be considered. In Herbert, J. and Ausubel, D.P. (Eds.), *Psychology in teacher preparation.* Toronto, Ontario: The Ontario Institute for Studies in Education Monograph Series No. 5, 1969.

Tabachnick, B., Popkewitz, T., Zeichner, K. *Teacher education and the professional perspectives of teachers.* Paper presented at the annual meeting of the American Educational Research Association, Toronto, March, 1978.

Tabachnick, B., Popkewitz, T., and Zeichner, K. Teacher education and the professional perspectives of student teachers. *Interchange,* 10(4), 1979/1980.

Tabachnick, R., Zeichner, K., Densmore, K., Adler, S., and Egan, K. *The impact of the student teaching experience on the development of teacher perspectives.* Paper presented at the annual meeting of the American Educational Research Association, New York City, March, 1982.

Waller, W. *The sociology of teaching.* New York: John Wiley and Sons, Inc., 1932.

Watts, H. *Starting out, moving on, running ahead or how the teachers' center can attend to stages in teachers' development.* Teacher's Centers Exchange (Occasional Paper No. 8) San Francisco: Far West Laboratory for Educational Research and Development, 1980.

Webb, C. Theoretical and empirical bases for early field experiences in teacher education. In C. Webb, N. Gehrke, P. Ishler and A. Mendoza (Eds.), *Exploratory field experiences in teacher education (Chap. 2).* Provo, UT: 1981.

Weber, L. The teacher as learner. In R. Dropkin (Ed.), *The center and the summer institute.* New York: City College Workshop Center for Open Education, 1977.

Wright, B., and Tuska, S. From dream to life in the psychology of becoming a teacher. *School Review,* 1968, 253–293.

Wright, B. Identification and becoming a teacher. *Elementary School Journal,* April 1959, 361–73.

CHAPTER 2

Teacher Preparation

Structural and Conceptual Alternatives

This paper focuses on different ways of conceiving and carrying out teacher preparation.[1] It examines some of the ideas that Americans have had about how teachers should be prepared and offers some frameworks for looking at distinctive approaches and alternatives.[2] The paper also discusses the state of the art concerning programs of initial teacher preparation and indicates where conceptual, empirical and practical work is needed.

The organization of this paper reflects a basic distinction in the professional literature and public debate. In discussing needed changes in teacher preparation, people tend to emphasize either structural or conceptual issues. Many of the current reforms, for example, call for adding a fifth year, increasing the amount of field experiences, limiting the number of credit hours in education, creating alternative routes to teaching by providing on-the-job training for liberal arts graduates. Tied to policy mandates and questions of supply and demand, these structural alternatives reflect political and economic considerations more than clear thinking about what teachers need to know or how they can be helped to learn that.

At the same time, one can hardly pick up a professional journal or attend a professional meeting these days without encountering the terms "reflective teaching and teacher education." Fifteen years ago, the same would have been true of the terms "competency-based" or "performance-based" teacher education. These conceptual alternatives reflect different views of teaching and learning to teach and suggest different orientations to the preparation of teachers.

Distinguishing between structural alternatives and conceptual orientations provides a way to highlight some of the major efforts that have dotted the teacher education landscape. At the same time, the need for such a strategy underscores the immature state of a field in which different forms of teacher preparation are only loosely tied to explicit traditions of thought, and conceptual orientations lack well developed traditions of practice. Instead of mandates and models, we need to learn from the past, experiment with alternatives and clarify what is entailed in helping people in different settings learn to teach.

HISTORIC TRADITIONS IN PREPARING TEACHERS

Today most teachers enter teaching by means of a four-year, undergraduate program. There was a time, however, when few believed that elementary teachers needed a college education, that high school teaching required professional preparation, or that teacher education was a fit undertaking for a major, research university. To appreciate how teacher preparation acquired its characteristic shape and where some of the major ideas about learning to teach have come from, we need to know something about the history of teacher education.

Three historic traditions have influenced ideas about and approaches to teacher preparation. Each tradition can be linked to a different institution offering a different kind of preparation to a different group of clients (see table 2.1 "Historical Traditions in Teacher Preparation"). The normal school tradition was intimately connected with the preparation of elementary teachers. The liberal arts tradition had early ties to the preparation of secondary teachers in liberal arts colleges. The tradition of professionalization through graduate preparation and research was promoted by the modern university which sought to prepare educational leaders.

The Normal School Tradition

The idea of teacher education as a special kind of academic training did not exist before there were normal schools. Prior to their appearance in the second quarter of the nineteenth century, few elementary teachers had any specific instruction for their work. Figuring out what kind of training to offer was the central challenge.

The early normal schools provided a brief course of study to help students master the subjects they would teach and acquire some techniques for managing instruction. With the spread of secondary education, normal

TABLE 2.1   Historical Traditions in Teacher Preparation

Institution	Elements/Themes	Clientele
Normal schools and teachers colleges	• institutional autonomy • professional esprit de corps • professional treatment of subject matter • art and science of teaching	Elementary teachers
Liberal arts colleges	• liberal arts as preparation for teaching • education as liberal art • intellectual values, knowledge and skills • common learnings	Secondary teachers
University schools of education	• research ideal • education as applied social science • professionalization through graduate study • devaluing of experience	Educational leaders

schools began to require a high school diploma for admission and to offer a two-year course of study. The typical curriculum consisted of reviews of elementary subjects (e.g., reading, spelling, arithmetic), some secondary academic subjects (e.g., geometry, philosophy) and pedagogical subjects (e.g., history of education, psychology, teaching methods, observation and practice [Monroe, 1952]).

When students had barely completed elementary school, it made sense to review the "common branches." Once normal schools required a high school diploma, some leaders felt that these schools should not duplicate academic instruction available in secondary schools and colleges. Rather they should offer a "strictly professional" curriculum. There were two approaches to this goal. One school of thought emphasized the "professional treatment of subject matter;" a second, emphasized training in special methods (Cremin, 1953).

Professional treatment of subject matter. Proponents of the professional treatment position believed that a teacher's knowledge of subjects differed from "academic" knowledge. This idea was promoted at Indiana State Normal School where faculty developed a distinctive kind of instruction in which "the method of the subject" became the main object of attention. Subject matter courses modeled principles taught in professional courses on the psychology of learning. Methods courses engaged students in reflection on their own experience as learners of school subjects as a way of sensitizing them to problems their pupils might encounter (Borrowman, 1956; Randolph, 1924). In this way, the entire program was organized around the professional goal.

Technical theory and methods. The second approach to creating a "strictly professional" curriculum emphasized technical theory and training in method. Edward Sheldon, president of Oswego Normal and Training School, developed a philosophy and methodology called "object teaching" based on ideas about the dignity and worth of children and the role of the senses in learning. Under this system, students learned special rules for teaching various subjects and practiced them in the training school. Sheldon considered the training school the heart of the professional program. Here students could observe model lessons and practice approved methods under close supervision. Recognized as part of the necessary equipment for training teachers, the practice school fostered close ties between pedagogical theory and practice. "Object teaching" was replaced by a second general method developed by the Herbartians. Also influenced by European pedagogical theory, the Herbartians emphasized technical competence. They believed that sound teaching consisted of five formal steps: preparation, presentation, association, generalization, and application. These ideas, which sound like contemporary models of direct instruction, were popular during the last quarter of the nineteenth century (Woodring, 1975).

While we tend to associate normal schools with narrow training, this judgment ignores the historic context in which they evolved and their hard-won gains in differentiating professional from liberal arts education. Commenting on their contribution, Clifford and Guthrie (1988) write:

> Although, in fact, the nineteenth century normal schools were never the single-minded and essential teacher education centers that their supporters had wished, their disappearance took with it two professional assets: First, the ideal of the autonomous professional school devoted solely to the exalted preparation of teachers and second, a dominating concern with "practical pedagogy." (p. 61)

Normal schools had a clear sense of their mission. They championed the idea of teaching as a noble calling or vocation and fostered a professional esprit de corps. Unlike modern-day schools of education with their fragmented mission and defensive posture, normal schools knew that their major purpose was to serve the profession by educating practitioners. They "formed" their students more effectively than the large university schools and departments of education that replaced them (Powell, 1980, p. 59). They also "glorified and supported the ideal of superb craftsmanship" (Borrowman, 1956, p. 19). The normal school curriculum gave explicit attention to pedagogical training and supervised practice and the practice school, at least in the stronger normal schools, fostered close ties between theory and practice (Clifford and Guthrie, 1988).

The Liberal Arts Tradition

The older, liberal arts tradition predates any thought of teacher preparation as a special kind of schooling. Linked in the nineteenth century with the preparation of secondary teachers, the liberal arts tradition highlights the unique relationship between liberal education and teaching. According to this tradition, "to be liberally educated and to be prepared to teach are equivalent" (Borrowman, 1965, p. 1).

In the nineteenth century, liberal arts colleges and secondary schools formed a "closed circle." The colleges offered a classical education to a select group of students who mostly entered the higher professions and became leaders in the community. A few taught in secondary schools which were elite, college preparatory institutions (Borrowman, 1956; Church and Sedlak, 1976). The expansion of secondary education brought a more diverse student population and the need to adapt the high school curriculum to a broader set of purposes. Still, liberal arts colleges kept their distance from school reform and persisted in the view that a liberal arts program was the best preparation for teaching, especially at the secondary level (Borrowman, 1956; Church and Sedlak, 1976; Cremin, 1953).

The idea that "liberal" and "useful" knowledge were incompatible dominated collegiate education for a long time. Harking back to the Greeks who reserved the liberal arts for free citizens, supporters of the classical curriculum believed that liberal study was only possible when students were not preoccupied with the immediate demands of vocational preparation (Borrowman, 1956). Although not designed with vocational goals in mind, the traditional college program served both liberal and professional aims. It inducted students into a common body of cultural knowledge. It fostered intellectual habits and skills deemed necessary for continued learning. It sought to develop humane values and a sense of social responsibility. At the same time, the classical curriculum exposed students to the best available thinking about education. Texts encountered in courses on mental and moral philosophy such as Aristotle's *Ethics* and Cicero's *Orations* discussed the meaning of a good life, the role of education in society, the nature of learning and human development, even methods of teaching.

The "modern" research university that emerged at the end of the 19th century altered the traditional definition of liberal arts education by attacking the notion that only certain subjects were inherently "liberal." New disciplines like the natural sciences were developing and some university leaders thought they should be taught. The rejection of the classical curriculum inspired various experiments in general education during the early decades of the twentieth century. Designed to balance the traditional liberal arts ideal of a common course of study with growing specialization, these experiments typically involved a prescribed curriculum in the first two years to ensure breadth of exposure and understanding with opportunities for electives in the last two years to respond to students' specialized interests. While the liberal arts tradition represented a defense against early specialization, both academic and professional, it became increasingly difficult in the 20th century to preserve those values in the university and even in the liberal arts college.

While the liberal arts tradition concerns the education of teachers as individuals, citizens and professionals, it does not prescribe a particular course of study. Rather, each generation must define the meaning of liberal education for its own time (Tom, n.d.). Kimball (1986) argues that the idea of liberal education embraces two contradictory traditions—the tradition of the philosophers with their commitment to reason and the tradition of the orators with their commitment to tradition and community. Historically, the liberal arts college sided with the orators' emphasis on language and texts while the modern research university allied itself with the philosophers' pursuit of knowledge. The challenge for teacher educators is to recover elements of both traditions and link them with the theme of democracy (Featherstone, 1988).

The liberal arts tradition underscores the special ties that link intellectual arts, academic content, and teaching. While some people associate a liberal arts education with subject matter preparation, this interpretation misses the larger message. What makes the relationship between liberal education and teacher education unique is the fact that the goods intrinsic to liberal education—humane values, critical thinking, historic perspective, broad knowledge—are central to teaching (Travers and Sacks, 1987). They are, in short, the very tools of the teacher's trade. Moreover, the liberal arts tradition construes education itself as a liberal art. "The study of education,"

writes Silberman (1970), "is the study of almost every question of importance in philosophy, history, and sociology . . . there can be no concept of
the good life or the good society apart from a concept of the kind of education needed to sustain it" (p. 384). From this perspective the academic study
of education belongs at the center of a liberal arts curriculum.

Professionalizing Education Through Scientific Research and Graduate Preparation

The creation of university schools of education at the turn of the century
was part of a larger movement to professionalize various occupations. Like
their counterparts in law and medicine, educators sought to place teacher
education in the modern research university, hoping that the new location
would dignify education as a career, lead to the development of a specialized
knowledge base, and support the professional preparation of educational
leaders (Clifford and Guthrie, 1988; Powell, 1976).

Graduate preparation for careers in education. Early on, leading university schools of education bypassed the preparation of new teachers, concentrating instead on graduate programs for experienced teachers interested
in careers outside the classroom. Previous efforts to transform high school
teaching into a respected profession through graduate preparation proved
unrealistic and inappropriate in the face of mass secondary education. The
unanticipated growth of secondary schools did create a need for administrators, supervisors, and specialists; and schools of education found a new
social mission in training experienced, male teachers for these roles (Powell, 1976). Education faculty recognized that gender played a part in the low
esteem many had for teaching and teacher education. They sought to overcome the stigma by focusing on career opportunities for ambitious school-
men. Unfortunately by increasing the status of those leaving the classroom,
they lowered the status of those who remained (Clifford and Guthrie, 1988,
p. 119).

The research ideal. While fields like law and theology found the codification
of experience to be a useful strategy for creating a knowledge base, schools
of education adopted the approach of the natural sciences. Developing a
"science of education" through research became an overriding concern.
The science of education movement embraced experimental and quantitative methods. Psychologist Edward Thorndike of Teacher College discovered general laws of learning through laboratory experiments and led the

development of intelligence and achievement tests. The new fields of administration and supervision eagerly applied the tools of quantitative measurement to problems of school organization and pupil classification.

As the number of education faculty with social science training and research interests increased, the focus shifted from psychology and measurement. A growing confidence in the capacity of social science research to solve broad, social problems led to a new wave of research that rarely addressed problems confronting teachers in classrooms. The emphasis on research and academic specialization had a fragmenting effect on the curriculum. Courses, organized along disciplinary or occupational lines, proliferated. Even courses for practitioners treated students as though they were preparing to do research (Powell, 1976).

Devaluing experience. In searching for a special expertise that could not be supplied by experience, education faculty cut themselves off from models of good practice. Though early schools of education often drew inspiration from medical education, the idea of the teaching hospital as a setting for experimental treatment, research and professional training did not transfer. Even the label "laboratory" school applied to some campus or affiliated schools was an "empty promise." Educational researchers were not interested in studying classroom problems, supervision of practice teaching carried little status, and developing exemplary training sites required considerable resources (Clifford and Guthrie, 1988, pp. 109–121).

The historic distinctions between the normal school and the liberal arts traditions did not disappear when teacher education took up residence in the modern university. Rather they increased as schools of education found themselves caught between pressures from the university and pressures from the field. During their formative period, leading schools of education accommodated these academic and professional pressures by ignoring initial teacher preparation and concentrating instead on graduate training and research. These policies may help explain why Borrowman (1956) characterizes the opening decades of the twentieth century as a time when the purposes of teacher education received little serious attention. Still, the leading schools of education did bequeath a mixed legacy that continues to influence the character of teacher preparation and proposals for its improvement. That legacy includes the precedent of professionalization through graduate training, the ideal of scientific research as the key to an authoritative knowledge base, a devaluing of experience, and a continuing estrangement from teachers in the field and academic colleagues in the university (Judge, 1982).

STRUCTURAL ALTERNATIVES

> 3 + 2 programs will become the more likely professional pattern among innovative programs by the middle of the 1990s and the 3 + 3 teaching program . . . will evolve from the integrated five-year programs and will probably be rather common within another generation. (Monahan, 1984, p. 43)

> The 4 + 1 model creates a relatively inexpensive program of short duration which can be subsidized if necessary when shortages become critical. (Wise, 1986, p. 39)

> Our experience suggests that the two-year, postbaccalaureate Teacher Corps model is superior to the one-year MAT program and also to the four year undergraduate model. (Bush, 1977, p. 6)

These three passages reflect a particular way of thinking about teacher preparation. They describe programs in terms of their general organization, specifying the length of the two main components. They imply that four-year, undergraduate programs are inadequate and should be replaced with a different model. They give the impression that this kind of general description is a meaningful way to characterize different approaches to teacher preparation. The passages also reflect the escalation of credentials that has characterized the field. From the days of the normal schools to the present, reformers have sought to improve the status and quality of teaching and teacher preparation by lengthening programs and adding requirements. The tendency to impose structural changes in the hopes that substantive changes will follow or to link quality with particular institutional arrangements is all too familiar.

Most teachers enter teaching by way of a four year, preservice program. The object of much criticism, undergraduate teacher education is the norm against which various structural alternatives have been proposed. One alternative involves extending the undergraduate program to five years. A second involves shifting or delaying professional studies until the graduate level. A third involves bypassing professional studies completely in favor of on-the-job training. Designed to address various limitations associated with undergraduate teacher preparation, these alternative structures differ in the extensiveness of the preparation they offer and in the ways they define the boundaries of their responsibility.

Undergraduate Programs

Despite considerable variation among the institutions that offer undergraduate programs, many people assume that such programs, like Gertrude

Stein's proverbial rose, are all pretty much the same. Certainly common ways of talking give the impression that there is such a thing as a "typical" program. Four-year programs are so uniform, notes Kerr (1983), that "a Trollope would surely mistakenly believe that a national curriculum has been imposed" (p. 133). The impression of sameness in content, organization and structure is reinforced by surveys of preservice preparation (American Association of Colleges of Teacher Education, 1987; Joyce, Yarger, and Howey, 1977). For example, the Preservice Teacher Education Study (Joyce, Yarger, and Howey, 1977; Yarger and Howey, 1977), which surveyed faculty, students and heads of education units in a random sample of 238 institutions preparing teachers, found "limited variation" in programs across the country. Commenting on the findings, Howey (1983) observes: "Initial training or teacher preparation programs across the country tend to appear quite similar at least in terms of the number and general type of experiences they afford students and the structure and framework in which these are organized" (p. 11).

A *"plain vanilla" program.* When people talk about a traditional preservice program, they have in mind a four-year program in which the first two years are devoted to general education and the last two to professional studies. The modern formula of breadth plus depth defined in terms of three or four grand divisions of knowledge (humanities, social sciences, natural sciences, fine arts) and calculated in courses and credits shapes general education requirements for teachers. Secondary education students major in an academic field close to their teaching subject; elementary majors construct a collection of academic minors supposedly related to the elementary school curriculum.

The professional sequence is also differentiated by teaching level. For elementary teachers, it consists of some sort of introduction to education, a course in educational psychology; six or seven methods courses for teaching reading, social studies, arithmetic, science, art and music; and student teaching. For secondary teachers, it involves a course in adolescent psychology, a general methods course, a subject-specific methods course and student teaching (Clark and Marker, 1975; Howey, Yarger, and Joyce, 1978). Typically the sequence begins with more theoretical courses often accompanied by some form of field experience and culminates in practice teaching (American Association of Colleges of Teacher Education, 1987). In terms of time, which many see as a major constraint, elementary education students complete an average of 50 of their 125 hours of credit in education, compared with secondary education students who average only 26 hours of credit in education (American Association of Colleges of Teacher Education, 1987, p. 12).

Where did this familiar structure come from? Cremin (1978) attributes the "present day paradigm of professional training in education" to James Earl Russell, dean of Teachers College (1894–1927), and his colleagues. According to Cremin, this model emerged at the turn of the century alongside different models in other fields as a response to widespread dissatisfaction with professional training at that time (e.g., apprenticeships for lawyers, proprietary schools for doctors, academies and normal schools for teachers).

Russell's paradigm: spirit or letter? In Russell's terms, a proper curriculum for teachers should contain four components: general culture, special scholarship, professional knowledge, and technical skill. Cremin summarizes what Russell had in mind:

> By general culture, he meant . . . the kind of preparation that would enable the student to see the relationships among the various fields of knowledge. . . . By special scholarship, he meant not only further academic study but the kind of reflective inquiry that would equip an aspiring teacher to select different sequences of material and adapt them to the needs of different students. . . . By professional knowledge, he implied . . . systematic inquiry into the theory and practice of education in the United States and abroad. . . . And, by technical skill, he implied . . . expert ability in determining what to teach and by what methods, when and to whom. Technical skill would be acquired in an experimental or model school, serving as a laboratory for pedagogical inquiry and a demonstration center for excellent practice. . . . The teachers in the school would be critic-teachers, capable of exemplifying first-class reflective pedagogy at the same time that they oversaw the training of novices (pp. 10–11).

While we can discern the basic structure of Russell's curriculum in the familiar components of the typical undergraduate program, it is the letter not the spirit of the proposal that stands out. The dominance of the general education sequence reflects widespread agreement about its importance. In practice, however, general education is more like a supermarket where students make independent choices from a wide array of offerings. Rarely does it provide broad cultural knowledge or deep and flexible subject matter understanding.

Organizationally and conceptually, general education and professional education are separate and distinct. This makes it difficult to orient the study of academic content around problems of teaching and learning despite the fact that such an orientation might be as helpful to students who do not intend to teach as to those who do. In the professional sequence, the balance between what Borrowman (1956) calls the "liberal" and the "technical" seems tilted in the direction of the technical. Methods courses dominate, taught not by master teachers but by university professors. Foundational knowledge comes mostly from educational psychology. The development of technical skills is limited to a brief stint of student teaching. In short, the typical undergraduate program seems more like an organizational compromise, the offspring of an unhappy union between the normal school and the liberal arts traditions.

Critics. From their beginnings, undergraduate programs have been the object of intense criticism. Academics (e.g., Bestor, 1953; Conant, 1963; Koerner, 1963) charge that education courses lack rigor; teachers claim they lack practical relevance (Lortie, 1975). Despite the fact that faculty in the arts and sciences provide most of the undergraduate courses that future teachers take, criticism about teacher preparation has often meant criticism of the professional sequence.

Some researchers blame structural features in the undergraduate context for constraining programs and undermining improvement efforts. They point to persistent underfunding, second-class status, the diffuse nature of program responsibility and accountability (Clark and Marker, 1975; Clark, 1986; Kerr, 1983; Peseau, 1982). While future teachers take most of their undergraduate courses in academic departments, for example, these units are organized with little attention to their teacher education function (Lanier and Little, 1986). Until teacher education is removed from the undergraduate context, the argument goes, it will not be able to overcome these barriers.

Recent studies in higher education have focused on the need to improve the quality of undergraduate education overall (Association of American Colleges, 1985; Boyer, 1987; Department of Education, 1984). From the standpoint of teacher preparation, the criticism is timely. Still, the prospects for genuine reform are unclear. As Tom (1986) points out, the real task is to rethink general education and subject matter preparation, not simply expand requirements in these areas since "the problem with general education is its quality and coherence, not its length" (p. 31).

Supporters. Not all critics of undergraduate teacher preparation question its viability. Even a harsh critic like Conant (1963), whose study of American teacher education became a best seller, thought teachers could be adequately prepared for initial employment in four years provided they had a good high school education and an appropriate balance of general education, academic concentration, and professional studies. Conant outlined programs for elementary and secondary teachers that emphasized broad academic studies, minimal professional education, and a combination of methods instruction and practice teaching supervised by a "clinical professor," an expert teacher with high university rank.

Contemporary supporters of baccalaureate approaches to teacher preparation agree that the present size of the preservice curriculum is sufficient given the current status of pedagogical knowledge. They also claim that undergraduate programs allow for the integration of general and professional education, capitalize on the youthful idealism of students, provide a more cost-effective alternative than postbaccalaureate programs and support a developmental curriculum. Combined with a careful induction program for first-year teachers, they argue that undergraduate teacher preparation is a viable option (Hawley, 1986; Tom, 1986).

Extended (Five-Year) Programs

In an extended or five-year program, students begin their professional work as undergraduates and continue through a fifth year of professional study and supervised internship. While most extended programs culminate in a master's degree and certification, some end only in certification.

Supporters argue that the five-year structure offers a more flexible framework and results in better integration of theory and practice. The extended time frame allows the possibility of greater emphasis on academic preparation and fieldwork and has encouraged some rethinking of the professional sequence (Denemark and Nutter, 1984; Scannell, 1987; Weinstein, 1988).

Some extended programs try to improve on conventional undergraduate programs by avoiding the proliferation of methods courses. At the University of Virginia, for example, separate methods courses have been replaced by six-credit "blocs" in language skills (reading, language arts, children's literature, creative arts) and reasoning skills (mathematics, science, social studies, and creative arts [Weinstein, 1988]). The reduction of subject-specific methods courses tends to reinforce a generic view of teaching.

Another common feature of extended programs is the emphasis on field experiences that begin early, continue throughout the undergraduate years, and culminate in a semester of student teaching or a fifth-year internship. Compared with an undergraduate- or a graduate-level program, an extended program offers the possibility for a gradual induction into the study and practice of teaching.

Sometimes the promise of the five-year structure is compromised when a significant number of students transfer in as juniors or fifth-year students or cannot meet the requirements for graduate study (Zeichner, 1988a). Moreover, the graduate status of integrated programs may also be questionable if fifth-year courses do not build on prior knowledge and experience and offer greater intellectual challenge than undergraduate courses (Weinstein, 1988).

Graduate-Level Programs

Since the turn of the century, graduate-level preservice programs have been associated with efforts to professionalize teaching (Wise, 1986). Popular during times of teacher shortage, graduate programs are supposed to attract stronger candidates, offer more rigorous instruction and carry greater prestige than undergraduate programs. Supporters claim that having students spend four years acquiring a liberal arts education before they undertake professional studies means they will be better educated and have a strong grounding in their teaching subjects. Two types of postbaccalaureate preservice programs can be discerned—an MAT (master of arts in teaching) model emphasizing academic knowledge and practical experience and a professional model combining professional studies with guided practice.

Academic model. The MAT program originated in the 1930s when James Conant, president of Harvard, proposed a new kind of teacher preparation for secondary teachers that would help bridge the gap between education and the arts and sciences (Powell, 1980). The program combined advanced study of a scholarly discipline with a sequence of professional seminars and an internship. While the program attracted few students, it provided the prototype for MAT programs that flourished in the 50s and 60s with support from the Ford Foundation (Cogan, 1955; Stone, 1968; Woodring, 1957). Recruitment of liberal arts students into teaching was an overriding goal. The Foundation supported programs at Ivy League institutions and directed resources toward elaborate recruiting schemes. The emphasis on a scholarly curriculum and the creation of a new academic degree were also designed to lure students wary of traditional education courses (Powell, 1980; Woodring, 1957). Stone (1968) offers the following description of a "typical" MAT program:

> The graduate student arrives at the university in June. The first week of the summer, he (approximately two-thirds of the students were women)

enrolls in six to eight units of education courses at the same time assisting in teaching high school classes on campus or at a public school. During the second six weeks of the summer session he takes regular academic courses. Then the MAT candidates are divided, half beginning full-time teaching internships at nearby schools and the other half continuing on campus as full-time graduate students. At the end of the fall semester, the two groups reverse their activities. By the following June, candidates are eligible for the Master of Arts in Teaching degree and have qualified for their teaching credentials. (p. 96)

While MAT programs succeeded as a recruiting strategy (Coley and Thorpe, 1985; Stone, 1968; Zeichner, 1988b), they did not lead to new conceptualizations of subject matter knowledge or pedagogical understanding and skill (Clifford and Guthrie, 1988; Powell, 1980). Students took regular academic courses, designed for potential researchers and scholars, and most programs relied on a disciplinary approach to educational foundations. When external funding ran out and the teacher shortage ended, many programs disappeared. Although MAT programs left behind good ideas about financing internships and using summer school as a laboratory for demonstrating pedagogy, they did not advance our understanding about how to institutionalize such practices.

Professional model. The professionally oriented, preservice master's degree program represents a contrast with the academically oriented MAT approach. The idea has been promoted by educators who believe that the key to upgrading the quality of teaching lies in professional education not recruitment. One such educator was Henry Holmes, dean of the Harvard Graduate School of Education in the 20s, who vigorously promoted the EdM (master of education) as the highest practitioner degree in professional education. Influenced by other professional schools at Harvard, Holmes advocated a two-year, professional preparation sequence that would follow the completion of a liberal arts college course; the goal—to train educators rather than craftsmen, professionals who could interpret issues, policies, and decisions in terms of their impact on educational goals (Powell, 1980).

The success of this "radical adventure" depended on the development of a curriculum that would transform novices into educators. Holmes envisioned an intense, prolonged, integrated experience that would fuse knowledge, understanding, skills and outlook into an "active whole" (Powell, 1980, p. 159). Holmes sought but never succeeded in identifying a set of fundamental principles around which to organize the professional curriculum. After a decade of trying, he sadly concluded that the problem seemed to lie in the state of the field (Powell, 1980). It is fitting and a bit ironic that a major national effort to reform teaching and teacher education today should carry Holmes' name (Holmes Group, 1986). The Holmes Group, a consortium of education deans and chief academic officers from 120 research universities in each of the 50 states, is dedicated to the improvement of teacher education and the construction of a genuine profession of teaching. Like its namesake, the Holmes Group advocates the elimination of undergraduate degrees in education in favor of graduate-level programs; however, the Holmes Group's emphasis on scientific knowledge and research and their endorsement of a hierarchy of teacher roles reflect different values from those advocated by Holmes himself (Johnson, 1987).

The group's first report, *Tomorrow's Teachers*, calls for a rethinking of liberal arts education including the design of more coherent majors, graduate-level professional studies, better articulation between pedagogical and clinical studies, the creation of exemplary training sites along the lines of a teaching hospital, and the establishment of a new career structure in teaching based on different kinds of professional preparation. The report claims that "a vital program of professional studies" can now be designed because scientific research has produced a body of professional knowledge helpful to teachers. According to the report, the "science of education promised by Dewey, Thorndike, and others at the turn of the century, has become more tangible." (p. 52) If this were so, a central problem that has plagued teacher education since its inception—the lack of a specialized knowledge base derived neither from the academic disciplines nor from experience alone—is closer to being solved than ever before.

Both critics and supporters of the Holmes Group point out that such claims are excessive and imply a devaluing of teachers' practical knowledge (Jackson, 1987; Zumwalt, 1987). Holmes himself emphasized practitioner training over scientific research because he saw how the university's emphasis on research widened the gap between researchers and practitioners and created a hierarchy in the education profession with researchers at the top and teachers at the bottom (Johnson, 1987). The Holmes Group proposals call for the redesign of every aspect of teacher preparation and require collaboration among groups that have historically not worked well together. It is too soon to tell what kinds of structural and conceptual changes will result from this latest effort at promoting graduate-level teacher preparation as part of a comprehensive reform effort (Woolfolk, 1988a, 1988b).

Alternative Certification Programs

Alternative certification programs are designed to increase the supply of teachers in areas of critical need during times of teacher shortage. A form of nontraditional teacher preparation, alternative certification programs provide on-the-job training to college graduates with no previous education background. Supporters claim that alternative certification programs attract talented people who might otherwise not go into teaching by avoiding certain features of traditional teacher preparation. For example, the traditional undergraduate program requires an early commitment (e.g., junior year), consumes a third of one's college education, and offers little or no financial assistance. Alternative certification programs do not require an early commitment and they reduce the costs of training by shortening the time frame and paying a salary (Carey, Mittman, and Darling-Hammond, 1988).

Alternative certification programs rely on provisional teachers' undergraduate programs to provide a good general education and an adequate grounding in subject matter. The program itself emphasizes learning by doing and the wisdom of practice. Sponsored by school districts and state education departments, alternative certification programs are oriented toward helping new teachers learn their jobs in particular contexts. The distinction between preservice and inservice teacher education disappears as alternative certification candidates learn to teach while teaching.

The typical program includes some formal instruction and work with an experienced teacher. Offered in the evenings, on weekends and during the summer, the formal instruction often focuses on practical "how to" topics (Adelman, 1986). Support and advice are provided by "mentor" teachers, usually classroom teachers, who receive a stipend for their work. For example, New Jersey's Provisional Teacher Program requires 200 hours of formal instruction, 80 during the first six weeks of the program and the rest throughout the year. Offered in regional training centers managed by a school of education, the training addresses broad topics mandated by the state—curriculum and instruction, classrooms and schools, student learning, and development.

The local school district assumes responsibility for the practical aspects of the training. Each teacher is assigned a three-member support team consisting of a principal, experienced teacher, and another educator. In the first phase of the clinical component, the provisional teacher works for a month with an experienced teacher undergoing a gradual introduction to the classroom. During the 10 weeks of the second phase, the provisional teacher is supervised at least once a week by one member of the support team, usually the experienced teacher. At the end of Phase Two, the first formative evaluation is performed by the principal who also solicits feedback from other members of the support team. Phase Three includes the remaining 20 weeks of the academic year. During this time the provisional teacher must be supervised at least once a month and two more evaluations are carried out. A final summative evaluation occurs after the 30th week of full-time teaching (Natriello, 1988).

Because alternative certification programs are new, we know relatively little about the kind of preparation they offer and the sort of teaching they promote. Clearly their success hinges on the caliber of the recruits and the quality of the supervision. In terms of recruitment goals, however, they seem to be attracting strong candidates from a variety of labor market pools (Adelman, 1986; Carey, Mittman, and Darling-Hammond, 1988; Natriello, Zumwalt, Hansen, and Frisch, 1988). Many policymakers regard alternative certification programs as a promising strategy for balancing the competing demands of quantity and quality (Carey, Mittman, and Darling-Hammond, 1988; Oliver and McKibbin, 1985). In the last few years, 23 states have enacted provisions for alternative certification (Feistritzer, 1986). But critics argue that such programs undermine efforts to professionalize teaching. At a time when the work of teachers is becoming increasingly complex, alternative certification programs allow people to teach with little formal preparation.

Discussion

Reforms in teacher education tend to pit one set of institutional arrangements against another—normal schools vs. teachers colleges in the past, undergraduate programs vs. graduate or alternative certification programs in the present. In fact, we know relatively little about what goes on inside these different program structures.

The forms of teacher preparation discussed in this section differ in the extensiveness of the preparation they offer, in the way they define the boundaries of their responsibility, and in their location on the preservice-inservice continuum. Four- and five-year programs encompass both general and professional education; graduate and alternative route programs assume that candidates will come with a solid liberal arts background and adequate grounding in their teaching subjects. The widespread criticism of general education, however, raises questions about the adequacy of teachers' academic preparation whether or not it falls inside or outside the boundaries of the program's responsibility.

In terms of professional education, all forms must confront the question of what teachers need to know and how they can be helped to acquire and develop that knowledge. Except for alternative certification programs which take a clear stand on the matter, none of the other program forms is uniquely associated with a particular point of view. All must determine what counts as "knowledge for teaching" and decide how to embody it in a preservice curriculum.

Obviously differences in the time frame and timing of the professional sequence affect what is possible. Four- and five-year programs, for example, allow for a spiral curriculum and a staged induction into the study and practice of teaching. Fifth-year programs do not, especially when they are largely taken up with an internship.

Four-year programs fit completely within the preservice phase of learning to teach; five-and fifth-year programs may bridge the preservice-inservice continuum. Because alternative certification route programs provide on-the-job training to novice teachers, they could technically be considered a form of inservice. While quality programs require adequate time, time alone does not guarantee quality. The important question is how that time is spent. Such a question cannot be answered by focusing on the structure alone.

While reformers debate the relative merits of one form over another, the dominance of a given program structure at a particular historic moment depends as much on compelling social forces as it does on the demonstrated strengths or weaknesses of the form itself. There are several contemporary trends that may influence the popularity and availability of different forms of teacher preparation. These include efforts by state legislators to limit undergraduate credits in education, the availability of alternative certification route programs, the challenge to vocationalism at the undergraduate level by the reform movement in liberal arts education, and an increase in the number of "at risk" students in schools (Wilkinson, 1988). Ironically, as the work of teaching is becoming more complex and challenging, suggesting the need for more extensive preparation, forces are in operation which permit college graduates to begin teaching with minimal preparation.

Finally, the history of teacher education suggests the importance of institutional norms in shaping the character and quality of preservice programs (Rhoades, 1985). As Clark and Marker (1975) observe: "The critical variance in teacher education programs among institutions is more a function of overall variance by institutional types than a systematic variation attributable to the professional training itself" (p. 58). While an undergraduate teacher education program in a liberal arts college may have the same components as an undergraduate program in a state university, what goes on inside the components may be very different (Howey and Zimpher, 1989; National Center for Research on Teacher Education, 1988a). To some extent, the impression of sameness among four-year programs may be an artifact of survey research that focuses on surface features and ignores institutional variation.

CONCEPTUAL ORIENTATIONS

An orientation refers to a set of ideas about the goals of teacher preparation and the means for achieving them. Ideally, a conceptual orientation includes a view of teaching and learning and a theory about learning to teach. Such ideas should give direction to the practical activities of teacher preparation such as program planning, course development, instruction, supervision, evaluation. This section surveys five conceptual orientations in teacher preparation: (a) academic; (b) practical; (c) technological; (d) personal; and (e) critical/social.

Unlike structural alternatives, conceptual orientations are not tied to particular forms of teacher preparation. They can shape a single component or an entire professional sequence, apply to undergraduate- as well as graduate-level programs. Nor are the conceptual orientations mutually exclusive. By design or default, they can and indeed do exist side by side in the same program.

Since the mid-seventies, several typologies for examining conceptual variations in teacher education have been proposed (Hartnett and Naish, 1980; Joyce, 1975; Kennedy, 1987; Kirk, 1986; Zeichner, 1983; Zimpher and Howey, 1987). A comparison of these typologies reveals considerable overlap in the theoretical perspectives, models, paradigms discussed. Of the six typologies identified for this review, all include something resembling the critical, technological, and practical schools of thought; three acknowledge a personal tradition; and two an academic orientation (see table 2.2 "Conceptual Orientations in Teacher Education"). The major difference between the present formulation and previous ones is the treatment of the practical and academic orientations. By linking the practical orientation with a more respectful stance toward the "wisdom of practice," and the academic ori-

TABLE 2.2   Conceptual Orientations in Teacher Education

	Academic	Practical	Technological	Personal	Critical/Social
Joyce (1975)	academic	traditional	competency	personalistic	progressive
Harnett and Naish (1980)		craft	technological		critical
Zeichner (1983)	academic	craft	behavioristic	personalistic	inquiry
Kirk (1986)			rationalism		radicalism
Zimpher and Howey (1987)		clinical	technical	personal	critical
Kennedy (1987)		deliberate action; critical analysis	application of skills; application of principles and theories		

entation with new research on subject matter pedagogy, both categories are extended beyond their traditional associations.

Reflective teaching as a generic professional disposition. Some readers may wonder about the absence of a reflective orientation. Analyzing various descriptions of "reflective" teacher education programs (e.g., Beyer, 1984; Cruichshank, 1987; Feiman, 1979; Goodman, 1984; Noordhoff and Kleinfeld, 1987; Posner, 1985; Zeichner and Liston, 1987) and considering recent attempts to distinguish different versions of reflective teacher education (Clift, Houston and Pugach, in press; Liston and Zeichner, 1988a; Tom, 1985; Valli and Taylor, 1987) led to the conclusion that reflective teacher education is not a distinct programmatic emphasis but a generic professional disposition. This position is supported by the fact that many of the programs described in this section explicitly endorse the goal of reflection.

What differentiates advocates of reflective teaching and teacher education are their substantive goals which suggest different levels or foci for reflection (Van Manen, 1977). For example, a technological orientation may focus reflection on the most effective or efficient means to achieve particular instructional objectives, while a practical orientation may encourage reflection on practical dilemmas or tensions among competing goals in particular situations while illustrating different conceptual observations.

Describing orientations. Each orientation has a focus or thesis that highlights certain aspects of teaching, learning and learning to teach, directs attention to a central goal of teacher preparation and is manifest in particular practices. While the orientations do not have uniform and explicit positions on each of these dimensions, it is possible to summarize what supporters have to say about the teacher's role, teaching and learning, knowledge for teaching and learning to teach. To illustrate the practical expression of different orientations, programs or components are described. These brief sketches, based mostly on efforts by faculty to explain, document, and evaluate their own work, often reflect the espoused rather than the enacted curriculum. Still the descriptions reveal some of the diversity within each category and provide a basis for thinking about the value and limitations of describing teacher preparation in terms of conceptual orientations.

The Academic Orientation

The academic orientation in teacher preparation highlights the fact that teaching is primarily concerned with the transmission of knowledge and the development of understanding. Traditionally associated with liberal arts education and secondary teaching, the academic orientation emphasizes the teacher's role as intellectual leader, scholar, subject matter specialist. Supporters of the academic tradition, even those skeptical of teacher preparation, have always stressed the importance of teachers' academic preparation, but there is a growing appreciation that the kind of subject matter knowledge teachers need is not likely to be acquired through academic study alone.

The academic orientation embraces various images of good teaching ranging from didactic instruction to Socratic inquiry. In terms of general goals, proponents talk about inducting students into different ways of knowing and thinking, teaching the "structures of the disciplines," fostering "meaningful" understanding of academic content. Different interpretations of these goals yield different ideas about how particular subjects should be taught. In mathematics education, for example, there are at least three competing views of effective teaching. One view emphasizes student performance and mastery of mathematical rules and procedures; a second stresses students' grasp of mathematical concepts and processes; a third focuses on students' personal construction of mathematical ideas. These views imply different ideas about what knowing, learning and teaching mathematics entails (see, for example, Ball, 1988a; Good and Grouws, 1977; Lampert, 1986).

Because teacher educators have not been responsible for teachers' subject matter preparation, they have tended to ignore the question of what teachers need to know about their subjects to teach them effectively and where that knowledge is acquired. In the case of elementary teaching, many assume that the content is easy to learn or already familiar because prospective teachers have "had" it in school themselves. In the case of secondary teaching, majoring in one's teaching field as an undergraduate is supposed to provide adequate subject matter background.

Research on subject matter pedagogy. Conceptual and empirical research on teachers' subject matter knowledge challenges these assumptions and provides a beginning knowledge base for the academic orientation. Besides clarifying what it means to know one's subjects for the purposes of teaching them, investigators are exploring how teachers' ideas of and about their subjects interact with other kinds of knowledge to influence teaching and learning in classrooms (See, for example, Ball, 1988b; Brophy, in press; Leinhardt and Smith, 1985; McDiarmid, Ball and Anderson, in press; Shulman, 1986 and 1987; Stodolsky, 1988). Subject matter or content knowledge includes knowledge of the facts, concepts and procedures that define a given field and an understanding of how these "pieces" fit together. It also includes knowledge about knowledge—where it comes from, how it grows, how truth is established (Anderson, 1988; Buchmann, 1984; Schwab, 1978).

But teachers need more than content knowledge. They need a special blend of content and pedagogy that Shulman (1986) has labeled "pedagogical content knowledge." The unique province of teachers, pedagogical content knowledge includes useful ways to conceptualize and represent commonly taught topics in a given subject plus an understanding of what makes learning those topics difficult or easy for students of different ages and backgrounds (Wilson, Shulman, and Rickert, 1986). The academic orientation turns the attention of teacher educators back to the "professional treatment of subject matter" theme associated with the normal school tradition. It challenges the familiar division of labor between arts and science faculty and teacher educators and suggests the need for new conceptualizations as well as new institutional arrangements.

The MAT programs of the early 60s with their emphasis on disciplinary rather than professional knowledge illustrate one version of the academic orientation. The Academic Learning Program at Michigan State University illustrates another. Designed as a two-year sequence, the Academic Learning Program represents a serious effort to work out some of the conceptual and organizational problems associated with the academic orientation at the undergraduate level.

The Academic Learning Program. The Academic Learning Program is centrally concerned with helping elementary and secondary teachers learn to teach school subjects in ways that promote conceptual understanding. To prepare for that kind of teaching, the program emphasizes three areas of understanding: (a) a broad understanding of the disciplinary roots of school subjects; (b) knowledge about how pupils learn in different subject areas; (c) knowledge of effective teaching strategies and learning environments that promote conceptual understanding. The faculty also aim to prepare teachers who will "reflect on their own learning and teaching practice" (Rosean, Lanier, and Roth, 1988).

The program consists of an integrated sequence of core courses and ongoing field experiences. The first two core courses, Learning of School Subjects and Curriculum for Academic Learning, draw on concepts from cognitive psychology, philosophy of science and curriculum to explore the major themes of the program—that knowledge is socially constructed, that learning is an active process of making meaning, that good teaching depends on a deep understanding of disciplinary knowledge and a repertoire of ways to represent key ideas in their fields (Amarel, 1988).

At the beginning of the program, students are paired with a local teacher ("mentor teacher"). Each term they visit their mentor teacher's classroom to carry out field assignments and, in the second year, to student teach. The field assignments are designed to help students link concepts taught in university courses with classroom practice. For example, students analyze how knowledge is represented in lessons and curricular materials and interview pupils to discover how they "make sense" of particular lessons.

Elementary education majors are also required to take a specially designed, three course math sequence taught by a mathematics professor and a math educator. The first course focuses on number theory, the second on geometry and the third on statistics. The sequence emphasizes conceptual understanding and actively engages students in making sense of mathematical situations. The course was motivated by the realization that elementary teachers cannot teach for understanding when they themselves have never been taught to understand the conceptual foundations of school mathematics. Preliminary findings on the impact of the first course suggest that students were beginning to understand for the first time why rules and procedures they had memorized years ago really worked. Still at least half remained skeptical about whether instructional processes that had enabled them to reach such understanding such as group problem solving were realistic in elementary classrooms (Schram, Wilcox, Lanier, and Lappan, 1988).

The Practical Orientation

The practical orientation focuses attention on the elements of craft, technique, and artistry that skillful practitioners reveal in their work. It also recognizes that teachers deal with unique situations and that their work is ambiguous and uncertain. Long associated with apprenticeship systems of training, the practical orientation endorses the primacy of experience as a source of knowledge about teaching and a means of learning to teach.

Advocates of the practical orientation do not necessarily share the *same* image of good teaching. They would, however, agree on its essential character. Both researchers (e.g., Jackson, 1968, 1986; Lortie, 1975) and practitioners (e.g., Kohl, 1976; Lampert, 1985; McDonald, 1986) have described the localized, uncertain, often conflicting nature of teaching with its concomitant demand for personal artistry, adaptability, invention.

Lampert's (1985) analysis of her own teaching practice, for example, reveals how these characteristics affect teachers' work. In trying to solve many common pedagogical problems, she argues, teachers have to balance a variety of interests. Often this results in "practical dilemmas," situations which present equally important but conflicting alternatives. Rather than resolving these dilemmas, teachers "manage" them, inventing and improvising a succession of temporary responses.

Schon's (1983) insights about the nature of professional practice further illuminate ideas about teaching associated with the practical orientation. Schon discusses the kind of artistry or tacit "knowing-in-action" that competent practitioners reveal in their work. Highlighting those situations where established theory and codified technique do not apply, he describes how thoughtful practitioners engage in on-the-spot reflection and experimentation. In these internal conversations with the situation, they consider different interpretations or courses of action, drawing on a repertoire of images, theories, actions to construct an appropriate response.

Apprenticeship learning. From the practical orientation to teaching, it follows that learning to teach comes about through a combination of firsthand experience and interaction with peers and mentors about troublesome situations. Through these experiences, the novice is inducted into a community of practitioners and a world of practice.

The apprenticeship is the standard mode of learning associated with the practical orientation. Working with a master over a period of time, the apprentice acquires practical skills and learns what works in real situations. Ever since Dewey (1904) distinguished the "laboratory" view of practice work with its emphasis on intellectual methods from the "apprenticeship" view with its focus on technical proficiency, the apprenticeship has had bad press in teacher education circles. Apprenticeships, say the critics, encourage imitation rather than understanding and foster the maintenance of existing standards and practices (Arnstine, 1975; Wilson, 1975). Certainly research on student teaching confirms these outcomes.

While the apprenticeship model does encourage novices to learn the practices of the master, it does not necessarily preclude a consideration of underlying principles or the development of conceptual understanding (Ball, 1987; Tom, 1984). Collins, Brown, and Newman (in press) have coined the term "cognitive apprenticeship" to describe experiential learning situations in which teachers think aloud so that learners can not only observe their actions but also "see" how their teachers work through particular problems or tasks.

Using the architectural design studio as his prototype, Schon (1987) proposes the idea of a "reflective practicum" as an important element in professional education. In contrast to an apprenticeship, a practicum provides a simplified or protected encounter with the world of practice. In a practicum situation, students engage in activities that simulate or simplify practice or they take on real world projects under the guidance of a senior practitioner. To support the goals associated with the practical orientation, the focus would have to be on helping prospective teachers think through situations where there are no "right" answers. By trying out multiple interpretations and considering alternative courses of action, prospective teachers would be helped to recognize and even accept the endemic uncertainties of teaching (Floden and Clark, 1988).

The Teachers for Rural Alaska Program, located at the University of Alaska in Fairbanks, prepares teachers to work in situations of extreme ambiguity and uncertainty. Perhaps this explains why the program directors were drawn to ideas about teaching and learning to teach associated with the practical orientation.

The Teachers for Rural Alaska Program. The TRA Program prepares liberal arts graduates to work in rural Alaskan high schools. In these small, isolated communities, teachers are expected to teach many subjects and grade levels and assist communities faced with complicated political, social and economic challenges. Initially attracted to the rhetoric of "reflective inquiry," the program developers found the concept too general to provide direction to staff and students.

> We wanted to stress the problematic nature of practice and to orient our students to the complexities of the kinds of situations they could encounter. As we came to see it, however, the term "reflective inquiry" doesn't help much in talking about *what* it is to be reflected upon, *how* that reflection is to occur, and to *what ends* it is directed. (Noordhoff and Kleinfeld,1987, p. 6.)

Instead of reflective teaching, they adopted the metaphor of teaching as a design activity.

To give students practice in deliberating about uncertain situations, the staff developed three major case studies based on the experiences of rural Alaskan teachers. Each case study describes a problem situation familiar to rural teachers in cross-cultural and multicultural communities—Native students' feelings about being "dumb" in a class with middle-class Caucasian students, a rural teacher's experiences in a community where alcoholism is rampant, a teacher harassed by a village and told to leave. Students analyze the cases from different vantage points, imagining a range of possible actions and their consequences. Students also complete a series of "design" projects during the professional seminar which meets daily on campus during the fall term. For example, students are given information about a particular context and culture (e.g., a village economy based on salmon fishing, parental ambivalence about sending children to college) and descriptions of individual students (e.g., seven Yu'pik Eskimo children of varying ages). Their job is to design a biology curriculum, formulating goals, exploring curricular materials, developing an instructional plan and justifying it on the basis of knowledge about students, subject and setting.

The practical wisdom of expert teachers has a prominent place in the TRA program. During the planning summer, five master teachers, selected by their colleagues, helped the project staff identify problems and dilemmas that teachers in rural settings face. Linked to the teaching of particular subjects, these problems provide the framework for the professional seminar that student take during the fall term. Master-teachers also serve as mentors during a six-week, afternoon apprenticeship and a semester of student teaching.

The TRA Program seems oriented to fostering the capacity for what Kennedy (1987) calls "deliberate action," a form of professional expertise that enables teachers to choose among alternative goals that may be sought in a given situation. Like critical analysis, deliberate action recognizes multiple ways of interpreting situations but it goes beyond analysis to yield action.

Technological Orientation

The technological orientation focuses attention on the knowledge and skills of teaching. The primary goal is to prepare teachers who can carry out the tasks of teaching with proficiency. Learning to teach involves the acquisition of principles and practices derived from the scientific study of teaching. Competence is defined in terms of performance. The technological orientation goes hand in hand with a search for a scientific basis for teaching. Proponents believe that the future of teaching as a profession rests on improvements that will come from the accumulation and application of scientific knowledge (Berliner, 1985; Gage, 1978; Lortie, 1975).

The past 10 years of productive research on teaching effectiveness have yielded a technology that can be taught to prospective teachers. It consists of generic teacher behaviors and strategies associated with student achievement gains. (For a recent summary of the research, see Brophy and Good, 1986). Based on studies of math and reading instruction in conventional classrooms, the findings cohere around a direct instructional model of teaching. How should this research-based technology be used by teacher educators? Some proponents regard effective teaching behaviors as content for teacher training and criteria for the assessment of teaching competence. Others believe that findings from teacher effectiveness research should be taught as principles and procedures to be used by teachers in making decisions and solving problems. The former suggests the metaphor of teacher as technician; the latter, teacher as decision maker. In both cases, professional knowledge is basically procedural knowledge—ways to achieve specified goals and solve familiar problems.

Training model. The technological orientation is primarily associated with a training model of learning to teach. Joyce and Showers (1980, 1984) have outlined the components of effective teacher training. First, teachers should learn about the theory or rationale behind a given strategy or procedure. Second, they should see a demonstration. Third, teachers need a chance to practice and get feedback on their performance. Ideally this should initially take place in a relatively "safe" environment where teachers can concentrate on mastering the skills and concepts without having to deal with all the complexities that arise in real classrooms. Finally, teachers need help transferring the new behaviors to the classroom from a coach who can detect errors in application and point out correct responses.

Teacher as decision maker. The rational version of the technological orientation is captured by a description of an educational psychology course in an undergraduate preservice program organized around the theme of "teacher as decision maker". The description comes from an exploratory study of what was taught and learned in this preservice program (Feiman-Nemser, 1987; Feiman-Nemser and Buchmann, 1989). The course focused on instructional decision making from a systems perspective. Students received an instructional packet containing an overview of the course, a list of "terminal behaviors" and a description of the projects they would complete to demonstrate their attainment of the course objectives.

The course was organized around five topics: goals and objectives, task analysis, evaluation, information and practice. The instructor presented a format for daily lessons—introduction, instruction, practice and feedback, daily evaluation, application. Students were told that if they plan systematically and their plans reflect empirically validated principles of motivation and instruction, they can be reasonably certain that their pupils will learn what they are trying to teach. The course exemplified the training model approach. The instructor explained and demonstrated the elements in lesson planning. Students had an opportunity to practice each step separately and then to put them together in designing an instructional unit. Students were also expected to transfer their newly acquired planning skills to the field. All term they developed and taught mini-lessons. Field instructors reinforced the systematic approach to planning by using the lesson plan framework as a basis for classroom observation and feedback.

Competency-based teacher preparation. No discussion of the technological orientation is complete without a reference to competency-based teacher education (CBTE). The reform movement of the late 60s and 70s, competency-based teacher education requires that teacher educators state explicitly the competencies students will acquire in their program and the criteria by which they will be assessed. Typically a competency-based program consists of instructional modules, sets of learning activities designed to help students achieve specific objectives (Elam, 1971; Houston and Howsam, 1972; Houston, 1974). Students' rate of progress through the program is determined by demonstrated competence rather than course completion.

In 1969, the U.S. Office of Education funded the design of nine comprehensive, competency-based elementary preservice models (Burden and Lanzilloti, 1969). While the project stimulated considerable talk about CBTE, lack of funding and an inadequate research base kept the idea from becoming much of a reality. Currently, competency-based teacher preparation is getting a boost from state legislatures who have mandated performance assessments of beginning teachers based on generic teaching principles. To help graduates meet the teaching competencies identified by the state, some universities have revised their preservice programs.

PROTEACH, a five-year preservice program at the University of Florida at Gainesville, provides an interesting case in point. Adopted in 1983 in response to the expanding knowledge base in teaching and state-mandated assessments of beginning teachers, PROTEACH aims to prepare "professional teachers" who make instructional decisions based on research and clinical insights (Smith, 1984). Widely publicized for its attention to teacher effectiveness research, the PROTEACH program actually embraces multiple commitments. Thus it illustrates some of the problems of trying to classify a program in terms of a single orientation.

Statewide use of the Florida Performance Measurement System (FPMS) has influenced the PROTEACH program. Based on generic research on teaching, the FPMS is organized into six domains: (a) instructional planning, (b) management of student conduct, (c) instructional organization, (d) presentation of subject matter, (e) communication, and (f) testing. Each domain consists of specific behaviors grouped into sets of competencies. Overall, the six domains include 128 behaviors organized into 28 competency categories. The faculty of the Elementary PROTEACH program are committed to helping students understand and become proficient in the performance domains of the FPMS. A new course, Research in Elementary Education, introduces students to research on teaching, the Florida Performance Measurement System, and other classroom observation systems organized around discrete teaching skills. During the program, students study and practice the FPMS and have it used on them in the field. Several faculty and graduate advisors (the program's term for supervisor) have become state certified in the use of the FPMS.

At the same time, faculty want students to view the FPMS as only one of many sources that professional teachers draw on in making instructional decisions and to use it intelligently not mechanically (Zeichner, 1988a). A core group of faculty have adopted the term "reflective teaching" to express the stance they are trying to promote in the PROTEACH program. They have also created program components that stress the role of teachers as producers not simply consumers of classroom research (Ross and Kyle, 1987). For "purer" examples of competency-based programs, see case studies of programs at the University of Toledo (Howey and Zimpher, 1989) and the University of Houston (Ginsburg, 1988).

The Personal Orientation

The personal orientation places the teacher-learner at the center of the educational process. Learning to teach is construed as a process of learning to understand, develop and use oneself effectively. The teacher's own personal development is a central part of teacher preparation. "A good teacher," Combs (1965) claims, "is first and foremost a person, a unique personality" striving to fulfill himself (p. 6). Students also share this basic drive toward self-adequacy and enhancement. It follows that teaching is less a matter of prescribing and molding and more a matter of encouraging and assisting. The teacher is a facilitator who creates conditions conducive to learning. To do this, teachers must know their students as individuals. With this knowledge they can select materials or set learning tasks that respond to individual interests, needs, abilities.

Advocates of the personal orientation favor classrooms where learning derives from students' interests and takes the form of active, self-directed exploration. They emphasize concepts like readiness and personal meaning and appreciate the interconnections of thinking and feeling. Just as teachers must come to know students as individuals, so students are allowed to know their teacher as a person (Combs, 1982).

The general description of teaching and learning set forth above also applies to learning to teach which advocates of the personal orientation describe as a process of "becoming" or "development." Teacher educators in preservice preparation attach various meanings to these phrases. For some, becoming a teacher means making a psychological shift from the partly dependent role of student to the fully responsible role of teacher (Biber and Winsor, 1967). For others, it means developing a personal psychology and finding one's own best ways of teaching (Combs, 1965; Combs, Blume, Newman, and Wass, 1974). Still others focus on helping prospective teachers make the transition from early concerns about self-adequacy to more mature concerns about pupils and their learning (Fuller and Bown, 1975).

Different versions of the personal orientation draw their rationale and guiding principles from developmental, humanistic, and perceptual psychology. From these sources, proponents derive content for the preservice curriculum such as dynamic concepts of learning and development and theories of human behavior and potential. They also drew ideas about the kinds of enabling conditions that promote meaningful learning on the part of prospective teachers. Most proponents talk about creating a supportive atmosphere where preservice students feel safe to take risks and discover personal meaning. They advocate field experiences where students can learn what they need to know and try their wings in encounters with "real" professional problems. They stress the importance of personal interactions with teacher educators who function as counselors or facilitators, helping prospective teachers explore problems, events, themselves and others (e.g., Combs, 1978; Fuller and Bown, 1975).

One dilemma facing advocates of the personal orientation is how to balance openness to individual teaching styles with a commitment to particular values. Can a personally oriented preservice program promote a view of good teaching and, at the same time, encourage students to develop their own theories and discover methods that work for them? The programs described below illustrate two resolutions to this question.

Personalized teacher education. The Personalized Teacher Education Program (PET) at the University of Texas was an effort to make teacher preparation more "relevant" by gearing the curriculum to the "developmental" concerns of preservice students. The program grew out of research on teacher concerns conducted by Frances Fuller and her associates at the university's Research and Development Center on Teacher Education. Fuller (1969) discovered not only that prospective teachers have common concerns but that their concerns emerge in a fairly regular sequence. The sequence goes from early concerns about self to later concerns about pupils and their learning. If teacher educators want to engage the interests of their preservice students, Fuller (1970) concluded, they should start with content related to concerns about the self as teacher such as how to control a class, and hold off on content related to concerns about educational goals, instructional design, pupil evaluation.

The PET Program was designed to help undergraduate students resolve concerns about themselves as teachers so they could move toward concerns about pupils. To address teaching concerns early in the program, for example, students were required to plan and teach a 15-minute lesson to a real class. This early teaching experience, which was videotaped, did not allay concerns about self-adequacy, but it certainly elicited teaching related concerns (Newlove, 1969). While the program succeeded in moving students from concerns about self to concerns about teaching, few undergraduates made the transition to concerns about pupils which Fuller regarded as the most difficult yet most important transition teachers ever make (Fuller, 1970). The PET program seems to give teacher educators a clear message about where they should put their energies—helping prospective teachers make a transition from concerns about self to concerns about students. In fact, a descriptive model of teacher concerns can never tell teacher educators what to do unless they first endorse the implicit goal of teacher development (Feiman-Nemser and Floden, 1981).

The advisement program at Bank Street College. Whereas the PET program seems to regard teacher development as an end in itself, the advisement program at Bank Street College in New York City views it as a vehicle for promoting a particular way of working with children. Since its founding in 1931, Bank Street College has been dedicated to "a clear system of values about education" and "a model of teaching excellence deemed essential to that system of values" (Biber and Winsor, 1967, p. 115–117). The advisement program is conceived as an analogue to that system of values and model of teaching. It allows students to experience on an adult level the kinds of learning opportunities and personal relationships which they, in turn, will enact with their pupils (Shapiro, 1988).

Shapiro (1988) describes the advisement program as "the intersection of learning in coursework, in fieldwork, in informal exchange with peers, and in the development of a personal style of teaching" (p. 10). Advisors help students integrate the different parts of the program and reflect on what they are learning and how they are changing (p. 29). Advisors work with students in three settings—field placements, weekly group conferences and individual sessions. Advisors help students function in the field and relate experiences there with what they are learning in courses. As students try on the role of teacher, they discover questions and problems to raise in conference group and individual sessions. The conference group is an occasion for learning from and with peers, a forum for group problem solving and reflection. While the content comes from the students, the advisor guides the discussion and summarizes the salient points.

Personal material is most likely to be discussed in individual sessions where advisors function as counselors. Advisors recognize that the quality of their relationship with students is the key. Shapiro (1988) characterizes that relationship as "personal but not intimate, supportive but not maternal, non-didactic but not laissez-faire. It is, at base, a relationship of teacher and student, based on mutual trust and respect" (p. 28).

Advisors must balance their commitment to a particular view of good teaching with their wish to help students find their own teaching style. Shapiro (1988) quotes an advisor who tells her students: "I don't want you to become a 'Bank Street teacher' but the best teacher you can be" (p. 12). Still, this openness to individual styles is bounded by the larger ethos of the institution.

The Critical/Social Orientation

The critical orientation in teacher preparation combines a progressive social vision with a radical critique of schooling. On the one hand, there is an optimistic faith in the power of education to help shape a new social order; on the other, a sobering realization that schools have been instrumental in preserving social inequities. Just as the teacher plays an important role in social reform in this orientation, so teacher education is part of a larger strategy to create a more just and democratic society.

The teacher is both an educator and a political activist. In the classroom, the teacher creates a learning community that promotes democratic values and practices through group problem solving. In the school, the teacher participates in curriculum development and policymaking. In the community, the teacher works to improve school conditions and educational opportunities through community involvement and political activity. Ginsburg (1988) offers the following rationale:

> As educators of teachers, we must . . . operate as activists in broader struggles for social transformation . . . because these broader structural and ideological struggles are . . . dialectically related to the struggles within teacher education, because we need to be models for the people we seek to educate as teachers; and because becoming involved in such political activity will help us to establish relations with others whose lives are similarly enabled by these broader structures. (p. 214)

Contemporary proponents of the critical orientation in teacher preparation speak about "progressive education," "critical pedagogy," "emancipatory teaching," "student empowerment," but they rarely translate these terms into concrete classroom practices. There is a general consensus about the importance of promoting democratic values, helping students find their voice and develop their identity, linking schooling with students' experiences in the larger community. Still, it is easier to visualize the kind of teaching that supporters reject than the kind of teaching they seek to promote through teacher preparation. The discourse about critically oriented teacher preparation is often quite theoretical, and practices to achieve particular purposes have not been clearly articulated.

There are discussions of the sorts of issues and topics that a critically oriented preservice curriculum should address and examples of the kinds of teacher education practices that promote critical analysis and action. Giroux and McLaren (1986) recommend the critical study of such themes as language, history, culture, and power. They also stress the value of direct experience in helping teachers understand the relationships and forces that influence their pupils. For example, they suggest that student teachers compile oral histories of the communities in which they teach or work in and analyze the role of different community agencies. Such experiences would help them develop curricula around the traditions, histories, and forms of knowledge that are often ignored within the dominant school culture.

The literature also contains descriptions of how individual methods courses, curriculum courses, and field experiences have been designed to promote critical analysis and critical pedagogy (e.g., Goodman, 1986a, 1986b; Zeichner and Liston, 1987). From such work, Zeichner (1987) culls five instructional strategies used by teacher educators associated with the critical tradition: ethnographic studies, journal writing, emancipatory supervision, action research, and curriculum analysis and development. Of course, it is not the strategies themselves but the purposes to which they are put that justifies the link with the critical orientation.

The description of New College, an unorthodox experiment in teacher preparation mounted at Teachers College, Columbia University, between 1932 and 1936, illustrates the continuity of the critical orientation with earlier progressive reforms. The description of the student teaching component at the University of Wisconsin illustrates the more analytic practices associated with contemporary expressions of the critical orientation.

The New College experiment. The New College program attempted to integrate general education, professional education, and laboratory experiences. The entire program was shaped around a definition of the teacher as a social leader. The faculty believed that "teachers should view their work against the background of world events and conditions and regard community involvement and leadership as a professional responsibility" (New College, 1936, p. 29–30).

In their first two years, New College students attended a central seminar organized around broad problem areas supplemented by divisional seminars in philosophy, natural sciences, the arts and human relationships. New York City served as a natural laboratory for developing general cultural understandings. In the last two years, the emphasis shifted from general cultural background to professional preparation. The central seminar took up educational implications of persistent social problems while divisional seminars focused on a particular teaching specialization. New College students were also required to spend time in the New College Community, a student-run farm in North Carolina and to study and travel abroad for at least a summer. Student teaching provided contacts with many phases of the teacher's work. In addition to opportunities for curriculum development, child study and instructional planning, student teachers surveyed local resources and needs and took part in various community activities.

The faculty continually tried to encourage political activity among the students. For example, in 1937, the director announced that two scholarships would be awarded to students "who go furthest beyond 'academic neutrality' in active participation in life outside the walls of the university" (Cremin, Shannon, and Townsend, 1954, p. 226).

Student teaching at the University of Wisconsin. The activist stance of the New College program with its varied opportunities for direct experience contrasts with the analytic stance of the University of Wisconsin student teaching component. Designed by teacher educators closely identified with the critical orientation, student teaching at Wisconsin is designed to foster critical reflection and pedagogy. Earlier statements of the program's rationale stressed the need for teachers to reflect on the moral and political implications of school structures and pedagogical practices and participate in curriculum development and educational policymaking (e.g., Zeichner, 1981–82); recent refinements call for teachers to add the role of political activist outside the classroom to their primary role as educators. The underlying metaphor of the program is "liberation" (Liston and Zeichner, 1988b; Zeichner and Liston, 1987).

The curriculum for the student teaching semester has five elements. The first is a teaching component that combines the gradual assumption of classroom responsibilities with an emphasis on curriculum development. The second is an inquiry component that focuses attention on the culture of schools and classrooms and their relationship to the larger political milieu. Students are required to carry out some investigation related to their own practices or the settings where they work. For example, students have analyzed the assumptions in various curricular materials, studied pupils' perceptions of school, experimented with different grouping strategies and their effects on pupil involvement.

The third component, a weekly seminar, is designed to help students "broaden their perspectives on teaching, consider the rationale underlying alternative possibilities for classrooms and pedagogy, and assess their own developing perspectives toward teaching" (p. 32). Journals, the fourth component, encourage student teachers to reflect systematically on their own development and their actions in classrooms and in the school. Finally, supervisory conferences emphasize analysis of classroom instruction, focusing on student teachers' intentions and beliefs, the social context of teaching, the content of instruction, and the hidden curriculum. Studies of the student teaching component at Wisconsin suggest partial implementation of goals (Zeichner, Malios, and Gomez, 1988), but limited impact on student teachers' perspectives (Tabachnick and Zeichner, 1985; Zeichner and Grant, 1981).

Discussion

A plurality of orientations and approaches exists because people hold different expectations for schools and teachers and because, in any complex human endeavor, there are always more goals to strive for than one can achieve at the same time. Teacher educators cannot avoid making choices about what to concentrate on. Thus deliberation about worthwhile goals and appropriate means must be an ongoing activity in the teacher education community. These deliberations would be aided by a conceptual framework that identifies central tasks of teacher preparation, those core activities that logically and practically belong to the preservice phase of learning to teach. Helping prospective teachers make a transition to pedagogical thinking, to thinking about teaching in terms of what students are and should be learning is an example of such a task. Generally, teacher education students have not thought much about the reciprocal relationship of teaching and learning that defines the essence of their professional responsibilities. Such a framework could provide guidance to teacher educators in program development and evaluation by identifying issues or tasks that programs should address whatever their orientation. In a field like teacher education that has been shaped more by external factors than by a clear sense of purpose, this kind of conceptual clarity is essential.

While some of the orientations focus on essential tasks of teacher preparation, collectively they do not represent a set of equally valid alternatives from which to choose. Rather they constitute a source of ideas and practices to draw on in deliberating about how to prepare teachers in a particular context. Each orientation highlights different issues that must be considered, but none offers a fully developed framework to guide program development.

The personal orientation reminds us that learning to teach is a transformative process, not only a matter of acquiring new knowledge and skills. Because prospective teachers are no strangers to classrooms, resocialization is necessary especially if new ways of teaching are to be fostered.

The critical orientation highlights the teacher's obligations to students and society, challenging teacher educators to help novices learn to align school practices with democratic principles of justice and equality. The critical orientation also underscores the need to develop the habit of questioning taken-for-granted assumptions about teaching, learning, knowledge, schooling, and so forth.

The technological and practical orientations represent different ideas about the nature and sources of knowledge about teaching and how it can be acquired and developed. The former stresses scientific knowledge and systematic training; the latter, the "wisdom of practice" and learning from experience. Clearly both have a contribution to make to the content and processes of teacher preparation.

Finally, the academic orientation focuses attention on the distinctive work of teaching. What distinguishes teaching from other forms of human service is its concern with helping students learn worthwhile things they could not pick up on their own. It follows that preparing someone to teach means helping them develop ideas and dispositions related to this goal (Buchmann, 1984; Feiman-Nemser and Buchmann, 1989; Wilson, 1975). The academic orientation has been a "missing paradigm" in teacher education. Historically viewed as someone else's responsibility, preparing teachers to teach academic content has rarely been a central concern of teacher educators. The current reform movement with its concern for improving the academic quality of teaching and the new research emphasis on the role of subject matter knowledge in teaching provide the impetus to give serious attention to this neglected aspect of teacher preparation.

STUDYING DIFFERENT APPROACHES AND ALTERATIONS

Many contemporary proposals for reforming teacher preparation echo earlier efforts. Still, the lack of systematic data makes it difficult to learn from past experience. Existing data do not permit clear portraits of the explicit preservice curriculum in different settings (Lanier and Little, 1986); nor do they help us understand the relative effects of selection compared with socialization or the relationship between opportunities to learn and learning outcomes in different types of preservice programs.

In a recent review of research on graduate-level preservice programs over the past 35 years, for example, Zeichner (1988b) laments the paltry findings despite millions of dollars spent on program development. While various studies do show that the quality of teaching displayed by MAT graduates was superior or comparable to that of teachers from undergraduate programs, there is no way of telling whether this outcome reflected the kinds of students recruited or the sort of preparation offered.

To consider the relative strengths and limitations of alternative approaches to teacher preparation, we need at least three kinds of research—program studies that examine what different programs are like as educational interventions, implementation studies that examine the factors promoting the success or failure of various programmatic reforms, and impact studies that explore the effects of particular program components and learning opportunities on teachers' ideas and practices.

Research-in-Progress

Recently several large-scale investigations have been undertaken to generate information about different approaches to teacher preparation in different types of institutions. These studies promise to yield a body of information and insights that can inform the work of policymakers and practitioners. While they differ in their scope and purpose, research design, and methodology, the projects all use teacher education programs as a major unit of analysis.

Research About Teacher Education. The Research About Teacher Education Project (RATE) is an ongoing data collection project of the American Association of Colleges of Teacher Education. Launched in 1985, the project is designed to generate a national database about the substance of teacher education programs and the perceptions of faculty and students. Each year 90 programs, stratified according to the highest degree offered, are sampled from the membership of 713. One person at each site fills out an institutional questionnaire and ten faculty and students complete a faculty or student survey that focuses on a specific program component (e.g., foundations, secondary methods).

The RATE project can be helpful in documenting program trends within and across different types of institutions. Two reports (American Association of Colleges of Teacher Education, 1987, 1988) provide a variety of "facts and figures" concerning the preparation of teachers. This kind of research is less effective in exploring issues related to program quality. For example, the 1987 report tells us that both faculty and students consider secondary education methods courses to be as "rigorous" or "more rigorous" than comparable courses in English and history, but less rigorous than science and math courses. As Zeichner (1988c) points out, since we know nothing about the criteria people used to reach this judgement or the courses they have in mind, this kind of finding does not say very much about the quality of teacher education.

Case studies of elementary teacher preparation. In conjunction with the first RATE survey, Kenneth Howey and Nancy Zimpher conducted field studies of six elementary education programs. Their goal was to provide "in-depth, personal accounts" of initial teacher preparation as it is carried out in different institutions of higher education. Six research sites in the midwest were chosen because they represent major types of institutions preparing teachers (research universities, comprehensive state universities, liberal arts colleges) and because their programs were nominated as "distinctive and/or exemplary." Besides generating descriptions of the "lived experience" of teacher education in particular settings, researchers sought "conditions and practices worthy of emulation." Influenced by the "school effectiveness" literature that identifies school-wide characteristics associated with a particular view of effective schools, they hypothesized that similar dimensions of program quality might exist for preservice programs.

During brief visits to the sites, researchers talked with program participants, observed various activities, and collected documents. From these data they have produced a set of case studies describing how teacher preparation is carried out in quite different settings (Howey and Zimpher, 1989). They have also generated a list of conditions and practices that appear to contribute to "coherent" or "effective" preservice programs. Examples include a clear conception of teaching/schooling, the use of student cohorts, high expectations, curriculum articulation, and adequate "life space" (e.g., time and space). The portraits will help fill a void in the descriptive literature and the conceptualization of "effective" program features provides one framework for thinking about potentially desirable practices. It would be a mistake, however, to assume that the features of "effective" programs derived from the data alone. Rather they reflect the researchers' views about what makes for a "coherent" teacher education program. Like any other normative concept, "coherence" must be defined and justified as a desirable quality in a preservice program.

Studying the Education of Educators. Values provide an explicit starting point for the SEE project which is looking at the preparation of teachers (and principals) in 29 institutions of higher education. Researchers are seeking evidence about the extent to which current practices fit the project's working assumptions about the ideal features of a good teacher education program. Starting from an explicit vision of what teaching and schooling should be like, researchers have formulated a set of postulates regarding a well conducted teacher education program. For example, one postulate specifies: "Teacher preparation programs will admit the number of candidates for whom they can guarantee exposure to and participation in at least six different modes of exemplary teaching actually practiced in available school settings" (Goodlad, 1988, p. 110). Such a criterion seeks to remedy casual selection of sites for student teaching and encourages colleges and universities to collaborate with school districts in creating exemplary settings. Differences between what the postulate recommends and what researchers find will determine the project's recommendations regarding student teaching.

A sample of 29 institutions, located in eight states, was chosen to maximize the diversity of educational programs across a range of institutional types (Sirotnik, 1988). Drawing on multiple sources of data gathered over three, two-day site visits during the 1987–88 academic year, researchers are producing "information-based portraits" of each institution. They will also describe trends across institutions or trends moderated by such institutional factors as size, history, student population. As John Goodlad (1988), director of the study, points out, the research is not designed to address such matters as "whether the education of educators should be a graduate or undergraduate enterprise, whether all teachers should have masters degrees . . . or similar matters that crop up frequently in the current rhetoric of reform" (p. 111). Rather the project is interested in broader issues of institutional commitment, faculty support, program philosophy, and so on. By studying a set of representative programs in relation to an explicit normative framework, researchers hope to generate ideas about improving teacher preparation that go beyond piecemeal programmatic changes.

Teacher Education and Learning to Teach. The National Center for Research on Teacher Education, located at Michigan State, is examining the role of teacher education in teacher learning (National Center for Research on Teacher Education, 1988b). The Teacher Education and Learning to Teach Study combines case studies of different teacher education programs with longitudinal studies of teachers' learning. The two-part design allows the Center to describe the purpose and character of different programs, determine whether and how teachers' ideas and practices change as they participate in programs and move into teaching, and explore the relationship between opportunities to learn and learning outcomes. Eleven programs representing important ideas in contemporary teacher education and different types of learning opportunities serve as settings for the research. The sample includes preservice, induction, inservice and alternative route programs so that the Center can explore questions about teachers' learning at different stages of their careers.

A distinguishing feature of the work is the focus on teacher learning in relation to two subject areas, mathematics and writing. Within each site, the Center is following a sample of teachers over time, tracking changes in knowledge, skills, and dispositions as teachers move through teacher education and into independent teaching (Ball and McDiarmid, 1988). The overall goal of the research is to uncover the reasoning behind different ways of helping teachers learn to teach and describe their impact on teachers' learning. This project will yield a rich body of information about different approaches and alternatives to teacher preparation as well as conceptual frameworks for thinking about issues of program quality and teacher learning.

A major strength of the work-in-progress reviewed above is the effort to supplement what people say by observing what they do. In at least three of the projects, researchers are collecting observational data in classes and field experiences. While the intensity of the effort varies, there is a clear recognition that claims about the character and quality of programs must ultimately be grounded in more than self-reports.

The research projects also reflect an appreciation for the fact that programs are nested within larger institutional, historical, geographical, and policy contexts. By reporting insights and information in the form of program case studies, researchers will be telling stories about how and why programs have taken on their particular shape and character. This kind of information is essential in understanding the impact of various policy initiatives designed to improve teacher education.

Finally, at least one project is exploring the issue of program effects. Many people believe that teacher education is a weak intervention incapable of overcoming the powerful influence of teachers' own personal schooling or the impact of experience on-the-job. In addition, various claims have been made about the strengths and limitations of different program structures. By generating systematic data about the impact of different kinds of programs on teachers' ideas and practices, the National Center for Research on Teacher Education will enable the field to test these and other claims against some real evidence.

The research will inform and enrich the debate about how teachers should be prepared for their work. It will also provide a database and a set of frameworks for thinking about different approaches and alternatives to teacher preparation. As a result, when the Association of Teacher Educators undertakes its next *Handbook of Research on Teacher Education,* there should be a more robust body of research to draw on in discussing structural and conceptual alternatives in teacher preparation.

REFERENCES

Adelman, N. (1986). *An exploratory study of teacher alternative certification and retraining programs* (Data Analysis Support Center Contract No. 300-85-0103). Washington, DC: Policy Studies Associates.

Amarel, M. (1988). *Site report: Academic Learning Program.* Unpublished paper, National Center for Research on Teacher Education, Michigan State University, East Lansing.

American Association of Colleges for Teacher Education. (1987). *Teaching teachers: Facts and figures.* Washington, DC: Author.

American Association of Colleges for Teacher Education. (1988). *Teaching teachers: Facts and figures.* Washington, DC: Author.

Anderson, C. (1988). The role of education in the academic disciplines in teacher education. In A. Woolfolk (Ed.), *Research perspectives on the graduate preparation of teachers* (pp. 88107). Englewood Cliffs, NJ: Prentice-Hall.

Arnstine, D. (1975). Apprenticeship as the miseducation of teachers. In R. Pratte (Ed.), *Philosophy of Education 1975* (Proceedings of the 31st annual meeting of the Philosophy of Education Society, pp. 113-123). San Jose, CA: Society for Studies in Philosophy and Education.

Association of American Colleges. (1985). *Integrity in the academic curriculum.* Washington, DC: Author.

Ball, D. (1988a). *Research on teaching mathematics: Making subject matter knowledge part of the equation* (Research Report 88-2). East Lansing: Michigan State University, National Center for Research on Teacher Education.

Ball, D. (1988b). *The subject matter preparation of prospective mathematics teachers: Challenging the myths* (Research Report 88-3). East Lansing: Michigan State University, National Center for Research on Teacher Education.

Ball, D. (1987, April). *"Laboratory" and "apprenticeship": How do they function as metaphors for practical experience in teacher education?* Paper presented at the annual meeting of the American Educational Research Association, Washington, DC.

Ball, D., and McDiarmid, W. (1988). Research on teacher learning: Studying how teachers' knowledge changes. *Action in Teacher Education, 10*(2), 17–24.

Berliner, D. (1985). Laboratory settings and the study of teacher education. *Journal of Teacher Education, 36*(6), 2–8.

Bestor, A. (1953). *Educational wastelands.* Urbana: University of Illinois Press.

Beyer, L. (1984). Field experience, ideology, and the development of critical reflectivity. *Journal of Teacher Education, 35*(3), 36–41.

Biber, B., and Winsor, C. (1967). An analysis of the guidance function in a graduate teacher education program. In *Mental health and teacher education* (46th yearbook of the Association for Student Teaching, p. 81–119). Dubuque, IA: Brown.

Borrowman, M. (1956). *The liberal and technical in teacher education.* New York: Columbia University, Teachers College, Bureau of Publications.

Borrowman, M. (1965). Liberal education and the professional preparation of teachers. In M. L. Borrowman (Ed.), *Teacher education in America* (pp. 1–53). New York: Teachers College Press.

Boyer, E. (1987). *College: The undergraduate experience in America.* New York: Harper and Row.

Brophy, J. (in press). *Advances in research on teaching: Vol. 2 Teachers' subject matter knowledge and classroom instruction.* Greenwich, CT: JAI Press.

Brophy, J., and Good, T. (1986). Teacher behavior and student achievement. In M. C. Wittrock (Ed.), *Handbook of research on teaching* (3rd ed., pp. 328–375). New York: Macmillan.

Buchmann, M. (1984). The priority of knowledge and understanding in teaching. In L. Katz and J. Raths (Eds.), *Advances in teacher education* (pp. 29–50). Norwood, NJ: Ablex.

Burdin, J., and Lanzillotti, K. (1969). *A reader's guide to the comprehensive models for preparing elementary teachers.* Washington, DC: American Association of Colleges of Teacher Education.

Bush, R. (1977). We know how to train teachers: Why not do so! *Journal of Teacher Education, 28*(6), 5–9.

Carey, N., Mittman, B., and Darling-Hammond, L. (1988). *Recruiting mathematics and science teachers through nontraditional programs: A survey.* Santa Monica, CA: Rand Corporation, Center for the Study of the Teaching Profession.

Church, R., and Sedlak, M. (1976). *Education in the United States: An interpretive history.* New York: Free Press.

Clark, D. (1986). Transforming the structure for the professional preparation of teachers. In L. Katz and J. Raths (Eds.), *Advances in teacher education* (Vol. 1, pp. 1-19). Norwood, NJ: Ablex.

Clark, D., and Marker, G. (1975). The institutionalization of teacher education. In K. Ryan (Ed.), *Teacher education* (74th yearbook of the National Society for the Study of Education, pp. 53–86). Chicago: University of Chicago Press.

Clifford, G., and Guthrie, J. (1988). *Ed school: A brief for professional education.* Chicago: University of Chicago Press.

Clift, R., Houston, W. R., and Pugach, M. (Eds.). (in press). *Encouraging reflective practice: An examination of issues and exemplars.* New York: Teachers College Press.

Cogan, M. (1955). Master of arts in teaching at Harvard University. *Journal of Teacher Education, 6*(2), 135–142.

Coley, R., and Thorpe, M. (1985). *A look at the MAT model of teacher education and its graduates: Lessons for today* (Final report sponsored by the Ford Foundation). Princeton, NJ: Educational Testing Service, Division of Education Policy Research and Services.

Collins, A., Brown, J., and Newman, S. (in press). Cognitive apprenticeship: Teaching the craft of reading, writing and mathematics. In L. B. Resnick (Ed.), *Cognition and Instruction: Issues and Agendas.* Hillsdale, NJ: Erlbaum.

Combs, A. (1965). *The professional education of teachers.* Boston: Allyn and Bacon.

Combs, A. (1978). Teacher education: The person in the process. *Educational Leadership, 35,* 558–561.

Combs, A. (1982). *A personal approach to teaching.* Boston: Allyn and Bacon.

Combs, A., Blume, R., Newman, A., and Wass, H. (1974). *The professional education of teachers: A humanistic approach to teacher education.* Boston: Allyn and Bacon.

Conant, J. (1963). *The education of American teachers.* New York: McGraw-Hill.

Cremin, L. (1953). The heritage of American teacher education. Part I. *Journal of Teacher Education, 4*(2), 163–170.

Cremin, L. (1978). *The education of the educating professions* (The 19th Charles W. Hunt Lecture). Chicago: American Association of Colleges for Teacher Education.

Cremin, L., Shannon, D., and Townsend, M. (1954). *A history of Teachers College.* New York: Columbia University Press.

Cruickshank, D. (1987). *Reflective teaching: The preparation of students of teaching.* Reston, VA: Association of Teacher Educators.

Denemark, G., and Nutter, N. (1984). The case for extended programs of initial preparation. In L. Katz and J. Raths, (Eds.), *Advances in teacher education* (Vol. 1, pp. 203–246). Norwood, NJ: Ablex.

Department of Education. (1984). *Involvement in learning: Realizing the potential of American higher education.* Washington, DC: National Institute of Education.

Dewey, J. (1904). The relation of theory to practice in education. In C. A. Murry (Ed.), *The relation of theory to practice in the education of teachers* (Third yearbook of the National Society for the Scientific Study of Education, Part I, pp. 1–30). Chicago: University of Chicago Press.

Elam, S. (1971). *Performance-based teacher education.* Washington, DC: American Association of Colleges of Teacher Education.

Featherstone, J. (1988). A note on liberal learning. *NCRTE Colloquy, 2,*(1), 1–8.

Feiman, S. (1979). Technique and inquiry in teacher education: A curricular case study. *Curriculum Inquiry, 9,* 63–79.

Feiman-Nemser, S. (1987). *Talking to prospective teachers: Lessons from educational psychology.* Paper presented at the annual meeting of the American Educational Research Association, Washington, DC.

Feiman-Nemser, S., and Buchmann, M. (1989) Describing teacher education: A framework and illustrative findings from a longitudinal study of six students. *Elementary School Journal, 89,* 365–377.

Feiman-Nemser, S., and Floden, R. (1981). A critique of developmental approaches in teacher education. *Action in Teacher Education, 3*(1), 35–38.

Feistritzer, E. G. (1986). *Profile of teachers in the U.S.* Washington, DC: National Center for Education Information.

Floden, R., and Clark, C. (1988). Preparing teachers for uncertainty. *Teachers College Record, 89,* 505–524.

Fuller, F. (1969). Concerns of teachers: A developmental conceptualization. *American Educational Research Journal, 6,* 207–226.

Fuller, F. F. (1970). *Personalized education for teachers: One application of the teacher concerns model.* Austin: University of Texas, Research and Development Center for Teachers.

TOURO COLLEGE LIBRARY

Fuller, F. F., and Bown, O. (1975). Becoming a teacher. In K. Ryan (Ed.), *Teacher education* (74th yearbook of the National Society for the Study of Education, pp. 25–52). Chicago: University of Chicago Press.

Gage, N. (1978). *The scientific basics of the art of teaching.* New York: Teachers College Press.

Ginsburg, M. (1988). *Contradictions in teacher education and society: A critical analysis.* Philadelphia: Falmer.

Giroux, H., and McLaren, P. (1986). Teacher education and the politics of engagement: The case for democratic schooling. *Harvard Educational Review, 56,* 213–238.

Good, T., and Grouws, P. A. (1977). Teaching effects: A process-product study in fourth grade mathematics classrooms. *Journal of Teacher Education, 28*(3), 49–54.

Goodlad, J. (1988). Studying the education of educators: Values-driven inquiry. *Phi Delta Kappan, 70,* 105–111.

Goodman, J. (1984). Reflection and teacher education: A case study and theoretical analysis. *Interchange, 15*(3), 9–26.

Goodman, J. (1986a). Teaching preservice teachers a critical approach to curriculum design: A descriptive account. *Curriculum Inquiry, 16,* 179–201.

Goodman, J. (1986b). Making early field experience meaningful: A critical approach. *Journal of Education for Teaching, 12,* 109–125.

Hartnett, A., and Naish, M. (1980). Technicians or social bandits? Some moral and political issues in the education of teachers. In P. Woods (Ed.), *Teacher strategies* (pp. 254–274). London: Croom Helm.

Hawley, W. (1986). A critical analysis of the Holmes Group's proposals for reforming teacher education. *Journal of Teacher Education, 37*(4), 47–51.

Holmes Group. (1986). *Tomorrow's teachers.* East Lansing, MI: Author.

Houston, W. R. (Ed.). (1974). *Exploring competency-based teacher education.* Berkeley, CA: McCutchan.

Houston, W. R., and Howsam, R. (1972). *Competency-based teacher education: Progress, problems and prospects.* Chicago: Science Research Associates.

Howey, K. (1983). Teacher education: An overview. In K. R. Howey and W. E. Gardner (Eds.), *The education of teachers* (pp. 6–37). New York: Longman.

Howey, K., Yarger, S., and Joyce, B. (1978). *Improving teacher education.* Washington, DC: Association of Teacher Educators.

Howey, K., and Zimpher, N. (1989). *Profiles of preservice teacher education.* Albany: SUNY Press.

Jackson, P. (1968). *Life in classrooms.* New York: Holt, Rinehart and Winston.

Jackson, P. (1986). *The practice of teaching.* New York: Teachers College Press.

Jackson, P. (1987). Facing our ignorance. *Teachers College Record, 88,* 384–389.

Johnson, W. (1987). Empowering practitioners: Holmes, Carnegie, and the lessons of history. *History of Education Quarterly, 27,* 221–240.

Joyce, B. (1975). Conceptions of man and their implications for teacher education. In K. Ryan (Ed.), *Teacher education* (74th yearbook of the National Society for the Study of Education, pp. 111–145). Chicago: University of Chicago Press.

Joyce, B., and Showers, B. (1980). Improving inservice training: The message of research. *Educational Leadership, 37,* 379–385.

TOURO COLLEGE LIBRARY

Joyce, B., and Showers, B. (1984). *Power for staff development through research on train-ing*. Washington, DC: Association for Supervision and Curriculum Development.

Joyce, B., Yarger, S., and Howey, K. (1977). *Preservice teacher education*. Palo Alto, CA: Booksend Laboratory.

Judge, H. (1982). *American graduate schools of education: A view from abroad*. New York: Ford Foundation.

Kennedy, M. (1987). Inexact sciences: Professional education and the development of expertise. In E. Rothkopf (Ed.), *Review of research in education* (Vol. 14, pp. 133–167). Washington, DC: American Educational Research Association.

Kerr, D. H. (1983). Teaching competence and teacher education in the United States. In L. S. Shulman and G. Sykes (Eds.), *Handbook of teaching and policy* (pp. 126–149). New York: Longman.

Kimball, B. (1986). *Orators and philosophers*. New York: Teachers College Press.

Kirk, D. (1986). Beyond the limits of theoretical discourse in teacher education: Towards a critical pedagogy. *Teaching and Teacher Education, 2*, 155–167.

Koerner, J. (1963). *The miseducation of American teachers*. Baltimore: Penguin Books.

Kohl, H. (1976). *On teaching*. New York: Schocken Books.

Lampert, M. (1985). How do teachers manage to teach? Perspectives on problems in practice. *Harvard Educational Review, 55*, 178–194.

Lampert, M. (1986). Knowing, doing, and teaching multiplication. *Cognition and Instruction, 3*, 305–342.

Lanier, J., and Little, J. (1986). Research on teacher education. In M. C. Wittrock (Ed.), *Handbook of research on teaching* (3rd ed., pp. 527–569). New York: Macmillan.

Leinhardt, G., and Smith, D. (1985). Expertise in mathematics instruction: Subject matter knowledge. *Journal of Educational Psychology, 77*, 247–271.

Liston, D., and Zeichner, K. (1988a). Reflective teacher education and moral delibera-tion. *Journal of Teacher Education, 38*(6), 2–8.

Liston, D., and Zeichner, K. (1988b, April). *Critical pedagogy and teacher education*. Paper presented at the annual meeting of the American Educational Research Association, New Orleans.

Lortie, D. (1975). *Schoolteacher: A sociological study*. Chicago: University of Chicago Press.

McDiarmid, G. W., Ball, D. L., and Anderson, C. (in press). Why staying ahead one chap-ter just won't work: Subject-specific pedagogy. In M. Reynolds (Ed.), *Knowledge base for beginning teachers*. Washington, DC: American Association of Colleges of Teacher Education.

McDonald, J. P. (1986). Raising the teacher's voice and the ironic role of theory. *Harvard Educational Review, 56*, 355-378.

Monahan, W. (1984). *Teacher education in the '90s: A working paper*. Charleston, NC: Appalachia Education Laboratory.

Monroe, W. (1952). *Teaching-learning theory and teacher education: 1890–1950*. Urbana: University of Illinois Press.

National Center for Research on Teacher Education. (1988a). *Dialogues in teacher edu-cation* (Issue Paper 88-4). East Lansing: Michigan State University, National Cen-ter for Research on Teacher Education.

National Center for Research on Teacher Education. (1988b). Teacher education and learning to teach: A research agenda. *Journal of Teacher Education, 39*(6), 27–32.

Natriello, G. (1988). *Site report: New Jersey Provisional Teacher Program.* Unpublished paper, National Center for Research on Teacher Education, Michigan State University, East Lansing.

Natriello, G., Zumwalt, K., Hansen, A., and Frisch, A. (1988, April). *Who is choosing different routes into teaching?* Paper presented at the annual meeting of the American Educational Research Association, New Orleans.

New College. (1936). *Teachers College Record, 38,* 1–73.

Newlove, B. W. (1969). *The fifteen minute hour: An early teaching experience* (Report Series No. 23). Austin: University of Texas, Research and Development Center for Teacher Education.

Nordhoff, K., and Kleinfeld, J. (1987, October). *Rethinking the rhetoric of "reflective inquiry": What this language came to mean in a program to prepare rural teachers.* Paper presented at the Reflective Inquiry Conference, Houston.

Oliver, B., and McKibbin, M. (1985). Teacher trainees: Alternative credentialing in California. *Journal of Teacher Education, 36*(3), 20–23.

Peseau, B. A. (1982). Developing an adequate research base for teacher education. *Journal of Teacher Education, 33*(4), 13–15.

Posner, G. (1985). *Field experience: A guide to reflective teaching.* New York: Longman.

Powell, A. (1976). University schools of education in the twentieth century. *Peabody Journal of Education, 54*(1), 3–20.

Powell, A. (1980). *The uncertain profession: Harvard and the search for educational authority.* Cambridge: Harvard University Press.

Randolph, E. (1924). *The professional treatment of subject matter.* Balitmore: Warwick and York.

Rhoades, G. (1985). *The costs of academic excellence in teacher education* (Working Paper #5). Los Angeles, CA: University of California, Graduate School of Education, Comparative Higher Education Research Group.

Rosaen, C., Lanier, P., and Roth, K. (1988, April). *Educative field experiences: The faculty perspective.* Paper presented at the annual meeting of the American Association of Colleges of Teacher Education, New Orleans.

Ross, D., and Kyle, D. (1987). Helping teachers learn to use teacher effectiveness research. *Journal of Teacher Education, 38*(2), 40–44.

Scannell, D. (1987). Fifth year and extended programs. In M. Haberman and J. Backus (Eds.), *Advances in Teacher Education,* (Vol. 3, pp. 168–180). Norwood, NJ: Ablex.

Schon, D. (1983). *The reflective practitioner.* New York: Basic Books.

Schon, D. (1987). *Educating the reflective practitioner.* San Francisco: Jossey-Bass.

Schram, P., Wilcox, S., Lanier, P., and Lappan, G. (1988). *Changing mathematical conceptions of preservice teachers: A content and pedagogical intervention* (Research Report 88-4). East Lansing: Michigan State University, National Center for Research on Teacher Education.

Schwab, J. (1978). Education and the structure of the disciplines. In I. Westbury and N. Wilkof (Eds.), *Science, curriculum and liberal education: Selected essays* (pp. 229–272). Chicago: University of Chicago Press.

Shapiro, E. (1988). *Teacher: Being and becoming*. New York: Bank Street College.

Shulman, L. (1986). Those who understand: Knowledge growth in teaching. *Educational Researcher, 15*(2), 4–14.

Shulman, L. (1987). Knowledge and teaching: Foundations of the new reform. *Harvard Educational Review, 57*, 1–22.

Silberman, C. (1970). *Crisis in the classroom: The remaking of American education*. New York: Random House.

Sirotnik, K. (1988). Studying the education of educators: Methodology. *Phi Delta Kappan, 70*, 241–247.

Smith, D. (1984). PROTEACH: Teacher preparation at the University of Florida. *Teacher Education and Practice, 1*(2), 5–12.

Stodolsky, S. (1988). *The subject matters*. Chicago: University of Chicago Press.

Stone, J. (1968). *Breakthrough in teacher education*. San Francisco: Jossey-Bass.

Tabachnick, T., and Zeichner, K. (1985). *The development of teacher perspectives: Final report*. Madison: University of Wisconsin, Wisconsin Center for Education Research.

Tom, A. (1984). *Teaching as a moral craft*. New York: Longman.

Tom, A. (1985). Inquiring into inquiry-oriented teacher education. *Journal of Teacher Education, 36*(5), 35–44.

Tom, A. (1986). *The case for maintaining teacher education at the undergraduate level*. Paper presented at the Coalition of Teacher Education Programs, Washington University, St. Louis.

Tom, A. (Ed.). (n.d.). *Teacher education in liberal arts settings: Achievements, realities and challenges*. Washington, DC: American Association of Colleges for Teacher Education and American Independent Liberal Arts Colleges for Teacher Education.

Travers, E., and Sacks, S. (1987). *Teacher education and the liberal arts: The position of the consortium for excellence in teacher education*. Swarthmore, PA: Swarthmore College.

Van Manen, M. (1977). Linking ways of knowing with ways of being practical. *Curriculum Inquiry, 6*, 205–228.

Valli, L., and Taylor, N. (1987, October). *Reflective teacher education: Preferred characteristics for a content and process model*. Paper presented at the Reflective Inquiry Conference, Houston.

Weinstein, C. (1988). Case studies of extended teacher preparation. In A. Woolfolk (Ed.), *Research perspectives on the graduate preparation of teachers* (pp. 30–50). Englewood Cliffs, NJ: Prentice-Hall.

Wilkinson, L. (1988). Prospects for graduate preparation of teachers. In A. Woolfolk, (Ed.), *Research perspectives on the graduate preparation of teachers* (pp. 352–369). Englewood Cliffs, NJ: Prentice-Hall.

Wilson, J. (175). *Educational theory and the preparation of teachers*. Windsor, England: NFER.

Wilson, S., Shulman, L., and Richert, A. (1986). "150 different ways" of knowing: Representations of knowledge in teaching. In J. Calderhead (Ed.), *Exploring teachers' thinking* (pp. 104124). Eastbourne, England: Cassell.

Wise, A. E. (1986). Graduate teacher education and teacher professionalism. *Journal of Teacher Education, 37*(5), 36–40.

Woodring, P. (1957). *New directions in teacher education*. New York: Fund for the Advancement of Education.

Woodring, P. (1975) The development of teacher education. In K. Ryan (Ed.), *Teacher education* (74th yearbook of the National Society for the Study of Education, Part 2, pp. 1–24). Chicago: University of Chicago Press.

Woolfolk, A. (1988a). Graduate preparation of teachers: The debate and beyond. In A. Woolfolk (Ed.), *Research perspectives on the graduate preparation of teachers* (pp. 1–11). Englewood Cliffs, NJ: Prentice-Hall.

Woolfolk, A. (Ed.) (1988b). *Research perspectives on the graduate preparation of teachers*. Englewood Cliffs, NJ: Prentice-Hall.

Yarger, S., and Howey, K. (1977). Reflections on preservice preparation: Impressions from the national survey. *Journal of Teacher Education, 28*(6), 34–37.

Zeichner, K. (1981–82). Reflective teaching and field-based experience in teacher education. *Interchange, 12*, 1–22.

Zeichner, K. (1983). Alternative paradigms of teacher education. *Journal of Teacher Education, 34*(3), 3–9.

Zeichner, K. (1987). Preparing reflective teachers: An overview of instructional strategies which have been employed in preservice teacher education. *International Journal of Educational Research, 11*, 565–575.

Zeichner, K. (1988a). University of Florida, Gainesville, Elementary PROTEACH and Secondary English PROTEACH: Site Report. In National Center for Research in Teacher Education, *Dialogues in teacher education* (Issue Paper 88-4, pp. 55–81). East Lansing: Michigan State University, NCRTE.

Zeichner, K. (1988b). Learning from experience in graduate teacher preparation. In A. Woolfolk (Ed.), *Research perspectives on the graduate preparation of teachers* (p. 12–29). Englewood Cliffs, NJ: Prentice-Hall.

Zeichner, K. (1988c). *Understanding the character and quality of the academic and professional components of teacher education* (Research Report 88-1). East Lansing: Michigan State University, National Center for Research on Teacher Education.

Zeichner, K., and Grant, C. (1981). Biography and social structure in the socialization of student teachers. *Journal of Education for Teaching, 1*, 198–214.

Zeichner, K., and Liston, D. (1987). Teaching student teachers to reflect. *Harvard Educational Review, 57*, 23–48.

Zeichner, K., Mahlios, M., and Gomez, M. (1988). The structure and goals of a student teaching program and the character and quality of supervisory discourse. *Teaching and Teacher Education, 4*, 349–362.

Zimpher, N., and Howey, K. (1987). Adapting supervisory practice to different orientations of teaching competence. *Journal of Curriculum and Supervision, 2*(2), 101–127.

Zumwalt, K. (1987). Tomorrow's teachers: Tomorrow's work. *Teachers College Record, 88*, 426–431.

CHAPTER 3

From Preparation to Practice

Designing a Continuum to Strengthen and Sustain Teaching

INTRODUCTION

After decades of school reform, a consensus is building that the quality of our nation's schools depends on the quality of our nation's teachers. Policy makers and educators are coming to see that what students learn is directly related to what and how teachers teach; and what and how teachers teach depends on the knowledge, skills, and commitments they bring to their teaching and the opportunities they have to continue learning in and from their practice. The National Commission on Teaching and America's Future (1996) puts it this way: "What teachers know and can do makes the crucial difference in what teachers can accomplish. New courses, tests, curriculum reforms can be important starting points, but they are meaningless if teachers cannot use them productively. Policies can improve schools only if the people in them are armed with the knowledge, skills and supports they need" (p. 5).

This paper rests on a single premise with far-reaching consequences—if we want schools to produce more powerful learning on the part of students, we have to offer more powerful learning opportunities to teachers. Conventional programs of teacher education and professional development are not designed to promote complex learning by teachers or students. The typical preservice program is a weak intervention compared with the influence of teachers' own schooling and their on-the-job experience. "Sink or swim" induction encourages novices to stick to whatever practices enable them to survive whether or not they represent "best" practice in that situation. Professional development opportunities are usually sporadic and disconnected, rarely tied to teachers' classroom work and lacking any follow up. Unless teachers have access to serious and sustained learning opportunities at every stage in their career, they are unlikely to teach in ways that meet demanding new standards for student learning or to participate in the solution of educational problems (Ball & Cohen, 1999).

Placing serious and sustained teacher learning at the center of school reform is a radical idea. It challenges dominant views of teaching and learning to teach. It calls for a major overhaul in provisions for teacher preparation, induction, and continuing development. It requires capacity building at all levels of the system. No one should underestimate the depth or scope of the agenda. As Fullan, Galluzzo, Morris, and Watson (1998) contend: "We are dealing with a reform proposition so profound that the teaching profession itself, along with the culture of schools and schools of education, will have to undergo total transformation in order for substantial progress to be made" (p. 68).

This paper was written to stimulate discussion and debate about what a professional learning continuum from initial preparation through the early years of teaching could be like. Drawing on a broad base of literature and my own research and experience in teacher education, I propose a framework for thinking about a curriculum for teacher learning over time. I also consider the fit (or misfit) between conventional approaches and the challenges of learning to teach in reform-minded ways and offer some examples of promising programs and practices in preservice preparation, new teacher induction, and early professional development.

The paper is organized around three questions: (a) What are the central tasks of teacher learning in the early stages of learning to teach? (b) How well do conventional arrangements for teacher preparation, new teacher induction, and early professional development address these central tasks and what are some major obstacles that get in the way? (c) What are some promising programs and practices that promote reform-minded teaching and enable teachers to become active participants in school reform?

The first question invites us to consider the learning needs of teachers at different stages in their learning to teach over time. The notion of "central tasks" suggests that each phase in a continuum of teacher learning has a unique agenda shaped by the requirements of good teaching and by where teachers are in their professional development. Delineating central tasks of preservice preparation, induction, and early professional development allows us to see the special challenges associated with different stages as well as the necessary threads of continuity that create a coherent and powerful curriculum for becoming a learning teacher and an agent of change.

The second question calls for an appraisal of current practice in light of the central tasks of learning to teach and for an analysis of major obstacles that limit our ability to prepare reform-minded teachers and help them develop their practice over time. The third question invites a description of some promising programs and practices in initial preparation, induction, and early professional development. These examples demonstrate the possibility of creating powerful opportunities for teacher learning directed toward reform-minded teaching and appropriate for teachers at different stages. The challenge is not only to connect such opportunities across a learning-to-teach continuum but also to make them a regular feature on the educational landscape.

Before turning to this agenda, a brief explanation of the underlying image of teaching is in order, since we cannot talk about a learning to teach continuum without clarifying the kind of teaching we want teachers to learn. Many contemporary reforms call for content-rich, learner-centered teaching, which emphasizes conceptual understanding and gives all students opportunities to think critically, solve problems, and learn things that matter to them and have meaning in the world outside of school. If conventional models emphasize teaching as telling and learning as listening, reform-oriented models call for teachers to do more listening as they elicit student thinking and assess their understanding and for students to do more asking and explaining as they investigate authentic problems and share their solutions.[1]

New curriculum frameworks and standards documents represent this image of ambitious teaching in the form of subject specific goals and principles; however, what this means and what it looks like in practice must be worked out by teachers themselves. It follows that teachers who embrace this kind of teaching must also be practical intellectuals, curriculum developers, and generators of knowledge in practice. The continuum for learning to teach proposed here is oriented around this vision of teaching and around an expanded view of professional practice that includes teachers working together for educational change.

TEACHER LEARNING DURING PRESERVICE PREPARATION

Dewey (1938) warned that "preparation" was a "treacherous" idea when applied to education. He believed that every experience should prepare a person for later experiences of a deeper, more expansive quality. He argued that educators should not use the present simply to get ready for the future. "Only by extracting the full meaning of each present experience are we prepared for doing the same thing in the future" (p. 49).

I think of Dewey when I hear cooperating teachers insist that student teachers need a lot of experience with whole-class teaching since that is what they will be expected to do on their own the following year. I wonder about the powerful learnings that could come from child study, classroom inquiry, coplanning, coteaching and other forms of assisted performance that would enable teacher candidates to learn with help what they are not ready to do on their own. I also think of Dewey when I see university teacher educators trying to cram too much into their courses, because they believe this is their last chance to influence prospective teachers. If preservice teacher educators could count on induction programs to build on and extend their work, they could concentrate on laying a foundation for beginning teaching and preparing novices to learn in and from their practice.

Central Tasks

The central tasks of preservice preparation build on current thinking about what teachers need to know, care about, and be able to do in order to promote substantial learning for all students. They also reflect the well established fact that the images and beliefs which preservice students bring to their teacher preparation influence what they are able to learn. Although the tasks are discussed separately, they form a coherent and dynamic agenda for initial preparation.

Analyzing Beliefs and Forming New Visions

The images and beliefs that prospective teachers bring to their preservice preparation serve as filters for making sense of the knowledge and experiences they encounter. They may also function as barriers to change by limiting the ideas that teacher education students are able and willing to entertain. The paradoxical role of prior beliefs in learning takes on special significance in teacher preparation. Unlike students of engineering or law or medicine, students of teaching do not approach their professional education feeling unprepared. Images of teaching, learning, students, and subject matter formed during elementary and secondary school provide a basis for interpreting and assessing ideas and practices encountered during teacher preparation (Lortie, 1975). These taken-for-granted beliefs may mislead prospective teachers into thinking that they know more about teaching than they actually do and make it harder for them to form new ideas and new habits of thought and action.

Researchers have documented the nature and persistence of preservice teachers' entering beliefs. For instance, many preservice students think of teaching as passing on knowledge and learning as absorbing and memorizing knowledge (Ball & McDiarmid, 1990; Calderhead & Robson, 1991). When they imagine themselves teaching, prospective teachers often picture themselves standing in front of a group of attentive students presenting information, going over problems, and giving explanations (Ball, 1988). These views are incompatible with conceptions of teaching, learning, and knowledge that undergird new visions of reform-minded practice. Before they can embrace these new visions, prospective teachers need opportunities to examine critically their taken-for-granted, often deeply entrenched beliefs so that these beliefs can be developed or amended.

Teacher candidates must also form visions of what is possible and desirable in teaching to inspire and guide their professional learning and practice. Such visions connect important values and goals to concrete classroom practices. They help teachers construct a normative basis for developing and assessing their teaching and their students' learning. Unless teacher educators engage prospective teachers in a critical examination of their entering beliefs in light of compelling alternatives and help them develop powerful images of good teaching and strong professional commitments, these entering beliefs will continue to shape their ideas and practices.

Developing Subject Matter Knowledge for Teaching

If teachers are responsible for helping students learn worthwhile content, they must know and understand the subjects they teach. Scholars have identified three aspects of subject matter knowledge for teaching: (a) knowledge of central facts, concepts, theories, and procedures within a given field; (b) knowledge of explanatory frameworks that organize and connect ideas; and (c) knowledge of the rules of evidence and proof (Shulman, 1986). Besides knowing content, teachers must understand the nature of knowledge and inquiry in different fields. How is a proof in mathematics different from a historic explanation or a literary interpretation? Such understandings influence the questions teachers ask, the tasks they set, and the ideas they reinforce. If teachers do not understand how scholars working in different fields think about their subjects, they may misrepresent those subjects to their students (Ball & McDiarmid, 1990).

Teachers also need to know their subjects from a pedagogical perspective (Wilson, Shulman, & Richert, 1987). This means understanding what students find confusing or difficult and having alternative explanations, models, and analogies to represent core concepts and processes. It means framing purposes for studying particular content and being familiar with some well-designed curricular materials. It means understanding how core concepts and processes connect across fields and how they relate to everyday life.

Developing Understandings of Learners and Learning

In order to connect students and subject matter in age-appropriate and meaningful ways, prospective teachers must develop a pedagogical stance rooted in knowledge of child/adolescent development and learning. What are students like at different ages? How do they make sense of their physical and social worlds? How are their ways of thinking and acting shaped by language and culture? Informed perspectives on development and learning provide necessary frameworks for understanding students, designing appropriate learning activities, justifying pedagogical decisions and actions, and communicating with parents, students, administrators, and colleagues.

A related task is learning about the cultures that students bring to school. Increasingly many teachers find themselves teaching students whose racial, cultural, and socioeconomic backgrounds differ markedly from their own. Some teacher educators advocate teaching about different cultures directly; others emphasize the importance of helping prospective teachers explore their own biases and personal experiences with diversity. All recognize the need to cultivate the tools and dispositions to learn about students, their families, and communities and to build on this knowledge in teaching and learning (Ladsen-Billings, 1999; Zeichner & Hoeft, 1996).

Developing a Beginning Repertoire

Good teachers do many things to promote student learning. They lead discussions, plan experiments, design interdisciplinary units, hold debates, assign journals, conference with students, set up classroom libraries, organize a writer's workshop, take field trips, and so on. Good teachers know about a range of approaches to curriculum, instruction, and assessment; and they have the judgement, skill, and understanding to decide what to use when. Wasley, Hampel, and Clark (1997) call this a teaching repertoire which they define as "a variety of techniques, skills, and approaches in all dimensions of education—curriculum, instruction and assessment—that teachers have at their fingertips to stimulate the growth of the children with whom they work" (p. 45).

Preservice preparation is a time to begin developing a basic repertoire for reform-minded teaching. This means becoming familiar with a limited range of good curricular materials, learning several general and subject specific models of teaching, and exploring a few approaches to assessment that tap student understanding. The focus should not be on variety for its own sake, but on helping teacher candidates figure out when, where, how, and why to use particular approaches.

Developing the Tools to Study Teaching

Preservice preparation is a time to begin forming habits and skills necessary for the ongoing study of teaching in the company of colleagues. Preservice teachers must come to see that learning is an integral part of teaching and that serious conversations about teaching are a valuable resource in developing and improving their practice.

The study of teaching requires skills of observation, interpretation, and analysis. Preservice students can begin developing these skills by analyzing samples of student work, comparing different curricular materials, interviewing students to uncover their thinking, studying how different teachers work toward the same goals, and observing what impact their instruction has on students. Carried out in the company of others, these activities can foster norms for professional discourse such as respect for evidence, openness to questions, valuing of alternative perspectives, a search for common understandings, and shared standards.

A Critical Appraisal of Conventional Preservice Programs and Practices

How well do conventional preservice programs address these central tasks? What programmatic and institutional factors limit their effectiveness? This section reviews some major problems and obstacles that contribute to widespread skepticism about teacher preparation and help explain its weak impact on teachers' beliefs and practices.

Most teachers enter teaching through a 4-year undergraduate program that combines academic courses and professional studies or a 5th-year program that focuses exclusively on professional studies. Academic requirements consist of arts and science courses including an academic major. Professional preparation includes courses in educational foundations and general and/or specific methods of teaching. Educational psychology is a staple in educational foundations, but courses in philosophy or history have been replaced with an "introduction to teaching" course. All programs require some supervised practice called student teaching.

These arrangements have been regularly criticized on conceptual and structural problems (Goodlad, 1994; Howey & Zimpher, 1989; Tom, 1997). Separate courses taught by individual faculty in different departments rarely build on or connect to one another, nor do they add up as a coherent preparation for teaching. Without a set of organizing themes, without shared standards, without clear goals for student learning, there is no framework to guide program design or student assessment. No wonder students have difficulty developing a vision of good teaching or making connections among different domains of knowledge and skill.

The weak relationship between courses and field experiences is further evidence of the overall lack of coherence. Teacher education students regard student teaching as the most valuable part of their preparation. Still, they cannot count on regular opportunities to observe, analyze, and practice reform-minded teaching. At the same time, cooperating teachers often feel the need to protect student teachers from "impractical" ideas promoted by education professors who are out of touch with classroom realities. When the people responsible for field experiences do not work closely with the people who teach academic and professional courses, there is no productive joining of forces around a common agenda and no sharing of expertise.

Fragmentation, weak pedagogy, and lack of articulation also extend to the arts and sciences and their relationship to education. For a long time, teacher educators took subject matter preparation for granted, relying on the fact that prospective teachers completed a specified number of courses in the arts and sciences. Recently, serious questions have been raised about the adequacy of teachers' subject matter knowledge (Borko & Putnam, 1996). Some studies have shown that even when teachers major in their teaching subjects, they often have difficulty explaining basic concepts in their disciplines (National Center for Research on Teacher Learning, 1991).

Undergraduate education is currently under siege. The survey courses that dominate these programs provide limited opportunities to develop deep understanding and critical perspectives or to experience firsthand the modes of inquiry associated with different fields. Thus it is not surprising that teachers lack conceptual and connected knowledge of the subjects they teach.

The pedagogy of teacher education mirrors the pedagogy of higher education where lectures, discussions, and seat-based learning are the coins of the realm. Too often teacher educators do not practice what they preach.

Classes are either too abstract to challenge deeply held beliefs or too super-ficial to foster deep understanding. All this reinforces the belief that the K–12 classroom is *the* place to learn to teach.

Also missing are well-designed opportunities to link theory and prac-tice, develop skills and strategies, cultivate habits of analysis and reflection through focused observation, child study, analysis of cases, micro-teach-ing, and other laboratory experiences (Dewey, 1904; Howey, 1996; Smith, 1980). Nor do preservice programs make effective use of the peer social-ization processes employed in other programs of professional preparation (Goodlad, 1994).

Obstacles to Effective Preservice Preparation

The obstacles to effective preservice preparation are legion. They include the low status of teachers and teacher educators, overregulation of preser-vice programs by the state, a pervasive anti-intellectualism, weak leadership, limited resources, and a lack of imagination on the part of teacher educa-tors. In this discussion of teacher development, it seems particularly relevant to highlight the ways in which the culture and organization of universities and schools work against effective teacher preparation.

The university culture favors research over teaching and accords low sta-tus to clinical work. The primacy of academic freedom makes it difficult to engage faculty in programmatic thinking. The departmental structure dis-courages collaboration across specializations. There are no incentives for arts and science faculty to take responsibility for developing teachers' sub-ject matter knowledge. There are few incentives for teacher educators to undertake the labor-intensive and time-consuming work of program devel-opment. Collaborating with practitioners may count as service, but it does not help in decisions about tenure and promotion. The university expects teacher education to generate revenue through high enrollments and large classes. There are few mechanisms to stimulate faculty renewal.

The culture of teaching and the organization of schools also serve as obstacles to effective field-based teacher preparation. Schools are not orga-nized for teachers to work together on problems of practice in serious and sustained ways. With no tradition of inquiry, collaboration, or experimen-tation, there is a strong press to maintain the status quo. A culture of politeness and consensus makes it hard to confront differences in teaching philosophy and practice. Egalitarian norms make it difficult to single out some teachers for participation in teacher preparation. Teachers are supposed to work with students. Anything that takes them away from their main responsibility is considered a problem rather than an opportunity for professional development or professional service.

Promising Programs and Practices

While teacher preparation faces major obstacles, reformers are beginning to address some of the familiar problems. In the past decade, much solid groundwork has been accomplished through the efforts of organizations like the Holmes Group (now Partnership) and the National Network for Educational Renewal and through ongoing program development in institutions with long-standing traditions of innovation in teacher education. Despite the perceived wisdom that teacher preparation is a weak intervention, preservice programs can make a difference, especially when they are organized around an explicit and thoughtful mission and conceptual framework, integrate courses and fieldwork, use student and/or faculty cohorts to intensify the experience and attend to students' entering beliefs and their evolving professional identity and practice (Barnes, 1987; Howey & Zimpher, 1989; National Center for Research on Teacher Learning, 1991).

Support for this claim comes from recently completed case studies of seven well-regarded preservice programs oriented toward "learner-centered and learning-centered teaching" (Darling-Hammond & MacDonald, 2000). Located in different types of institutions (liberal arts college, single purpose institution, research university), the programs differ in structure (4 year, 5 year, 5th year) and focus (early childhood, elementary, secondary). Beyond their structural differences, the programs share certain characteristics which help account for their distinctive quality and impact. These programs derive more from their substantive orientation and commitments and their ways of working with students.

The influence of substance over structure fits with findings from the Teacher Education and Learning to Teach (TELT) study, a study of over 700 teachers and teacher candidates in 11 structurally diverse teacher education programs across the United State. Conducted by the National Center for Research on Teacher Learning, the TELT study was designed to shed light on what actually goes on in diverse teacher education programs and what teachers learn as they participate in these programs over time. Summarizing the findings, researchers concluded,

> Although the debates in teacher education tend to be about the structure of teacher education programs, the TELT data suggest that the content

and orientation of programs are more likely to influence teacher learning. Differences in beliefs and knowledge about teaching practices, diverse learners, and subject matter among teacher candidates at the end of the preservice programs studied were largely a function of their entering beliefs and knowledge of the conceptual orientation of the program. Differences across program structures did not produce noticeable differences in teacher candidates' beliefs. (NCRTL, 1991, p. 6)

Because of their clear association with a reform agenda consistent with this discussion, I draw on a set of case studies of preservice programs sponsored by the National Commission on Teaching and America's Future (Darling-Hammond, 2000) to illustrate some promising practices in context. Often accounts of promising practices in preservice teacher education highlight isolated practices. In learning to teach, however, the educational whole is greater than the sum of its parts. Individual strategies such as the use of student/faculty cohorts, case-based teaching, well-structured field assignments, and portfolio assessments may represent important changes in practice, but their meaning and impact depend on the overall purposes they serve. And these, in turn, are influenced by a program's conceptual orientation.

Conceptual Coherence

The lack of articulation and the fragmented nature of most conventional preservice programs underscore the need for conceptual coherence. Howey (1990) makes the case in the following way: "Advocacy for more coherence seems appropriate given the number of preservice programs that superficially engage students in a large number of disparate and unconnected ideas and practices" (p. 150). I am not arguing that coherence is a good in itself, although a coherent program is more likely to have desired effects. Everything depends on the quality of the ideas that give the program direction and purpose.

A conceptual framework is the "cornerstone" of a coherent program (Howey, 1990). It provides a guiding vision of the kind of teacher the program is trying to prepare. It offers a view of learning, the role of the teacher, and the mission of schooling in a democracy. It provides a set of understandings about learning to teach. More than rhetoric, the values and ideas that make up a program's mission and conceptual framework inform the design and sequencing of courses and field experiences. They may get translated into specific themes or core abilities. They shape curriculum, culture, pedagogy, and assessment practices.

Each of the seven programs has a set of guiding values and beliefs which give it a distinctive ethos and provide the basis for a cohesive curriculum and a sequence of integrated learning opportunities. Some of the programs, especially those for early childhood and elementary teachers, derive much of their conceptual coherence from a strong developmental orientation which shapes their approach to teaching. For example, faculty at Wheelock College combine the traditional notion of development as an unfolding of abilities and interests with attention to issues of culture, diversity, and inclusion. Students talk about "the Wheelock way" which is "child-centered, community-based, and family focused" (Miller & Silvernail, 2000). Bank Street College, deeply rooted in a progressive vision of educational goals and possibilities, also projects and promotes a developmental stance toward learners and learning. One of the signature courses, "Observation and Recording, teaches prospective teachers to look closely at children and their development, to see them as growing individuals, and to find ways to foster their learning" (Darling-Hammond and MacDonald, 2000).

Clear goals and vision animate the elementary education program at Alverno College. The entire program is designed around a set of eight general education abilities and five professional abilities that define the kind of teacher the program seeks to prepare. The abilities, which must be "validated" at several developmental levels in multiple contexts, spell out the knowledge, skills, and dispositions students must demonstrate to complete the program and receive their elementary certification. The ability-based curriculum and its associated performance-based assessment system give faculty, students, cooperating teachers, and principals a common language for talking about teaching and learning and communicating clear expectations (Zeichner, 2000).

Purposeful, Integrated Field Experiences

The purposeful design and use of field experiences is another manifestation of program coherence. I treat it separately because of the critical and complex role that classroom experiences play in learning to teach during preservice preparation. Observation, apprenticeship, guided practice, knowledge application, and inquiry all have a place in field-based learning. Teacher candidates need opportunities to test the theories, use the knowledge, see and try out the practices advocated by the academy. They also need opportunities to investigate problems and analyze situations that arise in the field. Recent reform proposals call for teacher candidates to spend extended periods of time in professional development schools, internships, and other clinical sites. The real challenge for teacher educators is to see that prospective teachers not only have appropriate and extended field experiences but that they learn desirable lessons from them.

The seven preservice case studies are full of promising practices in field-based teacher preparation. All the programs use carefully structured field assignments to situate theoretical learning in practice and to promote reflection. Several programs require systematic child study as a vehicle for connecting perspectives on human development and learning with the study of individual students. One assigns the design, teaching, assessment, and public presentation of an interdisciplinary unit as a way to help teacher candidates "knit it all together" (Whitford, Ruscoe, and Fickel, 2000). Most use some combination of reflective logs, dialogue journals, weekly cohort-based seminars, and individual conferences to help teacher candidates develop the capacity to learn from the experience and analysis of their own and other's practice.

Through a careful sequence of multiple placements, some with their own graduates, programs make it possible for teacher candidates to see and practice the kind of teaching they are learning about in their courses as they move from observation to limited participation to full responsibility with appropriate modeling and supervision. For instance, Bank Street students take some of their courses and do some of their fieldwork in the Bank Street School for Children, an independent, progressive demonstration school which features an interactive process of curriculum building across all grade levels and subjects. Elementary education students at Alverno College experience a variety of grade levels, socioeconomic and cultural groups, and educational approaches in a careful sequence of field experiences and student teaching spread over 5 semesters. At least two of the field placements and one of two 9-week student teaching placements occurs in the Milwaukee Public Schools. All student teachers work with cooperating teachers who have completed a special course offered three times a year. Mentoring and assessment are closely tied to the ability framework. The University of Southern Maine immerses teacher education students in classroom practice during a 9-month internship organized around 2-semesterlong placements. Clear guidelines spell out expectations for instructional planning, degree of lead responsibility for teaching, required videotaping, and dialogue journals. Weekly visits by site coordinators and a weekly seminar help interns analyze and document their learning in relation to 11 program outcomes. Such careful attention to preservice teachers as learners is another distinguishing feature of exemplary programs.

Attention to Teachers as Learners

Just as student learning is the desired outcome of teaching, so teacher learning is the desired outcome of teacher education. Exemplary preservice programs support continuity in preservice students' learning by providing a dynamic culture and a coherent curriculum, by monitoring students' personal responses to new ideas and experiences, and by offering an appropriate mixture of support and challenge in response to students' changing knowledge, skills, and beliefs.

A focus on teachers as learners begins with a recognition that preservice students come with images and beliefs that must be extended or transformed. It is reflected in deliberate efforts by teacher educators to model the kind of interactive, content-rich teaching they are trying to promote and to create opportunities for preservice students to experience that teaching as learners. (This is especially critical when preservice students have not been exposed to such practices in their own K–12 schooling.) It is supported by opportunities to put into words one's evolving philosophy of teaching and to engage in ongoing assessment in relation to personal goals and shared professional standards.

The advisement system at Bank Street College provides a clear example of how one exemplary program insures continuity in preservice teachers' learning and pays careful attention to their personal and professional development. Researchers call advising the "glue" that holds the different learning experiences together and the "linchpin" for the enactment of a caring learning community. Advisors are faculty members with extensive classroom experiences. They work closely with six to eight students for at least a year, meeting them individually every other week, convening weekly conference group meetings, arranging placements, and supervising field experiences. Advisors help students integrate and interpret their experiences in the program, develop self-understanding, and evolve a personal philosophy of teaching. The personal/professional relationships between advisors and students reflect the centrality of relationships in teaching and learning and model the kind of relationship graduates are supposed to form with their own pupils (Darling-Hammond and MacDonald, 2000).

How do the graduates of these programs fare as beginning elementary and secondary teachers? Interviews and observations with one or two graduates from each program show them working hard to teach as they were taught in their preservice preparation, although some face skepticism from colleagues wary of their ambitious goals for learners and their progressive teaching methods. Yet even these well-started novices have more to learn if they are to master the kind of demanding teaching they learned about in their teacher preparation and are to work effectively with their colleagues to improve education for all students.

"No matter what initial preparation they receive," writes Carol Bartell (1995), a leader in California's efforts to develop new teacher programs and policies, "teachers are never fully prepared for classroom realities and for responsibilities associated with meeting the needs of a rapidly growing, increasingly diverse student population" (p. 28–29). Recognizing the inevitable limitations of preservice preparation provides an important justification for induction programs. Educators still have to figure out how to help novices connect the "text" of their preservice program to the "contexts" of contemporary classrooms (Dalton & Moir, 1996).

TEACHER LEARNING DURING THE INDUCTION PHASE

New teachers have two jobs—they have to teach and they have to learn to teach. No matter how good a preservice program may be, there are some things that can only be learned on the job. The preservice experience lays a foundation and offers practice in teaching. The first encounter with real teaching occurs when beginning teachers step into their own classroom. Then learning to teach begins in earnest.

The first years of teaching are an intense and formative time in learning to teach, influencing not only whether people remain in teaching but what kind of teacher they become. As Bush (1983) explains,

> The conditions under which a person carries out the first years of teaching have a strong influence on the level of effectiveness which that teacher is able to achieve and sustain over the years; on the attitudes which govern teachers' behavior over even a forty year career; and, indeed, on the decision whether or not to continue in the teaching profession. (p. 3)

Researchers characterize the first years of teaching as a time of survival and discovery, adaptation and learning (Nemser, 1983). According to one school of thought, novices rely on trial and error to work out strategies that help them to survive without sacrificing all the idealism that attracted them to teaching in the first place. They continue to depend on these strategies whether or not they represent best practice (Lacey, 1977; Lortie, 1975). According to another school of thought, beginning teachers face personal concerns about acceptance, control, and adequacy which must be resolved before they can move on to more professional considerations about teaching and student learning (Fuller, 1969; Kagan, 1990). Many assume that classroom management is the major preoccupation, but case studies of new teachers provide a more dynamic and contextualized picture (Bullough, 1989; Grossman, 1990). Clearly the experience of beginning teaching and the lessons learned derive from a complex interaction of personal and situational factors.

Teacher induction is often framed as a transition from preservice preparation to practice, from student of teaching to teacher of students. As these phrases imply, induction brings a shift in role orientation and an epistemological move from knowing about teaching through formal study to knowing how to teach by confronting the day-to-day challenges. Becoming a teacher involves forming a professional identity and constructing a professional practice. Both aspects of learning to teach must unfold in ways that strengthen the beginning teacher's capacity for further growth.

Central Task of Teacher Induction

What do novices in the first 3 years of teaching need to learn? What are the central learning tasks of a reform-oriented curriculum for new teacher induction? Some general answers to these questions can be offered based on an understanding of beginning teacher learning and a commitment to meet new teachers where they are and move their practice toward ambitious, standards-based teaching and learning. The actual curriculum in a given program must take into account the preparation new teachers bring and the realities they encounter and must extend across a reasonable span of time (2–3 years).

The situation in which new teachers find themselves is inherently paradoxical. Like all beginning professionals, they must demonstrate skills and abilities that they do not yet have and can only gain by beginning to do what they do not yet understand (Schon, 1987). This places beginning teachers in a vulnerable position. Moreover the work of teaching, itself complex, uncertain, and full of dilemmas, sharpens the paradox by reminding beginning teachers at every turn of what they cannot yet do.

Gaining Local Knowledge of Students, Curriculum, and School Context
Charged with the same responsibilities as their more experienced colleagues, beginning teachers are expected to perform and to be effective. Yet most aspects of the teaching environment are unfamiliar—students, curriculum, administrative policies and procedures, testing requirements, professional norms, the larger community. While novices deserve relevant information in

a timely fashion and easy access to answers as questions arise, much of what they need to understand cannot be explained once and for all.

Beginning teachers need to learn what the expected goals and outcomes are for students at their grade level and what materials and resources are available. They need to understand how these expectations fit into the larger school or departmental curriculum and how they relate to district, state, and national standards and testing. Most important, they need to figure out how to interpret and to use this information in their teaching.

Beginning teachers need to learn about the larger community. What structures are in place for teachers to communicate with parents? What community services and resources are available? How do other teachers establish productive relationships with families and work together on behalf of students and their education?

Besides learning what is generally expected and taught in specific subjects for particular grade/age levels, novices must learn about their students—who they are and what knowledge, interests, and life experiences they bring—and use this knowledge in developing curriculum.

Designing Responsive Curriculum and Instruction

To create a responsive curriculum, new teachers must bring together their knowledge of content and their knowledge of particular students in making decisions about what and how to teach over time and then make adjustments in response to what happens. To teach in ways that are responsive to students' thinking, they must also learn how to elicit and interpret students' ideas and to generate appropriate pedagogical moves as a lesson unfolds. Learning to listen to what students say and to construct appropriate responses on a moment to moment basis places special demands on new teachers. This challenging aspect of ambitious teaching takes time to learn and can only be developed in the context of teaching.

Enacting a Beginning Repertoire in Purposeful Ways

If preservice preparation has been successful, beginning teachers will have a compelling vision of good teaching and a beginning repertoire of approaches to curriculum, instruction, and assessment consistent with that vision. A major task of induction is helping new teachers enact these approaches purposefully with their students by developing the necessary understanding and flexibility of response. The multiple challenges of teaching alone for the first time can discourage new teachers from trying ambitious pedagogies. Good induction support can keep novices from abandoning these approaches in favor of what they may perceive as safer, less complex activities. It can also help novices attend to the purposes not just the management of the learning activities and their meaning for students.

Creating a Classroom Learning Community

Every year teachers must create and maintain a classroom learning community that is safe, respectful, and productive of student learning. This task covers a wide range of responsibilities from setting up the physical environment and establishing rules and routines, to promoting cooperation, managing disruptions, and teaching democratic processes and problem solving strategies. It involves building a classroom culture that supports intellectual risk-taking.

Issues of power and control lie at the heart of this task which is tied up with novices' evolving professional identity. Compounding the uncertainties about what stance to take and how to respond to the myriad situations that arise is the fear of judgment from students, colleagues, administrators, and themselves. If teachers are judged by how quiet and well behaved their classes are, they may avoid active or complex learning activities because they do not yet know how to manage them.

Developing a Professional Identity

Beginning teachers must consolidate a professional identity. Often beginning teachers struggle to reconcile competing images of their role, for example, the need to be an authority in areas of discipline and classroom management with the desire to be perceived as a friendly person, the need to prepare students for the "real world" with the desire to be a nurturing caregiver who is responsive to individual differences (Bullough & Knowles, 1991; Ryan, 1970). Constructing a professional identity is a complex, ongoing process. Beginning teachers form a coherent sense of themselves as professionals by combining parts of their past, including their own experiences in school and in teacher preparation, with pieces of the present in their current school context with images of the kind of teacher and colleague they want to become and the kind of classroom they want to create (Featherstone, 1993).

Learning in and from Practice

To develop their practice and improve as teachers, novices must learn to use their practice as a site for inquiry (Ball & Cohen, 1999). This means turning confusions into questions, trying something out and studying the effects, and framing new questions to extend one's understanding. Such work depends on skills of observation and analysis and the dispositions to seek evidence, take risks, and remain open to different interpretations.

The ongoing study and improvement of teaching is difficult to accomplish alone. Novices need opportunities to talk with others about their teaching, to analyze their students' work, to examine problems, and to consider alternative explanations and actions. If novices learn to talk about specific practices in specific terms, if they learn to ask for clarification, share uncertainties, and request help, they will be developing skills and dispositions that are critical in the ongoing improvement of teaching.

Induction by Default and Design: A Critical Appraisal of Current Practice

Induction happens with or without a formal program, and it is often an abrupt and lonely process. The problems with "sink or swim" induction are well documented. In far too many places new teachers must learn the ropes on their own. The cost is high. Up to one third of new teachers leave the profession within the first three years, a fact that falls heaviest on urban schools. Even when teachers remain, they may lose their ideals and lower their expectations for student learning.

Sometimes a beginning teacher gets help from a well-meaning colleague. This kind of informal buddy system may work for the fortunate novice who gets adopted, but it hardly represents an adequate response to the larger need. Relying on the good will of experienced teachers to reach out on their own initiative ignores the learning challenges that beginning teachers face and the need for a more sustained and systematic approach to their development.

The emergence of formal programs for beginning teachers in their early years on the job is a relatively recent phenomenon. Currently 27 states have a formally approved and implemented statewide support system for beginning teachers; and most urban districts, especially the larger ones, offer some kind of support to beginning teachers, usually in the form of mentoring (Fideler & Haselkorn, 1999).

Despite widespread interest, however, the overall picture is uneven. Most induction mandates do not rest on an understanding of teacher learning, a vision of good teaching or a broad view of the role formal induction can play in new teacher development. Often they lack the necessary resources to support effective programs. Even when formal programs exist, they may not help beginning teachers teach in ways that foster complex learning on the part of students. Research shows that mentoring, the most popular induction strategy, sometimes reinforces traditional norms and practices rather than promoting more powerful teaching (Feiman-Nemser & Parker, 1993).

Narrow Vision

Most induction programs confine their attention to the 1st year of teaching, maintaining a narrow vision of what they should accomplish. Instead of viewing induction as part of a broad continuum of professional learning opportunities for teachers, induction is regarded as short-term support designed to ease new teachers' entry into teaching and help them cope with their first year on the job. The narrow vision goes hand in hand with a lack of coordination between preservice providers and those responsible for induction programs.

Support is the dominant orientation and focus of most induction programs (Gold, 1996; Huling-Austin, 1990). Support is the omnibus term used to describe the materials, advice, and hand-holding that mentors offer new teachers. While supporting new teachers is a humane response to the very real challenges of beginning teaching, it does not provide an adequate rationale. Unless we take new teachers seriously as learners and frame induction around a vision of good teaching and compelling standards for student learning, we will end up with induction programs that reduce stress and address immediate problems without promoting teacher development and improving the quality of teaching and learning.

Constraints on Mentoring

Assigning experienced teachers to work with novices is the favored induction strategy, and most programs have a mentoring component. Still mentor teachers may not have adequate preparation or time to work with beginning teachers, and they may not define their role and responsibilities in educational terms. Moreover the widespread assumption that good teachers automatically make good mentors does not hold (Feiman-Nemser, 1998b).

In one comparative study, researchers found striking differences in the way mentor teachers defined and enacted their role which they linked to differences in selection, training, and time for mentoring (Feiman-Nemser & Parker, 1993). Some mentors defined their responsibilities in terms of emotional support and short-term technical assistance. They explained local policies and procedures, shared materials, answered questions, and gave advice. Willing to help with any problem, they often pulled back as soon as their novice seemed more confident. Researchers called these mentors "local guides."

Some mentors defined their role in educational terms. They still helped novices with immediate problems, but they also kept their eye on professional goals such as helping novices focus on student thinking and on developing sound reasons for their actions. Often they worked toward these goals by inquiring with novices into the particulars of their teaching situation, asking questions such as, "What sense did students make of the assignment?" "Why did you decide on this activity?" "How could we find out whether it worked?" Researchers called these mentors "educational companions."

A few mentors saw themselves as "agents of change." They deliberately worked to reduce the traditional isolation among teachers by encouraging collaboration and shared inquiry. They built networks among novices and between novices and their more experienced colleagues by arranging visits to other classrooms and facilitating serious conversations among teachers about teaching.

Mentors with limited ideas about their role tended to have limited time to mentor. Forced to fit mentoring in around the edges of full-time teaching, they leaned toward "fixing" novices' problems rather than treating them as occasions for joint problem solving or shared inquiry. Nor did their training promote an expanded vision of mentoring. Mentors who saw their work in educational terms had regular opportunities to develop their skills as mentors and form a vision of mentoring as a vehicle for educational change.

Forced Choice Between Assistance and Assessment

Many leaders in the induction movement believe that assistance and assessment are incompatible functions which should not be carried out in the same program and certainly not by the same person (Huling-Austin, 1990). They argue that new teachers, eager to make a good impression, will be reluctant to share problems and ask for help if they have to worry about being evaluated. They point out that high stakes evaluation for purposes of licensing or continued employment is traditionally an administrative function.

The sharp dichotomy between assistance and assessment seems shortsighted if we think of induction in terms of a broad continuum of learning opportunities for teachers. New teachers and those responsible for their learning need a defensible basis for deciding what to work toward and some means of determining how they are doing. This is the role of formative assessment. The biggest danger in linking induction and high stakes assessment is the possibility that states and district will adopt new assessments and licensing standards without providing adequate resources to help new teachers learn to meet those standards in practice.

Constraining Conditions in Schools

Even the best induction programs cannot compensate for giving beginning teachers the most difficult classes or for assigning them to teach subjects for which they have little or no preparation. Nor does the dominant culture of teaching and the social organization of schooling support quality induction programs (Little, 1990).

When staffing needs and teacher contracts work against appropriate and responsible placements for beginning teachers, induction is only a Band-Aid. Nor will assistance do much good when novices work in schools where poor facilities, inadequate resources, low morale, and high teacher turnover undermine efforts to teach or to learn to teach. Many beginning teachers find themselves coping with more classes than usual, teaching outside their areas of qualification, or dealing with known behavior problems (Fideler & Haselkorn, 1999). Such inappropriate assignments jeopardize student learning, devalue teacher expertise and experience, and ignore the fact that beginning teachers are novices.

The social organization of schooling and the culture of teaching also make it difficult for mentors and novices to work together in productive ways. While some schools promote active collaboration among teachers, such interactions are the exception, not the rule. For the most part, teaching is a highly personal, often private activity. Teachers work alone in their classrooms, out of sight of other colleagues and protected by norms of autonomy and noninterference (Little, 1990; Lortie, 1975). This means that most teachers have little experience with the core activities of mentoring—observing and talking with other teachers about teaching and learning. They rarely see another teacher's practice, and they have limited opportunities to talk about teaching in systematic and rigorous ways (Feiman-Nemser, 1998a).

Norms of politeness and the desire for harmony create additional barriers to productive mentoring interactions. Many beginning teachers are reluctant to reveal problems or ask for help, believing that good teachers work things out for themselves. Mentors may withhold assistance due to the enduring belief that teaching is a highly personalized practice of finding one's own style.

Promising Programs and Practices

In the last decade or so, researchers, state policy makers, and various professional organizations have put forward recommendations and standards regarding quality induction programs.[2] Most call for a multiyear, integrated approach to new teacher support, development, and assessment based around high standards for teaching and learning, built on school/university partnerships, and featuring a strong mentoring component. Descriptions of well-regarded programs provide some picture of what this looks like in practice. Besides these programmatic features, effective induction depends on appropriate assignments and a collaborative school culture.

Appropriate Assignments

Effective induction depends on workplace conditions that meet the beginning teacher's need for assisted entry into professional roles, responsibilities, and school norms (Fideler & Haselkorn, 1999). In strong induction settings, principals see that novices get assignments where they are most likely to succeed. This means assignments that can be handled at a level appropriate to their stage of development. A big challenge is figuring out what to do in districts that face severe teacher shortages and end up assigning novices to classes that they are not ready to handle. One solution is to have strong teachers team up with novices so that they can teach and learn side-by-side with highly skilled mentors. To make this possible, unions and districts will have to accept responsibility for creating appropriate structures and incentives. For example, in some districts with career ladders, peer assistance, and review programs, lead teachers coordinate grade-level teams composed of experienced and novice teachers.

Connected to the issue of appropriate assignments for new teachers is the idea of a reduced teaching load. Howey & Zimpher (1999) state the case succinctly: "Beginning teachers should experience a reduced load, perhaps sharing a classroom or teaching assignment, so that specific times during the school day can be dedicated to working with their mentor in the assessment of their teaching" (p. 298). This echoes a proposal by the National Commission on Teaching and America's Future (1996) that the first two years of teaching be structured like a residency in medicine with teachers regularly consulting an experienced teacher about the decisions they are making and receiving ongoing advice and evaluation. This kind of continuing support and guidance requires adjustments in the assignments of both resident teachers and their mentors, a situation which will require collaboration and negotiation between schools and universities (see discussion on partnerships later in this chapter).

Developmental Stance, Time Frame, and Curriculum

Strong induction programs have a multiyear time frame and a "developmental" stance. Two years is common, but three might be preferable given the time it takes for beginning teachers to develop a professional identity and consolidate a professional practice. In a multiyear program, the induction curriculum can help new teachers with immediate concerns and also move them toward more sophisticated understandings and practices over time. Programs with a developmental stance work from individual teacher's needs and strengths within a shared understanding of good teaching practice. One thoughtful support (mentor) teacher captured this dual focus in explaining how he sees his role: "Being a support teacher means helping people grow and become good teachers. It's a combination of basing teaching techniques on what we know about children and learning and what we are like as people, our personalities, interests, inclinations" (Feiman-Nemser, 1998a).

The Santa Cruz New Teacher Project (SCNTP), the longest running formal induction program in California, has translated a developmental stance into a 2-year program that offers individualized assistance to 1st and 2nd year teachers. Full-time mentors, called advisors, meet weekly with each new teacher for 2 hours before, during, or after school. During these visits they do demonstration lessons, observe, coach, coteach, and assist with emergent problems (Moir, Gless, and Barron, 1999).

Advisors also gather performance data to help new teachers assess their progress on a "Developmental Continuum of Teaching Abilities" developed by the Project and aligned with California's Standards for the Teaching Profession. The continuum helps new teachers and advisors visualize concretely what growth or development looks like by mapping teacher behavior onto a 5-step scale (Moir & Dalton, 1996). Based on their assessments, advisors and new teachers create individual learning plans which get revised over time.

Monthly after-school seminars give 1st-and 2nd-year teachers a chance to share successes and discuss challenges with their peers. They also allow the SCNTP to focus the attention of new teachers on different teaching standards and topics such as literacy, language development, and strategies for working with diverse teaching populations. The individualized curriculum of the advisor/novice pair and the common curriculum of the monthly seminars allow the SCNTP to address both short-and long-term goals for new teacher development.

Integrating Assistance and Assessment

Serious induction programs combine new teacher support, development, and assessment. They rely on common frameworks (e.g., professional teaching standards) and use performance assessments (e.g., observations, portfolios). The integration of these functions takes different forms, suggesting new directions for induction policy and practice.

Formative assessment is a central feature of California's Beginning Teacher Support and Assessment (BTSA, 1997) Program, which serves first- and second-year teachers who have completed preservice preparation. Support providers and beginning teachers work together to identify each new teacher's strengths and areas of growth through a formative assessment process. Using assessment data, they develop an Individual Learning Plan that identifies professional development activities to improve the new teacher's knowledge and practice. The California Standards for the Teaching Profession provide a framework for ongoing formative assessment and a common language for talking about teaching.

Connecticut's Beginning Teacher Support and Training Program integrates assistance with formative and summative assessment, but different people are responsible for the two kinds of assessment. All new teachers work with a school-based mentor or team who responds to their instructional and noninstructional needs and helps them prepare for assessments in their 1st and 2nd year of teaching. First-year teachers participate in an assessment process that reflects Connecticut's "essential teaching competencies." Second-year teachers compile a teaching portfolio that is assessed by trained assessors using criteria from content-specific professional teaching standards. When beginning teachers meet the acceptable standard, they are recommended for provisional certification (Connecticut State Department of Education, 1997).

A third approach is found in peer assistance and review programs. Following the example of Toledo, Ohio, three additional cities—Cincinnati and Columbus, Ohio, and Rochester, New York—have negotiated induction programs in which veteran teachers, on leave for up to 2 years, provide assistance to beginning teachers and make recommendations about contract renewal. Union leaders argue that practicing teachers should make decisions about who enters the teaching profession. Clearly the move to connect initial licensing to demonstrated performance must be coupled with appropriate learning opportunities that help new teachers develop a strong teaching practice and that prepare them to meet professional teaching standards.

Strong Mentoring Component

Just as all students deserve caring and competent teachers, all beginning teachers deserve caring and competent mentors. Well-prepared mentor teachers combine the knowledge and skills of a competent classroom teacher with the knowledge and skills of a teacher of teaching. In the words of one elementary mentor teacher: "I really need to help my novice learn to teach. That's my job. I'm in a teaching role" (quoted in Feiman-Nemser, 1998b, p. 72).

Strong mentoring programs use careful processes to select, prepare, and support mentor teachers in their ongoing work with novices. They insure adequate time for mentoring and appropriate compensation. In some programs, mentors are released from their classrooms full-time to work with novices for 1–3 years. In others, mentors combine mentoring with classroom teaching. Most programs provide training before mentors begin working with novices. Strong programs also bring mentor teachers together on a regular basis to talk about their work with novices and deepen their knowledge and skills as mentors. In general this is only possible when mentors are full-time.

Mentoring can be a powerful professional development experience for veteran teachers. As they hone their skills of observation and analysis, coaching and assessment, collaboration and inquiry, mentor teachers are developing the tools for the study and ongoing improvement of teaching with fellow teachers. In this way mentor teachers become a resource for schools and districts as well as for teacher education programs.

Partnerships and Collaboration

Serious induction that builds on preservice preparation, promotes thoughtful standards-based teaching, and prepares new teachers for initial licensure requires partnerships. No single institution has the expertise, authority, or financial resources to create the necessary structures and learning opportunities. Schools, universities, teacher unions, and the state all have an important part to play.

"Nowhere is the absence of a seamless continuum in teacher education more evident than in the early years of teaching," Howey and Zimpher (1999) write. "At the same time, no point in the continuum has more potential to bring the worlds of the school and the academy together into a true symbiotic partnership than the induction stage" (p. 297). Universities need schools to help them prepare and induct beginning teachers. Schools cannot extend initial preparation through the early years of teaching unless they coordinate their efforts with providers of preservice education.

Since there are few examples of such relationships, we can only imagine the benefits to new teachers, schools, and universities. New teachers would experience greater coherence and continuity in learning to teach if their induction into teaching were in the hands of school-based educators who understood and valued what preservice programs were trying to accomplish because they were part of its design and delivery. With some practical experience under their belts, new teachers might revisit some of the subjects they had previously studied and discover new meaning.

Building an induction program that extends and enriches initial preparation and addresses the realities of specific teaching contexts would provide a forum for school and university educators to think together about the learning needs of teachers and K–12 students. It would also provide a basis for designing more powerful and coherent forms of ongoing professional development.

PROFESSIONAL DEVELOPMENT

In the past, work-related learning opportunities for practicing teachers were more likely to be called "inservice training" or "staff development." These days the preferred term is "professional development." Inservice training connotes a deficit model of teacher learning in which outside experts supply teachers with knowledge they lack. Staff development evokes images of teachers implementing new programs in response to external mandates. The "new" paradigm of professional development calls for ongoing study and problem solving among teachers in the service of a dual agenda—promoting more powerful student learning and transforming schools (Lieberman, 1995).

The term *professional development* has an interesting ambiguity. On the one hand, it refers to the actual learning opportunities which teachers engage in—their time and place, content and pedagogy, sponsorship and purpose. Professional development also refers to the learning that may occur when teachers participate in those activities. From this perspective, professional development means transformations in teachers' knowledge, understandings, skills, and commitments, in what they know and what they are able to do in their individual practice as well as in their shared responsibilities.

We know something about the kinds of opportunities that promote these changes, but researchers are just beginning to study how teacher learning bears on student learning (Wilson and Berne, 1999).

Thompson and Zeuli (1999) add a further layer of meaning to professional development by connecting teachers' learning to the collective learning of the profession. They define professional development as "learning by widening circles of teachers, so that it is not only these teachers' knowledge but the whole profession that develops" (p. 367). Implicit in this definition of professional development is a view of teachers as constructors of knowledge and transformers of culture.

Central Tasks of Early Professional Development

Following the induction stage in learning to teach, researchers have identified a second stage of experimentation and consolidation and a third stage of mastery and stabilization (Berliner, 1986; Huberman, 1989; Watts, 1980). The stages are loosely tied to experience, with stabilization occurring around the 7th year of teaching. They suggest that, over time, most teachers develop instructional routines, learn what to expect from students, and settle into teaching patterns with confidence and with a sense of having arrived.

These generic and generalized models of learning to teach provide limited help in thinking about how teachers learn ambitious forms of teaching. Silent about the kind of teaching being learned, they assume individual teachers learn conventional practices on their own. At the same time, they support the case that achieving initial mastery even of conventional teaching takes much longer than most people believe, that it requires 5 to 7 years. Obviously, learning continues for thoughtful teachers as long as they remain in teaching.

In discussing the central tasks of *early* professional development, I focus on this time period, imagining "next steps" in learning to teach for teachers who are no longer rookies but who are still in the early stages of their career. I have in mind 3rd- to 5th-year teachers who have completed a strong preservice program, made a successful transition to beginning teaching, and are ripe for continuing professional development oriented around a reform agenda.

Deepening and Extending Subject Matter Knowledge for Teaching

A continuing task for teachers who want to connect students and subject matter in powerful ways is deepening and extending knowledge of subject matter as represented by the disciplines and understood by students. This is a particularly important task for elementary teachers who teach a broad range of subjects. Secondary teachers also have to keep up with new developments in their field and continue learning how "big ideas" connect within and across fields and to the world outside school.

With a better grasp of what they are responsible for teaching, postinduction teachers are in a good position to identify areas of content they want to strengthen. With more contextualized knowledge of students, they can concentrate on building both content knowledge and pedagogical content knowledge to enrich their curriculum and help them deal more effectively with concepts, topics, and procedures that students find difficult or confusing.

Extending and Refining One's Repertoire

The postinduction phase is a critical time for repertoire development in all areas of teaching—curriculum, instruction, and assessment. With a few years of classroom experience, teachers at this stage can concentrate on refining the interactive, inquiry-oriented instructional strategies they favor. Less tied to textbooks or a prescribed curriculum, they can work on gathering materials and designing units that build on student interests. Besides experimenting with different approaches to assessment, they can work on interpreting the information they gather and figuring out how to use it to support student learning.

Well-prepared, beginning teachers may use innovative strategies and create rich classroom environments without knowing how to realize fully the learning potential of these strategies and contexts with their students. For instance, they may use cooperative learning, math journals, manipulatives, or group inquiry projects without knowing how to structure these activities, when and how to intervene in ways that move thinking forward, and how to assess student understanding. No longer overwhelmed with the newness of everything, postinduction teachers can target aspects of their repertoire that they want to refine and strengthen.

Strengthening Dispositions and Skills to Study and Improve Teaching

In order to continue learning in and from teaching, teachers must be able to ask hard questions of themselves and their colleagues, to try something out and study what happens, to seek evidence of student learning, and explore alternative perspectives. Because of their preservice and induction experiences, postinduction teachers should be more comfortable having someone observe their teaching or comment on their students' work. They should also be open to working on critical problems with colleagues that invite deeper inquiry and critique.

Expanding Responsibilities for Leadership Development

While beginning teachers have their hands full with the challenges of classroom teaching, postinduction teachers are ready to play a more active role in the larger school community, sitting on committees, working with families, planning faculty meetings, and participating in school-based decision making. First year teachers are still learning the context; postinduction teachers can learn to work with colleagues to improve that context. If postinduction teachers have been socialized into a professional view of their role as curriculum developers, child advocates, and agents of change, they will seek opportunities to participate more fully in the life of the school and the profession; and they will develop their leadership skills in the process. Toward the end of this phase, some postinduction teachers may be ready to begin working with preservice students, an opportunity that will help them see and appreciate the growth of their own knowledge and skills.

Conventional Approaches and Their Limitations

Professional learning opportunities for experienced teachers generally take two forms: mandated staff development sponsored by school districts and university courses offered as part of a graduate degree program. Both rest on a problematic view of learning in which teachers "get" knowledge or skills from outside experts which they somehow "apply" in their work. Neither is well suited to helping teachers transform complex knowledge and skills into powerful teaching practices.

Conventional staff development is largely a dissemination activity. Teachers attend full- or half-day sessions in which outside experts give inspirational lectures, report the latest research findings, and introduce new techniques and strategies. Teachers have little say about the content of the sessions. There are limited opportunities for meaningful interaction or follow-up. Teachers may go home with a new idea, but the design of these sessions makes it unlikely that teachers' practice will change in any significant ways.

Besides attending these required events, teachers also enroll in courses at local universities. Even when these courses offer intellectual stimulation— something teachers hunger for—their academic content may not connect to teachers' practice. When university courses offer no opportunity for classroom application, teachers have trouble seeing how continuing education contributes to the improvement of teaching.

Geared to traditional modes of teaching and learning, conventional approaches to staff development and continuing professional education do not fit with the learning requirements of ambitious reforms and standards. They offer teachers a set of disconnected and decontextualized experiences. They do not help teachers bring new knowledge to bear on practice or generate new knowledge in practice.

A New "Paradigm" of Professional Development

Dissatisfaction with conventional approaches and the realization that teacher learning is central to any serious efforts to redefine teaching, professionalize teachers, and transform schools have led to new images and forms of professional development. Research syntheses identify key characteristics (Darling-Hammond & McLaughlin, 1995; Hawley and Valli, 1999; Little, 1993; McDiarmid, 1994). Professional organizations and advocacy groups echo the same themes (e.g., Abdal-Haqq, 1995; National Staff Development Council, 1994). Based on a combination of research and rhetoric, various researchers argue that a consensus is emerging about the kinds of professional development opportunities teachers need to teach in new ways and to substantially improve the learning opportunities of all students.

In place of superficial, episodic sessions, teachers need sustained and substantive learning opportunities. Instead of discrete, external events provided for teachers, professional development should be built into the ongoing work of teaching and relate to teachers' questions and concerns. Although teachers need access to knowledgeable sources outside their immediate circle, professional development should also tap local expertise and the collective wisdom that thoughtful teachers can generate by working together.

Discussions of new approaches to professional development cite a wide variety of formats, processes, and organizational arrangements. Professional development takes place in district-sponsored action research projects, grass roots teacher study groups, and school improvement initiatives. It occurs through curriculum development, peer observation and critique, and student assessment events. Creative use of time and flexible scheduling provide opportunities for teachers to work together during the school day. In some places, money is used to subsidize teachers' participation in workshops, conferences, and summer institutes (Little, 1999). There is a place for learning opportunities both inside and outside schools and some evidence that the latter serves as a catalyst for the former (Lieberman & Grolnick, 1996).

Looking at this array of possibilities, we need to remember that forms and structures do not guarantee consequential teacher learning. As Thompson and Zeuli (1999) put it, "Inquiry groups in name can turn out to be emotional support groups in practice, valuable to the moral and mental health of participants, but unlikely to effect real changes in their beliefs or knowledge" (p. 353).

As I analyze the current discourse on professional development in light of the central tasks of early professional development, three themes stand out. Professional development takes place through serious, ongoing conversation. The conversation occurs in communities of practice. It focuses on the particulars of teaching, learning, subject matter, and students. By engaging in professional discourse with like-minded colleagues grounded in the content and tasks of teaching and learning, teachers can deepen knowledge of subject matter and curriculum, refine their instructional repertoire, hone their inquiry skills, and become critical colleagues.

Serious Talk as a Medium of Professional Development

In conventional forms of inservice training and staff development, outside experts do most of the talking and teachers do the listening. In "new" approaches to professional development, teachers do the talking, thinking, and learning. Talk is the central vehicle for sharing and analyzing ideas, values, and practices. Through critical and thoughtful conversations, teachers develop and refine ways to study teaching and learning.

The kind of conversation that promotes teacher learning differs from usual modes of teacher talk which feature personal anecdotes and opinions and are governed by norms of politeness and consensus. Professional discourse involves rich descriptions of practice, attention to evidence, examination of alternative interpretations, and possibilities. As teachers learn to talk about teaching in specific and disciplined ways and to ask hard questions of themselves and others, they create new understandings and build a new professional culture. Over time, they develop a stronger sense of themselves as practical intellectuals, contributing members of the profession, and participants in the improvement of teaching and learning (Ball and Cohen, 1999; Stein, Silver, and Smith, 1994).

Professional Communities of Practice

Teachers do their work out of the sight of other adults. Current school structures provide few opportunities for teachers to confer with fellow teachers about their work. Regular opportunities for substantive talk with like-minded colleagues help teachers overcome their isolation and build communities of practice.

In order to teach in new and challenging ways, teachers need to rethink their pedagogy, their conceptions of subject matter, and their role in curriculum development. Many reformers agree that this intellectual work can best be accomplished when teachers work together over time, conducting inquiries centered in their practice. In a national study of secondary schools, McLaughlin (1993) found that every teacher engaged in the challenging pedagogy of "teaching for understanding" in which students and teachers construct knowledge together, belonged to a strong, collegial group.

Whether they draw members from the same school or from different schools, groups of "teachers helping teachers" offer many benefits. Based on accounts of five diverse teacher groups oriented around the challenges of reform, Helen Featherstone (1996) identifies the following benefits:

> They address particular problems of practice, they contribute to the professional development of members; they provide social, emotional and practical support; they nurture the development of professional identities; they craft a collective stance on issues related to teaching. (p. 2)

What distinguishes professional learning communities from support groups, where teachers mainly share ideas and offer encouragement, is their critical stance and commitment to inquiry. Exercising what Lord (1994) calls "the traits of critical colleagueship," teachers ask probing questions, invite colleagues to observe, and review their teaching and their students' learning and hold out ideas for discussion and debate. Among critical colleagues, disagreements are viewed as opportunities to consider different perspectives and clarify beliefs, not something to be avoided (Ball and Cohen, 1999).

Besides the support of local colleagues, teachers need access to a wider community of discourse. School/university partnerships, subject matter organizations, and networks of various kinds can expand the community of educators and resources that inform and support teachers in their work (Lieberman and Grolnick, 1996).

Grounded in the Particulars of Teaching and Learning

In new approaches to professional development, the specifics of teaching and learning provide a grounding for inquiry-oriented conversation and classroom experimentation. Opportunities for teacher learning are situated in the tasks of teaching—planning, enacting instruction, assessing student understanding, reflecting on teaching—and in samples of student work.

When teachers undertake these tasks together and study these materials, they clarify their goals and beliefs, gain new knowledge, and learn from the ideas and experience of others.

Designing curriculum together gives teachers an opportunity to examine their purposes and articulate the bases for decisions about what and how to teach. Suppose teachers also design a way to assess students understanding and undertake an investigation of what students actually learn. The process of interviewing students or looking at samples of their work could surface different interpretations of students' understanding and different ideas about what counts as evidence. Talking through these differences might lead teachers to reexamine their standards or rethink their pedagogy in light of the presence or absence of evidence. It could easily raise new questions for further inquiry into student thinking and learning.

Similar cycles of inquiry could grow out of joint efforts to work on some challenging new aspect of teaching such as leading Socratic discussions or orchestrating problem-based lessons in mathematics built around student reasoning and the sharing of different solutions. Teachers could learn about pedagogical moves by analyzing classroom videotapes and experiencing such teaching as learners. Once they began to experiment in their own classrooms, they could observe each other or videotape their efforts. This would allow for a more focused discussion of specific approaches and their effects on students. As teachers worked through problems and questions that arose in the course of their teaching, they would refine their performance capabilities and deepen their conceptual understanding.

Situating professional development in records and artifacts of teaching such as classroom videotapes, curricular materials, or samples of student work also provides a common referent for discussion. Instead of relying on vague reports and unsupported claims, teachers can support their claims with evidence and compare their interpretations with those of their colleagues. Basing professional discussions in records of practice helps teachers develop a more descriptive and discriminating language for talking about teaching. Studying such records together helps them build usable knowledge about subject matter, students, teaching, and learning (Ball and Cohen, 1999; Lampert and Ball, 1998).

Some Promising Examples

To show how these themes come together in practice, I offer three quite different examples of professional development. In the first, teachers use a specific format to shape an "oral inquiry" that builds on the multiple perspectives of participants. In the second, English and History teachers make discoveries about the different ways that they read texts and respond to students' interpretations. In the third example, teachers experience a new kind of mathematics learning which provokes them to reassess their mathematical knowledge and rethink their mathematics instruction. All three have been the focus of study by researchers interested in how transformative professional development works.

Descriptive Review and Other Protocols

Around the country some reform-minded educators have been developing and using various formats or protocols to structure conversations among teachers (Allen, 1998). One of the earliest and most influential of these protocols is the Descriptive Review. Developed by Pat Carini (1986) and her colleagues at the Prospect School in Vermont, the Descriptive Review brings teachers together to talk about particular students they find difficult to reach or teach. The goal is not to change the child, but to help the teacher see the child in a new light and use the child's interests to support his or her learning.

A chairperson guides the group through a series of descriptions which begin with the presenting teacher describing the child. The initial description is framed around a set of broad headings (physical presence and gesture, disposition, relationships with children and adults, interests and activities, formal learning) which insure that the teacher will see more about his or her student than the problematic behavior or learning difficulty which led the teacher to request a review in the first place. After the chairperson summarizes themes in the description and participants ask clarifying questions, the group returns to the presenting teacher's guiding question and offers recommendations.

The structure of the Descriptive Review not only organizes talk, it promotes certain kinds of thinking. Reading accounts of Descriptive Reviews, one sees how careful and respectful efforts at description lead teachers to new ways of looking at children and new ideas about how to support their learning. Teachers who regularly participate in Descriptive Reviews agree that studying one child provides insights into other children (Featherstone, 1998a; 1998b).

"Community of Learners" Project

To engage teachers in conversations about subject matter, teaching, and learning and to learn about the role of intellectual community in teacher development, Pam Grossman and Sam Wineburg from the University of Washington started a book club with English and History teachers in an urban Seattle high school. The group, which consisted of experienced teachers as well as some beginning teachers and special educators, met monthly to read and discuss works of fiction and history. Monthly meeting were supplemented by after-school meetings every other week and by a 5-day retreat during the summer. The group read widely, using their discussions to create a community of teacher-learners who would eventually design an interdisciplinary humanities curriculum.

Central to the project was the belief that before teachers can create interdisciplinary curriculum they must understand the disciplines they plan to integrate. Confronting their differing reactions toward and interpretations of texts pushed teachers to articulate and reflect on their assumptions and ways of knowing. Over time they came to realize that history and English teachers read differently, that they pay attention to different kinds of evidence, and that they react differently when students make personal connections to texts. Understanding literary characters by identifying with them may be acceptable in English class, but assuming that historic figures share contemporary values and worldviews is problematic in studying history (Wineburg, 1999).

According to the researchers who both studied and participated in the process, teachers came to notice and value these substantive differences:

> The act of surfacing and naming assumptions created the conditions for self-awareness and intersubjectivity. We don't necessarily agree any more than we did, but our disagreements are richer and more productive . . . . [O]ur discussions of different ways of reading are now understood as reasoned and legitimate differences from which we can all learn. (Wineburg & Grossman, 1998)

The group offered intellectual nourishment and renewal to veteran and novice teachers alike, a rare commodity in most urban high schools. Students saw their teachers participating in the same activities that occupy so much classroom time—reading and discussing text. Teachers also reported trying to create similar discussions in class where they modeled their own thinking for students and listened for differences in students' interpretations (Wineburg & Grossman, 1998). By cultivating intellectual community among teachers, the project enriched the learning possibilities for students (Grossman, Wineburg, & Woolworth, 2000).

Summer Math for Teachers

Summer Math for Teachers rests on a "constructivist" view of learning which holds that individuals must construct their own understanding of mathematics principles and concepts. During an intense, 2-week summer institute, the staff engages teachers in activities that help them take a new look at the learning and understanding of mathematics. In groups of three or four, teachers work on nonroutine problems, exploring mathematical ideas and devising ways to represent their solutions. In small groups and whole group sessions, staff members ask probing questions and invite teachers to take issue with each other.

Teachers also interview students and observe videotapes of students attempting to solve some of the same problems teachers struggled with. As they probe students' thinking, teachers begin to wonder whether students really understand even if they have the correct answer. Toward the end of the institute, teachers teach a lesson based on what they learned from interviewing a student about a mathematical idea. All these experiences unsettle teachers as they confront the limits of their mathematical knowledge and begin to question their teaching and their students' learning. At the same time, they experience the power of learning to think through and solve problems with peers and on their own.

During the school year, a staff member visits each teacher's classroom once a week to observe, interview students, and assist teachers as they experiment with new instructional strategies based on the learning principles they encountered in the summer. According to Schifter and Fosnot (1993), significant changes in teachers' practice take anywhere from 6 months to 3 years. Once teachers have new instructional routines in place, they begin to focus on student thinking as the basis for planning and interactive decisions. At that point, they are ready to rethink their curriculum. The staff has found that gaining the deeper understanding necessary for insights into student thinking poses the most difficult challenge for teachers.

These brief descriptions of rich opportunities for teacher learning help us see that consequential professional development can occur in different places, times, and formats, with teachers from the same school and teachers from different schools. The important ingredients have less to do with structural features and more to do with guiding purposes and ideas, the pedagogy of the leader, norms of discourse that favor discovery, and connections to teachers' context, content, and students. It should not surprise us that powerful learning opportunities for experienced teachers, which often engender productive disequilibrium, have much in common with powerful learning opportunities for preservice and beginning teachers.

SUMMARY AND CONCLUSIONS

The argument has come full circle. Learning to teach, especially the kind of teaching reflected in ambitious standards for students and teachers, is a complex, lengthy undertaking. It requires coherent and connected learning opportunities that link initial preparation to new teacher induction and new teacher induction to continuing professional development. Creating a curriculum for learning to teach over time, anchored in a vision of reform-minded teaching, depends on the contributions of universities, schools, and unions working as partners at each stage along the continuum.

Learning to Teach over Time

Teachers need to know about many things, including subject matter, learning, students, curriculum, and pedagogy. At the same time, knowledge for teaching cannot remain in separate domains if it is going to be usable in practice. An important part of learning to teach involves transforming different kinds of knowledge into a flexible, evolving set of commitments, understandings, and skills.

Some knowledge can best be gained at the university, but much of what teachers need to know can only be learned in the context of practice. This does not mean that good professional education and development only take place "in" schools and classrooms. It does mean that a powerful curriculum for learning to teach has to be oriented around the intellectual and practical tasks of teaching and the contexts of teachers' work.

Looking at table 3.1, "Central Tasks of Learning to Teach" (over time), we see important threads of continuity related to subject matter knowledge, inquiry, and repertoire development. The use of terms like "deepening," "refining," and "extending" to frame these tasks implies that learning to teach involves continuing growth and development in core aspects of teaching. At the same time, each phase in the continuum has a special agenda.

Preservice educators must start the process of transforming common-sense ideas about teaching and personal experiences of schooling into professional commitments and lay a strong foundation in subject matter knowledge for teaching. Those responsible for teacher induction must help new teachers construct a professional identity and practice consistent with their vision of good teaching yet responsive to the realities of schools and

TABLE 3.1   CENTRAL TASKS OF LEARNING TO TEACH

Preservice	Induction	Continuing Professional Development
1. Examine beliefs critically in relation to vision of good teaching	1. Learn the context—students, curriculum, school community	1. Extend and deepen subject matter knowledge for teaching
2. Develop subject matter knowledge for teaching	2. Design responsive instructional program	2. Extend and refine repertoire in curriculum, instruction, and assessment
3. Develop an understanding of learners, learning, and issues of diversity	3. Create a classroom learning community	3. Strengthen skills and dispositions to study and improve teaching
4. Develop a beginning repertoire	4. Enact a beginning repertoire	4. Expand responsibilities and develop leadership skills
5. Develop the tools and dispositions to study teaching	5. Develop a professional identity	

classrooms. Those who work in professional development can concentrate on repertoire development with not-so-new teachers, helping them gain the flexibility and depth of understanding that high quality teaching entails. Of course, a coherent and connected professional curriculum also enables teachers to revisit subjects they have already studied through the lens of their ongoing experience.

If teachers are going to participate in building a new professional culture, they must be introduced early on to the skills of inquiry and given many opportunities to develop the habits of critical colleagueship. They must be inducted into communities of practice where they can learn with and from reform-minded teachers working to improve the education and life chances of all students. We can only prepare teachers for schools as they should be in schools that are moving toward a shared vision of powerful teaching and learning.

The Lack of Connective Tissue

The problems of preservice preparation, induction, and professional development have been documented. The charge of fragmentation and conceptual impoverishment applies across the board. There is no connective tissue holding things together within or across the different phases of learning to teach.

The typical preservice program is a collection of unrelated courses and field experiences. Most induction programs have no curriculum, and mentoring is a highly individualistic process. Professional development consists of discrete and disconnected events. Nor do we have anything that resembles a coordinated system. Universities regard preservice preparation as their purview. Schools take responsibility for new teacher induction. Professional development is everybody's and nobody's responsibility.

Building the System

The need for a continuum of serious and sustained professional learning opportunities for teachers is clear. The task of building such a system is daunting. Yet there has never been a better time to tackle the problem. An infrastructure of standards for teacher development has emerged at the national level and the idea of a professional development continuum has captured the attention of reformers, educational leaders, and policy makers at all levels. Promising programs and practices exist at each stage in the continuum, and their effectiveness can be strengthened by supplying the connective tissue.

The outlines of a professional learning continuum have been drawn by three national organizations. The National Council for Accreditation of Teacher Education (NCATE, 1997), the Interstate New Teacher Assessment and Support Consortium (INTASC, 1992) and the National Board for Professional Teaching Standards (NBPTS, 1989) have developed compatible standards for the accreditation of preservice programs, the licensing of beginning teachers, and the certification of accomplished practitioners. Treated as living documents to be interpreted and discussed, not as the final word on what teachers need to know and be able to do, these standards can help local groups of educators construct a shared vision to guide their work.

Finally, building a professional learning continuum depends on partnerships of schools, unions, and universities. Each has a critical role to play and none can do the job alone. Some school/university partnerships have reshaped the preservice curriculum and created school communities where teacher candidates can learn the complex, messy, and uncertain business of reforming teaching with and from more experienced colleagues. How could that work be extended through the induction years, and how could induction become part of a larger vision and plan for professional development? Once we recognize that induction is a form of professional development, this makes good sense. Unions and schools must also work together around issues like appropriate assignments for new teachers, release time for mentor teachers, and other roles for teacher leaders at all stages in the continuum.

Preparing, inducting, and developing teachers who are deeply concerned about students, well grounded in their subjects, and excited about learning is critical to the improvement of K–12 education. We know about the projected need for 2,000,000 teachers in the next decade. Now is the time for groups of school and university educators to turn the idea of a professional learning continuum into a reality.

REFERENCES

Abdal-Haqq, I. (1995). *Making Time for Teacher Professional Development* (Digest #95–4). Washington, DC: ERIC Clearinghouse on Teaching and Teacher Education.

Allen, D. (Ed.). (1998). *Assessing Student Learning: From Grading to Understanding.* New York: Teachers College Press.

Ball, D. L. (1988). *Unlearning to Teach Mathematics.* (Issue Paper 88–1). East Lansing, MI: National Center for Research on Teacher Learning, Michigan State University.

Ball, D. L., & Cohen, D. K. (1999). Developing practice, developing practitioners: Toward a practice-based theory of professional education. In G. Sykes & L. Darling-Hammond (Eds.), *Teaching as the Learning Profession: Handbook of Policy and Practice* (pp. 3–32). San Francisco: Jossey-Bass.

Ball, D. L., & McDiarmid, G. W. (1990). The subject matter preparation of teachers. In W. R. Houston (Ed.), *Handbook of Research on Teacher Education* (pp. 437–449). New York: Macmillan.

Barnes, H. (1987). The conceptual basis for thematic teacher education programs. *Journal of Teacher Education, 36* (6), 2–8.

Bartell, C. (1995). Shaping teacher induction policy in California. *Teacher Education Quarterly, 22* (4), 27–43.

Beginning Teacher Support and Assessment *(BTSA).* (1997). *California standards of quality and effectiveness for beginning teacher support and assessment: A description of professional induction for beginning teachers.* Sacramento, CA: California Commission on Teacher Credentialing.

Berliner, D. (1986). In pursuit of the expert pedagogue. *Educational Researcher, 15* (7), 5–13.

Borko, H., & Putnam, R. T. (1996). Learning to teach. In D. Berliner & R. Calfee (Eds.), *Handbook of educational psychology* (pp. 673–708). New York: Simon & Schuster Macmillan.

Brooks, D. M. (Ed.). (1987). *Teacher induction: A new beginning.* Reston, VA: National Commission on the Teacher Induction Process.

Bullough, R. (1989). *First year teacher: A case study.* New York: Teachers College Press.

Bullough, R., & Knowles, J. (1991). Teaching and nurturing: Changing conceptions of self as teacher in a case study of becoming a teacher. *Qualitative Studies in Education 4* (2), 121–140.

Bush, R. N. (1983). *The beginning years of teaching: A focus for collaboration in teacher education.* Paper presented to the World Assembly of the International Council on Education for Teachers. Washington, D.C.

Calderhead, J., & Robson, M. (1991). Images of teaching: Student teachers' early conceptions of classroom practice. *Teaching and Teacher Education, 7* (1), 1–8.

Carini, P. (1986). Building from children's strengths. *Journal of Education, 168* (3), 13–24.

Cochran-Smith, M. (1991). Learning to teach against the grain. *Harvard Educational Review, 61*(3), 279–310.

Cohen, D. (1988). *Teaching practice.* (Issue Paper 88–3). East Lansing, MI: Michigan State University, National Center for Research on Teacher Education.

Cohen, D. K., McLaughlin, M., & Talbert, J. (1993). *Teaching for understanding: Challenges for practice, research and policy.* San Francisco: Jossey Bass.

Conant, J. B. (1963). *The education of American teachers.* New York: McGraw Hill.

Connecticut State Department of Education. (1997). *A guide to the BEST program for beginning teachers and mentors.* Hartford, CT: Author.

Dalton, S., & Moir, E. (1996). Text and context for professional development of new bilingual teachers. In M. McLaughlin & I. Oberman (Eds.), *Teacher learning: New policies, new practices* (pp. 126–133). New York: Teachers College Press.

Darling-Hammond, L., & MacDonald, M. (2000). Where there is learning there is hope: The Preparation of teachers at the Bank Street College of Education. In L. Darling-Hammond (Ed.), *Studies of excellence in teacher education; Preparation at the graduate level* (pp. 1–95). Washington, DC: National Commission on Teaching and America's Future, American Association for Colleges of Teacher Education.

Darling-Hammond, L., & McLaughlin, M. W. (1995). Policies that support professional development in an era of reform. *Phi Delta Kappan 76* (8), 597–604.

Dewey, J. (190401964). The relation of theory p in education. In R. Archambault (Ed.), *John Dewey on education: Selected writings.* Chicago: University of Chicago Press.

Dewey, J. (1938). *Experience and education.* New York: Simon & Schuster.

Featherstone, H. (1993). Learning from the first years of classroom teaching: The journey in, the journey out. *Teachers College Record, 95* (1), 93–112.

Featherstone, H. (1996). Teachers helping teachers. *Changing Minds.* Bulletin 12.

Featherstone, H. (1998a). Studying children: The Philadelphia Teachers' Learning Cooperative. In D. Allen (Ed.), *Assessing student learning: From grading to understanding.* New York: Teachers College Press.

Featherstone, H. (1998b). Teachers looking closely at students and their work. *Changing Minds.* Bulletin 13. East Lansing: Michigan State University.

Feiman-Nemser, S. (1998a). Linking mentoring and teacher learning. *Velon, 3* (June/July), 5–13.

Feiman-Nemser, S. (1998b). Teachers as teacher educators. *European Journal of Teacher Education, 21* (1), 63–74.

Feiman-Nemser, S., & Parker, M. (1993). Mentoring in context: A comparison of two U.S. programs for beginning teachers. *International Journal of Educational Research, 19* (8), 699–718.

Fideler, E., & Haselkorn, D. (1999). *Learning the ropes: Urban teacher induction practices in the United States.* Belmont, MA: Recruiting New Teachers, Inc.

Fosnot, C. (Ed.). (1996). *Constructivism: Theory, perspectives and practice.* New York: Teachers College Press.

Fullan, M., Galluzzo, G., Morris, P., & Watson, N. (1998). *The rise and stall of teacher education reform.* Washington, D.C.: American Association of Colleges of Teacher Education.

Fuller, F. (1969). Concerns of teachers: A developmental conceptualization. *American Educational Research Journal, 6* (2), 171–179.

Gold, Y. (1996). Beginning teacher support: Attrition, mentoring and induction. In J. Sikula (Ed.), *Handbook of research on teacher education, 2nd ed.* (pp. 548–594). New York: Macmillan.

Goodlad, J. (1994). *Educational renewal: Better teachers, better schools.* San Francisco: Jossey-Bass.

Griffin, G. A. (1986). Clinical teacher education. In J. V. Hoffman & S. A. Edwards (Eds.), *Reality and reform in clinical teacher education* (pp. 1–23). New York: Random House.

Grossman, P. (1990). *The making of a teacher.* New York: Teachers College Press.

Grossman, P., Wineburg, S., & Woolworth, S. (2000). *In pursuit of teacher community.* Paper presented at the annual meeting of the American Educational Research Association, New Orleans, April 2000.

Hawley, W. D., & Valli, L. (1999). The essentials of effective professional development: A new consensus. In L. Darling-Hammond & G. Sykes (Eds.), *Teaching as the Learning Profession: Handbook of Policy and practice* (pp. 127–150). San Francisco: Jossey-Bass.

Holmes Group. (1990). *Tomorrow's schools: A report of the Holmes Group.* East Lansing, MI: Holmes Group.

Howey, K. R., & Zimpher, N. L. (1989). *Profiles of preservice teacher education: Inquiry into the nature of programs.* Albany, NY: State University of New York Press.

Huberman, M. (1989). The professional life cycle of teachers. *Teachers College Record, 91* (1), 31–57.

Huling-Austin, L. (1990). Teacher induction programs and internships. In R. W. Houston (Ed.), *Handbook of research on teacher education* (pp. 535–548). New York: Macmillan.

Interstate New Teacher Assessment and Support Consortium (INTASC). (1992). *Model standards for beginning teacher licensing and development: A resource for state dialogue.* Washington, DC: Interstate New Teacher Assessment and Support Consortium.

Kagan, D. M. (1990). Professional growth among preservice and beginning teachers. *Review of Educational Research, 62* (2), 129–169.

Lacey, Colin (1977). *The socialization of teachers.* London: Metheun.

Ladsen-Billings, G. (1999). Preparing teachers for diversity: Historical perspectives, current trends, and future directions. In L. Darling-Hammond & G. Sykes (Eds.), *Teaching as the learning profession: Handbook of policy and practice* (pp. 86–123). San Francisco: Jossey-Bass.

Lampert, M., & Ball, D. L. (1998). *Teaching, multimedia, and mathematics: Investigations of real practice.* New York: Teachers College Press.

Lieberman, A. (1995). Practices that support teacher development: Transforming conceptions of professional learning. *Phi Delta Kappan, 76* (8), 591–96.

Lieberman, A., & Grolnick, M. (1996). Networks and reform in American education. *Teachers College Record, 98* (1), 7–45.

Little, J. W. (1990). The "mentor" phenomenon and the social organization of teaching. In C. Cazden (Ed.), *Review of research in education*, Vol. 16 (pp. 297–351). Washington, DC: American Educational Research Association.

Little, J. W. (1993). Teachers' professional development in a climate of educational reform. *Educational Evaluation and Policy Analysis, 15* (2), 129–151.

Little, J. W. (1999). Organizing schools for teacher learning. In L. Darling-Hammond & G. Sykes (Eds.), *Teaching as the learning profession: Handbook of policy and practice* (pp. 233–262). San Francisco: Jossey-Bass.

Lord, B. (1994). Teachers' professional development: Critical colleagueship and the role of professional communities. In N. Cobb (Ed.), *The future of education: Perspectives on national standards in education* (pp. 175–204). New York: College Entrance Examination Board.

Lortie, D. (1975). *Schoolteacher: A sociological study*. Chicago: University of Chicago Press.

McDiarmid, G. W. (1994). *Realizing new learnings for all students: A framework for professional development of Kentucky Teachers*. East Lansing, MI: National Center for Research on Teacher Learning.

McLaughlin, M. (1993). What matters most in teachers' workplace context? In J. Little & M. McLaughlin (Eds.), *Teachers' work: Individuals, colleagues, and contexts* (pp. 79–103). New York: Teachers College Press.

Miller, L., & Silvernail, D. (2000). Learning to become a teacher: The Wheelock way. In L. Darling-Hammond (Ed.), *Studies of excellence in teacher education: Preparation at the graduate level*. Washington, DC: National Commission on Teaching and America's Future, American Association for Colleges of Teacher Education.

Moir, E., Gless, J., & Barron W. (1999). A support program with heart: The Santa Cruz project. In M. Scherer (Ed.), *A better beginning: Supporting and mentoring new teachers* (pp. 106–115). Alexandria, VA: ASCD.

National Board for Professional Teaching Standards (NBPTS). (1989). *Toward high and rigorous standards for the teaching profession*. Detroit, MI: Author.

National Center for Research on Teacher Learning. (1991). *Findings from the teacher education and learning to teach study: Final report*. (SR 6–91). East Lansing: National Center for Research on Teacher Learning, Michigan State University.

National Commission on Teaching and America's Future. (1996). *What matters most: Teaching for America's future*. New York: Author.

National Council for the Accreditation of Teacher Education. (1997). *Standards, procedures and policies for the accreditation of professional education units*. Washington, DC: Author.

National Staff Development Council. (1994). *Standards for professional development*. Oxford, OH: Author.

Nemser, S. (1983). Learning to teach. In L. Shulman & G. Sykes (Eds.), *Handbook of teaching and policy* (pp. 150–170). White Plains, N Y: Longman.

Newman, F., & Associates. (1996). *Authentic achievement: Restructuring schools for intellectual quality*. San Francisco: Jossey-Bass.

Odell, S., & Huling, L. (Eds). (2000). *Quality mentoring for novice teachers*. Washington, DC: Association of Teacher Educators.

Ryan, K. (1970). *Don't smile until Christmas: Accounts of the first year of teaching*. Chicago: University of Chicago Press.

Schon, D. (1987). *Education the Reflective Practitioner: Toward a New Design for Teaching and Learning in the Professions*. San Francisco: Jossey-Bass.

Shifter, D., & Fosnot, C. T. (1993). *Reconstructing mathematics education: Stories of teachers meeting the challenge of reform*. New York: Teachers College Press.

Shulman, L. (1986). Those who understand: Knowledge growth in teaching. *Educational Researcher 15* (2), 4–14.

Smith, B. O. (1980). *A design for a school of pedagogy* (Publication No. E-80–42000). Washington, DC: U.S. Government Printing Office. ERIC document.

Stein, M. K., Silver, E., & Smith, M. S. (1998). Mathematics reform and teacher development: A community of practice perspective. In J. G. Greeno & S. Goldman (Eds.), *Thinking practices in mathematics and science learning*. Mahwah, NJ: Erlbaum.

Thomas, G., Wineburg, S., Grossman, P., Myhre, O., & Woolworth, S. (1998). In the company of colleagues: An interim report on the development of a community of teacher learners. *Teaching and Teacher Education, 14* (1), 21–32.

Thompson, C. L., & Zeuli, J. S. (1999). The frame and tapestry: Standards-based reform and professional development. In L. Darling-Hammond & G. Sykes (Eds.), *Teaching as the learning profession: Handbook of policy and practice* (pp. 341–375). San Francisco: Jossey-Bass.

Tom, A. (1997). *Redesigning teacher education*. New York: State University of New York Press.

Wasley, P., Hampel, R., & Clark. R. (1997). *Kids and school reform*. San Francisco: Jossey-Bass.

Warren, H (1980) *Starting out, running on, running ahead, or how the teachers' center can attend to stages in teachers' development*. (Teachers' Centers Exchange Occasional Paper no. 8). San Francisco: Far West Laboratory for Educational Research and Development.

Whitford, B., Ruscoe, G., & L. Fickel (2000). Knitting it all together: Collaborative teacher education in Southern Maine. In L. Darling-Hammond (Ed.), *Studies of excellence in teacher education: Preparation at the graduate level* (pp.173–257). Washington, DC: National Commission on Teaching and America's Future, American Association for Colleges of Teacher Education.

Wilson, S., & Berne, J. (1999). Teacher learning and acquisition of professional knowledge: An examination of research on contemporary professional development. In A. Iran-Nejad & P. D. Pearson (Eds.), *Review of research in education*, Vol. 24 (pp. 173–209).

Wineburg, S. (1999). Historical thinking and other unnatural acts. *Phi Delta Kappan, 80*, 448–449.

Wineburg, S., & Grossman, P. (1998). Creating a community of learners among high school teachers. *Phi Delta Kappan, 79*, 350–353.

Wilson, S., Shulman, L., & Richert, A. (1987). "150 different ways" of knowing: Representations of knowledge in teaching. In J. Calderhead (Ed.), *Exploring teachers' thinking* (pp. 104–124). London: Cassell.

Zeichner, K. (2000). Ability-based teacher education: Elementary teacher education at Alverno College. In L. Darling-Hammond (Ed.), *Studies of excellence in teacher education: Preparation in the undergraduate years*. Washington, DC: National Commission on Teaching and America's Future, American Association for Colleges of Teacher Education.

Zeichner, K., & Hoeft, K. (1996). Teacher socialization for cultural diversity. In J. Sikula (Ed.), *Handbook of research on teacher education*, 2nd ed. (pp. 525–547). New York: Macmillan.

CHAPTER 4

Multiple Meanings of New Teacher Induction

Interest in supporting and assisting beginning teachers is currently on the upswing, motivated by concerns about teacher retention and teacher quality. The 2000 Schools and Staffing Survey revealed that 83 percent of new teachers participated in some form of induction, up from 51 percent in 1990 (Smith and Ingersoll, 2004). Whether this leads to comprehensive systems of new teacher induction depends in part on whether educational leaders and policy makers embrace the fact that beginning teachers are novices to teaching and newcomers to their schools and, then, consider what these facts imply for induction programs, policy, and research.

This chapter examines these realities and their implications by analyzing three meanings of induction that appear in the discourse of researchers, educators, and policy makers. Each meaning highlights enduring issues of induction policy and practice. Each meaning also points to tensions that must be confronted if induction is to realize its potential as a lever for educational change. The high cost of teacher attrition and the persistent achievement gap among diverse groups of students underscore the importance of seeing induction as part of a larger effort to strengthen the quality of teaching and learning in our nation's schools.

Sometimes the term induction is used to label a unique phase in learning to teach. Stories by beginning teachers and studies of beginning teaching concur that the early years of teaching are a special time in a teacher's career, different from what has gone before and what comes after. The literature on new teacher induction tends to privilege teachers' immediate concerns, but a serious approach to induction must ultimately reconcile the tension between teachers' self-defined needs and the requirements of effective teaching and learning (Buchmann, 1993; Feiman-Nemser, 2001).

The term induction also refers to a process of socialization. This meaning highlights the institutional contexts and professional cultures that surround new teachers; the messages they send about what it means to teach in a particular school; and their impact on new teachers' identity, practice, and career trajectory. Thinking of induction as a process of socialization highlights the tension between helping new teachers fit into schools as they are and helping them participate in transforming schools into more effective sites for teacher and student learning (Little, 1990a).

Conceptions of induction as a phase in teacher learning or a process of teacher socialization remind us that, for better or worse, induction happens with or without a formal program. Still, in contemporary discussions of education practice and policy, induction most often refers to a formal program for beginning teachers. What counts as an induction program ranges from a statewide system of support and assessment to a district-sponsored orientation for new teachers. Most often it is equated with mentoring. Thinking about induction as a formal program for beginning teachers highlights the tension between the short-term, instrumental purpose of eased entry and the long-term, educative purpose of new teacher development (Odell and Huling, 2000; Wang and Odell, 2002).

This chapter is organized around these three meanings and their associated tensions or dilemmas. Drawing on relevant literature, I examine induction as a phase in learning to teach, a process of enculturation, and a program of support and development and show how each meaning points to critical issues and dilemmas. I also argue that more effective induction programs and policies depend on an understanding of all three meanings and what they imply for teacher education, professional development, school leadership, school reform, and educational policies at all levels.

INDUCTION AS A PHASE IN LEARNING TO TEACH

The notion of induction as a unique phase in the life of a teacher encompasses two related ideas. First, it underscores the special character of the new teacher's first encounter with the reality of being completely in charge of a classroom, as opposed to supervised practice teaching. Second, it highlights the place of induction as part of a comprehensive approach to ongoing, job-embedded teacher development. In that sense, induction is like Janus, the two-faced Roman god, looking backward to teacher preparation and forward to professional development.

A Unique Learning Agenda

The first year of teaching is a time of survival and discovery when the learning curve is steep and emotions run high (Huberman, 1989). Charged with the same responsibilities as their more experienced colleagues, beginning teachers are expected to perform and to be effective. Yet most aspects of the situation are unfamiliar. Moreover, the complexities of teaching confront the novice with daily dilemmas and uncertainties (Jackson, 1963; McDonald, 1980; Ryan, 1970). Having limited experience or little practical knowledge increases beginning teachers' uncertainty and frustration.

Some of the most important things new teachers need to know can only be learned on the job. As Judith Warren Little (1999) put it, "The learning demands that inhere in the work [of teaching] cannot be fully anticipated or met by preservice preparation, even when that experience is stellar" (234). A good preservice program can lay a strong foundation and help new teachers understand what they need to learn and how to go about it, but new teachers face a learning agenda that goes beyond what we typically assume.

The daily realities of teaching challenge all beginning teachers, even those with extensive preparation. Beyond maintaining order, generally viewed as the primary concern of new teachers (Veenman, 1984), the learning needs of novice teachers include issues of curriculum, instruction, assessment, management, school culture, and the larger community. As more and more teachers enter teaching with reduced preparation and face increasingly diverse students, the idea of induction as a critical phase in learning to teach takes on increased urgency (Grossman and Loeb, 2008).

Expert/novice comparisons reinforce the idea of induction as a distinct phase in learning to teach by uncovering qualitative differences in the thinking and performance of teachers at different stages in their careers. Berliner (1986) identified six dimensions on which novices and expert teachers differ. These include their abilities to interpret classroom phenomena, discern important events, use routines, make predictions, judge typical and atypical events, and evaluate performance. "What looks easy for the expert and so clumsy for the novice is the result of thousands of hours of experience and reflection" (15). In this heuristic model of skill development in teaching, novices and advanced beginners achieve competence by the third or fourth year. Proficiency may come to some teachers by the fifth year of teaching, but only a few attain the highest stage of expertise, which is characterized by fluid and efficient performance.

Novice/expert comparisons underscore the point that competence, proficiency, and expertise take time to develop and do not automatically flow from experience. They do not, however, tell us how novices gain skill and develop competence over time. That requires longitudinal research that takes into account the interaction of teachers' background, preparation, and school context.

In one longitudinal study, for example, researchers followed a group of beginning elementary and secondary teachers from their last year of teacher education through their first three years of teaching (Grossman, Smagorinsky, and Valencia, 1999). They found that the teachers used the reflective stance they had developed during their teacher education program to make sense of their teaching situation. Although some struggled as first-year teachers, by the second year most were able to use specific pedagogical tools (e.g., Writers' Workshop) they had learned about in their teacher preparation. The research team also identified particular aspects of the school and district context, including access to curricular materials and professional development opportunities, which dramatically affected teachers' on-the-job learning and their ability to use ideas and strategies introduced in teacher education. (These aspects of school context come to the fore in discussing the second meaning of induction.)

Part of a Professional Learning Continuum

The flip side of understanding induction as a distinct phase in learning to teach is seeing its place in a professional learning continuum (Feiman-Nemser, 2001). This means looking at induction as both an extension of initial preparation and a bridge to professional development. From this perspective, induction is justified not because it eases the new teacher's entry into teaching or compensates for inadequate preparation but because it contributes to the ongoing study and improvement of teaching.

The beginning years of teaching offer a natural opportunity to situate novices' learning in the central tasks of teaching—planning, instruction, assessment of student learning, and reflection on teaching. Unfortunately the induction literature rarely asks what kind of teaching new teachers should be learning and how they can be helped to learn new concepts (Ball and Cohen, 1999; Borko and Putnam, 1996; Feiman-Nemser and Remillard, 1995). Making beginning teaching a time of intentional, rather than incidental, learning is especially important if we want new teachers to practice the kind of standards-based teaching advocated by reformers (National Commission on Teaching and America's Future, 2006; Wang and Odell, 2002).

If preservice preparation has been successful, beginning teachers will have a compelling vision of good teaching; a beginning repertoire of approaches to curriculum, instruction, and assessment; and the tools to learn in and from their practice (Darling-Hammond and Bransford, 2005). A major task of induction is helping new teachers adapt and enact what they bring to teaching in ways that fit their students and local context. Sometimes the challenges of teaching alone for the first time lead novices to abandon pedagogies they learned in their preservice preparation.

In cases where induction support is continuous with initial preparation, it may keep novices from giving up on more demanding approaches in favor of what may seem like safer, less complex activities. This presumes a level of continuity between the principles and pedagogies studied during teacher preparation and the kind of teaching and learning required by the school or mandated by the district (Clift and Brady, 2005).

Besides conceptualizing induction as an extension of preservice instruction, the induction phase has been viewed as an "entry piece to a career-long professional development program for teachers" (Huling-Austin, 1990, 545). This highlights the necessary connection between induction and in-service education. Because of the patchwork nature of professional development, most induction programs, like most in-service programs, operate as discrete, isolated entities (Wilson and Berne, 1999). Thinking about induction as a form of professional development pushes us to consider how principles of effective professional development apply to learning opportunities for new teachers and move induction from short-term assistance for first-year teachers to the beginning of ongoing, job-embedded professional development (Hawley and Valli, 1999).

INDUCTION AS A SOCIALIZATION PROCESS

In the literature on the professions, induction traditionally refers to influences exerted by systems of recruitment, professional education, and work initiation as novices move along a path toward full membership in a professional community. Through a process of interaction and learning, recruits are "induced" to take on the dominant language, values, norms, and knowledge of their field. Looking at teacher induction through a socialization lens means looking at how new teachers are incorporated into the profession of teaching and into a particular work setting. It also highlights the tension of helping new teachers fit into schools as they are and expecting them to become change agents.

Traditional models of induction, like traditional theories of teacher socialization, stressed the one-way fitting of rookies into the existing system (Waller, 1932). Both have been criticized for portraying teachers as passively taking on the coloration of their surroundings (Lawson, 1992). Zeichner and Gore (1990) argued that teachers are not only shaped by institutional and cultural forces but also shape them as well, a process that contemporary studies of teacher socialization uncovered (Lacey, 1977).

This section focuses on the socialization that occurs as new teachers are inducted into a particular school community. If the process helps new teachers fit into schools as they are, it serves as a force for continuity. If it connects new teachers to educators who are working to transform existing norms and practices, induction can serve as a force for change. Viewing induction through a socialization lens highlights this tension between adaptation and transformation.

The Dominant Narrative

Many studies of teacher socialization have documented the tendency of new teachers to abandon their ideals and lower their expectations in order to conform to occupational or organizational realities (Richardson and Placier, 2005). From personal accounts by beginning teachers and studies by academic researchers, the story line is remarkably consistent (Codell, 1999; Grossman, 1990; Herndon, 1965; Ryan, 1980; Sentilles, 2005). New teachers struggle to succeed in an uncertain environment that demands much but offers little in the way of support. The main themes are reality shock, loneliness, and loss of idealism. Reviewing seven longitudinal studies of first-year teachers, Wideen, Mayer-Smith, and Moon (1998) concluded that the first year of teaching was one of dashed expectations.

This story line underscores how the practice and conditions of teaching shape the experience and outlook of beginning teachers. The primary mechanism of induction as socialization is everyday experience. By doing the work of teaching and interacting with colleagues, new teachers learn what is expected of them. They also form dispositions toward their work and their own learning. If we want to understand the induction process and direct it toward desired ends, we must attend to the socializing influence of school culture and structures.

Workplace Conditions

Since the 1980s, numerous studies have confirmed the power of school contexts to shape what teachers do and what they learn (Johnson, 2004; Little, 1982, 1999; McLaughlin, 1993; Rosenholtz, 1989). Three aspects of school life are especially salient for beginning teachers—teaching assignment, access to curricular resources, and relationships with colleagues. These factors shape the experience of beginning teaching and mediate its impact.

Teaching Assignment

It is not unusual for new teachers to find themselves teaching outside their areas of training, coping with more classes than usual, or dealing with known behavioral problems (Fideler and Haselkorn, 1999; Johnson and Liu, 2004). Such inappropriate assignments are a "poor fit" with new teachers' background and interests. They jeopardize pupils' learning, devalue the expertise of veteran teachers, and discourage deliberative planning and reflection (Little, 1999). As Johnson and Birkeland (2003) learned from a study of participants in thirteen alternative certification programs in four states: "No amount of commitment to teaching, love of young people, subject matter knowledge, or just-in-time training could compensate for an unreasonable and unmanageable teaching assignment" (121).

Access to Curriculum

The responsibility of planning and teaching lessons in multiple subjects or classes can be daunting for new teachers who do not yet know what students of different age groups should be learning and do not yet have an extensive pedagogical repertoire. Yet, in a study of fifty new teachers in Massachusetts, researchers found that nearly all wanted more curricular guidance than they got (Johnson, 2004).

Some new teachers face a "curriculum void," and others receive highly prescriptive instructional materials. This occurs most often in "underperforming" districts serving students from low-income and minority backgrounds where such materials are supposed to raise achievement test scores. Critics of such "teacher-proof" curricula argue that they deskill teachers by ignoring their judgment about what their students need. Advocates counter that such materials ensure greater equity across districts and mediate the unevenness in teachers' backgrounds.

In a provocative study, Achinstein, Ogawa, and Speiglman (2004) contrasted the experiences of Liz, an uncredentialed beginning teacher in a low-income district, with those of Sam, a graduate of a teacher credential program teaching in a progressive public school. Liz appreciated the highly prescriptive reading curriculum mandated by her district because she did not know how to teach reading to her students. Sam welcomed the opportunity to figure out what his students needed and created a literacy program to support their learning. Based on these cases, the researchers argue that school and district responses to accountability pressures not only influence teacher socialization but also they may create a system of teacher tracking that reproduces inequities related to achievement.

Relations with Colleagues

The typical school organization, which Little (1999) wryly referred to as "individual classrooms linked by a common parking lot" (256), maintains teachers' independence and isolation from one another. This limits the possibility of serious collaboration and problem solving. One result is that teachers may feel reluctant to ask for help or share problems, believing that good teachers figure things out for themselves. Even if teachers do get together, they may not know how to talk about teaching and learning in productive ways. Too often the need to maintain comfort and harmony take precedence over asking for evidence or offering a different perspective (Ball and Cohen, 1999; Lord, 1994).

In the study of fifty beginning teachers mentioned above, researchers learned how professional cultures in schools do and do not support new teachers (Johnson, 2004). Some new teachers found themselves in schools with a veteran-oriented culture, where experienced teachers protected their autonomy at the expense of collegial interaction and new teachers felt alone and unsupported. Other beginning teachers found themselves in schools with a novice-oriented culture, where enthusiasm and idealism were high but there was no one to provide expert guidance. The most fortunate beginning teachers found themselves in schools with integrated professional cultures, where all teachers participated in ongoing professional development, and professional exchanges across experience levels were the norm.

Thinking about induction as a process of socialization focuses attention on the school site where key factors that influence new teacher induction converge. Unfortunately, most schools are not organized to support new teacher development, and it may not always be in the interests of new teachers to rely on colleagues as dependable sources of knowledge about students, subject matter, or pedagogy. Too often the dominant teacher socialization narrative results from "sink-or-swim" induction in a bureaucratic school context. If we want to rewrite this socialization narrative, we need to change the working conditions and professional cultures in schools.

INDUCTION AS A FORMAL PROGRAM

Most educators regard induction as a formal program of support for beginning teachers. Huling-Austin (1990) endorsed this meaning in an early review of the literature where she defined induction as "a planned program intended to provide some systematic and sustained assistance to beginning teachers for at least one school year" (536). More expansive definitions broaden the purposes of induction programs to include new teacher development and assessment, although the relationship between assistance and assessment remains contested (Yusko and Feiman-Nemser, 2008).

Thinking about induction as a formal program fixes attention on the needs of beginning teachers that may reinforce an individualistic orientation to teaching and weaken collaboration and a sense of collective responsibility among teachers. Thinking about induction as a formal program surfaces a second tension as well, a tension between the goals of teacher retention and teacher quality. As researchers redefine teacher shortages as a problem of retention and not as a matter of insufficient supply, induction programs become a strategy for keeping people in teaching. But increased rates of retention do not tell us anything about the quality of new teachers' practices or the learning of their students. Linking induction programs to such outcomes is a serious challenge for research (Strong, 2009).

Comprehensive Induction

Recent calls for comprehensive induction expanded our understanding of elements other than strong mentoring that make an effective induction program. For example, the Alliance for Excellent Education (2004) defined comprehensive induction as "a package of supports, development and standards-based assessments provided to beginning teachers during at least their first two years of full-time professional teaching" (11). The package includes (a) structured mentoring from a carefully selected and trained mentor, (b) common planning time to collaborate with mentors and other teachers, (c) ongoing professional development, (d) participation in an external network of teachers, and (e) standards-based assessment and evaluation. Comprehensive induction involves both formal and informal learning opportunities inside and outside the school.

The Alliance for Excellent Education (2004) also stipulated the conditions that enable induction programs to succeed, including (a) strong principal leadership; (b) high-quality support providers; (c) additional support for teachers with little preparation; (d) incentives to participate in induction activities; (e) adequate and stable funding; (f) alignment between induction, classroom needs, and professional standards. These conditions tie induction to professional standards, differentiate the kind and amount of support available to new teachers based on their preparation and experience, accord the principal a critical role in making induction an integral part of school culture, recognize the need for adequate fiscal resources, and acknowledge that "support providers" require training.

Inherent Tensions

Thinking about induction as a formal program highlights certain tensions. One concerns the pull between an individual versus a collective orientation toward teaching and teacher learning. A second concerns the potential incompatibility between the goals of teacher retention and teacher quality. A third turns on the question of whether it is productive to think of induction as a stand-alone program or part of a school improvement initiative.

Individual Versus Collective Orientation

It is easy to see how induction programs might promote an individual rather than a collective stance toward teaching and teacher learning. Focusing on the needs and concerns of beginning teachers invites an individual as opposed to a sociocultural model of learning. Moreover, the culture of teaching itself favors an individualistic orientation, which the practice of mentoring may inadvertently reinforce.

Most teachers work alone in the privacy of their classrooms, out of the sight of colleagues and protected by a culture of autonomy and noninterference (Little, 1990a). Many teachers are reluctant to share problems with colleagues or ask for help, believing that good teachers figure things out on their own. Making independent decisions on behalf of their students is a valued aspect of teaching (Lortie, 1975). Yet these norms and patterns of interaction can limit collegial influence and work against shared professional standards.

In such a context, mentoring can easily promote an individualistic orientation toward teaching and learning to teach. If mentors pull back as soon as novices begin to feel comfortable, they may send the message that learning to teach is something you do on your own with a little advice on the side. If mentors do not model a sense of shared responsibility for student learning, new teachers may not come to see themselves as part of a broader collectivity working toward improved teaching and learning for all students. Some mentors feel uneasy about the expectation that they are supposed to influence or direct new teachers' practice, which may also encourage a reliance on individual preference rather than shared standards of good teaching (Feiman-Nemser and Parker, 1993; Little, 1990b; Smylie and Denny, 1989; Strong and Baron, 2004).

Retention or Quality

Of all the outcomes associated with new teacher induction, improved retention has the most solid support from research (Strong, 2009). Still we should not mistake increased teacher retention with enhanced teaching quality. We have to discern whether the right teachers are being retained and whether induction improves their practice.

Teacher shortages place pressure on states and districts to grant emergency certificates and create fast-track pathways into teaching. Some believe these moves undermine efforts to professionalize teaching; others view new sources of teachers as a way to enrich the teaching population. In any case, we need to adjust the induction curriculum to fit the backgrounds of different teachers and document the impact on teachers' practice, their retention patterns, and their students' learning.

Discrete Program or Schoolwide Initiative

Defining induction as a formal program might suggest something discrete and freestanding, but a view of induction as a process of socialization and the idea of comprehensive induction both challenge this conception. Both highlight the ways in which formal and informal induction processes can strengthen beginning teaching and contribute to a more collaborative and accountable professional culture in schools.

When teachers across experience levels have regular opportunities to develop curriculum, analyze student work, discuss classroom problems, or participate in peer observation, new teachers can learn from the practical knowledge of their more experienced colleagues. Such exchanges can also build professional community and strengthen teaching and learning across the board. These activities are commonplace in schools with an integrated professional culture wherein teaching is regarded as a public practice and teachers share the responsibility for new teacher development.

The notion of comprehensive induction highlights the workplace conditions that enable effective support for beginning teachers, including strong administrative leadership and teacher collaboration. In a real sense, creating the structures and professional culture that support new teacher learning builds the schools' organizational capacity to support teacher learning more generally. From this perspective, induction becomes less a discrete program for new teachers and more of a lever for fostering professional community and promoting a continuum of teacher development across experience levels.

CONCLUSION

This chapter explored three interconnected meanings of the term induction as it applies to new teachers and their early years on the job. Each meaning highlights a different aspect of beginning teaching, but together they offer a rounded understanding of new teacher learning in context. If we took beginning teaching seriously as a time for professional learning and socialization and not just for short-term support, we would think differently about what constitutes an effective induction program.

Defining induction as a distinct phase in learning to teach reminds us that new teachers have two jobs. They have to teach and they have to learn to teach in a particular school context. If we want new teachers to learn well from experience, we must provide them with curricular resources, guidance, models, and feedback rather than leave their learning to chance. We must also be clear about the kind of teaching we want new teachers to learn and to practice.

As more teachers enter the field with limited formal preparation, the need to treat the early years of teaching as a critical time for learning to teach gains increased urgency. Some alternate route programs require beginning teachers to work toward a master's degree and certification by taking the same courses at night that are offered to preservice teachers. This may not be the best model for integrating teacher preparation and induction if it ignores the pressing questions and problems that arise during the school day. Such a situation calls for new models that honor the emergent needs of new teachers while integrating professional knowledge and skills needed to help all students learn. Urban teacher residency programs such as those in Boston, New York, and Philadelphia offer one such model.

Viewing induction as a process of socialization reminds us that school structures and cultures mediate new teachers' learning and influence their teaching and their decision to stay, move, or leave. If we want novices to stay in teaching long enough to become accomplished practitioners, then we must induct them into a professional culture of collaboration, high standards, and collective accountability. Because such a culture does not exist in most schools, induction must become part of an overall school change effort.

Assigning mentor teachers to work with beginning teachers can be a step in the right direction, especially when mentors are prepared for this new role and have time to carry it out. But placing the whole responsibility for induction in the hands of a mentor ignores the limits of mentoring (Carver and Katz, 2004; Kapadia, Coca, and Easton, 2007; Katz and Feiman-Nemser,

2003) and the impact of working conditions on new teachers' satisfaction, success, and retention. When school leaders provide new teachers with clear curricular guidelines, a transparent teacher evaluation process, opportunities to observe and be observed, and easy access to colleagues' guidance, they not only help new teachers succeed but also they make induction a schoolwide responsibility.

As the linchpin between initial preparation and continuing professional development, induction has the potential to connect teacher learning and school reform. Development-oriented induction (as distinguished from short-term, personally affirming support) blurs the boundary between induction programming for new teachers and ongoing learning for all teachers. When this happens, professional communities are strengthened as teachers across experience levels work together to improve their teaching and their students' learning.

Finally, policy makers can influence the quality of induction by the way they define the problem of beginning teaching, the time frame they stipulate for induction support, and the programmatic tools and financial resources they provide (Carver and Feiman-Nemser, 2009; Grossman, Thompson, and Valencia, 2002; Youngs, 2007). For instance, California and Connecticut mandate two years of induction support organized around standards and linked to state licensure, and both states have dedicated funds for local induction activities, although the amounts differ significantly. Still, the impact of induction policy will always be limited by the local context in which it occurs.

If we want more effective induction programs and policies, we need a richer understanding of the meanings of new teacher induction. When teacher educators, school leaders, state policy makers, and classroom teachers understand that induction is a formative phase in learning to teach and a powerful process of occupational socialization and appreciate what those meanings entail, they are more likely to create purposeful and effective induction programs and policies.

REFERENCES

Achinstein, B., R. T. Ogawa, and A. Speiglman. 2004. Are we creating separate and unequal tracks of teachers? The effects of state policy, local conditions, and teacher characteristics on new teacher socialization. *American Educational Research Journal* 41(3):557–603.

Alliance for Excellent Education. 2004. *Tapping the potential: Retaining and developing high-quality new teachers*. Washington, DC: Author.

Ball, D. L., and D. K. Cohen. 1999. Developing practice, developing practitioners: Toward a practice-based theory of professional education. In *Teaching as the learning profession: Handbook of policy and practice*, eds. L. Darling-Hammond and G. Sykes, 3–32. San Francisco: Jossey-Bass.

Berliner, D. C. 1986. In pursuit of the expert pedagogue. *Educational Researcher* 15(7):5–13.

Borko, H., and R. T. Putnam. 1996. Learning to teach. In *Handbook of educational psychology*, eds. D. C. Berliner and R. C. Calfee, 673–708. New York: Simon & Schuster Macmillan.

Buchmann, M. 1993. Role over person: Morality and authenticity in teaching. In *Detachment and concern: Conversation in the philosophy of teaching and teacher education*, eds. M. Buchmann and R. Floden, 145–57. New York: Teachers College Press.

Carver, C., and S. Feiman-Nemser. 2009. Using policy to improve teacher induction: Critical elements and missing pieces. *Educational Policy* 23(2):295–328.

Carver, C., and D. Katz. 2004. Teaching at the boundary of acceptable practice. *Journal of Teacher Education* 55(5):449–62.

Clift, R., and P. Brady. 2005. Research on methods courses and field experiences. In *Studying teacher education: The report of the AERA panel on research and teacher education*, eds. M. Cochran-Smith and K. M. Zeichner, 309–424. Hillsdale, NJ: Lawrence Erlbaum Publishers.

Codell, E. R. 1999. *Educating Esmé: Diary of a teacher's first year*. Chapel Hill, NC: Algonquin.

Darling-Hammond, L., and J. Bransford. 2005. *Preparing teachers for a changing world. Report of the committee on teacher education of the national academy of education*. San Francisco: Jossey-Bass.

Feiman-Nemser, S. 2001. From preparation to practice: Designing a continuum to strengthen and sustain teaching. *Teachers College Record* 103(6):1013–55.

Feiman-Nemser, S., and M. Parker. 1993. Mentoring in context: A comparison of two U.S. programs for beginning teachers. *International Journal of Educational Research* 19(8):699–718.

Feiman-Nemser, S., and J. Remillard. 1995. Perspectives on learning to teach. In *The teacher educator's handbook: Building a knowledge base for the preparation of teachers*, ed. F. Murray, 61–91. San Francisco: Jossey-Bass.

Fideler, E., and D. Haselkorn. 1999. *Learning the ropes: Urban teacher induction practices in the United States*. Belmont, MA: Recruiting New Teachers.

Grossman, P. 1990. *The making of a teacher: Teacher knowledge and teacher education*. New York: Teachers College Press.

Grossman, P., and S. Loeb. 2008. *Alternate routes to teaching*. Cambridge, MA: Harvard Education Press.

Grossman, P. L., P. Smagorinsky, and S. Valencia. 1999. Appropriating tools for teaching English: A theoretical framework for research on learning to teach. *American Journal of Education* 108(1):1–29.

Grossman, P., C. Thompson, and S. Valencia. 2002. Focusing the concerns of new teachers: The district as teacher educator. In *School districts and instructional renewal*, eds. A. M. Hightower, M. S. Knapp, J. A. March, and M. W. McLaughlin, 129–42. New York: Teachers College Press.

Hawley, W. D., and L. Valli. 1999. The essentials of effective professional development: A new consensus. In *Teaching as the learning profession: Handbook of policy and practice*, eds. L. Darling-Hammond and G. Sykes, 127–50. San Francisco: Jossey-Bass.

Herndon, J. 1965. *The way it spozed to be*. New York: Bantam Books.

Huberman, M. 1989. On teachers' careers: Once over lightly, with a broad brush. *International Journal of Educational Research* 13(4):347–61.

Huling-Austin, L. 1990. Teacher induction programs and internships. In *The handbook of research on teacher education*, ed. W. R. Houston, 535–48. New York: Macmillan.

Jackson, P. 1963. *Life in classrooms*. New York: Holt.

Johnson, S. M. 2004. *Finders and keepers: Helping new teachers survive and thrive in our schools*, 167–92. San Francisco: Jossey Bass.

Johnson, S. M., and S. Birkeland. 2003. Pursuing a "sense of success": New teachers explain their career decisions. *American Educational Research Journal* 40(3):581–617.

Johnson, S. M., and E. Liu. 2004. Making better matches in hiring. In *Finders and keepers*, ed. S. M. Johnson, 167–92. San Francisco: Jossey-Bass.

Kapadia, K., V. Coca, and J. Q. Easton. 2007. *Keeping new teachers: A first look at the influences of induction in the Chicago public schools*. Chicago: Consortium on Chicago School Research, University of Chicago.

Katz, D., and S. Feiman-Nemser. 2003. New teacher induction in a culture of professional development. In *The teaching career*, ed. J. Goodlad, 96–116. San Francisco: Jossey-Bass.

Lacey, C. 1977. *The socialization of teachers*. London: Methuen.

Lawson, H. A. 1992. Beyond the new conception of teacher induction. *Journal of Teacher Education* 43(3):163–72.

Little, J. W. 1999. Organizing schools for teacher learning. In *Teaching as the learning profession: Handbook of policy and practice*, eds. L. Darling-Hammond and G. Sykes, 233–62. San Francisco: Jossey-Bass.

———. 1990a. The mentor phenomenon and the social organization of teaching. In *Review of research in education*, ed. C. B. Cazden, 297–351. Washington, DC: American Educational Research Association.

———. 1990b. The persistence of privacy: Autonomy and initiative in teachers' professional relations. *Teachers College Record* 91(4):509–36.

———. 1982. Norms of collegiality and experimentation: Workplace conditions of school success. *American Educational Research Journal* 19(3):325–40.

Lord, B. 1994. Teachers' professional development: Critical colleagueship and the role of professional communities. In *The future of education: Perspectives on national standards in America*, ed. N. Cobb, 175–204. New York: College Board Publications.

Lortie, D. C. 1975. *Schoolteacher: A sociological study of teaching*. Chicago: University of Chicago Press.

McDonald, F. 1980. *The problems of beginning teachers: A crisis in training*, vol. 1. Princeton, NJ: Educational Testing Service.

McLaughlin, M. W. 1993. What matters most in teachers' workplace context? In *Teachers' work: Individuals, colleagues, and contexts*, eds. J. W. Little and M. W. McLaughlin, 79–103. New York: Teachers College Press.

National Commission on Teaching and America's Future. 2006, January. *New initiatives from NCTAF: Teacher induction.* Paper presented at the AACTE/CADREI, San Diego, CA.

Odell, S. J., and L. Huling, eds. 2000. *Quality mentoring for novice teachers.* Indianapolis, IN: Kappa Delta Pi.

Richardson, V., and P. Placier. 2005. Teacher change. In *Handbook of research on teaching*, 4th ed., ed. V. Richardson, 905–47. Washington, DC: American Educational Research Association.

Rosenholtz, S. 1989. *Teachers' workplace: The social organization of schools.* New York: Longman.

Ryan, K. 1980. *Biting the apple: Accounts of first year teachers.* New York: Longman.

———. 1970. *Don't smile until Christmas: Accounts of the first year of teaching.* Chicago: University of Chicago Press.

Sentilles, S. 2005. *Taught by America: A story of struggle and hope in Compton.* Boston: Beacon Press.

Smith, T., and R. Ingersoll. 2004. What are the effects of induction and mentoring on beginning teacher turnover? *American Educational Research Journal* 4(2):681– 714.

Smylie, M., and J. Denny. 1989, March. *Teacher leadership: Tensions and ambiguities in organizational perspective.* Paper presented at the annual meeting of the American Educational Research Association, San Francisco, CA.

Strong, M. 2009. *Assessing the evidence: How effective is teacher induction?* New York: Teachers College Press.

Strong, M., and W. Baron. 2004. Analysis of mentoring conversations with beginning teachers: Suggestions and responses. *Teaching and Teacher Education* 20(1):47–57.

Veenman, S. 1984. Perceived problems of beginning teachers. *Review of Educational Research* 54(2):143–78.

Waller, W. 1932. *The sociology of teaching.* New York: Wiley.

Wang, J., and S. J. Odell. 2002. Mentored learning to teach and standards-based teaching reform: A critical review. *Review of Educational Research* 72(3):481–546.

Wideen, M., J. Mayer-Smith, and B. Moon. 1998. A critical analysis of the research on learning to teach: Making the case for an ecological perspective on inquiry. *Review of Educational Research* 68(2):130–78.

Wilson, S., and J. Berne. 1999. Teacher learning and acquisition of professional knowledge: An examination of research on contemporary professional development. In *Review of research in education*, eds. A. Iran-Nejad and P. D. Pearson, 173–209. Washington, DC: American Educational Research Association.

Youngs, P. 2007. District induction policy and new teachers' experiences: An examination of local policy implementation in Connecticut. *Teachers College Record* 109(3):797–837.

Yusko, B., and S. Feiman-Nemser. 2008. Embracing contraries: Assistance and assessment in new teacher induction. *Teachers College Record* 110(5):923–53.

Zeichner, K. M., and J. M. Gore. 1990. Teacher socialization. In *Handbook of research on teacher education*, ed. W. R. Houston, 329–48. New York: Macmillan.

CHAPTER 5

Pitfalls of Experience in Teacher Preparation

There is a common belief in the educative value of firsthand experience. We say things like "that was a real learning experience," "practice makes perfect," "experience is the best teacher," and "let experience be your guide." Common sense casts experience as both the means and content of important learnings.

This implicit trust in firsthand experience is particularly evident in discussions about learning to teach. Teachers claim that most of what they know about teaching came from firsthand experience. In short, they learned to teach by teaching. When teachers look back on their formal preparation, they generally say that student teaching was the most valuable part. In deference to this belief, teacher preparation programs give more and more time to classroom experience, while in-service programs stress teachers' sharing their experiences with one another. Increasing, states are proposing alternative routes to teacher certification whereby college graduates can replace formal preparation with a yearlong internship.

But is experience as good a teacher of teachers as most people are inclined to think? To answer this question, we must take into account commonly used informal strategies of inference and judgment, the immediate impact of personal memories and classroom realities, the instructional purposes of teacher educators, and the normative context of schools as institutions.

This article focuses on the contribution of firsthand experience in the preservice phase of learning to teach. The discussion rests on a broad view of learning to teach as a process that begins before formal teacher preparation and continues afterward. Thus preservice field experiences are part of a con-

This article is coauthored by Margret Buchmann.

tinuum that includes powerful early experiences with parents and teachers as well as the learning that inevitably occurs on the job.

To get a concrete frame of reference for our discussion, we begin with three vignettes that describe different occasions for firsthand experience at the preservice level in elementary schools. More and more, preservice programs are providing exploratory field experiences so that future teachers can encounter the realities of classroom life early in their formal preparation. The first vignette describes such an opportunity. The second vignette illustrates another trend—linking field experiences with foundations courses. The third vignette is about student teaching, the most familiar way of giving preservice teachers firsthand experiences of schools and classrooms. The students discussed are imaginary, but the vignettes are based on observations and interviews.

Each vignette is followed by a commentary in which we explore what the imaginary student is learning from the experience. The commentary is guided by three questions. First, what is the preservice teacher learning in the here and now? We look at potential learnings—insights, messages, inferences, reinforced beliefs—about being a teacher, about pupils, classrooms, and the activities of teaching. We describe and analyze a particular type of inappropriate learning, which we call a *pitfall*. Second, how do these lessons of experience relate to the central purpose of *teaching*, that is, helping pupils learn? Third, to what extent do these lessons foster the capacity to learn from future experience, which should be a central purpose of teacher education?

Three basic pitfalls—the familiarity pitfall, the two-worlds pitfall, and the cross-purposes pitfall—are present in these three vignettes and our discussion highlights each of them in turn. It draws on studies of the social psychology of judgment, reinforcement theory, research on teaching and teacher education, and the educated imagination of a teacher educator with a philosophical bent and a philosopher interested in teacher education.

The scenes that follow deal with learning from experience in the preservice phase of learning to teach. The expectation that something will be learned in these different occasions is probably justified. Yet not all learning is productive or desirable. Thus the questions of whether we want future teachers to learn all the lessons of experience and how to make these lessons educative must be examined.

VIGNETTE 1: EARLY FIELD EXPERIENCES

Every Thursday at 8:15 a.m., Karen, a college sophomore, catches the bus to Central School, where she spends the day in the fourth grade. Karen loves children and has always wanted to be a teacher. She is excited about being a teacher's aide this term. This is the first time Karen has been inside an elementary school since she was a pupil, and she is surprised at how modern the building is and how knowledgeable the fourth graders seem. She had wanted the children to call her Karen, but the teacher introduced her as Miss Miller, which feels a little strange.

In the morning Karen works with Tommy on his spelling list. While the teacher runs a reading group, Karen helps individual pupils with their seatwork. At recess, she goes outside with the children and usually plays with the same three girls. At lunchtime she swaps experiences with other university students enrolled in the same introductory education course. During the silent-reading period after lunch, Karen talks a little with the teacher and then marks papers. She can see that some pupils understand their work better than others. The teacher has asked Karen to do a bulletin board on careers and to take the class to the library. Karen feels like a real teacher walking the class to the library and back.

What Is Karen Learning and How Does Experience Figure in It?

In trying to make sense of her first field experience, Karen naturally thinks about how this setting resembles the ones she remembers from her own schooling. Her judgment about the pupils implies a comparison with the past and thoughts about the future. Not only does she feel that they know more than she did at her age, she also feels apprehensive about whether she will know enough to teach these children. Yet much of what she sees is familiar. Past experience helps in making sense of spelling lists and reading groups, recess and bulletin boards, seatwork and ditto sheets. Actually, her familiarity with these classroom practices gives her a feeling of competence. Classroom life is not all that strange to Karen, even seen from the other side of the desk. Many things are fixed in the school day, and classroom activities have inherent and predictable patterns. Caught up in memories that help her understand much of what is happening around her, Karen identifies teaching with things she already knows. Still, there is a lot to learn, and Karen is unsure about how to define it and how to go about learning it.

The fact that she prefers to be called Karen and plays with the same three children at recess suggests that she feels more like a pupil than a teacher. Yet getting the class to and from the library without mishap gives her a sense of what it will feel like to be in charge and have students do what she wants. A sense of power is added to some sense of competence; acting like a teacher, Karen sees pupils acting in their matching roles. "Should the teacher be an authority or a friend?" Karen wonders. How she resolves this issue and whether her attention will be directed toward what goes on in children's heads will depend on what is modeled in the classroom and on the expectations she holds and encounters at the university and in the schools.

Similarly, what Karen makes of her observation that the children differ in their understanding will depend on how the teacher handles errors and misunderstandings and whether teacher educators explain the significance of errors for assessing and directing student learning. The observation she makes about the children's written work relates to the heart of teaching: helping students learn things and looking for what they have learned. Will this observation be turned into questions that Karen actively tries to answer in further field experiences and in her professional coursework? It probably will be if Karen has the inclination and capacity to connect classroom experience with formal knowledge and to learn from further experience by thinking about it. These capacities are central to teaching, but they must be learned. Most teachers do not bring an inquiring disposition to their preparation, and immersion in the classroom tends to preclude inquiry. Since it is unlikely that the habit of inquiry will be acquired on the job, it is important to cultivate it at the preservice level and to show its indispensable role in teaching and getting better at teaching over time.

In early field experience, *unquestioned* familiarity is a pitfall because it arrests thought and may mislead it. People generally do not recognize that their experience is limited and biased, and future teachers are no exception. The "familiarity pitfall" stems from the tendency to trust what is most memorable in personal experience. Karen approaches her early field experience with preconceptions about what classrooms are like and what teachers do. She has a selective interest, and her perceptions are personal and affectively charged. Ideas and images of classrooms and teachers laid down through many years as a pupil provide a framework for viewing and standards for judging what she sees now. Such frameworks will fit with social traditions of teaching and schooling; they have the self-evidence and solidity of the taken-for-granted.

Fundamental facts of classroom life, such as that teachers *are* in charge, may impress Karen; however, she may not relate this fact to the central tasks of teaching unless someone helps her to do so. One can learn to be in charge without learning to teach children something. Classroom experience in itself cannot be trusted to deliver lessons that shape dispositions to inquire and to be serious about pupil learning. On the contrary, it may block the flow of speculation and reflection by which we form new habits of thought and action.

VIGNETTE 2: CLASSROOMS AS LABS

As a college sophomore, Tom had an early field experience much the same as Karen's. Now he is a junior halfway through his preservice program. This term, in conjunction with his educational psychology course, Tom spends one afternoon a week in a second-grade classroom. Because he is there for only half a day, he does not know all the pupils' names. He is not even sure that they know his name. Nor is he sure of the classroom routine. Most of the time he observes. He is supposed to focus on three pupils whom the teacher has identified as in some way different from the others.

Tom spends fifteen minutes observing each pupil. His assignment is to describe what they are doing during academic activities—to note the specifics of their behavior and the setting in which it occurs. At first Tom thought this would be easy. But it is hard to watch and write at the same time, and he is not sure about what he is expected to write down. In her feedback, the university instructor said that Tom should try to be more objective and avoid so many inferences. Instead of noting that his focal pupil is not paying attention, he should describe what he sees, that is, that D goes to the pencil sharpener, returns to his desk, stares out the window, and so on.

Tom's difficulties stem in part from the fact that by the time he arrives, the class is already busy at work. His three focal pupils are at their desks doing assignments, and Tom has trouble figuring out what they are supposed to be doing, let alone whether they understand it. He does notice differences, though, in their ability to concentrate, their tendency to move around and talk to neighbors, and the accuracy of their work. Tom looks forward to the time after recess. Then his assignment will be easier, because he can hear what the teacher says. Still, for the last two weeks, the class has been rehearsing for Parent's Night, which does not strike Tom as an academic activity.

In his educational psychology course, the instructor said that focused observation can help you learn to think like a teacher. It gives you practice in noticing differences in children's responses to instruction, which, in turn, can help you decide whether pupils are learning something. Tom can see that he is beginning to pay closer attention to children's behavior, but he is uncertain about the value of writing such detailed notes. Certainly when he is a teacher he will not be able to watch individual pupils and find out about their learning that way. Because he is in the classroom for such a short time, Tom cannot become an integral part of the action. Also, getting involved would keep him from concentrating on just those things that he needs to practice for his university class. His observation assignment is meant to set him apart from what is going on. The children rarely approach him for help and the teacher does not count on Tom's assistance. It is Tom who is the learner, and he is learning ways of seeing, not acting.

What Shapes the Course and Outcomes of Tom's Laboratory Experience?

Tom's learning experience is largely shaped by the instructional purposes of his course in educational psychology. He appears to be learning how to take detailed notes on individual children's responses to academic activities. Based on practice and feedback, he will become more adept at distinguishing description from judgment and at providing some context for observed behavior. Over time he should also begin to see patterns in the behavior of individual pupils and differences among them. In that sense he is developing tools to see how children respond differently to instructional activities. The question is whether Tom himself relates this growing awareness to his future work as a teacher.

Is Tom learning habitual ways of seeing or is he acquiring a skill that he can apply to specific situations? There may be some transfer once he is actually teaching—that is, Tom may continue to look for differences in student responses to instruction. Still, he will have to decide whether teaching calls for the application of observational skills. He must come to believe that this kind of observation can (indeed should) inform instructional decision making. In other words, this "academic" skill must become part of his conception of teaching.

In either case, a lot depends on what happens with his observations, both in the classroom and in his foundations class. Building habitual ways of seeing requires instruction, critique, and reinforcement. Tom will need help in thinking about what these observations mean and what they may suggest for action. He can get help from two sources—the classroom teacher and his university professor. Suppose the teacher shows Tom that she, too, is a classroom observer, even though she does not have the time to observe that Tom has. Suppose she talks with him about what his data may mean, encourages him to observe the same children in nonacademic activities to round out his impressions of them, tells him when she can afford to observe, and explains how observation helps her to decide what to do. Suppose, on the other hand, that the teacher lets Tom go about his business without paying much attention to him, seems to ignore or miss the kinds of observational cues he is picking up, and treats the business of lengthy note taking as somehow irrelevant. Clearly these two alternatives would communicate different messages about the role of observation in teaching and learning to teach. Note that the second alternative is liable to reinforce beliefs about the irrelevance of academic learning for teaching that Tom might already hold.

Chance also plays a role. The cooperating teacher's conception of her work may include observation. Ordinarily, she makes time to act on this conception. This class of second graders, however, happens to be all over the place—literally, and in terms of what they need to learn. The teacher is busy keeping order while doing her best to diversify pupil work. She cannot give the pupils all the feedback she wants, let alone spend time with Tom.

Classrooms are busy places, and Tom sees that the teacher must attend to many things. The observational skills that he is developing are related to helping children learn. Without training in how to look and what to notice, it is easy to miss important clues about pupil response to instructional activities. Tom can afford to concentrate on mastering this way of looking precisely because he is not responsible for what goes on. But there is a pitfall. If Tom does well in this assignment, he will have the gratification of a good grade. This immediate reward, however, is indigenous to the university culture, not to the culture of schools and teaching. The very structure of Tom's assignment shows that university learning and classroom teaching are worlds apart.

Tom's experience illustrates what we are calling the "two-worlds pitfall." In teaching, observation is a means, not an end. Tom may succeed in becoming a skilled observer, but this will not guarantee that he will know how to act wisely on what he notices. Nor will further classroom experience in itself activate the acquired skills in situations that call for observation. Tom will need help to see how what he has learned as a university student can shape his thoughts and actions as a teacher. His university instructor may tell him that learning to look is important in learning to teach. Will Tom come to see observation as a valuable tool for the work of teaching or merely as something he must do, this term, for a course requirement?

The two-worlds pitfall has at least two aspects. The norms and rewards associated with Tom's formal professional preparation fit with the academic setting. Doing well at the university brings immediate and highly salient rewards that may not have much to do with success in teaching. On the other hand, the pressure to adapt to the way things are done in schools is great. Moreover, this pressure will resonate with commonsense notions of teachers and classrooms acquired through the personal experience of schooling. Confronted with such pressure, academic learning is liable to evaporate, regardless of its worth. Its availability in memory depends on attributions of relevance and connections to particular instances that have personal meaning and felt significance. Its availability in action depends on knowing how to adapt it to concrete situations. This requires much more than mastery of skills and formal knowledge.

VIGNETTE 3: STUDENT TEACHING

It is spring. Sue has just begun her third week of student teaching in a fourth-grade classroom. Today, she is supposed to take over the morning activities. Since Sue has been watching the teacher for the past two weeks, she has a good idea of what the morning schedule is like, and that makes her feel fairly comfortable. In addition, the teacher explained what lessons she should cover and gave Sue the teacher's guide to follow. This morning Sue is planning to play Simon Says after the reading lesson. She puts the math assignment on the board, just like the teacher does, and calls the first reading group to the front of the room. She calls on children in turn to read the story and then asks the questions spelled out in the guide. Everything goes smoothly and Sue thinks with some elation that she can actually teach.

Next week Sue will take over for the entire day, which means that she will also do spelling, science, and social studies. She plans to have a spelling bee for Friday. This will generate a lot of noisy excitement, since the pupils enjoy competing with each other. In science she will teach a unit on batteries and bulbs that the science methods teacher showed her; she wonders how the children will like discovering things on their own. So far she has not seen any science instruction in this classroom, but her cooperating teacher said she could try out this unit. Some movies have already been ordered for social studies, so the day will be pretty well filled. She hopes that she can keep the pupils busy and that she will not have to discipline anyone. She is eager to see if she can get through a whole day on her own. The outcome will mean a lot to her. Sue stands at the threshold of doing the work of teaching in earnest. Whatever will help her to come out of this experience in one piece will impress her as tried and trustworthy.

How Does Practice Teaching Help or Hinder Teacher Learning?

So what does it prove if Sue can make it on her own in student teaching? In the first place, it shows that she can keep the system running, which is basically how Sue sees her task. She is confident because she knows what her cooperating teacher does in the morning and she believes that she can step into the teacher's shoes. Moving children through the daily schedule is, of course, part of the teacher's responsibility, but a real teacher also has to decide what the schedule will be, how the children should be grouped, and what assignments to put on the board. The point is that student teaching occurs in someone else's classroom; this makes the requirements for action and thought in student teaching fundamentally different from those for the teacher.

Making it on one's own in student teaching is not the same as learning to teach or being a teacher. Sue's confidence is not well founded; she does not see clearly that the order around her was shaped and established over time and that, for the real teacher, there is a good deal of uncertainty to contend with. Classroom structure has to be created, and it can take different forms for different purposes. Sue's personal experiences as a pupil and her experiences in the field do not provide a reliable sample of the variation in classroom environments.

What can be experienced firsthand is necessarily limited and likely to be biased. Just because experiences seem plausible does not mean they are trustworthy. Sue's belief that she knows how classrooms work will be difficult to dispel since it grows out of things she has seen and participated in; these experiences are vivid and cathected. Yet inferences and generalizations based on firsthand experience are frequently unwarranted or at least premature.

One can see why Sue thinks she is learning to teach and why she feels competent at teaching. She rehearses behaviors that she identifies with teaching and that are familiar to the class. She and the cooperating teacher will see children at work, perhaps happily and with excitement. It is unlikely that her cooperating teacher will fail to commend her performance. Like everyone else, student teachers are particularly sensitive to things that bring about a feeling of success. Going through familiar routines and being praised will produce that feeling, independent of whether these practices lead to student learning or could have been established by the novice in the first place.

Sue's confidence is partly based on experience in the classroom, but vivid memories of her own schooling also help her figure out what to do. Take the spelling bee. Teachers often use competition as an incentive to get children through boring tasks. Unless Sue is helped to see the possible long-term consequences of such instructional strategies—shaping pupil conceptions of the purposes of classroom life in terms of rewards extrinsic to learning, for example—she may continue to think of a spelling bee simply as a "fun thing to do." If no one requires Sue to practice making and justifying instructional decisions or to consider the consequences of given actions in a concrete context, she may be confirmed in a view of teaching as filling time, keeping children busy, perpetuating familiar practices without considering their consequences for pupil learning, in the short *and* long run. Classroom experience alone, whether past or present, cannot justify what teachers do, nor teach teachers to think about their work.

Sue has the impression, common to many teacher candidates, that student teaching is the time to put it all together, the definitive test of the relevance and practical worth of formal preparation. In this context, it would be important to know what motivated Sue to try out the elementary science unit on batteries and bulbs. Did Sue's decision stem from an interest in science and a belief that children should understand how their everyday world works? Or was it motivated by a desire to try out something new and neat (being "creative" is a characteristic of student teachers that teachers and teacher educators often judge favorably). The problem is that the discovery approach to science teaching presupposes a deep understanding of subject matter and children's learning. Sue has never seen the teacher in this classroom teach science. Has Sue seen any demonstration of "open" pedagogy in science? Without understanding the value and limits of "messing about," she will have no basis for deciding when and how to intervene in order to nudge children's learning along.

What will the experience be like and what will Sue learn from it? Various scenarios are possible. The children could cooperate in this new kind of learning because the activities are fun, and the teacher could compliment Sue on her creativity. On the other hand, Sue could be unable to manage "hands-on" discovery learning, and the teacher could be displeased with the commotion and the amount of time being taken. While it is not clear whether either scenario would promote science learning in the pupils, both have potential for teaching Sue some things about teaching—if she were helped to articulate the lessons of this experience. Just as the pupils must make sense of their experiments with batteries and bulbs, so Sue must figure out what it takes from both pupils and the teacher for discovery learning to succeed. Promoting student learning through discovery is difficult, perhaps too difficult for a novice, but one unsuccessful experience should not lead a teacher to dismiss the whole approach.

Before one can assess what Sue has learned from her student teaching experience as a whole, one needs to know about the teacher's intentions as well as those of the university staff. Perhaps the teacher has judged that Sue needs a lot of guidance as she takes over a block of time. Or it may be that the teacher is not inclined to have her classroom schedule altered, especially at this time of year. Has Sue been encouraged by the university staff to fit herself into the teacher's overall plan and to propose activities that do not alter what is going on in the classroom? The university staff realizes that teachers need to keep their classrooms running and appreciates how easily even well-established, thoughtfully devised routines can be upset.

This analysis illustrates the "cross-purposes" pitfall. The legitimate purpose of teachers center on their classrooms, which generally are not designed as laboratories for learning to teach. In her role as teacher of children, the teacher will see the student teacher's attention to the way things are as praiseworthy since it is functional from the point of view of classroom life. Yet, without instructional intervention, Sue's adaptiveness to the here and now may be dysfunctional for the long-range purposes of learning to teach. Learning from practice teaching and further experience presupposes acting with understanding. If Sue cannot analyze practical successes, identifying critical variables presumably responsible, there is no reason to believe that she can replicate, let alone learn from them. Attending to the requirements for action in established settings does not foster the capacity to learn from further experience. In fact, immediate practical success in student teaching is almost a disincentive for analysis. Nor is one's success in this experience a reliable predictor of success at running one's own classroom for the purposes of pupil learning.

CONCLUSION

The three vignettes illustrate three basic pitfalls that must be overcome if classroom experience during teacher preparation is to serve the broad purposes of learning to teach. At best, field experience in teacher preparation can help in learning some parts of the job of teaching. The more serious problem is getting into pitfalls or learning things that are inappropriate in any teaching situation and that will be reinforced by further unanalyzed experience on the job. The familiarity pitfall arises from the fact that prospective teachers are no strangers to classrooms. The two-worlds pitfall arises from the fact that teacher education goes on in two distinct settings and from the fallacious assumption that making connections between these two worlds is straightforward and can be left to the novice. The third pitfall arises from the fact that classrooms are not set up for teaching teachers; it is a case of being at cross-purposes.

These pitfalls arrest thought or mislead prospective teachers into believing that central aspects of teaching have been mastered and understood. Premature closure comes from faulty perceptions and judgments that are supported, even rewarded, by trusted persons in the salient setting. For Tom, this setting is probably the university classroom; for Karen and Sue, the elementary classroom. What makes these perceptions pitfalls is that future teachers get into them without knowing it and have a hard time getting out. What makes them even more treacherous is that they may not look like pitfalls to an insider, but rather like a normal place to be. Clearly, help from the outside is necessary on both counts.

Overcoming the Pitfalls

The familiar is the most salient and the least amenable to inquiry. Overcoming the familiarity pitfall requires a break with the taken-for-granted and a recognition that people have devised what is familiar in schools and classrooms. Nor can future teachers be expected to recognize that what they know about classroom life is only a part of a universe of possibilities. They need help in appreciating how their personal history and experience of schooling influence their perceptions of classrooms in a way that makes it difficult to see alternatives. A larger and more flexible vision need not result in a rejection of traditional or familiar ideas and practices. There is, however, a big difference between mere habit and customary action that is understood and seen in perspective. Furthermore, plain thinking and doing empirical research do sometimes show that traditional ways of doing things are not always sound or effective. Overcoming the familiarity pitfall should keep future teachers from confusing what is with what can or should be, and heighten their receptivity to new data and ideas.

Overcoming the two-worlds pitfall requires acknowledging that the worlds of thought and action are legitimately different. Each has its unifying purposes and a potential for making a contribution to learning to teach. In other words, one does not overcome this duality by eliminating it. The goal of professional education is acting with understanding. Neither understanding nor action will suffice by itself, and belief alone does not produce action. Teacher education students need help in seeing how understanding can clarify and shape ways of doing. They also need instruction in judging ways of doing and in adapting them to particular settings as well as to their own capacities. Teacher education students cannot be expected to make the crucial distinction between enlightenment and application in considering the uses of knowledge in teaching. This is where teacher educators must take responsibility for guiding their students' learning.

Finally, the cross-purposes pitfall can be overcome by working toward a closer fit between the purposes of classroom life and those of learning to teach. This will require structural and normative changes in schools, including an expansion of the teacher's role.

If schools became places where teachers studied their own practice together and were rewarded for doing so, future teachers would be inducted into a professional community where collegiality and experimentation were norms. In such a setting, observation and conversation among persons at different career stages would expand the alternatives available to the novice and dramatize the limits of personal and local experience. Future teachers would get the message that learning from teaching was part of the job of teaching.

A second way around the cross-purposes pitfall turns on a recognition that teachers who invite novices into their classrooms take on a new role. While the goal of pupil learning is legitimate, it does not justify treating student teachers only as assistants in the ongoing life of classrooms. If classrooms are to become settings for learning to teach that go beyond adaptation and unreflective imitation, purposes of learning to teach cannot automatically be subordinated to the goal of pupil learning. Teachers also must see themselves as teacher educators willing to plan for the learning of a novice.

Such role expansion not only benefits the teacher candidate, it offers mature teachers new opportunities for teaching and learning on the job. Associated long-term gains such as increases in reflectivity and competence, in breadth and depth of communicable teacher knowledge, will benefit everyone concerned, including the teaching profession, and more than compensate for the time involved in talking and working with teacher candidates to further their learning.

The disposition of teachers to take seriously yet another set of responsibilities and opportunities to learn will be enhanced and supported by appropriate changes in school norms and structures. Beyond this, however, are questions of substantive preparation. Just as becoming a professional teacher involves a transformation from person to teacher, so becoming a teacher of teachers means shifting to another role. Here, too, experience alone will not suffice. Preparation must sensitize teachers to the pitfalls of experience in learning to teach so that they can guide teacher candidates around them.

REFERENCES

The inferences and generalizations in our discussion are based on the following: H. S. Becker, "A School is a Lousy Place to Learn Anything," *American Behavioral Scientist* 16, no. 1 (1972): 85–105; M. Buchmann and J. Schwille, "Education: The Overcoming of Experience," *American Journal of Education* 92, no. 1 (1983): 30–51; J. Dewey, "The Relation of Theory to Practice in Education," in *Teacher Education in America: A Documentary History*, ed. M. L. Borrowman (New York: Teachers College Press, 1965; originally published in 1904); S. Feiman-Nemser, "Learning to Teach," in *Handbook on Teaching and Policy*, ed. L. Shulman and G. Sykes (New York: Longman, 1983); S. Feiman-Nemser and M. Buchmann, *The First Year of Teacher Preparation: Transition to Pedagogical Thinking?*, Research Series No. 156 (East Lansing: Michigan State University, Institute for Research on Teaching, 1984); J. W. Little, "Norms of Collegiality and Experimentation: Workplace Conditions of School Success," *American Educational Research Journal* 19, no. 3 (1982): 325–40; R. Nisbet and L. Ross, *Human Inference: Strategies and Shortcomings of Social Judgment* (Englewood Cliffs, N.J.: Prentice-Hall, 1980); J. Platt, "Social Traps," *American Psychologist* 28 (1973): 641–51; S. B. Sarason, *The Culture of the School and the Problem of Change*, 2nd ed. (Boston: Allyn and Bacon, 1982); B. Tabachnick, T. Popkewitz, and K. Zeichner, "Teacher Education and the Professional Perspectives of Student Teachers," *Interchange* 10, no. 4, (1980): 12–29; and K. Zeichner, "Myths and Realities: Field-based Experience in Preservice Teacher Education," *Journal of Teacher Education*, November/December 1980, pp. 45–55.

CHAPTER 6

The First Year of Teacher Preparation

Transition to Pedagogical Thinking?

Teacher preparation is the first formal encounter with professional modes of thought and action. Still, prospective teachers do not come to this encounter feeling unprepared. From years of teacher-watching in elementary and secondary schools, they have many ideas about what teachers do. Thinking about teaching from a student's perspective, however, is not the same as looking at teaching in a pedagogically oriented way.

Teaching means helping people learn worthwhile things. It is a moral activity that requires thought about ends, means, and their consequences. Since teaching is concerned with learning, it also requires thinking about how to build bridges between one's own understanding and that of one's students. There is a difference between going through the motions of teaching (e.g. checking seatwork and talking at the blackboard) and connecting these activities to what students are learning over time. In the encounter between teacher and student, subject matter provides the common meeting ground.[1]

Ends–means thinking and attention to student learning are central to pedagogical thinking. While teachers cannot directly observe learning, they can learn to detect signs of understanding and confusion, of feigned interest and genuine absorption. Thus, pedagogical thinking is strategic, imaginative, and grounded in knowledge of self, children, and subject matter. Perhaps most difficult for the novice is the shift of attention from self or subject matter alone to what needs explaining to children. Highet puts this powerfully, "You must think, not what you know, but what they know; not what you find hard, but what they will find hard; then, after putting yourself

---

This article is coauthored by Margret Buchmann.

inside their minds, obstinate or puzzled, groping or mistaken as they are, explain what they need to learn."[2]

Puzzling about what is going on inside the heads of young people is difficult enough when teachers and students share a culture; it is even more so when they do not. Yet teachers must assume some responsibility for equal access to knowledge. This requires, in addition, that they examine their own beliefs about the capacities and needs of different students and pay attention to the effects of different teaching strategies on them.

A major challenge for teacher educators is to help prospective teachers make a complex conceptual shift from common-sense to professional views of teaching. In this paper we present two case studies based on an analysis of eight interviews across the first year of teacher preparation.[3] The case studies illustrate how personal experience, new knowledge, and professional training influence the thinking of two elementary education students. The stories of Janice and Sarah[4] offer different versions of an honest quest for understanding and competence in the context of contrasting teacher education programs.

Janice is enrolled in the Academic Learning Program, which emphasizes the importance of theoretical and subject matter knowledge in learning to teach. The first course, which is on the psychology and epistemology of school subjects, sets the tone for the year. Her field experiences are limited, brief, and connected with specific course requirements. Sarah participates in the Decision-Making Program, which emphasizes generic methods of teaching and research-based decision-making with personal reflection. Most of her program takes place in an elementary school, and she regularly spends time in classrooms aiding, observing, and teaching small- and large-group lessons.

For both students, teacher preparation is hard in different ways. Janice struggles with the academic part of her program that seems remote from teaching. She feels she is missing out on learning to teach. Sarah also finds professional preparation hard—not only because her program is demanding, but because teaching is difficult work. Janice and Sarah also begin their professional studies at different starting-points. While Janice does not feel ready to go to college, Sarah feels mature and confident in her decision to teach.

The case studies of Janice and Sarah highlight the difficulties in making the transition to pedagogical thinking and provide direction for thinking more clearly about how teacher educators can foster this conceptual change. In order to preserve the integrity of the cases and dramatize the contrast, we present both individuals first before drawing implications and conclusions.

JANICE

Not Being Ready

Janice comes from a sizeable farm family. Her youngest sister is three years old. Janice learned from her mother that reading is good for people but she sometimes feels she could do without it. Still, she thinks she ought to read more, even "things that don't really interest me, but I know that they are important." Her mother made her go to college although she did not feel ready:

> I kept dragging my butt, you know, I just, I wouldn't get the form, the application. I wouldn't sign up for the SAT test and those kinds of things. I wouldn't put out the application, and I finally did it . . . after I got accepted to MSU, then I got into it . . . but before that I just, I didn't know what I wanted to do, I thought, "Oh, I'm just not ready." I remember being really upset about it.

Janice's mother wants her girls to go to school so that "if anything ever happened to our husbands, we would be able to take care of ourselves."

Home and personal experience often come to Janice's mind as she thinks about teaching. She concludes her first interview by stating: "My experience with my mother and going to school, I think, you know, that's my attitude." Janice worries a lot about her "attitude"—patience and readiness. During her first year of professional preparation, she feels that readiness is at the heart of the matter. Until recently, Janice did not feel ready for teaching.

> A couple of years ago I didn't want to work with little kids, I didn't think I had the patience. But now I think I have the patience to, you know, I think that's just part of maturing that I've gotten used to it, little things like that, like standing in line, I have the patience to do it again.

Now Janice feels that she has the patience a teacher needs, but she is also aware of (perhaps troubled by) the fact that things that have affected her personally are shaping her orientations as a teacher.

> Sometimes I think I should have waited, because I got up here and I wasted so much time, so much money. And a lot of times I think that that will reflect on my teaching, my attitude towards my students and everything . . . Cuz, now I have this thing, you know, some kids just aren't ready and everybody is different, you know, and they're ready at different stages.

By the time she finishes student teaching, Janice hopes she will be ready to teach.

Teacher Preparation Is Hard

In her first year of professional study, Janice had courses in the Academic Learning Program that play into her personal concerns about readiness and reading, giving them poignancy. For one thing, there is a lot of reading to do, but books do not seem to get her into what she calls "the nitty-gritty" of teaching. Added to personal ambivalence is her question, asked hesitantly at first: "What is the point of all this reading in learning to teach?" Reading books may make one a good student, but it does not make one a good teacher, according to Janice. To learn teaching, Janice would rather be "out there," observing children and teachers who know what they are doing.

To Janice, her first professional course seems "just a course in philosophy," where she learns new terms, ideas, and theories to talk about. It is true that she had never thought about assessing students' understanding, an idea that instructors in this class emphasized and that Janice came to regard as important. The philosophy texts she reads for this class, however, exacerbate her feelings of being not ready and make her feel stupid, an experience that is new to her. As she talks about these texts, Janice says: "A couple of books, I just, there's no point in me ever saving, because I'll never want to ever pick 'em up again and I sold 'em." She says she saves case studies because they make her "stop and think." Still, her ambivalence about reading is always present:

> It bothers me that I don't like reading, and I think I should make an effort to read, and as I said, I would rather have more outside fieldwork and everything, because it bothers me that I don't like reading them [the case studies]. Maybe I could get the same experience out of both if I just sit for an hour and read something or sit for an hour and observe.

Modes of Learning to Teach: Reading and Remembering

Even when she buckles down to the task, Janice is aware that she doesn't get what she could from reading case studies: "I don't think I can get the full picture out of them all the time." It may be that descriptions of teaching lack the texture and vividness of firsthand experience, making it hard for a novice to imagine what is being described. In order to learn from vicarious experiences (e.g. case studies), teacher education students need help unpacking what is there and figuring out what to make of it.

Like most people, Janice already has a sense of what teaching is all about. She feels she started learning to teach at home, where she taught her brother and sister (twelve and thirteen years old) to drive the family tractor:

Because we live on a farm and they're about the age that they can learn how to do this and so I had to go through and show them every little thing about the tractor, because it's old and there's certain little things they have to do just to get it started. And I saw that, you know, *I really got into showing 'em and explaining it to 'em so that when they were all done, they would be able to do it as well as I and it made me, I was really pleased, I liked doing it, you know.* I was there giving, you know, positive reinforcement, "Oh, you're doing so well," and that type of thing. And that made me, you know, think: "Well, I can, I can keep going, I can do this, it won't be that hard."

Here are important elements of acting, thinking, and feeling like a teacher in the context of everyday life on a farm. Janice takes delight in helping her brother and sister do something well that she herself does well. In this setting, motivation and management are no problem, and Janice begins thinking that she likes teaching and can stick with it.

In reading for her teacher education classes, Janice feels she is missing out on something, or, maybe, that she is missing the point. "Am I getting it?" and "What am I *not* getting?" are questions that sum up her concerns as a student and as a student of teaching. At the beginning of the year, Janice wonders whether this sense of missing out on something—education for teaching—stemmed from her missing the point of instruction. At the end of her first year of professional preparation, Janice is more confident as a student and clearer about what she thought she was not getting:

Janice: Big deal, going through books from the library and do some research and write and type a paper. It is all stuff I know about and I am just . . . just, maybe, I don't want to write a paper anymore to show that I have learned. *I want to demonstrate that I know it in some other way.*

Interviewer: How would you rather do it? To show "that I know it in some other way," like what? What would you like to do?

Janice: Get out in the classroom. That is what I would really like to do is, *get out in the classroom.* Maybe work as a group with people . . . I don't think I get to see enough, actually of kids, students. A lot of the stuff we learn, and it gets real general but, they never get specific. What about a sixth grader and then what about the first grader? We talk about reading and writing but we never get specific about the different ages.

The Gap Between Theory and Practice

Janice wants practice in teaching, including its mental activities, and she wants to meet the realities of teaching face to face. She has one such encounter as part of a major assignment in the curriculum course in her second term. Working in groups, students are supposed to develop a spiral curriculum[5] around some topic. The instructor has emphasized the importance of finding out about children's preconceptions and knowledge prior to instruction and required the groups to conduct clinical interviews with children at different grade levels. Janice's group focuses on poetry. She talks about her experience interviewing three third graders for twenty minutes each:

> I was doing upper elementary. And I had to have a set of questions. And I wanted to find out, you know, what the students know, what prior knowledge they had, what preconceptions they had. *And I thought to myself, you know, I just don't know what to ask them.* I just, I don't know, and whether in my education, teaching education, am I going to get some experience and some practice and to know, like what are good questions to ask. And so, I think a lot of my questions just didn't help me at all, because a lot of times the kids just didn't seem to be able to answer them that well.

With one of her questions, though, she manages to get children to move beyond "I don't know." Janice asks:

> "Why do you think people write poems?" And a little boy said: "Because they like 'em." And then, the other little girl said: "So people will have something to read." And she was the one, yeah, she said when you get bored and you have nothing to do, you write these little "stories," she called them.

Pausing reflectively, Janice comments:

> Yeah. But, when we were developing our spiral curriculum, we were going on the idea that writing poems was a way of creating thoughts or expressing thoughts, and they didn't seem to really, you know, have that idea that it was a thought put into words.

What did Janice's group make of what they found out about children's conceptions and how these differed from what teacher educators had taught them about poetry? Nothing. The group simple decided that the children at the upper elementary level "could start writing and putting their thoughts into words." They ignored what the children said and went ahead with their university assignment.

Janice feels strongly that she is missing out on learning "the mechanics of actual teaching." While she may have acquired some new terms and ideas in the first year of her professional preparation, she cannot tie them in with teaching. She wants to get out into the classroom to watch teachers and children in action—learning to look at and to relate things (with advance preparation by an instructor)—and to see actual teaching in relation to lesson plans, and an instructional program beyond following the textbook. In the end, Janice concludes that she will have to learn how to teach "when I get right out into a classroom, actually my *own* classroom." She feels she will learn to teach by trial and error and through talking with other teachers.

Not Learning School Subjects

Janice also thinks she is missing out on learning subject matter. She recalls her first course, Psychology and Epistemology of School Subjects:

Janice: But I really don't remember ever learning *school* subjects. The title doesn't seem to go along very well with what we actually did.

Interviewer: What was what you actually did more like?

Janice: We did things more along the line of just in general the way students think. We didn't get specific about school subjects and the way students learn different school subjects. It was just in a more general way, the way students learn and think differently.

This problem comes up again when Janice considers her methods class: "We really didn't learn social studies, we just learned about social studies in the classroom and the way children learn it. The same way with math, different ways of teaching math to different age groups, reteaching." Asked by the interviewer about where she expects to learn social studies and math, Janice bursts out with: "Yeah, I know what you mean there. It means that you have to really know math in order to be able to teach math." Having to help her brother over the summer with his math (sixth grade going into the seventh) has made this clear to her.

Janice talks at length about the strategies she will use to try to deal with this serious gap in her preparation. She stresses that she will have resources that a subject expert might not have. For example, she will know how to teach addition or subtraction in different ways, and she can rely on textbooks and films. Recalling what she was taught in elementary school and finding out about math and about students ahead of time will also help, she believes. Still, she concludes, if she can't understand a sixth grade math book "there is something wrong with me."

Relying on her own schooling and textbooks to compensate for lacks in pedagogical and subject knowledge, however, presents new problems. Both are givens independent of teacher education, and Janice hears in her courses that textbooks are no substitutes for one's own ideas about teaching and curriculum:

> *Janice:* I keep hearing this over and over again, "get away from the text-books," you know, the textbooks are just a tool, they're just a teach-ing tool, the actual teaching comes from up here [taps her forehead], from you.
>
> *Interviewer:* In the head.
>
> *Janice:* And so when I get out there, the only guidelines I am going to have are the textbooks. So, so I'm going to end up using it again, and I think it just keeps reversing, it's the same cycle over and over again. If they don't, they don't give me some guidelines that I can work with, I'm going to have to follow the textbooks and keep teaching the way textbooks are.

Preconceptions and Misconceptions

Janice feels that she has not learned enough about being a good teacher in her first year. She also believes that some of what she was told was sim-ply common sense, or things she already knew. For example, Janice had an assignment to write a paper on children's tastes in books. From going to the library, she discovers that children like to read about subjects related to their own lives. This strikes Janice as pretty obvious:

> Yeah, and I can remember doing the same thing, you know, when I was in fifth grade. I got interested in Nancy Drew and that seems to be the thing. Boys at that age seem to get interested in more adventure, more action than girls do. Girls, sort of romance, and it was the same thing, it was common sense.

Janice makes this connection during the interview, not while doing the assignment:

> You know, I remember when I was 12 years old that I was interested in reading Nancy Drew and that type of book and I know a lot of other girls were too and I remember a lot of kids that did do reading, what type of books they read. Laura Ingalls Wilder, Little House books. I remember reading those when I was like in third or fourth grade.

Girls want romance, boys get into action. This idea fits with Janice's personal experience and has been validated by her teacher education class. What seems like common sense to Janice, however, is sexual stereotyping.

Janice also has views about what children who belong to out-of-power minorities (children of migrant workers, inner-city children, or ghetto children) are like. They are not interested in learning and learn slowly. They are low achievers oriented towards the present, culturally deprived ("no poetry in their homes" and "no use for it in their class structure") and from the lower classes. Bilingual and inner-city children fall into the same category. In short, they have difficulty with school. How did these stereotypes develop in Janice's mind? We can show how Janice puts information from different sources together during her first year in a way that appears to support her earlier beliefs.

When asked to describe a case study that really stood out for her from among those read in one of her courses, Janice selects "Social Class and School Knowledge," an article by Anyon that criticizes the unequal distribution of school knowledge by social class and school location.[6] She sums up what Anyon writes as follows:

> She dealt with class structures and the different social settings in schools. Some schools are like a working class; some are middle . . . It was interesting, you know, the aspects of what, what each school wanted for their students and the way they learned.

Continuing her response, Janice mentions reading something for another class on the topic of student motivation:

> I was reading that low-class people are the kids and students from, from like ghettos and urban areas, they, their goals are really present-oriented, so you have to work out the success, so it's every day, they are achieving immediate type of success.

The notion that children from ghettos and urban areas are more oriented towards the present and require immediate reinforcement to get them to do school work was communicated in a methods class on teaching elementary math. The even more invidious assumption that children from ghettos and urban areas are slow learners and underachievers was conveyed to Janice through the organization of the course: inner-city children were discussed in the section devoted to slow learners and underachievers.

When asked, in the same interview, whether she had any experiences with children from backgrounds different from her own, Janice talked at some length about Mexican migrants who worked on her family's farm:

One thing I always noticed that, when I was going to school and every-thing, *the kids, you know, they weren't all that interested in going to school*. A lot of times they wouldn't show up, 'cause they would just turn around and like, maybe, a couple of weeks go back to Texas, and so even the parents didn't seem to pressure 'em into going to school up here. They had trouble because they, a lot of times they didn't understand the lan-guage, *and it was more important that they work and get, you know, get enough money to go back*.

What Janice has seen and heard as a youngster makes what she hears in her math methods class ring true. For her, it vividly exemplifies the appar-ent lack of interest in school and learning that she expects some children to have. Moreover, linking these orientations to economic need makes them seem inescapable.

Adding a final piece to this picture, Janice connects discussion ques-tions from her curriculum class to her thoughts about the spiral curriculum assignment. In doing so, she equates school location, social class, and low achievement, as well as the importance and meaning of poetry, with the use it may have for people:

One of the things Kelly was mentioning to us, "What is the *importance of poetry* to an, you know, a low class, a kid that is from the ghetto? . . . A low achiever and things like that, poetry maybe doesn't *mean anything to him*, and does it really? Is it that important to him? What good is he gonna, you know, how is he ever gonna use poetry in the class structure he's in?"

There is a hard pedagogical question here. Janice wavers between pursuing it and dismissing poetry as unimportant in some schools.

It made me think about it, you know, is it really necessary, or, you know, *how would you stress the importance of teaching poetry to somebody that didn't want to learn it?* It was really hard, and I couldn't . . . It's hard to, it was hard to, just put that in words . . . And, you know, you can inter-est them through the humour of poetry and interest them in some idea, write poetry on some area that they're interested in. You know, you can do poetry with cars and things like that. But, it just made me think that, maybe, some things maybe aren't important, and maybe we should stress other things. *Certain things should be stressed in certain schools, depend-ing on where they're located.*

This example shows how Janice puts past experiences together with things she picks up in her formal preparation—reinforcing earlier beliefs that work against the equality of educational opportunity.

SARAH

Being Different

Sarah describes herself as different. While her friends and the people she knew where not "into academics," she was by her own description in the top half of her high school class. Sarah likes to read. Her mother used to get mad at her because she read instead of going outside to play. Sarah would read "stories of poor black kids in the ghetto and how they would be going to school" and "the teacher helped them and they really made it." Referring to these stories, Sarah said: "That really got me going. I always wanted to be a teacher." This desire to serve others through teaching may have special poignancy for Sarah because she is black.

Writing an essay in high school on how the media affect black people won Sarah a scholarship to a summer workshop on journalism at MSU. She worked on her high school newspaper and her teachers encouraged her to pursue a career in journalism. Sarah studied journalism for two years in college. An English teacher who Sarah considered to be one of her "really good teachers" suggested that she go into teaching, but she left college and took a job that paid well.

After she got laid off and had a baby, Sarah decided to return to school because, as she put it, "my mind had matured." She had always been the kind of person that people came to with their problems. She saw that as part of being a teacher "'cause students are gonna have problems . . . you're kind of like a social worker." Even now, as a teacher education student, Sarah sees herself as different: "I'm more mature than others in the program. They don't know what they really want to do."

Teacher Education: Difficult but Full of Object Lessons

This does not mean that going back to school to earn a teaching certificate has been easy for Sarah. In fact, the first year of formal preparation has been hard. Some of the pressure stems from the amount of work required. Looking back over the year, Sarah observes:

> It's a lot of work for a few credits . . . They are trying to throw everything in together in two years, when this program should be like a three-year program or something.

But some of the difficulty stems from the fact that Sarah took seventeen credits one term, has a small child to care for, and feels financially strapped. Despite the stress, Sarah says she is determined "to stick it out," but she adds: "I'll just be so glad when it is over."

Being a student in the Decision-Making Program also makes Sarah feel different from teachers she encounters in schools as part of her course work and field assignments:

> If we see a teacher that isn't doing the things that we're being taught to do, all you can say is they're doing the best they know how to do with what they've learned and they're doing it to the best of their ability.

Moreover, she sees her education courses as different from her other courses because there is more interaction and because "it relates to what I want to do . . . whereas a science class or something or a sociology class, who cares. It gets boring." This view of academic subjects fits with Sarah's notion that teaching is like social work.

After the first year, Sarah feels that her program hangs together: "All these classes are overlapping. You can't really use one without the other." She likes the close tie between coursework and fieldwork and sees many parallels between the way students in the Decision-Making Program are being taught and how they, in turn, should teach. For example, her educational psychology course first term is full of object lessons: opportunities to experience prescribed strategies and approaches.

The instructor said that teachers should give students a chance to practice what they will be tested on and he gave the class a practice mid-term exam. This made a strong impression on Sarah, who said that it helped her see the value of the advice: "We had it firsthand because that's what he [the instructor] did with us. So you know, it became meaningful for us and we saw how that would help." She also saw the problem-solving lab as a deliberate effort to have students in the Decision-Making Program "experience thinking through a problem so when we become teachers you can help a child think through a problem. If teachers don't know how to think," she observes, "they can't teach children to think."

Modes of Learning to Teach: Seeing, Doing, and Thinking

Seeing and doing are the dominant modes of learning for Sarah during her first year of professional study, the means by which she comes to understand what she is being taught. The program provides numerous opportunities (structured and spontaneous) for observation and practice, and Sarah learns from both.

Since the beginning of the program, Sarah has spent two days each week in an elementary school classroom, which gives her a chance to watch an experienced teacher at work. Sarah notices that her teacher uses some of the methods she is learning about:

She uses them in her own way but I see she's using them and you know it's helping me 'cause I can relate to how this subject we're learning in class is being used in the real world.

At times Sarah sees her teacher using things that she has been taught to avoid such as "high profile" techniques of classroom management. Still, Sarah sees that it works for her and she comments: "There's no set way."

A major feature of Sarah's program during the first year is the demonstration classroom where teacher candidates observe their reading-methods instructor teach fourth graders once a week. At first, Sarah (like many of her fellow students) did not know what to look for, but the reading instructor helped the group formulate a focus question each time so that they would benefit more from the experience. Gradually, Sarah learns how to observe in a productive way: "I'm picking out things that Julie does, strategies that she uses and how the children react to her strategies."

Doing or practice takes different forms: working with a low reading group, helping one child, developing and teaching a social studies unit, adapting a lesson in a basal reader, assisting the reading-methods instructor in the demonstration room, trying out mini lessons on small groups of children. What stands out for Sarah are her experiences with the social studies unit and working with one child in her reading group.

Learning About Planning

The Decision-Making Program teaches Sarah that a professional teacher "is one who sits down and thinks through all the processes to get to that product which you want them to do." As a teacher, Sarah believes that she must decide "what am I gonna teach, why am I gonna teach it, then how am I gonna teach it." At first, Sarah does not realize that teachers have many decisions to make. She learns about setting objectives, defining terminal behaviour, assessing students, doing a task analysis, and so on, in her first term in an educational psychology class. This does not come easily for Sarah, and during the third term, she sets as her term goal to:

> sit down and think about my objectives 'cause they [the program staff] say I'm a very good technical teacher right now but they're trying to turn out professionals, so I have to get into professional process.

Sarah contrasts planning with "grabbing a book and doing whatever the book says to do even if it's not appropriate with your students' attitudes." She plans to write objectives during her first year and hopes she will still believe in objectives after ten years of teaching. At this point in her professional studies, Sarah's faith in planning ahead is unqualified: "It's good to plan ahead . . . you can't go wrong after you plan ahead." She also believes that: "If your planning is good and motivating, then you won't have management problems."

Teaching her social studies unit gives Sarah a chance to test the adequacy of her plans and to discover the ubiquity of unforeseen events in teaching. Here is how she explained what she learned about the relationship between planning and teaching:

> If I'm gonna teach a certain concept and its gonna be taught over weeks, I can't just wait till next week, the day before, and think of something to do. Like last night I sat down . . . and planned out every step of the way. It went smooth and it just went great.

As Sarah sees it, preparation for teaching involves careful planning ahead of time, not making it up as one goes along.

Sarah also talks about the things she didn't plan for that came up during teaching: how to fill in students who are absent so that they won't be "left out in the cold," how to tell when students are "taking you for a ride," what to say to students who get a bad grade. Rather than taking the unforeseen as something inevitable, Sarah attributes problems to lack of planning, the fact that this was her first experience with the whole class, and time constraints—only two days a week to fit everything in. (According to her teacher, the students were testing Sarah, and the project she assigned was too hard.)

What Is Comprehension?

One of the biggest challenges for Sarah during her first year was trying to "teach comprehension" to one girl in her reading group. Not only was the concept of comprehension new to Sarah, but her focal student posed special problems.

Before her first reading course, Sarah said she "didn't even know what comprehension was." After reading a lot of material on the subject, she learns that "comprehension is understanding what you are reading, getting some meaning out of it." She says:

> If a child reads the story to you out loud, if he doesn't read every single word or if he reads a "this" for a "that," it's no big deal. "The child would know that word when it came up in context . . . he was leaping ahead in his thinking process and reading for what the rest of the sentence was

going to tell him or the rest of the story, versus reading specifically each word and getting nothing out of it.

Sarah has picked up a concept of comprehension that will allow her to listen to a child reading and focus on what is going on in the child's head, not whether the child can read every single word. While she believes she understands comprehension in theory, she says:

> actually putting it into practice is the hard part. I could tell you what comprehension is, I can give you examples of comprehension, but when it comes to teaching, I know some methods with all the material we've been reading . . . I'm wondering: Am I really teaching comprehension or what?

This difficulty is brought home to Sarah in the case of her focal student, who can recognize words and read books from the library but cannot talk about what she is reading. On top of it, she talks softly, mumbles, and stares into space. "It's frustrating," Sarah explains,

> because we have to write down what we've learned about the student in our group and what we think we've taught 'em and I just don't know. I'm frustrated because I am trying to find out why she's so withdrawn. It seems she has an emotional problem or something because it's just not so with the reading group.

The day the focal student was supposed to give her book report was a day when Julie, the reading instructor, observed Sarah:

> I had to keep asking and asking the question and Julie, the instructor, says she doesn't see the purpose, that she's not motivated, but *what could you do to motivate her? I don't know 'cause I've taken them away from the basal* . . . I take them to the library and they've gotten books that they want to read and I just threw away my whole lesson. I said all we're going to do is enjoy reading and we're going to write about it and you're going to tell me about a story you've read and you're going to write a story 'cause I wanted to see if the student, given a chance to write about a story, would be able to tell me about it.

Sarah had abandoned the basal reader and given students a chance to read books of their own choosing, which she assumes will be intrinsically motivating. Disappointed that this does not improve the motivation or comprehension of her focal student, Sarah blames herself: "I don't think I helped her at all." She suspects that the child has special problems but also recognizes that "I didn't have the background or the knowledge to test her right."

Practicality: Beyond the Personal

Sarah's first year of teacher preparation has reinforced some common-sense notions about teaching as practical activity. Much of what she says echoes the sentiments of experienced teachers: an individualistic stand towards teaching, reliance on first hand experience, a belief that good teaching is something you have to work out in your own classroom.[7] Sarah believes that, in teaching, no one can tell you what to do: "It has to be your own idea." Nor can someone tell whether something is "a good idea" until one tries it oneself or actually sees someone else using it. This partly stems from the fact that teaching occurs in a particular context, which is why a teacher can't just "take the book and go straight through."

For Sarah, seeing is believing and doing is the way to understanding. In fact, she believes the more experience, the better. Asked how she will learn the things she still needs to learn, Sarah answer:

> I think mostly it will be from the interaction with the class, of being there and experiencing it. Because for me its kind of hard to be told this is what you do and this is why you do it and then not be able to back it up with going out and really seeing it happen. *Because if I experience it more, I understand it better.* So I am going to learn some of it in the [education] classes and the most part is going to be learned in the classroom with the students.

Sarah's reliance on practical experience in learning to teach may be confounded with an emphasis in the Decision-Making Program on figuring things out for yourself:

> One thing we've learned this term is you don't get any answers here from Julie or anybody else. If you ask a question it's always: "Well, what do you think?" It's never: "I'll tell you." *You have to discover it your own way.*

Sarah is partially right in her notion of teaching as practical activity, but she does not go far enough. Doing is only a beginning in professional learning, and the policy "seeing is believing," can mislead. Besides the clarification of ends and means under particular circumstances, there are also questions of justification and considerations of consequences. In justifying belief and action in teaching, for example, one cannot only rely entirely on one's personal sense of what feels right.[8] Nor is it true that teaching and learning require discovering everything by oneself or doing it all one's own way. In becoming a professional, some things are properly learned through imitating experts and practising new modes of acting and thinking under guidance.

TOWARDS A CONCLUSION

These case studies illustrate how pedagogical thinking is different from teacher thinking that relies on common sense or the apprenticeship of observation. Sarah and Janice are good foils for each other. After her first year of teacher preparation, Sarah is making some progress in the transition to pedagogical teaching, while Janice seems behind in making this conceptual shift. Some of the differences between the two teacher candidates relate to their opportunities to learn, which differ in content, instructional setting, modes of supervision, and general ideology. Sarah and Janice also rely on who they are as individuals. Thus, our data highlight the influence of personal history and formal preparation in helping or hindering the transition to professional thinking.

How Far Have Sarah and Janice Progressed in Making the Shift to Pedagogical Thinking?

The world of teaching and learning is beginning to look different to Sarah. Sarah feels responsible for children's learning and works hard to foster it. She sees the need to think strategically and to plan for teaching with a larger scheme in mind. In trying alternatives, she thinks about what will help children learn. She is making connections between the way she has been taught in the program and the way she could teach.

Sarah is forming pedagogical habits of mind and ways of acting. She is trying to fit general notions (e.g. about planning) to particular situations (e.g. the social studies unit and her reading group). In the process, she sometimes discovers that these general ideas don't work—as in her attempt to apply a concept of comprehension and an approach to teaching reading to her focal student. "Putting ideas into practice" makes vivid and concrete to her the importance of planning and adaptation. It also shows Sarah that good intentions are not enough. Working with her focal student makes her realize that she still lacks specific professional knowledge.

So far, little has changed in Janice's ways of thinking about teaching. She continues to believe that patience makes ones ready for teaching—and standing in line for registration is one way the university helped her develop this personal quality. Memories serve as a primary source of ideas about teachers, students, and the content of instruction. In making sense of new experiences or ideas, she "takes things home" for validation, exemplification and explanation. This reliance on what she already knows contributes to a know-it-all attitude that shields her from change. An exception is the notion that teachers should pay attention to children's understanding and preconceptions.

Janice has little sense, however, of how she should think and act to uncover, deepen, redirect, or assess student understanding. Confronted with children, she gets some ideas (e.g. that she needs to know how to ask questions), and she feels, more concretely, that she is missing out on education for teaching. She is not getting enough particulars; general notions and injunctions (e.g. getting away from the basal) do not help her decide what to do with third rather than sixth graders. Like many teachers, Janice expects she will get her questions answered in student teaching and by learning on the job when she has her own classroom.

How Are Differences in Transition Related to Differences in Opportunities to Learn?

The Decision-Making Program helps Sarah begin the transition to pedagogical thinking. Different university assignments during her first year make her attend to goals, instructional activities, and the reactions of individual children. They all build an explicit sense of professional responsibility, exceeding good will and common sense. New ideas about teaching do not remain at a general level. In her field experiences, Sarah tries to put principles and procedures into practice (e.g. teaching comprehension, assessing students' understanding, stating purposes for a lesson, adopting a proactive rather than a reactive approach to classroom management). The program emphasizes being a "professional" and not merely a "technical teacher"; it tries to enforce conceptual change through direct instruction, supervised practice, criticism, and guided reflection as students face some of the demands of teaching.

There is a clear message that the Decision-Making Program can teach students what they need to know to be professional teachers. Often, theories and methods are presented as procedures to be followed in the field. Neither the limits of professional knowledge nor the endemic uncertainties of teaching get much attention during this first year.

Sarah's unqualified faith in planning will no doubt be challenged as she learns more about teaching first hand. At this point, we can only speculate on the consequences of letting her learn this from experience rather than from instruction about the nature of teaching and the difficulties of applying knowledge in the field.

For example, will Sarah abandon long-range planning when the rational model she has been taught does not prepare her to deal with the unexpected, or will she modify what the program has taught her? By fostering unrealistic views about how educational theory and research can help teachers, the Decision-Making Program may unwittingly strengthen teachers' tendency to reject formal knowledge and rely on first hand experience. Ironically, the program also has an overlay of constructivist psychology that reinforces this reliance on personal preference and experience.[9]

The Academic Learning Program resembles its name; in the first year, it emphasizes text-based instruction and is remote from teaching, perhaps to avoid premature immersion in the culture of schools. There is some reliance on cases to bring home points or to make principles and ideas vivid. Yet these "cases" are uneven; they include a Platonic dialogue and excerpts from *Zen and the Art of Motorcycle Maintenance*. Since case studies do not have the urgency of reality, they can provide the shelter often necessary for new and consequential learning. Still, their challenge of the taken-for-granted may not be obvious to the novice without instruction that takes students' preconceptions into account. Recall, for example, how Janice construes a critique of the unequal distribution of knowledge by school location as the way things ought to be.

The spiral curriculum assignment provides an opportunity for students in the Academic Learning Program to do some instructional planning during their first year. Here is a chance to find out about children's preconceptions, which are a major concern in the program and in pedagogical thinking. As the students receive little help in figuring out what to make of what they discover, the assignment becomes academic, something to complete for a grade.

So far, teacher education has not been a source of professional knowledge for Janice. She wants more contact with classrooms and what she calls the "nitty-gritty" of teaching, but such opportunities are not yet available in the Academic Learning Program. Thus it may not be surprising that she relies on her memories of school to make sense of teaching and hopes that practical experience will do the rest.

While Janice's program does introduce powerful ideas in the first year, it does not provide enough *teacher* education (instruction, supervision, practice, and reflection) to shape new ways of acting and thinking. For example, the Academic Learning Program calls attention to the importance of subject matter in teaching, but so far has not helped teacher candidates acquire such knowledge or provide guidance in adapting subject knowledge to teach particular children.

Equal Access to Knowledge and the Contingency of Starting-Points for Teachers

By her own testimony, Sarah has a personal interest in the fate of black children that shapes her commitment to teaching. During her first year, Janice's stereotypes are reinforced and elaborated in a way that makes unequal access to school knowledge seem unproblematic. While Sarah may seem closer to connecting issues of equity and diversity to the responsibilities of teaching, *both* teacher candidates rely on their personal experiences, which are limited and subject to bias. Teacher educators must help the novice see and understand the limitations and pitfalls of personal experience in learning to teach.[10] Like teachers, teacher educators must pay attention to what is going on in the heads of their students in order to identify and correct misconceptions.

Teacher educators cannot leave to chance the commitment of teachers to provide equal access to knowledge, and opportunities for excellence for diverse students. Future teachers need help in examining their own beliefs about the needs and capacities of different children. Goodlad explains clearly why this is a requirement of teacher education.

> If teaching practices are to reflect . . . the well-established notion that there are winners and losers in learning, as in everything else, teachers require only common sense and not much professional preparation.[11]

Dispositions and beliefs alone cannot do the job. Teachers' capacities for providing equal access to knowledge depend on knowledge of children and the subjects they are supposed to teach.

Teachers' Knowledge of Subject Matter

Janice and Sarah share a weakness in subject knowledge that has not yet been remedied by their professional studies. They both need to learn the subjects they will teach and the pedagogy—how they are taught and learned.[12]

Both Janice and Sarah bring to their professional preparation some sense of personal readiness for what they think teaching is. Sarah starts with an idea of teaching as social work: people turn to her a lot because of the kind of person she is. In the process of working hard and being supervised in working with particular children, she begins to change her view of what a teacher is. Maybe she will come to see that she needs to know her subjects in order to contribute to children's "success stories." Janice starts out worried about her personal readiness for college and teaching. Now she feels she has enough patience to be a teacher. Still, she lacks a good sense of what teaching is all about, though she is concerned about her weakness in subject matter knowledge.

This work in progress dramatizes the need for education and professional training in teacher education. Teachers must know their subjects from the inside; they are not social workers:

> If anything is to be regarded as a specific preparation for teaching, priority must be given to a thorough grounding in something to teach. There are other things which a teacher must know well—about children, for instance, and the social conditions which shape their lives. But social workers, therapists, and juvenile employment officers must also know about these things. A teacher, insofar as he is concerned with teaching and not just therapy, "socialization," or advice about careers, must have mastered something which he can impart to others. Without this he would be like an actor who was exquisitely sensitive to the reactions of an audience, a master of gesture and of subtle inflections of voice, but who omitted to do one thing—to learn his words.[13]

Furthermore, while teaching is, in some sense, an everyday activity, thinking pedagogically is not natural. The transition to professional thinking in teaching marks a divide—a move in which future teachers learn to look beyond the familiar worlds of teaching and learning. The pull of prior beliefs is strong, however, not least because of the long apprenticeship of observation that distinguishes teachers from other professionals.

Thus, in becoming a teacher, very little normatively correct learning can be trusted to come about without instruction that takes the preconceptions of future teachers into account—preconceptions that are warranted by common sense and the conventional practice that future teachers are already steeped in. In learning to teach, neither first hand experience nor university instruction can be left to work themselves out by themselves. Without help in examining current beliefs and assumptions, teacher candidates are likely to maintain conventional beliefs and incorporate new information or puzzling experiences into old frameworks. Our thesis has implications for the charge that teachers are conservative and individualistic. The lack of explicit teaching in teacher education, not unalterable facts about teachers, may explain these features of teacher thinking.

CHAPTER 7

When Is Student Teaching Teacher Education?

What kind of occasion for teacher learning is student teaching? How do interactions among the classroom setting, professional program, and participants shape opportunities to learn and learning outcomes? How do the nature and timing of student teaching affect what teacher candidates learn and how are they impressed by it? Do we want student teachers to learn the things they are learning? What needs to be done to make student teaching *teacher education*?

In this paper we consider these questions, in detail, for two prospective teachers enrolled in contrasting teacher education programs. Our purpose is to describe and analyze what kind of occasion for learning student teaching offered these individuals, to appraise the content and significance of the lessons they learned, and to discuss what teacher educators and policymakers can learn from these cases. To accomplish these goals of description, analysis, and appraisal, we present a conceptual framework that allows us to relate empirical aspects of student teaching to considerations of value (Scheffler, 1985). By empirical aspects we mean certain structural givens, such as the placement of student teaching at the end of formal preparation and relevant characteristics of programs, settings, and persons. By considerations of value, we mean what student teachers *ought* to learn and what sort of instruction that requires. We offer a conception of the central tasks of teaching and teacher education.[1]

The paper has three parts. First, we explain what we mean by calling student teaching "an occasion for teacher education and learning." Second, we

---

This article is coauthored by Margret Buchmann.

present two stories of student teaching that illuminate the relative influence of program, setting, and participants in determining opportunities to learn and learning outcomes. To preserve the integrity of the case material, we present them sequentially. Finally, we discuss the lessons learned in terms of our framework and describe how teacher educators can increase the educative power of student teaching.

STRUCTURAL GIVENS

Student teaching holds promise for helping beginners learn because it is experiential; that is, it offers a chance to teach under guidance, to watch an experienced teacher close up and to find out how he or she thinks about teaching, to get to know children and how they think, to discover what it "feels like" to be in charge of a class. These possibilities for learning derive from the fact that student teaching is an extended, first-hand encounter with teaching in someone else's classroom. Of course, the experiential nature of student teaching can also be a source of problems. Student teachers are not strangers to classrooms. Familiarity with classrooms and teachers may prevent beginners from searching beyond what they already know and from questioning the practices they see. In teacher preparation, experience is a trusted though not always reliable teacher (Feiman-Nemser & Buchmann, 1985).

Student teaching also has salience for prospective teachers and teacher educators because it comes at the *end* of formal preparation, serving as an occasion to evaluate whether or not the novice is ready to teach. Less obvious is the fact that student teaching can be a *beginning* that lays foundations for future learning (Feiman-Nemser, 1983). Prospective teachers are in a position to start learning from teaching, under guidance, and to see that some of the knowledge they need is "local": It can only be derived from interactions with particular students over time.

The Influence of Persons, Programs, and Settings

Participants, settings, and programs all help shape student teaching as an occasion for teacher learning (Zeichner, 1985). Student teachers have particular understandings and dispositions that influence their approaches to the experience and their capacities to learn from it. Social and intellectual skills, as well as expectations about themselves, influence their work. The classrooms in which student teachers work affect the boundaries and directions of what can be learned through their characteristic interactions and curricula. Cooperating teachers set the affective and intellectual tone and also shape what student teachers learn by the way conceive and carry out their role as teacher educators. School ethos and faculty norms may be sources of influence as well. Finally, professional programs aim to teach future teachers knowledge and skills. To identify program influences, we must know what was taught and learned in professional courses prior to student teaching. We can also look at university supervisors as representatives of program commitments during the experience.

CENTRAL TASKS OF TEACHING AND TEACHING PREPARATION

What distinguishes teaching from other helping professions is a concern with helping people learn worthwhile things in the social context of classrooms. Whatever else teachers do, they are supposed to impart knowledge and see that pupils learn (Wilson, 1975; Hogan, 1983; Buchmann, 1984). To promote learning, teachers must know things worth teaching, consider what is important, and find ways to help students acquire understandings. Since teachers cannot observe learning directly, they must learn to detect signs of understanding or confusion, feigned interest or genuine absorption (Dewey, 1904/1965).

Because teachers work with groups of students, they must consider the needs of many individuals as they orchestrate the social and intellectual sides of classroom life. Good teachers at their best moments manage both sides together, whereas novices usually cannot give them equal attention at the same time. By concentrating on the interactive side alone, however, student teachers may learn to manage pupils and classrooms without learning what it takes to promote learning. Teaching, in sum, requires knowledge of subject matter, persons, and pedagogy. It demands principled and strategic thinking about ends, means, and their consequences. Most important, it requires interactive skills and serious commitment to foster student learning.

Pedagogical Thinking and Acting

Whereas the lengthy personal experience of schooling provides prospective teachers with a repertoire of beliefs and behavior to draw from, this "apprenticeship of observation" (Lortie, 1975) does not prepare them for the central tasks of teaching. Looking at teaching from the perspective of a pupil is not the same as viewing it from a pedagogical perspective, that is, the perspective of a teacher. Prospective teachers must learn to look beneath the familiar, interactive world of schooling and focus on student thinking and learning. Perhaps the most difficult is learning to shift attention from themselves as teachers or the subjects they are teaching to what *others* need to learn. In *The Art of Teaching*, Highet (1966) describes what this shift entails:

> You must think, not what you know, but what they do not know; not what you find hard, but what they will find hard; then, after putting yourself inside their minds, obstinate or puzzled, groping or mistaken as they are, explain what they need to learn. (p. 280).

There is a big difference between going through the motions of teaching—checking seatwork, talking at the board, assigning homework—and connecting these activities to what pupils should be learning over time. Helping prospective teachers recognize that difference and laying the groundwork for the orientations and skills of pedagogical thinking and acting are central tasks of teacher preparation.

INTRODUCING THE STUDENT TEACHING CASES

The concrete meaning and challenge of these tasks will become clear as we report on the experiences of two student teachers enrolled in programs with contrasting structures and ideologies. The data are part of a larger study concerning what is taught and learned in teacher preparation.[2] Susan was a student in the Academic Program, which emphasized the importance of theoretical and subject-matter knowledge and provided limited field experiences prior to student teaching. Molly was a student in the Decision-Making Program, which emphasized generic methods of teaching and research-based decision making and offered different kinds of field experiences throughout formal preparation.

The cases which follow have a common format. First, we describe what each student teacher expected from student teaching. Then we sketch personal qualities in the student teachers and aspects of the program and setting that shaped their experiences and the impact. In these stories, we show how student teaching became a particular kind of occasion for teacher learning by illustrating how the three factors of person, program, and setting interacted over time. Finally, we examine in detail one teaching episode that elicited considerable pride in each student teacher. These prideful occasions not only highlight what and how these student teachers learned but also strengthen our basis for appraising the experiences in the terms of the central tasks of teaching and teacher preparation.

THE CASE OF SUSAN

Goals and Expectations

Considered by her instructors one of the strongest students in the Academic Program, Susan looked forward to student teaching with eagerness. "Finally," she said, "I'll be getting out and doing something practical." Like many teachers, Susan believed that "actual concrete experience" was "more valuable than all the reading and discussion and everything that can take place on a topic" (p. 37).[3] Whereas the Academic Program recommended five weeks of full-time responsibility, Susan said, "I want to do it for at least seven" (p. 34). At the same time, Susan recognized the need for someone to observe her, to offer guidance, and to stimulate reflection. She considered student teaching a kind of internship, a time to try out ideas about good teaching under supervision:

> You can't take someone and have them learn all the aspects of good teaching and then say, "Go out and teach," without giving them an opportunity to try it out, to have someone to give them feedback and guidance, and then to go back again and look at it in retrospect. (p. 34)

Susan wanted a chance to plan lessons in all the content areas and to be responsible for pupils' learning over time. She recognized that these instructional responsibilities would differ from the experience of planning and teaching "one-shot lessons" to a reading group, as she had done in conjunction with her reading practicum. There she only needed a single objective and did not have to worry about where her lesson was leading. Now, however, she said,

> I have to be very aware of what I'm doing and where I'm going and of the time that's spent in each of the times, for, maybe, math, for reading, for science, that sort of thing. I've never really gone through a day where I teach each of these things . . . *and I need experience with that*. (pp. 29–30)

Susan was hoping to "learn by doing," by getting experience. But she also saw student teaching as a testing period for herself as a person, and for her choice of career:

> Just being in the classroom . . . is going to be a big, I don't want to say shock, but that's going to be a big part of what student teaching is about— to know whether or not you can handle those kids, to know whether or not you actually want to do this for the rest of your life. (pp. 35–36)

Susan's entering goals and expectations referred both to the knowledge and the interactive dimensions of teaching, and both these elements were reflected in her image of a good teacher. According to Susan, a good teacher never has to raise her voice. She "has excellent things going on but there's no chaos" (p. 33). Susan described an idealized picture of an orderly classroom where pupils were busy and happy learning through "fun" activities and where the teacher was liked and respected. She was vague about what she meant by good classroom management (not "heavy handed") and innovative activities ("not boring seatwork"). Although her ideal included a commitment to foster learning, getting respect was very important to her:

> I've always wanted ever since I started the program to be a teacher that my students would love, respect, and look back on . . . That was the ideal image of a teacher in my mind. Someone who really taught them a lot, and yet they really respected and loved her for things that she put forth for them, and her attitude and actions, that sort of thing (p. 132).

Program Influences

Prior to student teaching, Susan had begun to incorporate the major themes of the Academic Program into her ways of thinking about teaching. Most striking was her belief that she had started to "think like a teacher." In describing her work with a reading group (in conjunction with the reading practicum), she revealed concerns and expectations about student thinking and learning that her program stressed:

> I'm trying to make the kids connect what they're doing with something they should be learning. I don't want them to just read and then sit down and close the book without thinking about "Why did we read this story? What did I get out of it? What's it saying to me? What good has it done me?"—that sort of thing. (p. 8)

Susan seemed to feel that *doing* schoolwork was not enough. She wanted students to think about the reasons for doing it, what they were *learning*, and what that meant to them as *persons*.

Susan credited the reading professor for showing her how to foster these attitudes by taking over her reading group and modeling what can be done even with the stories in the basal reader. His demonstrations of teaching to foster understanding and personal meaning made a big impression on Susan because they provided concrete models of the Academic Program's commitment. She said that this professor had really started to "press that into us" and she looked forward to working with him during student teaching. The Academic Program provided specialists in subject matter to supervise her. In addition to her reading professor, Susan was also supervised by a science teacher.

Susan's notion of learning through "fun" activities captured her interpretation of another message in the Academic Program: Good teachers do not rely on textbooks. She translated this message into a dichotomy between "meaningful" learning activities, usually created by the teacher, and "boring" seatwork, usually based on workbooks and dittos. Susan wrote in her student teaching application that she wanted to "get away from textbooks and learn to use the community as a resource" (p. 45).

Cooperating Teacher and Setting

Susan had a cooperating teacher who exemplified many of the commitments of the Academic Program. Bob taught science and reading to a combined third/fourth-grade class composed largely of children from professional families; he teamed up with the teacher next door for mathematics and social studies. Bob involved his students in projects and was especially skillful at giving clear explanations, asking challenging questions, and probing students' thinking. His expertise came out in large and small ways. He seemed to know when to persist and when to tell a student "I'll let you think about that" or "Let's leave it; we can't agree today" (p. 49).

Once, after Susan showed a film on longitude and latitude, Bob stimulated a lively exchange by asking the class: "What kinds of workers need to know about time zones?" Bob typically asked application questions that could be answered in several ways. The children's suggestions—businessmen, travel agents, pilots (p. 82)—showed that they had understood the concepts. Susan had never imagined opening up the discussion in such a way and was impressed that the students had so many different ideas.

Although he had never had a student teacher before, Bob chose Susan because he liked what she had written in her student teaching application. He encouraged her to set aside the basal to teach story elements and he asked her to plan a field trip to a local television station. Overall, Bob gave Susan a great deal of responsibility, but he did not talk much about his own teaching or hers. For example, toward the end of student teaching, Susan and Bob each taught a science lesson on rectangular grids to half the class, but they approached the topic in different ways. Whereas Bob presented the rectangular grid as a "system," a central concept in the science curriculum, Susan treated the topic of rectangular grids as a follow-up to the unit on polar coordinates that she had just finished teaching. Having no comprehensive view of the science curriculum, Susan was unaware that "system" was a unifying theme.

Despite these differences in treatment, Bob and Susan never discussed what each did and why. Susan found Bob somewhat aloof. She said he did not respect the other teachers at this suburban school even though they held him in high regard.

Susan the Person

Susan was rather shy. Describing herself before she transferred to the university, Susan said: "I was a very nice person, but a very quiet person" (p. 140). Over the course of her junior and senior years in college, Susan became noticeably more self-confident. She attributed that change to her job as a dormitory receptionist which gave her "a great boost": "Now I'm not just another person . . . I'm somebody there. I can help . . . I don't feel like an outsider. I feel like I'm one of the insiders now" (p. 2). Susan had a strong need to be noticed, to count as someone special. When the "guys" in the dorm where her fiance worked as a resident advisor included her in their thank-you letter at the end of the year, Susan was touched: "I never had that kind of feeling that, you know, that I counted as someone, that I wasn't just someone in the background . . . that someday, somebody would notice me for being the quiet person that I was" (p. 141). Susan connected the need to be important to others with her desire to teach and with the legacy she wanted to leave behind: "It makes me feel good to be needed and maybe that's why I want to teach so much, because I want to be able to give help . . . I want to be the kind of teacher that the kids will remember" (p. 4).

Despite her growing confidence, Susan depended greatly on others for assurance. Flattered that Bob had chosen her as a student teacher, she worried about making a good impression on him. Susan, who was accustomed to getting straight "A"s, wanted everything to be perfect right from the start.

The Story and Its Turning Points

Phase one: Deciding to get tough. At the end of the first week of student teaching, Susan announced: "I'm going to have trouble with discipline." She had sized up her cooperating teacher and decided that he might be "good at explaining things," but he was not a good model for her in the area of discipline. "He's too laissez-faire. He lets the kids talk and move around when he's talking, but I want stricter ground rules" (p. 83). Susan knew that the students went to the bathroom or their lockers and sharpened pencils while he was talking. Still, she measured their respect for her by their willingness to listen attentively and follow her directions. Throughout student teaching Susan maintained that being short, female, and soft-spoken put her at a disadvantage compared to Bob who was a tall male.

Taking over a reading group, Susan worked hard to prepare homemade dittos which she claimed were "more meaningful" than the regular workbook pages. For example, she had students find two- and three-syllable words in a newspaper to fill in the blanks of a ditto she had prepared on syllabification. But Susan had trouble getting her group of 11 boys to cooperate and often confused her inability to pace the lesson or attend to individual differences with their unwillingness to comply. Once, after asking everyone to wait for instructions, three boys completed a ditto before she was finished explaining it. Rather than consider the appropriateness of the assignment or the need to have additional work on hand, Susan got upset about what she saw as the students' lack of respect.

Another time, after the class had seen a film on different kinds of graphs (e.g., bar graphs, line graphs), Susan asked the students to find a graph in the newspaper and tell a little about it. Susan considered this a good idea because students would be working with information they had derived from a source other than a textbook. "I thought it would be a great idea, use newspapers, no books, actually have them searching for these things and interpreting what the graphs meant" (p. 109). The students, however, could not make sense of graphs about gold prices or the Dow Jones average. One girl burst into tears of frustration. Seeing that the task was too hard for fourth-graders, Susan changed her strategy when she taught the third-graders, asking them to make up their own graphs. She was greatly relieved that Bob had not been in the classroom to see "the big disaster" (p. 110).

When her science supervisor came to observe, Susan expected comments on her science teaching. Instead, the supervisor focused on her management and checked "needs improvement" in all categories of the observation form. Later that day, Susan told the interviewer that the science supervisor had recommended three studies on classroom management for her to read. Susan felt discouraged: "I want to be a miracle teacher. I want to do it right, right away" (p. 53). Her discomfort seemed to provide an impetus for change. With encouragement from her fiance and cooperating teacher, she decided "to be tough. No more nice Ms. T. I have to get respect and compliance" (p. 52).

Phase two: Taking charge. Susan took over the class, announcing: "I'm going to be your teacher for the next seven weeks, so I want you to listen. I'm not going to talk over you" (p. 56). Bob was absent frequently and even the substitutes looked to Susan for directions. Now Susan took action more quickly. She kept individual students in at recess, turned off the lights, stopped a game when there was too much noise, made students put their heads down on their desks. Still, she continued to be concerned about getting enough respect.

During the second phase, Susan also tried out various instructional activities, succeeding most in areas in which she had some specific preparation. In science, for example, Susan taught a unit on polar coordinates from the SCIS (Science Curriculum Improvement Study) unit because this was the curriculum Bob used and because she wanted "to see what it was like." For the most part, she followed the suggestions in the teacher's guide. She did, however, transform a pencil-and-paper exercise from the materials into a "concrete" activity by having students go out into the playground and pretend they were navigators locating objects at sea. Working with the SCIS materials, Susan saw firsthand what her science methods professor meant when he criticized the curriculum for being "activity-driven":

> SCIS I found was basically directed towards doing the activities and it was just assumed that the children would understand the concept behind it. It was never spelled out or given . . . And although the activities were very enjoyable, I don't think SCIS in itself . . . was sufficient for what I would want to teach. (p. 97).

Because she had a framework for thinking about SCIS, Susan was more aware of its strengths and limitations and was better able to adapt it for student learning.

In her higher ability reading group, Susan followed Bob's suggestion and planned a unit on elements of fiction (plot, character, setting, point of view). Although she had majored in English, Susan seemed to have a limited understanding of these terms. Asked for a definition of plot, she said, "It's the action, one thing leads to another" (p. 73). Susan was particularly pleased with her strategy for teaching the concept of character which she got from her children's literature textbook. Using the format of a radio interview, she developed a set of interview questions (e.g., What is your name? Where do you live? What do you do?). The students were supposed to fill in the names of the main character in their story and answer the questions as the character would. The reading supervisor criticized some of her lessons for being "too abstract," meaning that the students were "bored by workbooks and basals", and that she was attempting to challenge them (p. 73).

Whereas Susan was able to move the class through various lessons, applying sanctions when necessary, she rarely probed student responses or made explicit connections between the activities students were doing and the concepts they were supposed to be learning. For example, one day Susan tried a mathematics activity called "Mystery Pumpkins," designed to foster logical reasoning. Given a series of clues, students were to deduce the answer to a puzzle ("Which pumpkin?"). Susan put the problem on the overhead. She read each clue and called on students to give the answers. When a student gave a wrong answer, she called on someone else. She did not ask students to justify their answers, right or wrong, nor did she solicit discussion about the thinking entailed in the task. Although Susan felt that she had taught a lesson on problem solving, she missed the central point of focusing on students' thinking.

At midterm, Bob said she was doing fine in every area. His only suggestion was that she wait a bit longer before plunging into lessons so that the students had time to quieten down. Otherwise, he said, she was "well prepared, capable, in charge, punctual." Susan felt elated and focused on her teacher's positive evaluation rather than on the more critical feedback from her university supervisors who had pointed out areas for improvement in management and in the teaching of subject matter.

Phase three: Marking time. After receiving this positive midterm evaluation from her cooperating teacher, Susan seemed to lose interest in student teaching as a source of learning. She had done the things she wanted to do and said that if, for some reason, she could not continue, she would feel that she had accomplished her goals (p. 72). Her twin sister was about to be married and Susan confessed that she took the weekend off without taking any of her books, even though she had to go to school on Monday morning by 7:30 to prepare.

Susan also acknowledged that she was relying on dittos and workbooks, even though this conflicted with her idea of a good teacher. She said it would take enormous time and commitment to prepare appropriate exercises for all the children (p. 75). And Susan continued to worry about discipline and getting respect.

Furthermore, Susan did not feel she had developed her relationship with Bob or increased her capacity to learn from him. At the beginning of student teaching, the class had gone on a field trip to the planetarium and Susan had watched Bob extend the experience through a class project on the Big Dipper. At the end of student teaching, Susan planned a field trip to the local public television station. At Bob's suggestion, she even attended an inservice workshop on learning to use video equipment. Nevertheless she saw the trip as an end in itself and not as an impetus for further learning.

By contrast, Bob had a lot of ideas about how to use the trip to motivate worthwhile classroom work, yet he did not tell Susan about his ideas. When she asked him what to write on the permission form under "Purpose of the Trip," he said, "community resources enrichment." After the trip, Bob surprised Susan by teaching students how to use video equipment so that they could film interviews with each other. Watching the interviews, students not only saw the importance of lighting but also came to appreciate the challenge of interviewing someone who gave one-word answers. Bob planned to have students interview each other about their family histories and also videotape their tutoring in the kindergarten. Whereas Susan claimed that she had learned "how to plan field trips with an educational purpose," she still seemed to believe that the destination determined the educative value of a trip. She contrasted "educational" field trips to the planetarium and television studio with a trip to the circus which she had taken as an elementary student (p. 81).

Right up to the end of student teaching Susan was concerned about getting enough respect from children. She sought the advice of a friend from home, a veteran teacher of 11 years:

> I don't have the respect that I think I need. I can say "Stay in for recess," but don't feel that's going to be sufficient because it doesn't teach them anything . . . Even though I don't want to be a heavy punisher, there needs to be some kind of reminder or something about what they had done wrong. (p. 120)

The teacher suggested that Susan have students write sentences reminding them of their misdeeds. When Bob was not around, Susan followed this advice, asking students to write "I will not disturb the class" or "I will listen when Ms. T. talks" (p. 120).

While Susan's concerns about getting compliance and respect never abated, she did clarify and alter her ideas about what good classroom management entails. She used to think that she could simply tell students what to do: "I had no idea when I first started. I assumed I could tell the kids to sit down and be quiet and they would, but you can't. Kids aren't like that" (p. 112).

Susan said that being responsible for keeping 25 students occupied showed her the importance of having enough activities for students to do and of being prepared for those students who finish early: "You can't just have one lesson and expect all the kids to go through it at the same rate" (p. 114). Susan connected this insight to a lesson she had learned from babysitting—keeping children busy is a good way to control them. Susan's thoughts about management echoed the one lecture that the Academic Program presented on the topic before student teaching. The instructor had emphasized that management is a combination of many different elements, not simply a matter of being the authority. Susan summarized the instructor's message:

> It's a combination of having yourself prepared, having all the materials you need, being organized, knowing how you're going to present it, what order things will come in, having things that the kids will understand that build on something that they already know or that build on the lesson itself. (p. 114)

Prideful Occasion

Of all the things Susan did during student teaching, she was most proud of her book-making project. Susan said the project was worthwhile because it was "something out of the ordinary," which to her meant "not related to work in basal readers." She thought that having students make their own books would also motivate them to write. "We made the books first before we wrote the story," she explained. "That way they saw a need to fill in these pages. There were all these blank pages; this beautiful book was all theirs and they could put anything in it they want" (p. 105).

Book making. To initiate the project, Susan had students write letters to their parents saying that they would be making books in their reading class and asking if they could bring a piece of material for the cover. One mother volunteered to sew the pages together for all the books. Then, an entire school day was devoted to cutting cardboard, ironing the material onto the cover, and putting the books together. Since she had made books twice before—in her children's literature class and in her reading practicum—Susan felt confident about the procedure. Though eager, the children spent much time chatting and standing around, waiting for Susan or Bob to help them. Afterward Susan admitted, "They should have had another assignment to do, but they were all pretty excited cutting out their material and getting their books together" (p. 108).

Story writing. Once the books were made, Susan told the students that they could write anything they wanted "as long as it had an idea behind it." Without explaining what this requirement meant or giving examples, Susan changed the formula, saying: "Every story has a problem and a solution." To illustrate this point, Susan tried using a "story starter." She gave the class a story title, "The Day I was a Popsicle", and together they thought up problem situations that a popsicle could get into and then figured out solutions. It was not clear how this technique, which Susan had picked up in her children's literature course, fitted with her vague advice about story structure or her injunction that stories have ideas.

While Susan was competent in the book-making process, she did not structure the writing phase of her project for purposes of student learning. Students worked on their stories in class and at home without getting criticism or advice. There was no discussion about problems and solutions in the stories or any effort to identify and clarify the students' ideas. Spelling was the only standard applied to the final product and even here Susan turned the responsibility over to the students:

> I wanted them to work together to check each other's stories. Again that's something they hadn't done too often, so they would skim through it and say "OK" and hand it back and there were still spelling errors . . . but it was a start anyway with working together and correcting each other. (p. 106)

Before all the students had finished their stories, Susan was ready to turn the class back to Bob. One day during her last week of student teaching, Susan sat at a table in the back of the room writing out directions for making books which the teacher had requested. As far as she was concerned, the project was over.

Bob, however, saw a way to treat the students as authors. He moved to the front of the room and told those who had finished to put their books on a side table so that others could read them. Meanwhile, he invited one of the students to come sit beside him and read his story aloud. During the reading, Bob noticed a mis-spelling and sent the student to the dictionary saying, "This is really great, but can we make it better?" Later Susan explained that he had said to her: "Today why don't we take time out and just you and I will spend time correcting and reading the kids' books and showing them that we're excited and we care" (p. 106).

Susan had focused on the technique of book making rather than the process of story writing. Though Susan was proud of "doing her own thing," she did not seem to recognize the possibilities for important academic learning. Only the classroom teacher saw the opportunity to treat students as authors who could improve their craft and their stories as pieces of writing that others could enjoy.

THE CASE OF MOLLY

Goals and Expectations

Molly looked forward to student teaching but did so calmly. While the experience itself would not be new, there would be more of it. The Decision-Making Program had provided her with many and varied classroom experiences, which she expected to build on: "I see the learning as a building on what I already know. I see it as a practice time, not as something totally new . . . There will be some stuff that is new, but most of it, I see as building" (I-7, pp. 11–12).[4] Molly stressed that she was not worried about handling students or relating to a teacher because she had already done these things (p. 16).

In one sense, student teaching seemed like one more hoop to jump through. Molly compared it to working in a hotel kitchen before one becomes a chef. Still, Molly expected to benefit from the experience:

> My requirements will be more. I'll be in contact for more time during the day with the kids. I'll be communicating more with the teacher. I'll be expected to follow through on a lot of different kinds of things, keep in contact with more of a variety of people, such as the principal . . . I see an expanded role. (I-7, p. 11)

She wanted to find out about the children in her classroom, and "to be their friends" for a while.

Although expanding the scope and amount of her interactions to a larger time frame was important to Molly, she had one "knowledge use" goal for student teaching. She hoped to bring together all the things she had learned in her program from all the different sources—classroom experiences, ideas and concepts from courses. To Molly, being able "to put it all together" was the test of what she really knew. In this sense, student teaching was a culminating experience.

"Putting things together" had been a goal and personal concern for Molly from the start. She knew that she was somewhat slow at that and she devoted time between quarters and during the summer to work toward this goal. Molly realized that one cannot easily use knowledge wisely. She commented in an interview at the beginning of her program:

You're taught all this stuff and you want to use it so desperately—"I know this thing and I want to use it!" But the thing is, you're not really using it as you should. You're—you're *over*using it. I want to use it in the right proportion and at the right time. (I–1, p. 15)

In the same interview Molly also explained what she regarded as the crucial principle of curriculum and instruction: What is taught should already be of interest to children and should, in turn, be applicable to the "real world."

Program Influences

In Molly's program, the principle of interest and real-world application was operationalized as "meaningfulness" and "out-of-school application." Both categories appeared on the evaluation forms used throughout the program. One form, called "Instructional Discussion Observation and Data Collection" had the following category for supervisors to check under "Focus on Learners": It [discussion] draws out and integrates students' relevant, personal experience in order to reach the goal by way of a route that is meaningful to students" (p. 13). Another form, called "Science Inquiry Lesson Observation and Data Collection," listed among the categories to be checked under "Lesson Closure": "Where students might use the learning [application/transfer]" (p. 12).

The Decision-Making Program stressed the importance of planning and required regular planning times for student teachers, who were expected to use detailed, specific formats to write lesson plans for different curriculum areas. Molly simplified these formats for reading and mathematics and used them every day. She told an interviewer:

I had to put a picture on my plans to help motivate me to look at them. I put a book on the form that I use for reading and a price tag on the form that I use for math lessons. (p. 70)

Molly's goals for her own learning were compatible with her program's emphasis on "knowledge use" and "teacher decision making." They also fitted with what Martha, her program director, judged she needed to work on during student teaching. In looking at some of Molly's plans, Martha was concerned that Molly was not making enough connections in teaching content, especially between making what she taught fit into a "larger picture" and identifying relationships among the things that she was teaching (p. 93). Whereas Molly was observed frequently, she had different supervisors, some newcomers to the program staff. Molly thought that "they know what I did but not really *how* I did it" (p. 154). She considered herself and her cooperating teacher as the principal sources for evaluation.

Molly the Person

Molly had always written goals for herself, taking pains to figure out what she wanted to achieve as well as what she was actually learning from class or summer employment, for example. She seemed serious and mature, but was also vivacious and spontaneous. Molly had a capacity for becoming interested in things and enjoying them. Moreover, she had dramatic talents and a knack for working with visual aids.

In her program, Molly had a reputation for being "creative" and her "own person." The program director had hoped that Molly's cooperating teacher would support her in these areas of personal strength. During student teaching, however, Martha was concerned that what was "different" in Molly would be "squashed," and thought, "I hope she lives through this term" (p. 94). These worries were understandable, given the setting in which Molly taught.

Setting and Cooperating Teacher

The halls of Harrison School were light, clean and cheerfully decorated with children's pictures and artifacts. Walking down the halls, one rarely heard a sound. Built approximately 20 years ago to allow for teaming and flexibility, the school had 34% minority children. The current staff was a closely knit group; the newest teacher had been at Harrison for nine years. Teachers worked together in teams for grades K–2 and 3–5. The teachers shared expectations about student behavior which they took care to enforce in a number of settings (halls, classrooms, library).

The opening exercises for the lower grades took place in the "addition" (a large room used for different purposes) and demonstrated the ethos of the school and the camaraderie among the teachers. Four classes gathered each morning at 8:40 a.m. for about 20 minutes to take attendance, collect milk money, mark the calendar, and say the Pledge of Allegiance. Teachers took turns supervising these activities. The children had to sit up straight, with their feet on the floor, look at the teacher talking to them—usually over a microphone—refrain from talking or moving about, and enter and leave the room in single file. Reprimands were frequent, often personal, and sometimes sharp.

Although she disagreed at times with other teachers, Suzy, Molly's cooperating teacher, did not want "to rock the boat." According to Molly, Suzy did not like the playground rules at Harrison: Girls got ropes for jumping and boys got balls to play in teams. Girls were told to walk like "little ladies" and boys like "little gentlemen" (p. 53). Still, Suzy did not want to say something "because of the team; it doesn't seem worth it" (p. 79). She expressed her belief that "the kids need tightening up" (p. 29) in the formula: "A good listener is someone who sits tall with their feet flat on the floor, looking at the person who's talking" (p. 19).

Regarding the knowledge side of teaching, Suzy tended to follow the maxim "one and only one right answer." One day she gave directions for a seatwork assignment which involved choosing the *right* word from the list ("went," "want," "where," and "what") and putting it in a blank on a ditto. She directed students to read the sentences on the blackboard, trying every word until they found the one that made sense. As they moved through choices for the sentence, "I ____ to read a book," they came to the word "went." "Do you think that's the best choice?" asked the teacher. There was a pause. Suzy said, "Probably not," and the children all joined in and said "No" (p. 19).

A skillful manager, Suzy was good at keeping things moving and monitoring the class; a look or a word from her often quietened the class down. Molly was greatly impressed by her ability to anticipate what might happen and her ability to step in immediately when things got out of hand:

> One thing that really struck me was that "thinking ahead." I think ahead but I'm more slow to act and with her zipping, and zipping and bopping, I was like "Oh, wow, *I would have never gotten those things*." (p. 187)

The Story: The Power of Setting to Develop Molly's Different Teaching Personas

Socialization. Molly was a student teacher for 15 weeks—from the last week of August to the first week of December. The goals of her cooperating teacher, which fitted with the school ethos of control, loomed large in Molly's experience. At the beginning of the school year, Suzy gave a lot of attention to "grooving" her second-graders, expecting them to sit still and upright with their eyes on the teacher, to listen attentively. She was concerned that the children follow directions correctly when given.

Suzy spent time and effort at the beginning of the day and during transition periods to bring children to order and attention. To achieve these goals, she talked very slowly in a flat, monotonous voice. Before going to the library, for instance, Suzy said to the children, "I want you to know that I don't want *one single* sound." Children were sitting, heads down, at their desks. She continued, pointing to several of them, "I want these people to show what a nice job you can do standing in line. If I see you running, I will lose my patience" (p. 51). In Suzy's classroom, access to the toilet, the water fountain, and the pencil sharpener were strictly controlled, and children who talked more than once during a spelling test got "zeros." Curriculum and instruction were highly standardized at the beginning of the year, based on dittos, drills, and workbooks. Suzy grouped children for instruction by the comparative speed with which they completed workbook assignments.

Molly assumed the teacher's goals: "They need this," she said (p. 28). "The teacher wants to work on this" (p. 32). When asked during the second week of student teaching what she watched when observing Suzy, Molly replied, "I'm watching to see how she gets the kids to be good listeners" (p. 28). The following week she responded that she was learning a great deal about management, which Molly had come to see as her major problem (p. 35).

Molly rapidly took on an equal share of the classroom routines in mathematics drills, spelling tests, and reading skill instruction. In these instructional contexts, Molly developed a "teacherish persona." Tight-lipped, robot-like, often yawning, Molly seemed bland and authoritarian. Because she spoke very slowly, there was little evidence of thinking or involvement on her part. At times, an unpleasant note crept into what she said. Once, while Molly tried to get the class ready for spelling, two boys haggled over an eraser. "This is not the time to settle it," Molly insisted, but the boys did not stop even when she repeated herself:

> This is not the time to settle it. *My spelling test isn't on Friday, yours is.* Daniel, head down. I will not wait that long next time; you'll be sitting here with your heads down for five minutes during recess. (p. 46).

Amiable with one another, the two teachers seemed at times to be allied against the children. With the class in the library, Molly and Suzy had a cozy chat about a play based on "Three Billy Goats Gruff," which one reading group had practiced that morning. Suzy remarked to Molly in the same slow and wooden manner that the children had used: "Now this play is not going to get any better than it is . . . so we'll put it on this afternoon" (pp. 51–52). Both teachers laughed. They did not realize that the children were speaking as they were spoken to.

Despite this camaraderie, Molly's novice status stood out clearly to the students. She had difficulty getting compliance and attending to more than one classroom situation at a time. She often told the children to pay attention, or said that she would wait, or that they were not doing what they were supposed to be doing. Given all her classroom experiences in the Decision-Making Program and her specific preparation in management, Molly was surprised and aggravated to find that the children were testing her and that she had difficulties in controlling them. Molly reverted to strategies that were discouraged in her program but were customary at Harrison School where teachers raised their voices and punished children by giving "time out" from instruction. She explained that she was "following the teacher" in management technique because what Suzy did was "effective" and the "kids were used to it" (p. 185).

Molly also had difficulties dealing with the knowledge side of teaching. When she introduced homemade spelling dittos for "enrichment," her explanations were not helpful. Decorated with "word pizzas," these dittos were harder than the spelling lesson and their format was confusing. For example, one of them required students to unscramble nonsense words like "stla," "tna," "cta," and "dnah," and place them into appropriate categories according to the "word pizzas." Many children seemed unable to read the word "unscramble," figure out what they were supposed to do, or follow Molly's repeated directions (pp. 22–23).

Difficulties of this sort went unnoticed. Suzy observed Molly in management and gave her advice in that area. Although she thought it too advanced for "these children," Suzy allowed Molly to read *Charlotte's Web*, and the class was thrilled by her dramatic, exciting delivery. The teacher told Molly that "she had flunked in management." Still, Suzy had confidence in her student teacher, thought Molly a wonderful reader, and loved having her in the room (p. 46).

Self-assertion. Six weeks into the school year, classroom work became more diverse and interactions more relaxed, even though Suzy's concerns for curbing and controlling students never disappeared. Molly improved in classroom management. She was learning to monitor the rest of the class while working with individual students or a small group. The children continued to test her, but she carried on. Molly felt that the teacher had shifted attention from *her* improvement to shared focus on children (p. 55). Desks side-by-side, the teachers planned and administered classroom life.

In small but significant ways, Molly asserted herself. Grouping children for a game, she said "Instead of separating the boys and girls, I'd like people with blonde hair over here, brown hair over here" (p. 45). Molly was struck by the unequal treatment of boys and girls on the playground and found it frustrating to watch. Nor did she like the fact that, at Harrison, there were, "unwritten rules about speech, behavior, how little girls talk, how little boys walk. Boys get a lot more attention but they also get to hear the harsher voices," she explained, "all the research—it's true!" (p. 57). Molly stressed that she had noticed these patterns because of her social foundations course, which had focused on problems of equity in teaching.

When circumstances allowed, Molly used her own voice in management, and her voice reflected her program's view that management and instruction should not be separated. One day, for example, both Suzy and Molly taught art in the school's addition. Molly was cutting and gluing pumpkins with one group; Suzy was having children paint pumpkins on black paper. Whereas Molly started with instruction at the outset and permitted children to handle the materials, Suzy made children put back the brushes they had seized eagerly and ordered them to sit quietly, feet flat on the floor. Molly's voice was friendly; children made comments, talked and shuffled around. On the other side of the room, Suzy quelled all noise and commotion by giving directions in a robot-like voice, insisting, "I want everyone to be very controlled" (pp. 77–78).

Molly was not happy giving skill instruction "when kids can't immediately see the application" (p. 53) and she felt free enough to state her view that children were "skilled to death in reading." She did not see why students who could read well should continue to have skill instruction and she compared this to knowing how to ride a bike and then being told, "Now, get off the bike, and I'll teach you how to pedal" (p. 71).

This may explain why Molly's "teacherish persona" persisted in spelling tests and reading instruction. One typical 20-minute lesson contained silent story reading, recall questions, choral reading of unconnected sentences, base word recognition, and practice in the "qu" sound (p. 49–51). While Molly followed the teacher's guide and mirrored Suzy, who was teaching the same lesson to a second group, she felt exasperated about these lessons:

> They throw in structure, sight, phonetics, it's all thrown in. First they do prefixes, then there are vowels thrown in . . . It's just like a thousand shots in the hopes that one will hit. Where are their minds? (p. 71)

In her own classroom, Molly said she would first find out what the children know, spend "a couple of minutes" on skills, and then go on to comprehension, preferably using library books. She would test children to find out what kinds of learners they are, then group them accordingly.

In general, Molly wanted to add "quality": "Think about things more, improve, try to make them [children] think more instead of just getting through" (p. 71). She tried to do this in mathematics by using chip trading to teach place value. Molly acted the part of a friendly banker, yet when laying down the basic rules, she did not make a distinction between those bearing on behavior and those bearing on mathematics: "(a) When you have 10 yellow chips, you get a blue chip. (b) Roll your dice on the board and not on the table" (p. 138).

When Molly asked questions like, "Why are these chips worth 60, and not 6?," the children gave answers that sounded like a restatement of her question: "Because they're worth more" or, "Because it's 60 cents" (p. 138). Without probing what the children meant by the answers she accepted at face value, Molly could not know whether they had grasped the key point that *each* chip was worth more, in fact, 10 times more. Still, Molly "felt comfortable" teaching the concept in this way and thought that children "were real comfortable learning it" (p. 183). Suzy was impressed, and Molly proudly told an interviewer that she was teaching Suzy and an aide how to do chip trading (p. 70).

Having participated together in an inservice workshop, Molly and Suzy teamed up to introduce a writing program in which teachers acted as consultants and children wrote stories on topics that interested them, without worrying about spelling and punctuation. There were regular conferences in which teachers helped children develop their ideas and acted as critics. Students read each other's stories and commented on them.

Such ideas were new to Suzy, who worried about managing the program properly, but this innovation allowed Molly to work in ways that were more natural to her. Molly elicited children's ideas and talked to them with evident pleasure and ease. Many students showed considerable capacity for thought and imagination, and even Suzy was surprised at how much she was learning about their ways of thinking (p. 114).

Counting the days. Molly was "working hard and enjoying it," but at the same time she was "counting the days." In October, she announced, "There are four more weeks until Thanksgiving, and then it's downhill" (p. 71).

True to her prediction, Molly went into a holding pattern after Thanksgiving. She explained that student teaching had been very long and that she was very tired. Almost from the beginning, she had been taking attendance in the addition for 85 children each morning, and she wearily recited her daily responsibilities:

> Getting them [the class] down to the room, getting them quieted down, explaining their reading work, meeting with them in writing, transitioning to math . . . explaining directions, getting them down to the addition, getting them out of the door, I say "Out you go!" Watching them come down from the hall as they get back from lunch, making sure they're walking. Taking attendance again in the afternoon, getting them down to the room again, getting them to quiet down, ready for reading, doing their reading strategy lesson with them, getting them lined up for science or social studies . . . and throughout this whole thing, you know, figuring things out in my head, "How much do I have left for ____?" and, "Should I change that?" (pp. 175–176)

It "required a lot of effort to get mentally up for teaching now," and Molly wished "it were all over" (p. 157).

Suzy felt that classroom management was coming apart and began to intervene as she had done in the early phase of student teaching. During a lesson on vowels and consonants, Suzy felt that the children in Molly's group were getting "really out of hand." When Suzy questioned Molly whether she knew where she was going in the lesson, Molly responded curtly that she did (p. 158). Molly kept saying, "It's so busy; there's so much to do," and Suzy wondered whether she should remind Molly that she had only done *half* of the teaching, *half* of the grading (p. 158).

Nevertheless, her cooperating teacher was extremely enthusiastic about Molly's teaching and did not want her to leave student teaching with negative feelings. According to Suzy, the director of the Decision-Making Program took credit for Molly's many successes, but Suzy concluded, "Molly's a natural, a real colleague, and a joy to have around." As a fitting memento, all Decision-Making Program student teachers were presented with an engraved whistle—"Harrison School 1984"—by the staff.

Molly's Prideful Occasion

Molly was most herself when teaching an elections unit she had developed. She thought that children should know about the presidential elections as an important current event. She used social studies to expand their vocabulary with "words they would probably be seeing again," "words that they probably see in a newspaper or hear people talking about" (p. 125). The unit was also important to Molly because, "If I create it, I tend to be more motivated and directed, and the kids sense this and they meet my expectations" (p. 70).

How Molly planned the project. Molly put time and thought into planning her unit. To decide on content, she drew on her everyday knowledge. This is illustrated by the vocabulary words and definitions she created "out of her own head" (pp. 123–124). For instance, she defined "power" as "when you can do things your way;" "voting" as "giving your support;" "opinion" as "what you yourself believe" (p. 79). She assumed that children would be interested in the fact that the president must be a U.S. citizen, be at least 35 years old, that he earned $200,000 a year, and could do, as Molly put it, "whatever he wanted." She also thought that children ought to know about "gimmicks" for swaying opinions, such as television commercials, buttons, signs, and radio announcements.

Aiming for a tangible outcome to give her a sense of completion and to help the children remember what they had studied, Molly decided to have the children make a book with a ditto sheet for every lesson:

> It was important for me to give them something they could take home, that was something in their hand; this knowledge, floating around up there, it's in a book, and it's in an order kind of book, and it's in the same order that we covered it, and that should help their recall. (p. 125)

The dittos, for instance, required coloring the American flag and matching words to definitions.

For every lesson, Molly wrote out vocabulary words, objectives, and an abbreviated script. Her plan for the lesson on voting had these words at the top: vote, voting, booth, ballot, vote count, wrap-up. As objectives, Molly listed the following: students would be able to state that their vote was private and a matter of choice. Her script was a combination of things to do (count the votes; review opinions) and things to say ("You have a decision;" "It's time for you to vote"). Molly came up with the idea of using puppets (President Richard and Mr. Martin) for candidates and picked "issues" that she thought would be meaningful to the children (e.g., the lunch menu, recess). She realized that what she was teaching about presidential elections was simplified and not true to reality. Still, she believed the students could transfer what they learned to other elections (p. 126).

Molly as "her own person." On the last day of the sequence, Molly reviewed her lesson plans during lunch and commented that it was hard to keep everything straight and to remember everything she was going to do (p. 62). When it was time to start the lesson, she pretended that one of the puppets, President Richard, was calling, "Hey, take us out of the closet." Going over to a cupboard, she took the puppet out, saying "Hello everybody." The children called back, "Hi, President Richard." The puppet said, "I hope you'll vote for me." When Molly got the other puppet out, the children greeted it, "Hi, we are going to vote for you."

Launching into the lesson, Molly said, "I think we should go over our opinions on the issues. After all, the way you vote is because of what you think about the issues." Then, through a combination of recall questions to the children—"Can anyone remember what President Richard said about recess?"—and queries to the puppets themselves, she elicited their positions, and recorded them on the board.

The children were noisy and excited, and Molly interjected a few warnings. "I can't talk over people. Robert, go to the other side of the room. You know how to behave. Sam, you have your warning. Does anyone know what the word 'votes' means?" One girl said, "If you pick one person and they are 35, that means you vote." Molly let this confused answer pass and put down the right answer: "Vote is the way you support the candidate."

Now it was time to vote. Molly said, "I am looking for two people with good behavior who can go to the voting booth. Who knows what a voting booth is?" She wrote the definition on the board: "*Voting booth* is where you vote." Then she pantomimed stepping into a booth, closing the curtains, and stepping out. "A *ballot*," she explained, "is on what you vote." Molly distributed the remaining ditto sheets for the elections booklet. While the class worked on them, she took two children at a time to the voting booth she had set up in the listening center (p. 67). In the end, Molly ran out of time and asked the children to put their books together at home.

Afterward Molly considered what she would have to do differently in the future so that the booklets could be completed and the activities in her elections unit would go more smoothly. What happened during her elections unit stood in vivid contrast to much of the school work in this classroom, bringing Molly and the students to life. Watching her performance, Suzy commented spontaneously: "Isn't she fun to watch?" (p. 77).

WHAT DO THE CASES SHOW?

Looking back on these stories, one can compare what student teachers hoped for as they approached student teaching and what actually happened; how persons, program, and settings interacted to shape the experience; and how the realities of student teaching—its experiential quality and placement at the end of formal preparation—created significant impressions on Molly and Susan. Personal meaning, however, is not inconsistent with mislearning, Molly's and Susan's student teaching experiences were no exception.

The Test of Reality

Student teaching did not meet Molly's expectations. Having taken for granted her capacities concerning the interactive side of teaching, she found that she had many of the problems other student teachers have. The children tested Molly, and she had difficulty getting their attention and compliance. To her surprise, she had to put effort into learning how to manage Suzy's class.

Contrary to her hopes, Molly had limited opportunities to synthesize all she had learned in her formal preparation. Instead, she received an intensive and lengthy induction into the "daily grind" of schooling. Thus, the experience proved to be a test for her as a novice but failed to be the culminating test of what she knew as a teacher. Though understandable, Molly's hope reveals a limited view of practical knowledge in teaching and shows how views of teaching grow and change over time.

In contrast, Susan's expectations were largely met. She found out what it was like to be responsible for a class and she concluded that she could "handle it." Even though Susan never got the level of respect she wanted, she succeeded in taking charge. Thus she passed the personal test that student teaching represented for her.

In teaching subject matter, Susan *did* the things she had hoped to do— plan and teach in several curriculum areas over time. Up to a point, she also succeeded in doing what she had written about in her student teaching application—putting aside the basal and using the community as a resource. Lacking a sense of what she needed to learn to foster her students' understanding, she was satisfied that she had the experiences she wanted.

Interaction of Factors in the Experience

Susan's personal capacities and concerns set the boundaries for learning from student teaching. Drawing on a new-found confidence developed in personal relationships and work, Susan decided to take a hard line with the class. Her basic insecurity came through, however, when she continued to worry about not getting enough respect from her students. The need for personal recognition helped motivate the book-making project. But the potential of the project as a worthwhile learning experience for teacher and children was curtailed by Susan's limited understanding of story writing and its pedagogy.

Susan worked to realize her ideal of a good teacher, one who combines skillful management with learning activities that are "fun." Based on teachers she admired from her past, this ideal had been extended by what she had learned in the Academic Program. Whereas Susan came to student teaching with foundational knowledge of teaching and learning, she did not know how to connect this knowledge to pedagogical thinking and acting.

Although the classroom setting did not impede Susan, it did not offer the necessary structure for learning. Susan had a great deal of responsibility and latitude. She did not have to perpetuate practices that conflicted with her personal views or with those of her program. In fact, her cooperating teacher was an exemplary teacher of academic subjects. But because Susan did not see Bob as a model and because he did not act as a teacher educator, she had little opportunity to learn from him.

In Molly's experience, the setting dominated. Against her nature and the messages of her program, she adopted a "teacherish persona" consonant with the school. In instructional activities typical for the setting, Molly mirrored her cooperating teacher's bland and authoritative comportment. This compliance came at a cost: The pervasive ethos of control left its marks on children and on Molly. When circumstances allowed, Molly asserted herself, drawing on her personal talents, everyday knowledge and the ideas she had learned in the Decision-Making Program. Employing strategies from a social foundations class, she departed from the sexism of Harrison School. She simplified the program's planning formats and motivated herself to write daily lesson plans involving objectives, scripts, and behaviors.

Molly's knack for visuals, drama, and impersonation were prominent when she did "her own thing." Using puppets to relate the presidential election to children's lives, she was engaged and engaging in the activity. Doing things she believed in, such as chip trading and writing conferences, she was warm and attentive. In the interplay of setting, person, and program, Molly changed personas as she moved through different instructional contexts. The tension between socialization and self-assertion, played out in the different contexts, set limits on her learning.

Lessons of Experience and Their Limits

Despite differences in the amount of prior classroom experience, both Molly and Susan learned how hard it can be for a novice to take charge of someone else's classroom. Children recognize a lack of experience and behave accordingly; student teachers do not know (and may not like) the operating system of their classroom placement.

Being in charge and having to keep 25 students occupied showed Susan the value of setting limits and dealing with management through instructional planning that considers individual differences. She also saw how much time and effort that takes. Molly assumed that she already had teaching and management skills. When the children were difficult to handle, she imitated Suzy who was skilled at pacing and monitoring the class but preoccupied with control.

As for the knowledge side of teaching, both Molly and Susan were on their own during student teaching, and they succeeded within the limited understandings and skills they brought to student teaching. Molly's election unit showed that she was serious about planning and completing an activity she thought would be meaningful to children, but she lacked any grounded understanding of politics or children's interests. Her beliefs and decisions in this area were unchallenged.

While Susan's program stressed academic knowledge and teaching for understanding, she did not know how to recognize and develop possibilities for worthwhile academic learning. She was proud about *doing* what she thought were "meaningful" activities, such as going on fieldtrips or making books. Although the reading supervisor challenged some of Susan's plans, her sense that she had been "innovative" and "in charge" caused her to ignore his criticism.

From the standpoint of the central tasks of teaching and teacher preparation, Molly's and Susan's learning was systematically limited. Neither student teacher was helped to attend to pupil thinking in planning or teaching, or to clarify what counts as a worthwhile learning activity. While student teaching is not an occasion to learn subject matter it can be an opportunity to consider the adequacy and accuracy of what one is teaching and to practice probing students' thinking to see what they are learning.

Susan may have been closer to perceiving the central tasks of teaching, but neither cooperating teacher nor university supervisors focused her attention on the particular techniques she needed to use to accomplish her goals in practice. In some ways, Molly seemed more attuned to the purposeful, strategic aspects of pedagogical thinking, but she became saturated with "institutional activities" (Green, 1971) and received no help to further pupil understanding.

Personal Meaning and Mislearning

Because student teaching comes at the end of formal preparation and because it is experiential, it is a source of impressive, cathected learning, regardless of the merits of the lessons learned. Both Molly and Susan felt that they had proven themselves even before student teaching was over. Not only had they stood the test of time, they seemed to have succeeded as teachers. They felt they had learned by doing. Both received glowing recommendations from their cooperating teachers. This encouraged and reinforced these misconceptions. Thus, for Molly and Susan, student teaching was more an end than a beginning.

Molly received criticism and advice only about the management side of teaching. This, coupled with Suzy's generally enthusiastic evaluation, left Molly's personal and process-oriented view of teaching undisturbed. The pedagogy of subject matter eluded her (Shulman, 1986). Susan sought outside advice about discipline and management, but placed great stock in Bob's reassuring midterm and final evaluation. In her first extended encounter with teaching, she defined her success mostly in terms of getting respect and conducting innovative activities. Yet Susan lacked the skills to clarify the point of these activities. Because student teaching has great personal meaning, surviving the experience and receiving praise from teachers have great affective salience. Compared with such "hard evidence," the rhetoric of programs carries less weight with student teachers.

WHEN IS STUDENT TEACHING TEACHER EDUCATION?

Together with our framework, these stories of teacher learning during student teaching help to illustrate some answers to the question posed in the title of this paper. Student teaching is teacher education when intending teachers are moved toward a practical understanding of the central tasks of teaching; when their dispositions and skills to extend and probe student learning are strengthened; when they learn to question what they see, believe and do; when they see the limits of justifying their decisions and actions in terms of "neat ideas' or classroom control; and when they see experience as a beginning rather than a culminating point in their learning.

Meeting these conditions depends on teacher educators' perceiving and acting on the central tasks of teacher preparation.

By themselves, student teachers can rarely see beyond what they want or need to do or what the classroom setting requires. Without guidance, they cannot be expected to recognize that management skills may be necessary to teach classroom groups but are certainly not sufficient for teaching content. Nor can we expect novices to probe the validity of the knowledge they have to make curricula or question their beliefs about children's interests while they try to stay abreast of all aspects of classroom life within the constraints of someone else's classroom and their own limited expertise.

Teacher educators must be actively present in student teaching to give prospective teachers a concrete sense of pedagogical thinking and acting. As the trusted person in the setting, cooperating teachers are well positioned to induct novices into the invisible world of teaching. The job of cooperating teacher is to talk aloud about what they do and why, to demonstrate how to probe and extend student thinking, to alert student teachers to interpret signs of understanding and confusion in pupils, to stimulate student teachers to talk about their reasons for decisions and actions and the difficulties inherent in finding out what pupils know and what they need to learn. As an outsider to the setting, the university supervisor can help the student teacher relate the specifics of the classroom to larger frames of reference such as disciplinary knowledge, societal mandates, research on teaching, a broad view of learning to teach (see Buchmann, 1984). Through "situational teaching" (Cohn, 1979), the supervisor can connect foundational knowledge to particular actions and decisions and reinforce important concepts and orientations from the program. If cooperating teachers and university supervisors do not act as teacher educators, other factors (e.g., persons, setting) will dominate, shaping what can be learnt in student teaching (Griffin et al., 1983).

For student teaching to be teacher education, it must go beyond survival or extend practice in the outward forms of teaching to sort out appropriate from inappropriate lessons of experience. Well-meaning praise from cooperating teachers, coupled with a focus on management, fixes the attention of student teachers in the wrong direction. University supervisors cannot only be occasional visitors who mark observation forms; they must act in concert with cooperating teachers to make student teaching an occasion for teacher education.

The current structure of student teaching makes these goals difficult, at best, to achieve. Indeed, our case studies show how teacher learning can be limited or misdirected even with the best intentions and with some suitable preparation. For example, the case studies dramatize the failure of cooperating teachers to take seriously their roles as teacher educators. Current proposals (e.g., the Holmes Group report, 1986) to involve experienced teachers more fully in the education of novices will miscarry unless policymakers appreciate what is required in terms of preparation and support. Just as becoming a classroom teacher involves making a transition from being a student to being a professional, becoming a mentor involves making a transition from classroom teacher to teacher educator. Classroom teachers need time and commitment to develop the necessary understandings, skills, and orientations, and schools must broaden the scope of teachers' roles and rewards to include teacher education.

REFERENCES

Buchmann, M. (1984). The priority of knowledge and understanding in teaching. In L. G. Katz & J. D. Raths (Eds.), *Advances in Teacher Education* (Vol. 1, pp. 29–48). Norwood, NJ: Ablex.

Cohn, M. (1979). *The interrelationship of theory and practice in teacher education: A description and analysis of the Lite Program.* Published doctoral dissertation. St. Louis: Washington University.

Dewey, J. (1904). The relationship of theory and practice in education. In M. Borrowman (Ed.), *Teacher education in America: A documentary history.* New York: Teachers College Press, 1965).

Feiman-Nemser, S. (1983). Learning to teach. In L. Shulman & G. Sykes (Eds.), *Handbook of teaching and policy* (pp. 150–170). New York: Longman.

Feiman-Nemser, S., & Buchmann, M. (1985). Pitfalls of experience in teacher preparation. *Teachers College Record, 87,* 49–65.

Green, T. (1971). *The activities of teaching.* New York: McGraw-Hill.

Griffin, G., Barnes, S., Hushes, R., O'Noal, S., Defino, M., Edwards, S., & Hukhill, H. (1983). *Clinical preservice teacher education: Final report of a descriptive study.* Austin: University of Texas Research and Development Center for Teacher Education.

Highet, G. (1966). *The art of teaching.* New York: Knopf.

Hogan, P. (1983). The central place of prejudice in the supervision of student teachers. *Journal of Education for Teaching, 9,* 30–45.

Holmes Group, Inc. (1986). *Tomorrow's teachers: A report of the Holmes Group.* East Lansing: Michigan State University, College of Education, The Holmes Group, Inc.

Lortie, D. (1975) *Schoolteacher: A sociological study.* Chicago: University of Chicago Press.

Scheffler, I. (1985). *Of human potential: An essay in the philosophy of education.* Boston: Routledge & Kegan Paul.

Shulman, L., (1986). Those who understand: Knowledge growth in teaching. *Educational Researcher*, 15(2), 4–14.

Wilson, J. (1975). *Educational theory and the preparation of teachers*. Windsor, U.K.: NFER.

Zeichner, K. (1985, April). *Content and contexts: Neglected elements in studies of student teaching as an occasion for learning to teach*. Paper presented at the annual meeting of the American Educational Research Association, Chicago.

CHAPTER 8

Linking Mentoring and Teacher Learning

INTRODUCTION

While mentoring has been part of human history, the term itself first appears in The Odyssey, an epic poem by Homer. Odysseus is leaving Troy to fight in the Trojan Wars. He entrusts his household and especially his son, Telemachus, to the care and guidance of Mentor, his old friend and advisor. Odysseus is gone for over twenty years, so Mentor has the responsibility of shepherding Telemachus through adolescence and helping him find his father.

Some articles on the mentoring of preservice and beginning teachers take inspiration from Homer (e.g. Merriam, 1983; Anderson & Shannon, 1988; Galvez-Hjornevik, 1986). One writer claims that "the father-like relationship between young Telemachus and the wise, loving Mentor set a standard for characterizing future mentoring relationships" (Merriam, 1983, p. 162). Another concludes that mentoring is an intentional, nurturing, insightful, supportive, protective process based on "the activity which bears his [Mentor's] name" (Anderson & Shannon, 1988, p. 38).[1]

One problem with trying to base teacher mentoring on this classical source is that Homer tells us very little about what Mentor actually does in carrying out his responsibilities toward Telemachus. Another is that the person who really encourages, inspires, instructs and assists Telemachus is the goddess Athena, often disguised as Mentor. Homer's model(s) of mentoring may work in a mythological tale of war, gods and magic, but they do not fit the requirements of teacher mentoring very well (Cochran-Smith, 1995). Nor can educators derive much guidance from general definitions of mentoring drawn from developmental psychology, business or academia, fields where the term gained popularity long before it caught the imagination of the education community (Levinson, 1978; Speizer, 1981).

In the U.S. mentoring entered the vocabulary of educational reform in the early 1980's as part of a broader effort to professionalize teaching (Little, 1990). At first mentoring was associated mainly with beginning teacher induction. This often led to a narrow view of mentoring as a form of temporary support to help novices cope with the demands and stresses of their first year teaching. The mentoring idea was also extended to the preservice level where proposals for the redesign of teacher preparation call for teacher candidates to spend extended periods of time learning to teach in the company of experienced teachers (e.g. Holmes Group, 1990).

Through the early 1990's, researchers advanced various competing and complementary role definitions and specifications of mentors' functions, characteristics and qualities (e.g. Gehrke, 1988; Alleman, 1986; Gray & Gray, 1985; Healy & Welchert, 1990). Most studies relied on self report and took the form of program evaluation. Few reflected serious conceptual clarification or attention to mentors' practice and its consequences for novices' learning (Little, 1990).

The early prescriptive literature on mentoring uses terms like "support," "guidance" assistance" to describe what mentors are supposed to do (e.g. Bey & Holmes, 1990; Odell, 1989). A recent review of mentoring and teacher induction characterizes mentors as "support providers" (Gold, 1996). While these terms signal a general stance of helpfulness, they say little about mentoring as an educational activity aimed at helping novices learn to teach. To advance the cause of mentoring as an improvement over traditional arrangements for teacher preparation and induction, we need images of thoughtful mentors at work, studies of mentors' impact on novices' teaching and learning, and more powerful conceptualizations of the mentoring process.

This paper makes a contribution to that agenda by presenting a conceptual framework and two brief cases of educative mentoring. The framework and cases come from a comparative cross-cultural study of mentoring sponsored by the National Center for Research on Teacher Learning (NCRTL) at Michigan State University and conducted in selected sites in the U.S., England and China between 1991–1996. The purpose of the research was to learn more about how novices learn to teach, how mentoring contributes to that learning, and how various contexts (e.g. classroom and school, national policies and societal values) influence mentors' practice and novices' learning.

Altogether we studied 24 mentor/novice pairs in selected sites in the U.S., England and China. We framed the research as a cross-cultural study in order to see how mentoring, considered a reform in England and the U.S., appears in a culture with a longstanding tradition of teacher collaboration and joint study. The research sites included reform-oriented preservice and induction programs for both elementary and secondary teachers. Local researchers assisted outside researchers with data collection which included interviews with mentors and novices, observations and videotapes of their teaching and mentoring activities, weekly interaction logs which mentors and novices filled out at regular intervals across the year. The conceptual framework informed the data collection and analysis which, in turn, helped refine the framework.

CONCEPTUALIZING MENTORED LEARNING TO TEACH

In designing a study of mentoring, we had to think through our assumptions about the nature of teaching, consider the kind of teaching we wanted to study, conceptualize the process of learning to teach, and clarify our stance toward mentors and mentoring. That meant answering questions like the following: What do we know about teaching as a practice to be learned? What kind of teaching do we want novices to learn? What do assumptions about teaching imply for learning to teach? What views of learning are compatible with the task of learning teaching? How should we conceptualize the educational role of experienced teachers in novices' learning?[2]

We coined a phrase "mentored learning to teach" to signal a relationship between mentoring and teacher learning. The phrase highlights an important distinction between learning to teach on one's own, a common experience for many beginning teachers, and learning to teach in the company of an experienced teacher, a departure from the isolated and individualistic culture of teaching (Lortie, 1975). It also suggests that when novices learn to teach in the company of an experienced (mentor) teacher, their learning is "situated" in the context of teaching and in a relationship with a knowledgeable other.

Teaching as a Practice to be Learned

Questions about teaching as a practice focus attention on the content of learning to teach. We know that mentoring can be a force for continuity as well as a force for change. If mentors help novices learn conventional teaching practices, they contribute to maintaining the status quo. If mentors induct novices into new pedagogies and new professional relationships, they can contribute to the ongoing improvement of teaching. So in order to study educative mentoring, we had to clarify our assumptions about the practice of teaching and consider the kind of teaching we wanted mentors to promote.

We began with a basic observation that the practice of teaching involves both doing and thinking. At the level of visible practice, teaching encompasses a wide range of actions: explaining, advising, disciplining, prodding, organizing, assessing, demonstrating, listening, persuading, modeling, counseling, inspiring (Ayers, 1993). In addition, teachers make decisions, engage in planning, reflect on their actions, analyze and assess student work, interpret classroom events. These invisible aspects of teaching thinking combined with the visible aspects of teaching performance remind us that novices need to learn how to think and act like a teacher. This is an important point given the tendency in school-based teacher education and teacher induction to favor outward performance and to treat managing a class as the most important evidence of progress in learning to teach.

We know, of course, that teaching draws on many different domains of knowledge. Teachers must know about students, subject matter, curriculum, pedagogy; however, the practice of teaching involves putting together different kinds of knowledge in making decisions and taking action. For instance, in planning an instructional activity, a teacher may consider what concepts she wants students to learn, how that content fits with previous and future topics in the curriculum, how appropriate the activity will be for different learners and what might be difficult for some of them, how she will assess what individual students do and do not understand. Novices may learn about these different domains of knowledge in separate, university-based courses. Mentored learning to teach is an opportunity to learn how to weave different kinds of knowledge together in practice (Feiman-Nemser & Remillard, 1996).

The interactive character of teachers' knowledge stems from the contextualized nature of teaching. Teachers teach particular subjects to particular students. Consequently some of the most important knowledge they need is local. A teacher needs to know how her students feel about a particular learning activity and what they already know and believe about a particular subject. Over time teachers develop an appreciation for the concerns and confusions, ideas and interests that students in a given school at a given grade are likely to have and they build up a repertoire of ways to respond. Even so, they must still check their understanding in relation to the particular students they are teaching. Novices do not have contextualized knowledge of students and curriculum. So an important part of learning to teach involves learning to uncover and develop this kind of knowledge and to verify it in practice.

These general qualities of teacher knowledge and teaching practice take on special meaning when we consider the kind of teaching mentors should help novices learn. We were interested in how novices learn the kind of ambitious teaching currently advocated by reformers, teaching rich in content and responsive to student thinking. Various labels have been used to describe this kind of teaching, including teaching for understanding, learner-centered teaching, constructivist teaching (Prawat, 1989; Cohen, McLaughlin & Talbert, 1993).

Current instructional reform calls for classrooms where teachers and students develop knowledge together, where facts are challenged in discourse, where conceptual understanding of subject matter is fostered. Such teaching places new demands on teachers to know their subjects deeply and be able to represent them in authentic and appropriate ways, to understand how their learners think about subject matter and be able to promote critical thinking and active learning. Such teaching also invites teachers to take on new roles as designers of authentic tasks and orchestrators of classroom discourse and to manage new student roles.

One hallmark of this kind of teaching is its responsiveness to students. To teach in ways that support and extend students' thinking, teachers must be able to elicit and interpret students' ideas and generate appropriate pedagogical moves as a lesson unfolds (Lampert, 1985; Heaton & Lampert, 1990). The need to attend to what students say and to construct appropriate responses on a moment to moment basis rather than following a prepared lesson plan places special demands on teachers. It also highlights challenging aspects of teaching practice which must ultimately be learned in practice.

Learning Teaching

As one Chinese mentor told us, learning to teach outside of teaching is like trying to scratch an itch on the outside of your boot. Certain requirements of teaching such as knowledge of subject matter, child development, curriculum, teaching strategies can be learned in a variety of contexts, but teaching must ultimately be learned in practice. This is not the same as "having" first-hand experience. The pitfalls of experience in learning to teach have been conceptualized and documented in studies of teaching and student teaching (See, for example, Feiman-Nemser & Buchmann, 1983; Zeichner, 1980;

Tabachnick, Popkewitz & Zeichner, 1979). They include limited opportunities to see in practice the kind of teaching espoused by reformers, the inevitable press to act which restricts reflection and analysis, and the lack of a professional culture which supports teacher learning in and from teaching. If mentor teachers are part of the problem, they are also central to the solution of transforming learning to teach into an educative experience for novices.

In searching for a more suitable way to conceptualize the learning in mentored learning to teach, we were drawn to socio-cultural perspectives which emphasize the social and situated nature of learning through joint activity (Resnick, 1991; Lave & Wenger, 1991; Brown, Collins & Duguid, 1989; Collins, Brown & Newman, 1989). Theorists working in this tradition reject a view of learning as a passive process that occurs only in people's heads. They tell us that what people learn depends on the company they keep, the activities they engage in, and the talk that surrounds those activities.

Vygotsky's (1978) theory of assisted performance in the zone of proximal development (ZPD) accounts for how learning occurs through social interaction with a more capable other. The ZPD is the distance between what an individual can do independently and what he or she can do with assistance. Assistance from and co-operative activity with a more capable other enables a learner to perform at levels beyond his or her level of independent performance. The novice learns through observation and interaction, gradually internalizing the ways of thinking and acting that make up the activity. Traditional apprenticeships provide one model of this kind of learning. In an apprenticeship, a beginner ideally develops flexible skills and conditional knowledge by working on genuine tasks in the company of a master. Knowing cannot be separated from doing and from talk about the activity. The term 'cognitive apprenticeship' has been applied to classroom-based instructional models that incorporate key features of an apprenticeship (Brown et al, 1989; Brown & Newman, 1989). These features include authentic activity, social interaction and a teacher/coach who makes his or her knowledge and thinking visible to the learner(s). Adding 'cognitive' is intended to convey the idea that the same conditions or opportunities which support the development of physical skills can also support the development of cognitive skills.

Lave and Wenger (1991) talk about learning as a function of a novice's participation in a community of practice. Participation is a way of learning—of absorbing and being absorbed into a culture of practice. At first, the novice's participation is peripheral, but gradually it increases in engagement and complexity as the novice moves toward full participation. Part of the participation is linguistic. The novice is not only trying to learn from talk but also learning to teach. The idea of learning as a process of enculturation leaves open the question of cultural change. Can novices develop cultural competence in teaching and also learn how to change the culture of teaching?

These socio-cultural views of learning offer a compelling though idealized perspective on mentored learning to teach. They suggest that a novice could learn to practice like a teacher by observing and engaging in the work of teaching alongside a more experienced practitioner. Mentors would model and explicate their ways of thinking and acting, coach novices in their attempts to carry out particular tasks, adjust their support and guidance to novices' developing capacities. This process of enculturation assumes a community of practice with shared standards, norms of collaboration and inquiry, a language for talking about teaching. Since we cannot assume that these conditions are the norm, we must find such communities to study and work with practitioners to create them.

Educative Mentoring

Mentoring can be conceptualized as a role, a relationship, and a process. Our mentored learning to teach framework interprets each of these terms through an educational lens. The framework suggests that, in helping novices learn to teach, mentors take on an educational role, form a pedagogical relationship, engage in an educational activity.

Mentoring is often treated as a new social role for teachers. For instance, one rationale for the creation of mentor teacher roles is the desire to reward and retain good experienced teachers by enabling them to exercise leadership without leaving classroom teaching (Mitchel & Hough, 1990). While this is a worthwhile goal, it leaves room for a wide range of role orientations. When the culture of teaching or the conditions of mentoring prevent mentors from asserting their educational authority and expertise, the result may be a narrow role definition (Little, 1990; Shulman & Colbert, 1987; Feiman-Nemser, Parker & Zeichner, 1993).

The relational aspect or interpersonal side of mentoring has received a lot of attention. One question that frequently arises is whether an activity so dependent on affective qualities can be formalized in a program. If we adopt a socio-cultural perspective, we may discover that what mentors and novices do together is just as important as whether they like each other or become friends (Gallimore, Tharp & Steiner, n.d.). Of course, this does not diminish the importance of mutual respect in mentoring relationships.

We wanted to study mentors who teach for understanding. Having conceptualized mentoring as an educational process, we needed to understand mentors' goals for novices' learning and their ideas about mentoring and learning to teach. That meant asking mentors what they think novices need to learn, what kinds of experiences they believe foster such learning, how they see themselves contributing to novices' learning. To understand the learning opportunities available in a particular mentoring relationship, we had to know what a mentor and novice actually do together, including what they talk about, and how the mentor and novice make sense of those experiences. To understand novices' learning, we had to document changes in their teaching and their thinking about teaching over time. Through our research we refined our concept of educative mentoring and developed concrete images of thoughtful mentors at work in varied contexts. We came to see mentoring as a professional practice which takes different forms and involves careful judgment and principled actions based on mentors' ongoing assessment of the novice as a learner (Schwille & Wolf, 1997). We learned that effective mentors have a vision of good teaching and a working theory of learning to teach.

IMAGES OF EDUCATIVE MENTORING

To illustrate some of these ideas about mentored learning to teach, we present brief portraits of two U.S. mentor teachers. Both mentors teach in a professional development school, a regular public school where school and university faculty collaborate on teacher education, teaching and school-based inquiry. Based on more extensive case studies, the portraits highlight their practice as teachers and mentors and provide insights into their views of mentoring and learning to teach.

Nancy: Secondary Science Teacher as Mentor

As a Teacher

Nancy is a confident and competent high school science teacher.[3] When she began teaching over twenty years ago, Nancy taught science as she had been taught, following the textbook, giving multiple choice exams, "delivering information." The teaching Nancy practices today, which she calls "conceptual change science teaching," is dramatically different.

Nancy has recast her curriculum into units focused around key scientific questions or problems (e.g. How do plants eat? What are cells made of?) For every unit, she follows the same instructional routine. First, she introduces the scientific question and assesses her students' current conceptions and misconceptions. Next she models how scientists think about the question and helps students generate hypotheses and devise experiments to test their ideas. As students carry out their experiments in small groups, Nancy coaches on the side. Students share their findings and conclusions with the whole class, reconciling any discrepancies and contradictions. Finally Nancy tests students' understanding with a teacher-made essay exam.

Asking good questions in the right sequence is a key element in Nancy's teaching. She uses questions to "activate" students' prior knowledge and to help them rethink or reorganize their ideas, as she explains:

> Often kids have the pieces they need to solve a problem. But if you just give them the problem, they don't know how to do it. By asking the right sequence of questions, you can pull those pieces out and line them up and the kids end up solving it [the problem] themselves. That's very powerful for the kids and very hard to do as a teacher.

The changes in Nancy's teaching evolved through a long-term, collaborative relationship with two science educators. In particular the questioning strategy modeled by one of the professors helped Nancy move from being a "deliverer of content" to a "facilitator of learning."

> I worked with them for eight years and I picked up so much. In fact, they have probably been the most influential people as far as they way I teach. They would provide me with literature about this kind of teaching. They would model it. Bruce is probably the most outstanding teacher. He can take you from point A to point Z and you have no idea that you've traversed that distance just by questioning.

As a Mentor

Nancy believes that novices need guidance. "It's just like any kind of teaching. You have to be guided in the beginning and given help." Rather than learning from independent trial and error, she thinks it is more efficient and effective to work with an experienced teacher "who can show you things" and how they fit together.

> You may discover things on your own by trial and error. You may try it one day and see if it works. I think that would take a long time and it's pretty risky because you learn about little pieces that are not connected.

Nancy tries to do for her novices what her mentors, the science educators, did for her. Having broken the mold of delivering information, she tries to help them learn the same kind of science teaching she now practices. She approaches her work with novices in the same systematic way that she approaches teaching, using modeling, coaching and fading to structure learning over time. Nancy repeats this cycle for core tasks of teaching such as planning, managing instruction, writing and grading exams.

Nancy believes that productive talk about teaching must be grounded in firsthand experience. She has student teachers take responsibility for one class right from the start. She embeds this initial responsibility in a well thought-out structure.

> When they come to me as a student teacher, I feel it is important that I model my best teaching for them . . . What I like to do is have them take a class later in the day. They can work with me in the morning and then take ownership of a class right from the beginning. If they have the experience under their belt the first week, then everything we talk about they can relate to that experience. After they teach we will sit down and talk about what they felt went well, what they thought didn't go well, what did I see, and so on . . . Then we figure out what we need to do for the next time.

During our study, we saw a clear example of this structure. Nancy taught biology during the first period while her student teacher Betsy observed and took notes. Then Betsy taught the same content to a different class during the second period while Nancy observed and took notes. Third period Betsy watched Nancy teaching genetics and fourth period, they analyzed what happened in the biology classes and planned for the next day. At first Nancy did most of the planning, but over time, Betsy's participation increased until she was taking the lead.

> . . . The first unit, I would do all the planning with Betsy and get her input. Then the next unit we would kind of do it 50/50. I would get it started and then I would get her input more and more. The last unit we did we reversed roles. It was her plan and she would ask me what I thought. So I modeled how to do it, then I coached her how to do it, and then I faded out and she is now totally in control.

Nancy used the same sequence to help Betsy learn other tasks of teaching as well. The description below shows how Nancy structured an occasion for Betsy to learn how to grade exams.

We both had a batch of papers. I had my first hour and she had her second. We sat down, side by side. This is the first time she had graded anything like this and it was difficult to grade. A lot was subjective and you have to make decisions. And it's hard sometimes to tease out the pieces. So . . . I started grading mine and she was sitting around the corner grading hers. It was a funny assignment and we could laugh and share the funny things the kids did. Then when she got to the parts where she was stuck, she could lean over and say, "What do you think of this?" And she would read it to me and I'd say: "Well what do you see there? What do you see that's wrong? If it's worth this many points, how much do you think should come off of this?" We would talk it through and if I disagreed, I would tell her my rationale and she would give me her rationale and we would come to a solution.

As they worked together on grading their exams, Betsy could gain access to Nancy's thinking and Nancy could assess where Betsy was in her learning and provide needed guidance.

Nancy also involved Betsy in studying aspects of teaching which Nancy herself was still working on. For instance, one important issue for Nancy is attending to individual students and their understanding. This is a difficult challenge for teachers because they have to manage the learning of groups of students. Here is how Nancy framed the issue:

You have 24 bodies out there. You are running the show in a class discussion, trying to pull in those kids who are generally left out. You want the discussion to go well, so you often slip back and call on kids you know will give the correct response. Then it appears that everything is going well when in reality you know it isn't.

At Nancy's initiative, she and Betsy worked at helping each other include all the students in their lessons. They undertook a joint inquiry, observing each other teach and identifying students who were excluded from participation. This experience sent a powerful message to Betsy about the value of collaboration and inquiry in the ongoing improvement of teaching.

Beth: 2nd/3rd Grade Teacher as Mentor

As a Teacher

At the time of our study, Beth had been teaching for eight years. Four years earlier, she decided that she wanted to follow her second graders into third grade so that she could build on the strong classroom learning community she had developed and use her knowledge of individual students to support their learning over a two year period. She persuaded a third grade teacher to teach second grade so that she could pursue this experiment.

Beth's classroom reflects her values and commitments. Children's art covers the walls. A large classroom library, including books written and illustrated by the students, demonstrates the centrality of language arts. Clusters of desks encourage students to help each other and a carpeted area with comfortable chairs and a sofa offers a cozy setting for group discussions.

As a teacher Beth is always working on her practice. This lesson was not lost on Nikki, her student teacher, who commented: "It's very encouraging and refreshing to know that even after eight years I can still be refining my practice . . . I think that if you are a good teacher, you are always reflecting on your practice." During the year of our data collection, Beth worked especially hard on her mathematics teaching, trying to align her practice with new national standards. Specifically she wanted to learn how to use problem solving and oral and written discourse to help students reason with and about mathematical ideas. Beth described the teacher's role as having to "listen to what every single child says, try to understand it, and at the same time, connect it to where you're trying to go." Learning this kind of mathematics teaching presented challenges to Beth and to Nikki.

As a Mentor

Beth fully embraces her role as mentor. "I am Nikki's teacher," she said. "I spend a lot of time talking about what I believe and why I do things. I consciously try to do that." Beth did not always see herself as a teacher of teaching. She used to think that teaching was a "natural talent that you were born with." Now she believes that teaching can be taught and learned provided the novice is open-minded and takes the learning seriously. Beth changed her mind after collaborating with a university researcher/teacher educator on a year-long study of her mentoring practice.

Asked what is important for novices to learn, Beth first talks about the need to learn how to ask questions about your own practice and talk openly and analytically about your problems.

> You have to learn to say, "This is something I'm having a little problem with in my classroom. This is what I'm puzzling about." And be able to know how to kind of describe it and then to find ways to figure out what the pieces are of that problem so that we can work on it.

Beth thinks of teaching as a process of inquiry and she believes that a mentor teacher should model an inquiring stance. "You're always asking questions about your practice and learning more, collecting data and writing about it. A good mentor has to model these habits of mind for her student teacher."

Besides learning how to analyze and talk about teaching, Beth believes that novices need to learn to listen to and talk to students, to interpret what they are saying, to figure out what they need to be successful learners. Beth has accumulated a lot of knowledge about the messages implicit in children's talk and actions which she is eager to share with her novice. "I have all this stuff in my head that I've learned about children and I can start telling her those things."

Planning is a central focus of Beth's mentoring and an occasion to articulate her thinking and share her practical knowledge. When we asked Beth what we should videotape to capture important aspects of her mentoring practice, she replied: "I think you should film the actual planning that we do before a lesson . . . because that's where you'll see a lot of Nikki's learning taking place." Nikki offered the following description of her planning with Beth:

> She [Beth] might say: "The kids will love this book . . . Why don't you go home and read it tonight and bring it back and we'll talk about it tomorrow." So then I'll bring it back and say, "Well, I thought the most interesting part of the book was the illustrations." Then she would say: "How can we turn this into a learning activity?" I mean, it's very much bouncing the ball back and forth. She really prepares me first and helps me think, first of all, what activity am I going to do with this book that supports our big purpose? And what should I anticipate? . . . And the next step would be I write a lesson plan and then she looks at my lesson pan. We kind of worked out the system.

Through the PDS structure, Beth had a two hour block of released time each week which she devoted to planning with Nikki.

Co-planning laid the groundwork for coaching and co-teaching. With a shared understanding of what was to be taught, what the difficulties might be, and what directions they wanted to go, Beth and Nikki could share or exchange the leadership role during teaching. Sometimes Beth's mentoring took the form of coaching which she defines as "helping the novice keep going." Beth might give Nikki an encouraging nod. Or Nikki might invite Beth to help out by saying, "Ms. B., what do you think?" or by going over to Beth in the middle of a lesson and softly asking for advice. These forms of coaching were particularly prominent when Nikki was trying to learn how to lead discussions during mathematics lessons, as Beth explains:

> Nikki would take the lead, sort of set the lesson up with the kids, and start asking them questions. When the kids start saying things and writing problems on the board and getting to ideas that we hadn't been able to anticipate and Nikki doesn't know what to do, she'll just look at me, and then I'll say: "Ask if there are any more comments." Or if she doesn't know what to say next, I can give her a hint or a question to ask, and she'll carry on.

Even at the end of the year, when Nikki was doing a lot of independent teaching, she still took time to observe Beth's teaching. For instance, when she encountered situations which she didn't know how to handle, she would watch for a similar situation when Beth was teaching and take note of what she did.

> I really try to listen to how Beth talks to kids and the things she says because I really like the way she talks to kids. So the more I can get her to talk, the more I can learn about what she is saying to get the kids' attention and help them engage in learning.

This was especially true in learning to "orchestrate the discourse" in mathematics lessons. Nikki felt that her lack of subject matter knowledge combined with the challenges of this kind of teaching made learning to guide discussions and help students build mathematical understandings difficult. Beth wondered whether her own doubts and uncertainties contributed to Nikki's.

CONNECTING THE CASES AND THE FRAMEWORK

The concept of educative mentoring emerged from studying mentors like Nancy and Beth. Comparing these and other cases helped us identify some common characteristics of thoughtful mentoring and test the usefulness of sociocultural perspectives on mentored learning to teach. Mentors like Nancy and Beth taught us that mentoring depends on a vision of good teaching and a theory of learning to teach as well as a repertoire of mentoring moves. Like teaching, educative mentoring is a practice which must be learned.

Both Nancy and Beth had a vision of the kind of teaching they were trying to teach. As practitioners of conceptually oriented, learner-centered teaching, they deliberately sought to induct their novices into the intellectual and logistical challenges of this kind of practice. Attending to student thinking, getting inside subject matter, learning to think on your feet lay at the center of their learning-to-teach curriculum.

As teachers of teaching, Nancy and Beth viewed their novices as learners. Through observation and interaction, they continually assessed what their novice needed to learn and how they might best learn that. Through modeling, joint planning, co-teaching and coaching, they guided the novice's learning. Doing the work of teaching with their novice provided opportunities to share practical knowledge and ways of knowing. Nancy and Beth displayed a special kind of bifocal vision which we have come to associate with educative mentoring. Attending to the immediate needs of their novice, they kept their eye on long-term goals. Responding to here-and-now concerns, they tried to create learning opportunities that would move the novice forward. Realizing that learning to teach is an ongoing process, they helped their novice develop tools to continue learning in and from their teaching.

Beth and Nancy did not learn to mentor on their own. Each had extensive experience being mentored. Nancy worked closely with two science educators who helped her transform her science teaching. Beth participated in a study of her mentoring practice and also received on-site help in learning to teach mathematics for understanding. Both teachers used these experiences as sources of insight about what novices need to learn and how to help them learn to teach.

Assigning mentors to work with novices represents a change in the structure of teacher induction and a shift in the locus of power in preservice preparation. It may not, however, contribute to improvements in teaching and teacher education. For that to happen, we need to conceptualize mentoring as an educational intervention aimed at helping novices learn the most promising pedagogies. We must also provide teachers with images of educative mentoring and opportunities to develop and articulate their practice as mentors. Hopefully the framework and cases presented here can assist in that task.

REFERENCES

Alleman, E., 'Measuring mentoring—frequency quality impact'. In: W.A. Gray and M.M. Gray (Eds.). *Mentoring: Aid to excellence in career development, business and the professions* (pp. 44–51). The Xerox Reproduction Centre, British Columbia 1986.

Anderson, E.M. & Shannon, A.L., 'Toward a conceptualization of mentoring.' In: *Journal of Teacher Education*, 39(1), 1988; pp. 38–42.

Bey. T.M. & Holmes, C.T., *Mentoring: Developing successful new teachers*. VA: Association of Teachers Educators. Reston 1990.

Brown, J.S., Collins, A. & Duguid, P., 'Situated cognition and the culture of learning'. In: *Educational Researcher*, 18(1), 1989; pp. 32–42.

Cochran-Smith, M., 'Mentor and mentoring: Did Homer have it right?' In: J. Smyth (Ed.). *Critical discourses on teacher development*. Yorkhouse, Australia 1995; pp. 175–195.

Collins, A., Brown, J.S., & Newman, 'Cognitive apprenticeship: Teaching the craft of reading, writing and mathematics'. In: L.B. Resnick (Ed.). *Knowing, learning and instruction: Essays in honor of Robert Glaser*, Erlbaum, Hillsdale, NJ, pp. 453–494.

Dembele, M., *Mentors and mentoring: Frames for action, ways of acting, and consequences for novice teachers' learning* (Unpublished doctoral dissertation). MI: Michigan State University, East Lansing 1995.

Feiman-Nemser, S. & Buchmann, M., 'Pitfalls of experience in teacher preparation'. In: *Teachers College Record*, 87(1), 1995; pp. 53–65.

Feiman-Nemser, S., *Helping novices learn to teach: Lessons from an experienced support teacher* (Report 91-6). Michigan State University, National Center for Research on Teacher Learning, East Lansing 1992.

Feiman-Nemser, S. & Parker, M., 'Mentoring in context: A comparison of two U.S. programs for beginning teachers'. In: *International Journal of Educational research*, 19(8), 1993; pp. 699–718.

Feiman-Nemser, S., Parker, M., & Zeichner, Z., 'Are mentor teachers teacher educators?' In: D. McIntyre, H. Hagger, & M. Wilkin (Eds.). *Mentoring: Perspectives on school-based teacher education*. Kegan Paul, London 1992; pp. 147–165.

Feiman-Nemser, S., & Remillard, J., 'Perspectives on learning to teach'. In: F. Murray (Ed.) *The Teacher Educator's Handbook: Building a Knowledge Base for the Preparation of Teachers*. Jossey Bass, San Francisco 1996; pp. 63–91.

Gallimore, R., Tharp, R.G. & John-Steiner, V. (n.d.), *Developmental and socio-historical foundations of mentoring*. Manuscript.

Galvez-Hjornevik, C., 'Mentoring among teachers: A review of the literature'. In: *Journal of Teacher Education*, 6(2), 1986; pp. 207–262.

Gehrke, N.J. & Kay, R.S., 'The socialization of beginning teachers through mentor-protege relationships'. In: *Journal of Teacher Education*, 35(3), 1984; pp. 21–24.

Gold, Y., 'Beginning teacher support: attrition, mentoring and induction'. In: J. Sikula (Ed.), *Handbook of Research on Teacher Education*. MacMillan, New York 1996; pp. 548–594.

Gray, W.A. & Gray, M.M., 'Synthesis of research on mentoring beginning teachers'. In: *Educational leadership*, 43(3), 1985; pp. 37–43.

Healy, C.C. & Welchert, A.J., 'Mentoring relations: A definition to advance research and practice'. In: *Educational Researcher*, 19(9), 1990; pp. 17–21.

The Holmes Group, *Tomorrow's teachers: A report of the Holmes Group*. MI: Author, East Lansing 1990.

Huling-Austin, L., 'Research on learning to teach: Implications for teacher induction and mentoring programs.' In: *Journal of Teacher Education*, 43(3), 1992; pp. 173–180.

Lave, J. & Wegner, I., *Situated learning: Legitimate peripheral participation.* University Press, Cambridge 1991.

Levinson, D.J., *The seasons of a man's life.* Ballentine, New York 1978.

Little, J.W., 'The mentoring phenomenon and the social organization of teaching'. In: C.B. Courtney (Ed.), *Review of research in education.* Vol. 16. American Educational Research Association, Washington, DC 1990, pp. 297–351.

Lortie, D., *Schoolteacher: A sociological study.* University of Chicago Press, Chicago 1975.

Merriam. S., 'Mentors and proteges: A critical review of the literature.' In: *Adult Education Quarterly,* 33(3), 1983; pp. 161–173.

Resnick, L., 'Shared cognition: Thinking as a social practice'. In: L.B. Resnick, J.H. Levine & S.D. Teasley (Eds.), *Perspectives on socially shared cognition.* American Psychological Association. Washington DC, 1991; pp. 1–12.

Schwille, S. & Wolf, N., *The professional practice of mentoring.* National Center for Research on Teacher Learning, East Lansing, MI, 1997.

Shulman, J. & Colbert, J.A., *The intern teacher casebook: Cases and commentaries.* Far West Laboratory for Educational Research and Development, San Francisco 1988.

Speizer, J.J., 'Role models, mentors, and sponsors: The elusive concepts'. In: *Signs: Journal of Women in Culture and Society,* 6(4), 1981; pp. 692–712.

CHAPTER 9

Helping Novices Learn to Teach
Lessons from an Exemplary Support Teacher

> I want to be a cothinker with them so that I can help them to see new
> perspectives, new ways to solve the problems they have.
> —*Pete Frazer during an interview (1988)*

In this eloquent statement, Pete Frazer, a 30-year veteran teacher, summed up the essence of his work with beginning teachers.[1] Released from classroom teaching for 2 years, Frazer worked full-time as a support teacher in an induction/internship program jointly sponsored by a university and a local school district. Assigned to help 14 beginning elementary teachers, he spent most of his time visiting their classrooms and talking with them about their teaching.

I first met Pete Frazer in 1986 while conducting a study of an induction/internship program in which he was working. The research was part of the Teacher Education and Learning to Teach project, sponsored by the National Center for Research on Teacher Education at Michigan State University and carried out between 1985 and 1990. The project combined case studies of 11 teacher education programs (preservice, induction, in-service, and alternate route) with longitudinal studies of teachers' learning as they participated in the programs and moved into teaching (National Center for Research on Teacher Education, 1988). I decided to write about Pete Frazer's philosophy and approach to working with new teachers because he was so articulate about his practice and because he offers a vivid example of what I call "educative" mentoring (Feiman-Nemser, 1998).

The idea of educative mentoring builds on Dewey's (1938) concept of educative experiences, which are experiences that promote rather than retard future growth and lead to richer subsequent experiences. According to Dewey, the educator is responsible for arranging the physical and social conditions so that learners have growth-producing experiences.

> Every experience is a moving force. Its value can be judged only on the ground of what it moves toward and into. . . . It is the business of the educator to see in what direction an experience is heading . . . so as to judge and direct it. (p. 39)

In this article, I use the term *educative mentoring* to distinguish Frazer's approach to mentoring from more conventional approaches that emphasize situational adjustment, technical advice, and emotional support (Little, 1990).[2]

Educative mentoring rests on an explicit vision of good teaching and an understanding of teacher learning. Mentors who share this orientation attend to beginning teachers' present concerns, questions, and purposes without losing sight of long-term goals for teacher development. They interact with novices in ways that foster an inquiring stance. They cultivate skills and habits that enable novices to learn in and from their practice. They use their knowledge and expertise to assess the direction novices are heading and to create opportunities and conditions that support meaningful teacher learning in the service of student learning.

A close study of a support teacher who exemplifies this orientation is especially timely. There is growing interest in the problem of teacher induction, and the idea of assigning experienced teachers to work with beginning teachers has received widespread support. Currently, 28 states require districts to offer induction programs. Eight states plan to implement a program in the next few years, and five more expect to expand their current programs (Sweeney & DeBolt, 2000). Most urban districts provide some kind of support to beginning teachers, usually in the form of mentoring (Fideler & Haselkorn, 1999). These induction initiatives are part of a larger effort to improve the quality of teaching and learning in schools by focusing on the recruitment, preparation, induction, and renewal of teachers (National Commission on Teaching and America's Future, 1996).

Providing on-site support and guidance is especially critical during the beginning years of teaching. New teachers really have two jobs to do—they have to teach, and they have to learn to teach (Wildman, Niles, Magliaro, & McLaughlin, 1989). No matter what kind of preparation a teacher receives, some aspects of teaching can be learned only on the job. No college course can teach a new teacher how to blend knowledge of particular students and knowledge of particular content in decisions about what to do in specific situations.

Experienced teachers can help novices have a successful first year of teaching. They can also influence what novices learn from the experience. Little (1990) distinguishes between emotional support that makes novices feel comfortable and professional support that fosters a principled understanding of teaching. She argues that the promise of mentoring lies not in easing novices' entry into teaching but in helping them confront difficult problems of practice and use their teaching as a site for learning. As a result, participating in a serious mentoring relationship may actually make the first years of teaching more strenuous in the short run while promoting greater rewards for teachers and students in the long run.

Assigning mentors to work with beginning teachers creates new incentives and career opportunities for experienced teachers. It also challenges past assumptions about where knowledge for teaching comes from and how it can be learned. Implicit in the title "mentor" is "the presumption of wisdom . . . accumulated knowledge that can serve as the basis of sensitive observation, astute commentary, sound advice" (Little, 1990, p. 316). Yet, we know relatively little about what thoughtful mentors try to teach novices, how they make their knowledge accessible, and how they think about their mentoring in context. Some studies of thoughtful mentors at work have been conducted (see Dembele, 1995; Nevins, 1993), but more are needed if we are going to understand the insides of this important professional practice and its influence on novices and their teaching. This article contributes to that agenda by describing how one thoughtful support teacher defines and enacts his mentoring role and also how he learned to function so effectively in that capacity.

THE SUBJECT, THE DATA, AND THE ANALYSIS

Considered a legend in his district, Pete Frazer had been teaching elementary school for more than 30 years when I met him. He earned a doctorate in 1975 from the University of New Mexico where he worked with Marie Hughes, a prominent early childhood educator. A frequent instructor at the university and presenter at in-service workshops, Pete Frazer is a strong advocate of anecdotal records as a way for teachers to study children and keep track of their thinking and learning. When Frazer applied for the job of support teacher, the program director wondered whether others would be intimidated by his reputation: "It was obvious that he could work with children. It was obvious that he could work with adults. And it was obvious that he was open to learning. But was he so proficient that he would be threatening?" So she asked him, and his response allayed her concerns. "He was so modest and so willing to look at what other people could teach him. It was very obvious when I spoke to him."

This article is based on 10 hours of interview data and an equal amount of observational data gathered in four visits spread over a period of 2 years. Besides regular conversations with Frazer about the induction program, his participation in it, and the progress of his interns, we conducted two formal interviews designed to uncover Frazer's reasons for becoming a support teacher, his views of his role, how he learned it, and his thoughts about the impact of the work on his own teaching. In addition, we shadowed Frazer on three separate occasions, observing his interactions with eight beginning teachers/interns both in and out of the classroom and interviewing him about these interactions. We took notes about the teaching we observed, taped Frazer's conversations with his "clients," and interviewed him about what we had seen and heard. By watching Frazer in action and talking to him about his practice, we sought a better understanding of how he thought about helping beginning teachers learn to teach.

In analyzing the observational and interview data with regard to Pete Frazer, I was struck by the abundance of his strategic knowledge about teaching and mentoring and by the eloquence and precision with which he talked about his actions. Scattered throughout the interview transcripts were numerous instances when Frazer labeled a specific principle or strategy or offered a clear rationale for a particular intervention. As I thought about these examples in conjunction with the freestanding interviews, I began to see powerful connections between the way Frazer defined his role and the way he enacted it. Here was a fresh set of terms for describing particular mentoring moves along with a conception of role and purpose to give them unity.

Much of the language of beginning teacher support and assistance comes from the literature on clinical supervision (e.g., Cogan, 1973; Glickman, 1985; Goldhammer, 1969) and coaching (e.g., Joyce & Showers, 1985). Although these sources provide valuable models, perspectives, and strategies, they are often represented as technologies to apply or patterns of action to follow rather than as a set of ideas from which a variety of actions could be generated. Focused on reflective conversation and targeted feedback, they do not consider how mentor teachers can use their own practice as a site for novices' learning.

By fusing of values, theory, and action, Pete Frazer's formulations differ from the procedural, morally neutral vocabulary of scripting, pattern analysis, conferencing, coaching, and feedback. Frazer's "moves" add nuance to a complex practice, and his commentaries illuminate the kind of reasoning and improvisation called for in this form of professional development. Learning how one thoughtful mentor weaves showing and telling, listening and asking together in support of beginning teacher development enlarges our understanding and our images of mentoring as an educational practice.

This wisdom of practice study highlights the commitments, stance, and strategic knowledge of one thoughtful support teacher. I begin with Frazer's thoughts about teaching and learning to teach and his ideas about the role of the support teacher. Next, I show how Frazer enacts his role by describing eight different moves that he identified and that we observed or heard him talk about. Third, I use one extended example to show how several moves come together in a dynamic whole. Finally, I briefly discuss how Frazer learned to work with beginning teachers and consider what we can learn from his example. Throughout the text, I make connections between Frazer's skillful mentoring and key issues in the literature on beginning teacher support.

DEFINING THE SUPPORT TEACHER'S ROLE

Pete Frazer has very clear ideas about what it means to be a support teacher. His role definition embraces a central tension between encouraging personal expression and maintaining professional accountability, between supporting the unique qualities of an individual teacher's style and promoting a shared understanding of good practice. Frazer wanted to cultivate the particular strengths of his new teachers. At the same time, he felt responsible for seeing that the novices' teaching was responsive to the community, informed by developmental theories, and reflective of the best thinking about learner-centered teaching. These obligations have their parallel in Frazer's views of teaching.

Talking about what it means to be a support teacher, Frazer identified two elements: (a) helping novices find ways to express who they are in their work, and (b) helping novices develop a practice that is responsive to the community and reflects what we know about children and learning. "Being a support teacher," he said, "means helping people grow and become good teachers. It's a combination of basing teaching techniques on what we know about children and learning and what we are like as people, our personalities, interests, inclinations."

This role definition parallels Frazer's ideas about good teaching:

> Part of what I would call good teaching is just idiosyncratic to me and to my readings and my studies and my learning. Part of what I would call good teaching is more generalizable . . . and would be recognized by all.

By maintaining a double vision, Frazer tried to avoid two dangers in working with novices: "imposing his own style" and "sounding too laissez-faire." Committed to helping novices find their own way of doing things rather than copy his, he did not want to give the impression that anything goes. As he pointed out,

> We do know some things about teaching and learning. We know some things about people and schools and communities. Hopefully the things that I know about, I can help them use, and not just be there and say "Gosh, whatever you're becoming is wonderful."

Pete Frazer captured the essence of what being a support teacher means to him with the word *cothinker*.

> I want to be a cothinker with them so that I can help them to see new perspectives, new ways to solve the problems they have. . . . And always, as they're doing the thinking, I bring to that as a listener my whole worldview, my whole perspective about the nature of human beings and education. So when I make suggestions, of course they have some relationship to what I think is good schooling . . . but I try to keep an awareness that Frank or Ellen or Diane—each one of them is in the process of developing their own set of things. So I certainly don't want to impose my whole view on them. . . . *I just want to stand beside them and work and let them take from me what fits into the solution of the problem they're working on now* [italics added].

Adopting the stance of cothinker rather than expert, Frazer tried to balance his desire to share what he knows about good teaching with his concern with helping novices figure out what works for them as they construct their own professional practice and identity. As an "educational companion" to his novices, he offered personal support and professional perspectives tailored to individual needs and purposes.

ENACTING THE ROLE

The moves and strategies Frazer used to enact his role and stance embody these principles and values. Some reflect his respect for novices as individuals in the process of developing. Others express his commitment to base emerging practices on self-study and relevant knowledge. Most striking is the strong parallel between the way Pete Frazer treated beginning teachers and the way he hoped they would treat their students.

Finding Openings

A big issue for support providers and others who work with beginning teachers is deciding what to talk about so that the conversation will be productive. The literature on clinical supervision recommends that the supervisor and teacher choose a common focus during the pre-observation conference. The literature on advising advocates working from the teacher's self-defined concerns (see, e.g., Devaney, 1978). Neither source pays sufficient attention to the process of interpreting teachers' concerns, clarifying their self-identified problems, or attending to the challenges of problem framing as well as problem solving. Recent literature on inquiry communities, networks, and cooperating teachers and student teachers as collaborative teacher researchers (e.g., Lieberman & Grolnick, 1999; Lytle & Cochran-Smith, 1992) emphasizes problem posing, question asking, developing interpretations, and researching together; however, mentor training programs rarely tap these sources.

Frazer conceptualized the process of figuring out what to talk about in dynamic terms. He talked about finding "openings," fruitful topics that are salient to the novice and that lead to a consideration of basic issues that all teachers need to think about. The word *productive* characterizes the kinds of topics he looked for—not just anything the novice brings up, but something that would open up a "productive line of thinking."

The idea of "finding openings" came out in an interview following a visit to the classroom of Ellen, a beginning teacher. When I asked Frazer how the conference with Ellen went compared with what he had expected, he explained that they ended up discussing something quite different from what he had anticipated.

> Well, the only thing I had on my potential agenda going in was to do some follow-up on the Chinese New Year because the last time I had talked to her, she was real enthused about that. . . . As it turned out, the *opening* came in the direction of Ruben. And the key thing, I decided, was seeing if there was going to be *something productive* when I asked about the stu-

dent of the week and how well he does on reading the school newsletter. That just *opened the door* to all this talk about possible retention next year. It was so much *rich content* there that it took all but 5 minutes of our half hour. (italics added)

Ellen had been worrying about whether Ruben would be ready to go on to second grade by the end of the year. The school district required teachers to notify parents early in the year about the possibility of retention so that they would not be surprised later on by such a recommendation. When Frazer noticed that Ruben was student of the week and asked how he was doing, Ellen poured out her concerns about what to do. This led to an extended discussion about Ruben's accomplishments to date, his likely progress by June, the pros and cons of holding him back or sending him on to second grade, and the problems caused by rigid grade-level expectations. Frazer suggested that Ellen find out more about the philosophies of the second-grade teachers concerning reading so that she would be in a position to recommend an appropriate placement. Ellen had never considered taking such a proactive stance. By exploring Ruben's situation in depth, Frazer not only responded to Ellen's immediate concern but also raised broader issues about assessment, individual differences, and the teacher's responsibility to be an advocate for his or her students.

Because Frazer saw his novices once a week, he usually had some idea of what they were working on and some expectations about what they would talk about. At the same time, the unpredictability of classroom life meant that he had to be prepared to deal with issues as they arose. Because Frazer wanted to use his time in productive ways, he did not take a catch-as-catch-can approach, talking about whatever came up. For him, the challenge lay in finding something to discuss that was salient to the teacher but that would also move the teacher's practice in fruitful directions.

Pinpointing Problems

A related strategy involved what Frazer called "pinpointing problems." In *How We Think*, Dewey (1933) reminds us that problems are not ready-made, that they must be constructed out of a problematic situation. More recently, Donald Schon (1983) elaborated on the nature of problem finding and framing in the context of professional work.

When we set the problem, we select what we will treat as the "things" of the situation, we set the boundaries of our attention to it, and we impose on it a coherence which allows us to say what is wrong and in what directions the situation needs to be changed. (p. 40)

The notion of problems as constructed rather than given seems absent from the literature on beginning teacher concerns. For example, one frequently cited review (Veenman, 1989) identifies discipline and management as the most pressing problems of beginning teachers. Yet problems so classified may have more to do with curriculum and instruction. A little probing reveals that such problems frequently arise because the teacher is unclear about his or her purposes, has chosen an inappropriate task, has not given students adequate directions, or does not understand the content.

Frazer recognized that problems in teaching must be identified or, as he put it, pinpointed. When Diane told him that she was not feeling very good about reading, he suggested that they talk about it next time. Later, he explained his rationale to me:

> I want to help her clarify, what does she mean by, "Reading isn't going well"? I mean, let's sort out the elements because it's such a big statement— "Reading isn't going well." I'd like her to be able to get at this . . . to pinpoint the problem . . . to come up with some specifics about what about it isn't as good as it could be. . . . I'd like to think with her, to help her pinpoint more exactly what she means by "Reading is not going well." And that means looking for strengths as well as things she wants to change.

By working to pinpoint problems, beginning teachers practice talking about teaching in precise, analytic ways. This is a critical tool in joint problem solving and continuous improvement. Unless teachers can frame problems and communicate them clearly to others, they will not be able to get assistance.

Probing Novices' Thinking

To be a cothinker who engages in "productive consultations," Pete Frazer had to know what beginning teachers were thinking about an issue. Sometimes he issued beginning teachers an "invitation" to share what was on their minds by asking open-ended questions. Often, he asked probing questions to learn what novices meant by the things they said and to help them clarify their ideas. He did not assume that he automatically understood.

> I want to get at what they're thinking about an issue. . . . I don't want to just assume that I know from a few words. . . . So I keep coming back

with, What do you think? What's going on? I guess that's a style or technique I use to make sure I'm getting enough input from them.

When Ellen commented that the children were reading the school newspaper more quickly, Frazer asked, "Why do you think the work with the newsletter is going faster?" Later, he offered the following rationale for his question:

I was trying to get at what her picture is about why progress is occurring in reading. . . . What are her thoughts about why it is getting better? We don't just need to say, "They're better at this, now that's nice." A more productive line of thinking is, "Why did it get better? What has led to that?"

Frazer offered a similar rationale for his approach to Diane when she told him that "reading isn't going very well." Pete said he hoped she would clarify her reasons for using the basal as they talked it through:

I'm not sure how much she's thought of all the reasons, and I'm curious to know what her sequence is, why she's doing this, where do you go next, how do you help kids along the road to improvement? I'll think with her on that and we'll both learn from it.

Frazer sought knowledge about how his beginning teachers were thinking about their students and their work. By encouraging teachers to explicate their practice, he fostered an analytic stance and precision that is unusual in discourse among teachers (Ball & Cohen, 1999). Frazer wanted new teachers to have good reasons for the things they do and be able to explain themselves to others, including principals and parents. He also believed that teachers should inquire into their practice not only when they experience problems but also when things are going well so that they can develop grounded theories about teaching and learning.

Noticing Signs of Growth

As I observed Pete Frazer working with different beginning teachers, I noticed that he regularly complimented them on specific aspects of their teaching. He complimented Ellen on how nicely the children lined up and walked themselves down the hall, saying, "That's a testimony to the trust and respect that you give to them." He complimented Fran on the way she fostered thinking:

I don't think I've ever been in a class where so much thinking is going on. . . . You continually turn it back to them with an attitude that says, "Think about it because you'll probably be able to figure it out."

He complimented Diane on the way she handled the administrative intern: "You really showed you were a strong teacher."

When we questioned Frazer about this practice, he offered a general rationale based on the beginning teacher's psychological or emotional needs:

> In the 1st year, you have doubts, you need reassurance, you're so overwhelmed by all the things you think you're not doing. "I'm not teaching enough science. I'm not teaching social studies in the right way." You need to know all the ways that you're effectively working. I don't think you can ever get too much of that.

In reassuring his clients, Frazer tried to offer specific feedback about individual accomplishments rather than general praise for doing a good job. Each instance of praise that we observed reflected an assessment of the teacher's unique strengths and needs. Later, Frazer explained that he tries to give compliments "that are really true and aren't just phony pats on the back." For example, in response to our query about Ellen, he said:

> I want her to see, sometimes she says things to me that make me wonder if she knows how good she is. I think she needs to hear in many ways what an excellent job she is doing. I do that a lot with her because she says things like, "I don't know if I've been doing this right. What do you think?" I don't think it's fishing for compliments. I think she genuinely needs to hear a lot of times and in a lot of ways what a great job she's doing in that room.

He complimented Fran on how she fosters thinking because he wanted her to see how her teaching reflects her own intellectual style. "You're such a thinker. . . . The children in your room, their thinking is starting to parallel yours in so many wonderful ways."

Frazer called this "noticing signs of growth." Besides reinforcing his beliefs about good teaching and responding to novices' needs for reassurance, this practice fit with his view of learning to teach as a process of development. When he noticed Fran dealing with a student in a more direct way, for example, Frazer repeated what she said and related that to her own development.

> I can see you're now more directive. Jose was not doing what he was supposed to and you said, "I'm going to need to interrupt you. You really have a responsibility over there that isn't finished. Go get that done and then come back." *That was more direct and less beating around the bush than before* [italics added].

In the same vein, he reminded Diane that earlier in the year, she would not have been able to explain her position on reading to the administrative intern and principal. This kind of concrete and specific feedback helps novices visualize their evolving style, clarify what they need to work on, and concretize their own vision of good teaching.

Focusing on the Kids

In working with new teachers, Frazer kept his eye on students. He regarded information about students' thinking and sense making as invaluable feedback to the teacher and a rich source of ideas for curriculum development. Focusing on the kids also took some pressure off the beginning teacher by providing a "neutral ground" for conversation. For Frazer, the challenge was to "ask the question in a way that doesn't make the teacher think he's neglected Eric or that he doesn't know what he's doing."

When Frazer visited classrooms, he often got involved with the students, taking on the role of coteacher. This allowed him to gather information about pupils' learning, which he could share with the teacher. If Frazer visited Bonnie's room when the children were writing, he would pull up a chair, sit down, and start helping them with their editing. If he noticed something special about a pupil's writing, he might call it to Bonnie's attention on the spot by going over and telling her, "Jenny is doing this and this with her writing and that seems to be such an improvement." Alternatively, he might write a note about something a child did or said and give it to the teacher. The day Ellen introduced a reading activity using sentence strips, Frazer overheard one of her students say that the strips of paper reminded him of Chinese fortune cookies. Frazer made a note about that and handed it to the teacher. Afterward, he explained his purpose to me:

> I hope it helps her see. One of the ways you get feedback about your own work is from little indices like that during the day. For me, that kind of anecdotal information is so much more valuable for studying your own work than the test scores of children on standardized tests.

In focusing beginning teachers' attention on student thinking, Frazer departed from the conventional wisdom with regard to beginning teacher concerns. In her influential work on this subject, Frances Fuller (1969) argues that the preoccupations of beginning teachers follow a "developmental" pattern that starts with concerns about self, moves on to concerns about teaching, and finally arrives at concerns about pupils. Criticizing teacher educators for "teaching against the tide," Fuller advocates a better fit between the curriculum of teacher education and the concerns of beginning teachers.

Fuller's developmental theory of teacher concerns may have face validity, but it confounds description with prescription.[3] Even if beginning teachers are preoccupied with their own performance, it does not follow that mentor teachers should avoid focusing their attention on student learning. As Dewey (1938) explains in *Experience and Education*, there is no point in being more mature if the educator, instead of using his or her greater insight to organize the conditions of experience, throws away his or her insight. Pete Frazer models how a support teacher can help beginning teachers attend to pupils' thinking and sense making even when they are concerned about their own adequacy and teaching performance.

Reinforcing an Understanding of Theory

Increased reliance on experienced teachers to mentor beginning teachers means greater access to teachers' practical wisdom. When mentor teachers have relevant theoretical knowledge they can help beginning teachers make meaningful connections between theory and practice. Pete Frazer deliberately looked for such opportunities.

After listening to Ellen talk about reading, Frazer brought up Frank Smith's (1985) research about "how kids bring their own meaning to a page." Later, he explained his rationale to me:

> She knows that theory, but I think we can never know it enough. . . . It needs to be continually brought up because the new paradigms for teaching reading and writing and language are so completely different from the old ones that I think it's a career-long process to keep looking at that.

By reinforcing theoretical ideas in context, Frazer helped novices develop usable knowledge and principled understandings. He believed that teachers need a deep understanding of how children learn, enriched by theoretical knowledge and informed by firsthand experience. This was part of his induction curriculum for beginning teachers.

Giving Living Examples of One Person's Ways of Teaching

Teacher educators have long debated the merits of apprenticeship-type learning opportunities. Ever since Dewey (1904/1965) distinguished the "laboratory" view of practical work with its emphasis on intellectual methods from the "apprenticeship" view with its focus on performance, the apprenticeship has gotten bad press in teacher education circles. Critics argue that it encourages imitation rather than understanding.

While the apprenticeship model does encourage novices to learn the practices of the master, it does not preclude a consideration of underlying principles or the development of conceptual understanding (Ball, 1987; Schon, 1987). Collins, Brown, and Newman (1989) have coined the term "cognitive apprenticeship" to describe experiential learning situations in which teachers think aloud so that learners can not only observe their actions but also see how their teachers think about particular tasks or problems.

The idea of a cognitive apprenticeship fits the intent behind Frazer's use of demonstration teaching, which he called "giving living examples of one person's ways of teaching." Frazer hoped that novices would not only pick up particular teaching ideas but begin to clarify general characteristics of good teaching. This required them to separate out those qualities unique to Frazer's personality and style from more general features of good practice.

When Diane expressed concern about how to motivate her low reading group and what to do with them for a whole hour, Frazer volunteered to teach a reading lesson. He introduced and read a story from the basal reader about a mouse. Then he read aloud from *Stuart Little* by E. B. White (1945), a classic children's book about a distinguished mouse born into a human family. During the lesson, he stopped to explain to Diane what he was doing and why. Here is how he described the demonstration lesson to me:

> I got myself all jazzed up about mice and I said, "The first thing you need to do is get them so they want to know more about mice." So we did this activity to get them interested in mice and mice words. . . . I would stop as I was teaching and say, "This is why I'm doing this."

Frazer hoped that Diane would see "some specific methods for getting across a reading lesson." In particular, he wanted to show her how to integrate reading aloud good children's literature with lessons from the basal reader. At the same time, he hoped that she could look beyond the parts that were uniquely Frazer such as the way he imitated Donald Duck and pull out some general features of good teaching—"He responded positively to children. He really listened to children. He extended what they said."

Demonstrations can help beginning teachers visualize new practices and see how teachers enact particular values and principles. At the same time, beginning teachers may not see what experienced teachers notice or intend because their cognitive maps are less elaborated. To ensure that demonstrations are educative tools in teacher development, mentors need to point out what they regard as central and find out how novices interpret what they see. Frazer understood that giving living examples of another person's teaching could be an effective strategy, but he did not leave to chance what the beginning teachers made of the experience.

Modeling Wondering About Teaching

Educators generally associate modeling with actions. Frazer also modeled "wondering about teaching," which he saw as central to the improvement of teaching.

> It seems that wondering about our work and wondering about kids is a major element in being able to improve our teaching. . . . Part of the excitement of teaching and also the effectiveness depends on a sense of wondering.

The idea of modeling wondering about teaching came up in an interview with Frazer about working with Frank on how to teach multiplication to third graders. The extended example, which follows, illustrates how Frazer modeled wondering about teaching. It also shows how the other moves we have examined came together in practice. In this episode, we see Frazer probing Frank's thinking, focusing on students' sense making, bringing in research, giving a living example of his teaching, and modeling wondering about teaching.

Frank had asked Frazer to work with a small group of third graders who were having trouble with multiplication. Frank had been doing some skill and drill work with them, but he was not sure the students were getting it. On the way to school, Frazer described his purpose to me:

> I don't have a very specific goal except that both of us will think more about what goes on with kids. . . . I think we'll both be trying to clarify what are we trying to get kids to understand when they multiply and what can eight-year-olds [understand], what kind of sense of it can they make and what kind of manipulatives can we use to help make sense of that.

Frazer met Frank in his classroom at 8:00, 30 minutes before the children showed up. He brought a book about how children learn mathematics and a bag of small game pieces and rubber bands to use in helping students get the idea of separating things into sets. In his usual fashion, Frazer let Frank take the lead, listening patiently while Frank described his confusion with regard to the numbers in a multiplication problem—"Which is the number of sets and which is the number of items in a set?"

After a while, Frazer gently shifted the conversation from Frank's confusion to their plans for the morning. "Would Frank like to see what he was planning to do with the kids?" Frank listened eagerly as Frazer described how he would use the cubes and rubber bands to help students represent the times tables. He also accepted the extra materials Frazer had brought, putting aside the worksheet he had prepared for them. When the children arrived, Frazer worked with one small group while Frank worked with another. Then Frazer left for another appointment.

In the interview following the visit, Frazer (PF) explained to the researcher (R) that he wanted to show Frank the strategy of using game pieces and rubber bands, even though he did not necessarily intend for him to "do it that way." He also planned to use data gathered from working with the children to talk with Frank about how children make sense of mathematics. In the course of elaborating on this idea, he introduced the idea of modeling how he wonders about teaching:

R: What type of feedback will you give Frank?
PF: It depends on what he brings up. One of the things we can always keep thinking about . . . in a class of 24 kids . . . how much variety there is in their understanding of mathematics and how very individual it is. . . . I would like to highlight that with examples from his group and my group . . . . I want to model how important I think it is to . . . maintain a balance between the information you are dealing with and the individual realities of the kids.
R: When you say "model," what do you mean?
PF: Thinking about it, I guess. Say, for example, look at Luis. I wonder if he was thinking this or I wonder what he was thinking, but I don't have a theory. *It seems important to give him examples of how I wonder about the work, as a teacher, how questions come up, how I say, "I wonder what is going on here. It could be this, it could be this. What are the factors contributing to this?" So that's what I mean by modeling* [italics added].

In this example, we see Frazer working on multiple agendas. To help clear up Frank's subject matter confusion and add to his pedagogical content knowledge, Frazer brought a book and concrete materials to represent the operation of multiplication. He also came prepared to work with students and gather data about how they thought about mathematics. This would provide the basis for a conversation with Frank about what different children understood, what they found confusing, and what the teachers might do to clear up confusions and strengthen understanding. In all this, Frazer would take the stance of co-teacher and co-thinker, using his own practice as a site for learning about student thinking and for helping Frank learn about teaching mathematics for understanding.

LEARNING TO BE A SUPPORT TEACHER

How did Pete Frazer learn to work with beginning teachers in this way? Where did he develop his ideas about the support teacher's role? Without diminishing the contribution of Pete Frazer's educational background, teaching experience, and enormous personal resources, it is also true that he worked in an induction program that provided support teachers with the same kind of backing and guidance offered to novice teachers. Pete Frazer learned the role of support teacher and developed his practice in the context of a professional learning community.

Frazer was one of eight support teachers working for 2 years (1986 through 1988) in the Graduate Intern/Teacher Induction Program, a joint venture of the University of New Mexico and the Albuquerque Public Schools. Through an ingenious financial arrangement that involved no additional cost to the district, the program released 15 experienced teachers from classroom duties to work full-time with preservice and beginning teachers for 2 years. It did this by placing 28 interns in classrooms where they carried out all the responsibilities of a 1st-year teacher while earning half a beginning teacher's salary. Interns also worked on a master's degree at the university. The money saved allowed the district to continue paying the experienced teachers their full salaries.

Support teachers began learning about their role in a weeklong orientation before the start of the school year and continued studying their work in weekly, 3-hour staff seminars throughout the year. Conducted by the program director, a national expert on teacher induction, the staff seminars provided a regular opportunity for ongoing conversation about how to help new teachers. During the course of my research, I attended the orientation and observed six staff seminars over the course of 2 years. I also interviewed the program director about her goals and the support teachers about the contribution of the seminar to their work with interns and beginning teachers.

Presenting individual cases was a regular activity in staff seminars. Support teachers raised specific questions or described particular situations, which they needed help addressing. Besides talking about individual clients and how to help them, the support teachers also read and discussed various articles about teaching and learning to teach selected by the program director. Combining discussions of specific problems with more theoretical discussions and readings helped support teachers articulate their knowledge, clarify their beliefs, develop a shared language, and construct an understanding of their new role.

From his fellow support teachers, Pete Frazer learned a lot about how to work with beginning teachers. He also learned about the value of collaboration. Like most teachers, he had had few opportunities to learn with and from colleagues. "It means a lot to me," he explained. "As a teacher, I've gotten along well with my colleagues . . . but mostly I've done my own work and didn't work on a team." In an interview, Frazer described what he found most valuable about the staff seminar:

> The biggest part has been the review of individual cases, individual things that are actually going on with one of my team members. I've got this and this going on with a teacher and principal at my school. Then we all think together with that person. OK, what's going on, in what ways can we put our heads together to help you think of ways you can work with them? That has been the most continuously helpful thing for me.

Learning to Be More Direct

From colleagues and from firsthand experience, Frazer learned to be more direct about getting into people's classrooms. Compared with the other support teachers during his 1st year, Frazer said he was "the most cautious." By listening to colleagues talk about "ways to work their way into thinking with their clients about problems, ways to set mini-agendas or ways to get into conversations that have depth and potential" and by experimenting with different strategies, Frazer gradually learned to be more direct.

When we returned in the 2nd year of the study to observe Frazer and talk to him about his work, he reflected on how he had grown as a support teacher: "Last year, I waited more for the clients to bring things up. This year, I bring them up more myself. . . . I'm better at my job . . . and it feels good." Then he described in great detail how he had been trying to work his way into the classroom of a very resistant beginning teacher. He started out indirectly but quickly surmised that that would not work. So he brought in a 10-sided die and showed the teacher some quick activities to do, hoping "that would make her know that I have practical ideas." But she said, "Thank you very much." And no invitation followed. Finally, he said directly,

> You know, part of my job is to come in the room and help people. I work in the rooms of all my clients, and I would like to come in and work in your room, but I need to know when and if you would like me.

She said she would let him know. "I've done everything I can short of walking in there and sitting down. She doesn't seem to have anything to hide." He had gone in at lunch time to do miniworkshops on math and science for this beginner and the teacher next door. "I've given every hint I can in every direct way, and no way, she's not going to let me in her room." Although this seemed to be an extreme case, it was clear that Frazer would not have taken such actions the previous year.

Learning New Approaches to Writing

Not only did Frazer develop his practice as a support teacher; he also broadened his ideas about teaching children, particularly in the area of writing. Attending a district-sponsored workshop on the writing process with his interns and watching several of them start a writers' workshop in their classroom led Frazer to rethink his approach to the teaching of writing. In the past, Frazer had had his students write stories about artificial topics (e.g., "A Martian landed in your community. What did the community do about it?"). During his tenure as a support teacher, he came to see the significance of grounding students' writing in their own life experiences. "You're teaching them to look at the world and write about things that they've experienced, that they've been through, and turning those into essays or stories." The intense involvement of the students and the quality of their writing persuaded Frazer that he should consider incorporating writers' workshop into his own teaching.

> I'm so amazed how kids can stay involved. More and more, I'm thinking, "when I go back to a classroom, I'll try to make the writers' workshop the heart of our writing." It's been a slow change for me. I didn't know if it could work with kids, and it felt like all these steps and if they're spending so long on one piece of writing and thinking, "How will they do it?" And I see them doing it. It's very developmentally sound. Each child will be at their own level of writing and the process will help them write more and take them farther.

Pete Frazer not only contributed to the learning of beginning teachers, but he himself also learned. The things he learned helped him become a better support teacher and a better classroom teacher. Both Frazer's learning and the learning of the beginning teachers occurred within a community of practice where colleagues shared a vision of good teaching and a commitment to progressive public education and valued collaboration and inquiry.

CONCLUSION

Mentoring entered the vocabulary of U.S. educational reform in the 1980s as part of a broader effort to professionalize teaching (Little, 1990). The early association with beginning teacher induction often led to a narrow view of mentoring as a form of temporary support to help novices cope with the demands of their first year of teaching. Through the early 1990s, as the idea of mentoring was extended to the preservice level, researchers advanced various competing and complementary role definitions and specifications of mentors' functions, characteristics, and qualities (e.g., Gehrke, 1988; Gray & Gray, 1985; Healy & Welchert, 1990). Most studies relied on self-report and took the form of program evaluation. Few reflected serious conceptual clarification or attention to mentors' practice and the consequences for novices' learning (Little, 1990).

Situated in practice and in a relationship with an experienced educator, mentoring has the potential to foster powerful teaching and to develop the dispositions and skills of continuous improvement. At the same time, mentors may also perpetuate standard teaching practices and reinforce norms of individualism and noninterference. How mentors define and enact their role, what kind of preparation and support they receive, whether mentors have time to mentor, and whether the culture of teaching reinforces their work all influence the character and quality of mentoring and its influence on novices' practice (Feiman-Nemser & Parker, 1993).

This portrait of an exemplary support teacher provides a vision of the possible in mentoring rather than a view of the probable.[4] It shows how educative mentoring promotes beginning teacher development by cultivating a disposition of inquiry, focusing attention on student thinking and understanding, and fostering disciplined talk about problems of practice. Conventional approaches to mentoring may offer short-term, feel-good support. Educative mentoring bears a strong family resemblance to other forms of practice-centered, inquiry-oriented professional development that are linked to a vision of powerful learning for all students and supported by a collaborative professional culture (Ball & Cohen, 1999; Hawley & Valli, 1999; Little, 1990).

If teaching is the profession that shapes America's future (National Commission on Teaching and America's Future, 1996), then investing in new teacher development and the development of teachers' mentors is an investment in that future. As large numbers of new teachers are hired to meet growing needs and to fill gaps created by unprecedented amounts of retirement and high rates of attrition in the early years of teaching, serious attention to induction and mentoring becomes even more critical. Policy makers and the public must understand that new teachers, like other beginning professionals, need continuing opportunities to hone their knowledge and skills under the guidance of more knowledgeable and experienced practitioners (Darling-Hammond, Berry, Haselkorn, & Fideler, 1999). Educators and administrators must create the structures and culture that enable all teachers to continue learning in and from practice as they address the complex challenges of public education.

REFERENCES

Ball, D. (1987, April). *"Laboratory" and "apprenticeship": How do they function as metaphors for practical experience in teacher education?* Paper presented at the annual meeting of the American Educational Research Association, Washington, DC.

Ball, D., & Cohen, D. (1999). Developing practice, developing practitioners: Toward a practice based theory of professional education. In G. Sykes & L. Darling-Hammond (Eds.), *Teaching as the learning profession: Handbook of policy and practice* (pp. 3–32). San Francisco: Jossey-Bass.

Cogan, M. (1973). *Clinical supervision.* New York: Houghton Mifflin.

Collins, A., Brown, J. S., & Newman, S. (1989). The new apprenticeship: Teaching students the craft of reading, writing and mathematics. In L. Resnick (Ed.), *Knowing, learning, and instruction* (pp. 453–494). Hillsdale, NJ: Erlbaum.

Darling-Hammond, L., Berry, B., Haselkorn, D., & Fideler, E. (1999). Teacher recruitment, selection and induction: Policy influences on the supply and quality of teachers. In L. Darling-Hammond & G. Sykes (Eds.), *Teaching as the learning profession: Handbook of policy and practice* (pp. 183–232). San Francisco: Jossey-Bass.

Dembele, M. (1995). *Mentors and mentoring: Frames for action, ways of acting and consequences for novice teachers' learning.* Unpublished doctoral dissertation, Michigan State University, East Lansing.

Devaney, K. (Ed.). (1978). *Teachers' centers.* San Francisco: Far West Laboratory for Educational Research and Development.

Dewey, J. (1904/1965). The relation of theory to practice in education. In M. Borrowman (Ed.), *Teacher education in America.* New York: Teachers College Press.

Dewey, J. (1933). *How we think.* Chicago: D. C. Heath.

Dewey, J. (1938). *Experience and education.* New York: Collier Books.

Feiman-Nemser, S. (1998). Teachers as teacher educators. *European Journal of Teacher Education, 21*(1), 63–74.

Feiman-Nemser, S., & Beasley, K. (1998). Mentoring as assisted performance: The case of co-planning. In V. Richardson (Ed.), *Constructivist teacher education* (pp. 1–32). New York: Falmer.

Feiman-Nemser, S., & Floden, R. (1981). A critique of developmental approaches in teacher education. *Action in Teacher Education, 3*(1), 35–38.

Feiman-Nemser, S., & Parker, M. (1993). Mentoring in context: A comparison of two U.S. programs for beginning teachers. *International Journal of Educational Research, 19*(8), 699–718.

Fideler, E., & Haselkorn, D. (1999). *Learning the ropes: Urban teacher induction practices in the United States.* Belmont, MA: Recruiting New Teachers. Downloaded from jte.sagepub.com at Harvard Libraries on January 21, 2011

Fuller, F. (1969). Concerns of teachers: A developmental conceptualization. *American Educational Research Journal, 6,* 207–226.

Gehrke, N. J. (1988). Toward a definition of mentoring. *Theory into Practice, 27,* 190–194.

Glickman, C. (1985). *Supervision of instruction: A developmental approach.* Newton, MA: Allyn & Bacon.

Goldhammer, R. (1969). *Clinical supervision: Special methods for the supervision of teachers.* New York: Holt, Rinehart & Winston.

Gray, W. A., & Gray, M. M. (1985). Synthesis of research on mentoring beginning teachers. *Educational Leadership, 43*(3), 37–43.

Hawley, W., & Valli, L. (1999). The essentials of effective professional development. In L. Darling-Hammond & G. Sykes (Eds.), *Teaching as the learning profession: Handbook of policy and practice* (pp. 292–312). San Francisco: Jossey-Bass.

Healy, C. C., & Welchert, A. J. (1990). Mentoring relations: A definition to advance research and practice. *Educational Researcher, 19*(9), 17–21.

Joyce, B., & Showers, B. (1985). The coaching of teaching. *Educational Leadership, 40*(1), 4–11.

Lieberman, A., & Grolnick, M. (1999). Networks and reform in American education. In L. Darling-Hammond & G. Sykes (Eds.), *Teaching as the learning profession: Handbook of policy and practice* (pp. 292–312). San Francisco: Jossey-Bass.

Little, J. W. (1990). The mentor phenomenon. In C. Cazden (Ed.), *Review of research in education* (pp. 297–351). Washington, DC: American Educational Research Association.

Lytle, S., & Cochran-Smith, M. (Eds.). (1992). *Inside/outside: Teacher research and knowledge.* New York: Teachers College Press.

National Center for Research on Teacher Education. (1988). Teacher education and learning to teach: A research agenda. *Journal of Teacher Education, 39*(6), 27–32.

National Commission on Teaching and America's Future. (1996). *What matters most: Teaching for America's future.* New York: Author.

Nevins, R. (1993). *Classroom teachers as mentors: Their perspectives on helping novices learn to teach.* Unpublished doctoral dissertation, Michigan State University, East Lansing.

Schon, D. (1983). *The reflective practitioner: How professionals think in action.* New York: Basic Books. Schon, D. (1987). *Educating the reflective practitioner.* San Francisco: Jossey-Bass.

Shulman, L. (1983). Autonomy and obligation: The remote control of teaching. In L. Shulman & G. Sykes (Eds.), *Handbook of teaching and policy* (pp. 484–504). New York: Longman.

Smith, F. (1985). *Reading without nonsense* (2nd ed.). New York: Teachers College Press. Sweeney, B., & DeBolt, G. (2000). A survey of the 50 states: Mandated teacher induction programs. In S. Odell & L. Huling (Eds.), *Quality mentoring for novice teachers* (pp. 97–106). Washington, DC: Association of Teacher Educators and Kappa Delta Pi.

Veenman, S. (1989). Perceived problems of beginning teachers. *Review of Educational Research, 54,* 143–178. White, E. B. (1945). *Stuart Little.* New York: Harper & Row.

Wildman, T. M., Niles, J. A., Magliaro, S. G., & McLaughlin, R. A. (1989). Teaching and learning to teach: The two roles of beginning teachers. *Elementary School Journal, 89,* 471–493.

CHAPTER 10

Mind Activity in Teaching and Mentoring

INTRODUCTION

New teachers have two jobs to do—they have to teach and they have to learn to teach in a particular context (Wildman, Niles, Magliaro, & McLaughlin, 1989). Teacher education can equip new teachers with critical knowledge and skills and foster the habit of learning in and from teaching. Still, some of the most important things new teachers need to know can only be learned once they actually begin teaching. Only then it is possible to get to know one's students, assess their knowledge and skills, discover what they are supposed to learn, and begin developing or adapting a curriculum to enable their learning (Feiman-Nemser, 2003).

Increasingly educators and policy makers recognize that new teachers need help making the transition to independent teaching.[1] Many states and districts have formal induction programs and most of these programs rely on mentoring as the primary induction strategy (Fideler & Haselkorn, 1999); however, numerous studies have documented large variations in the purposes, length, structure, and intensity of these programs and in the selection, terms, training, and expectations of mentor teachers (see, for example, Huling-Austin, 1990; Fideler & Haselkorn, 1999; Ingersoll & Smith, 2003). The spread of induction and mentoring programs creates a pressing need to understand what kind of mentoring makes what sort of difference for new teachers and their students and under what circumstances such differences are most likely to occur.

Studies show that the benefits of formal mentoring and induction are possible but not automatic (Feiman-Nemser & Parker, 1993; Gold, 1996;

This article is coauthored by Patricia J. Norman.

Johnson et al., 2004). Analyzing data from the 1999–2000 Schools and Staffing Survey (SASS), Ingersoll and Smith (2003) found that participating in an induction program and working with a mentor teacher reduces the likelihood that new teachers will transfer to a different school or leave the profession altogether. Not surprisingly, these benefits are most likely to occur when new teachers have mentors in their same subject or grade level with time to mentor. Evertson and Smithey (2000) found that new teachers who worked with mentors in a formal induction program were better able to manage instruction, establish routines, and keep students engaged in academic tasks than new teachers paired with mentors who had no formal opportunity to develop their skills as mentors. The researchers concluded that the mere presence of a mentor is not enough. Knowledge and skill in mentoring is also necessary.

The impact of mentoring not only depends on appropriate matches, time, and training, but also on the expectations that mentors and novices hold for one another and what they actually do together. Prevailing images and expectations of mentoring often prevent mentor teachers from playing a significant role in new teacher learning. Reviewing research on the role of mentoring in helping novices learn standards based teaching, Wang and Odell (2002) conclude that, overall, mentors expect to provide and novices expect to receive psychological support, technical assistance, and guidance about local customs and policies. Neither sees mentoring as a substantial and meaningful influence on novice's learning to teach.

A narrow view of mentoring focuses on easing the new teacher's entry into teaching and helping with the immediate questions and uncertainties that inevitably arise when a teacher enters the classroom for the first time. A robust view of mentoring promises more. Linked to a vision of good teaching and a developmental view of learning to teach, such mentoring still responds to new teachers' present needs while helping them interpret what their students say and do and figure out how to move their learning forward. We call this "educative" mentoring to distinguish it from technical advice and emotional support and to suggest that mentoring can be a form of individualized professional development.

Mentors who see their work in educational terms have a clear idea of the kind of teaching they want to foster. They regard new teachers as learners and think about how to help them develop a principled teaching practice. Like good teachers, they have a kind of bifocal vision, keeping one eye on the immediate needs of the novice teacher and one eye on the ultimate goal of meaningful and effective learning for all students. Discerning observers of teaching, such mentors use their teaching and the teaching of others as a site for new teacher learning. Their mentoring practice blends showing and telling, asking and listening (Schon, 1987) in ways that promote new teacher learning.

Our title comes from a classic essay by Dewey (1904/1965) in which he argues that what (student) teachers need most of all is the capacity to see what is going on in the minds of their students. When observing an experienced teacher, for example, novices should not focus on the teacher's behavior in order to "accumulate a store of methods." Rather they should pay close attention to the way students make sense of what they are studying. In Dewey's words, they should focus on "the interaction of mind on mind, how teacher and pupils react upon each other" (p. 324). The currently popular phrase "teaching for understanding" signals a similar concern for a kind of content-rich teaching that builds on students' ideas and experiences, honors their questions, and aims for meaning and understanding (Cohen, McLaughlin, & Talbert, 1993).

Popular models of teacher development suggest that new teachers are too preoccupied with their own adequacy and performance to focus on student thinking and learning (Fuller, 1969; Fuller & Brown, 1975; Kagan, 1992). Such a focus will "naturally" emerge once beginning teachers resolve their initial concerns. In principle, however, having a mentor should enable new teachers to go beyond what they could do on their own (Wells, 2002). Some even suggest that serious (educative) mentoring could make the early years of teaching harder rather than easier by holding out higher standards than beginning teachers are likely to work toward on their own (Little, 1990a).

If we want to promote mentoring as a significant influence on new teacher learning, we need to know more about the kind of mentoring that makes such a difference. Survey research can provide general support for induction and mentoring, but we also need nuanced descriptions of interactions between thoughtful mentors and beginning teachers in order to understand how formal mentoring can be a strategy to promote effective teaching and learning. How do thoughtful mentors help new teachers focus on students' "mind activity"? What learning opportunities does serious mentoring afford beginning teachers? Under what conditions are the benefits of such mentoring most likely to occur? We explore these questions by presenting two extended cases of mentored learning to teach.

We developed these cases because they offer rich portraits of serious mentors at work and because they presented us with an interesting puzzle. In their first year of teaching, the two new teachers struck us and their mentors as unusually confident and capable, and we expected to learn a lot about how serious mentoring contributes to the development of well-started beginning teachers. By the end of the second year of teaching, one of the beginning teachers had made considerable progress in learning to teach for understanding while the other had not. In fact, in the words of her mentor, she had actually "worked backwards."

How could we account for these different trajectories? What could we learn from these cases of mentored learning to teach about the needs of beginning teachers, the content and pedagogy of educative mentoring, and the factors that enable or constrain its influence?

METHODOLOGICAL CHOICES

The two cases come from a larger study of mentoring in three well-regarded induction programs (Feiman-Nemser, 2000). We chose our study sites because of their reputation as strong induction efforts supported by state and district policies. While the literature contains numerous descriptions of "sink or swim" induction, we wanted to know what it was like to be a new teacher in places purported to take induction and mentoring seriously. As part of the research, we documented the interactions of a sample of mentors and new teachers in each program and traced the impact of mentoring on new teachers' practice and their students' learning. The two cases presented below come from one of the research sites, an induction project in California known for its developmental stance toward new teacher learning and its serious approach to the selection, preparation and ongoing support of mentor teachers.

The Induction Program

A local project of California's Beginning Teacher Support and Assessment initiative (BTSA), the program relies on fulltime mentors released from classroom teaching for 2–3 years to work with a group of beginning teachers during their first two years. The program selects mentors carefully and provides both initial training and ongoing substantive support and development through weekly staff meetings. In keeping with state policy, mentors combine individualized assistance with formative assessment. The program supplies mentors with various tools, including assessment rubrics and state teaching standards.

The California Standards for the Teaching Profession frame the mentors' work. Adopted in 1997, the standards are designed "to facilitate the induction of beginning teachers into their professional roles and responsibilities by providing a common language and new vision of the scope and complexity of teaching" (CDE, 1997, p. 1). The first teaching standard, "engaging and supporting all students in learning," focuses on the central work of interactive teaching—eliciting, assessing, and deepening children's subject matter understanding. The standard calls for teachers to build on students' ideas and experiences in order to extend their understanding and to adjust their teaching in response to students' comments and questions. In short, the standard uses contemporary reform language to describe what Dewey (1904/1965) seems to have in mind when he urges teachers to focus on "mind activity" in teaching.

The Mentors

Although we studied eight mentors in this program, we focus here on two—Rachel and Eileen. Rachel worked with a dozen new teachers in several school sites; Eileen worked with a handful of new teachers at a professional development school where she also served as the PDS coordinator. The two mentors, both experienced elementary teachers, shared the program's underlying vision of teaching for conceptual understanding. Rachel viewed teaching as "getting in there with the kids and really hearing from them and getting a grip on what they do and do not understand." Eileen described teaching as "scaffolding students' learning," finding ways to provide individualized support in their "zone of proximal development." Both mentors acknowledged their desire to help new teachers attend to and interpret students' questions and ideas and use them in planning and teaching. This goal became a common thread across their work with their new teachers, Vanessa and Anna.

The New Teachers

The two beginning teachers—Vanessa and Anna—had similar teaching assignments. Both taught a 4th grade class of second language learners in a Title 1 elementary school with a strong reputation in their respective districts. Although their initial teaching assignments were similar, their preparation was not. Vanessa entered teaching through an alternative certification program while Anna completed a highly regarded preservice program. We wondered how these different paths to teaching would influence their work with mentors.

Most significant for our purposes, both novices initially struck their mentors as quite capable and confident for beginning teachers. Rachel said of Vanessa at the end of her first year:

> She was feisty and thoughtful and decisive and really went after her own learning. She started out strong not because of her preparation but because of who she is . . . She's so smart that we've really been able to construct a program that's working. She has done incredible work.

Likewise Eileen said of Anna at the end of her first year of teaching:

> Her instructional practice is so congruent with current research and theory and her philosophy of education. You don't see that kind of development in one year. She has a real keen sense of what she needs to learn, and she has extraordinarily high expectations of herself . . . She's really brilliant.

When we asked Eileen near the end of the second year to describe Anna's learning, she responded that Anna was an "exceptional teacher" whose students had made "phenomenal progress" as readers and writers. In contrast, Rachel's view of Vanessa had radically changed. After two years of intensive work together, Rachel had a very different assessment of Vanessa's seeming confidence and her ability to look at teaching through the eyes of her students. Rachel had come to realize that Vanessa's understanding of teaching was much more elemental. She was simply "not in students' heads." In retrospect, it seemed to Rachel that they had been "working backwards." Trying to account for the different learning trajectories of the two beginning teachers—despite the fact that their mentors consistently emphasized the need to attend to students' "mind activity" in planning and teaching—led us to consider their background and teaching contexts, and to think more about the mentoring they received.

Data Sources and Analysis

In developing these cases, we drew on interview and observational data gathered over a two-year period and supplemental written records generated by the two pairs. Preliminary data analysis informed subsequent data collection. We analyzed the data independently and then worked through differences in interpretation. In addition, we shared draft cases with the mentor teachers.

Data Collection

At the beginning and end of each school year, we individually interviewed both mentors and novices. Initially we sought information about their background and preparation, views of teaching and learning, goals and expectations for their work together, and anticipated challenges. Over time, we elicited perspectives on the work of teaching, information about the school context, and specific examples of changes in the new teachers' practice that could be directly linked to mentoring. Twice a year we videotaped the new teachers teaching a literacy lesson. Then we videotaped subsequent post-observation conferences and interviewed the mentors and novices about the lessons and the conferences. To supplement these data, we asked mentors to audiotape twice yearly sessions where they analyzed student work with beginning teachers. Finally we collected all the written records produced by each pair which included collaborative logs filled in after each meeting, professional development plans created at the beginning of the school year, and lesson plans.

Data Analysis

Guided by our research questions, data analysis occurred on multiple levels. Moving back and forth between the interview and observational data, we tried to construct a picture of the novices' first two years of teaching, paying particular attention to what they had learned, how that learning was manifest in their teaching and their students' learning, and what role mentoring had played in their development.

Working with the interview data, we developed descriptive codes to help us identify dimensions of learning on the part of the new teachers (Miles & Huberman, 1994). The codes covered aspects of curriculum, planning, and instruction as well as aspects of professional socialization. We looked for evidence of changes in new teachers' attitudes, ideas, and practices, and their stance toward teaching, mentoring, and learning to teach. We also noted statements about salient influences on these changes. Moving from new teacher data to mentor data, we sought confirming and disconfirming evidence, especially about the effects of mentoring on new teachers' learning. We extended the analysis of new teacher learning to the observational record of lessons and conferences, testing claims, searching for corroborating evidence, developing our own independent assessments using the teaching standards to frame our analysis.

To construct a picture of mentors' practice and deepen our understanding of mentors' influence on novices' learning, we wrote summaries of each language arts lesson, then coded the post-observation conference transcripts. Using "inductive analysis," we segmented the conferences and analyzed the dynamics and content of each segment (Erickson, 1986). Looking across the conferences and lessons, we identified patterns of mentoring and evidence of influence which we further explored through the interview transcripts and written records.

To understand how mentors and new teachers interpreted their work together and to develop our own account of their actions and interactions, we drew on information about goals and aspirations, background and preparation, school and program contexts gleaned from transcripts and summaries.

Framing the Cases

Each case is organized chronologically and focuses on a central goal that unified the work of novice and mentor across the two years. After briefly summarizing what the novice learned in her first year of mentored teaching, we turn to the second year, describing in some detail two teaching episodes and the subsequent post-observation conferences. We follow each case with an analysis, highlighting critical dimensions of educative mentoring and showing how personal history and professional culture influence what new teachers can learn even from serious mentoring. In a closing discussion, we consider broad implications for mentors, educational leaders, and policy makers.

VANESSA AND RACHEL: A CASE OF "WORKING BACKWARDS"[2]

After earning her teaching credential through a state university's alternative certification program, Vanessa was hired to teach in a Sheltered English Immersion (SEI) classroom in a Title I elementary school serving low-income Hispanic children. SEI is a one-year program designed to help students fluent in their first language make a transition into an English-only classroom. Having grown up speaking French until she entered kindergarten in the United States, Vanessa empathized with her students as fellow second language learners. Vanessa's mentor, Rachel, had just left classroom teaching in order to begin working with beginning teachers and she looked forward to working with Vanessa. A central goal across their two years of work together was strengthening Vanessa's commitment and capacity to help students comprehend what they were reading.

Vanessa's First Year of Mentored Learning to Teach

Initially uncertain how to teach reading and writing, Vanessa asked Rachel for help in setting up her language arts program. Rachel described Vanessa's early efforts to teach reading as "putting the whole class in one book," then "giving them an assignment and letting students work in groups to finish it." To strengthen the reading program, Rachel helped Vanessa replace whole class instruction with reading centers so that she could work with small groups of children, helping them make sense of what they were reading. Besides modeling small group reading lessons, Rachel took Vanessa to observe other teachers who taught reading in small groups.

As Vanessa grew more adept at managing transitions between centers, Rachel focused on strengthening the quality of Vanessa's instruction at the teacher-led center. Instead of spending so much time listening to children read, Rachel wanted Vanessa to work on comprehension. Vanessa acknowledged that her desire to "get through the story" and develop students' fluency often meant that she "never got to the comprehension strategies and other planned activities."[3] Based on Rachel's suggestions, Vanessa began using a pre-reading strategy with students before they read on their own or in pairs while she monitored the other centers. When students finished reading, Vanessa returned to the teacher-led center to discuss the story. By the end of the first year, Rachel believed that Vanessa had "used her teacher time more and more effectively to actually teach skills rather than let them [the students] just read to her." Rachel looked forward to continued work with Vanessa on strengthening children's reading comprehension.

Vanessa's Second Year of Mentored Learning to Teach

Rachel was not available at the start of Vanessa's second year of teaching. Returning to her mentoring responsibilities in November, she was shocked to discover that Vanessa had dismantled the reading centers they had worked so hard to set up the previous year, replacing them with fast-paced, whole-class reading lessons. Vanessa explained that she had gotten the idea while observing a Reading Recovery teacher tutor a bilingual student. Impressed with the "quick transitions" and numerous "teaching strategies" that the Reading Recovery teacher had used, Vanessa decided that she wanted to try using "as many teaching strategies as possible" with all of her students. She hoped that Rachel would help her explore how to teach the whole group since she "already knew how to teach small groups."

Whole Class Reading Lesson

In November, we sat with Rachel as she observed Vanessa teach a whole class reading lesson. Before the lesson, Vanessa asked Rachel to focus on whether whole group instruction "was working", since she noticed that during such lessons, "six or seven kids are just completely fazed out." Vanessa asked: "Do I change my whole program around because of these seven kids or do I just let those kids fall through the cracks?" Rachel was deeply troubled that Vanessa would even consider "letting seven kids fall through the cracks." "That hurt my heart," she later told us.

From the standpoint of using multiple strategies in a single lesson and keeping up a snappy pace, Vanessa's lesson was a masterful performance. First she corrected students' spelling homework (7 min), then explained the new homework assignment which involved the use of editing symbols to proofread a passage (12 min). Holding up a book about Buddy, the first seeing eye dog, Vanessa next invited students to predict what the book was about and when the story took place by looking at the illustrations (12 min). Students' guesses, which Vanessa did not probe, ranged from 7 to 1000 years ago. The story actually took place in the 1950s. The final instructional segment of this 50 min lesson involved a lively interaction around word endings (13 min). Students were asked to stand if they heard "nt" at the end of a word or remain seated if they heard "nd." For the final 5 mins, they worked independently on a workbook page focusing on these word endings.

Post Observation Conference

Rachel worried that whole class instruction gave Vanessa "a false sense of control" and kept her from hearing how students made sense of their reading. Rachel entered the post-observation conference hoping to move Vanessa away from her "whole versus small group stance" to consider the place of whole and small group instruction depending on the teacher's purposes. When the two met over lunch to discuss the lesson, Rachel opened their conversation by asking Vanessa how things were going in general. Vanessa spent nearly 10 min describing a recent field trip to a haunted house, her stress about students' standardized test scores, and a child who was coping with a very difficult home situation. When she mentioned how pleased she was with her reading instruction, Rachel shifted the conversation back to the question Vanessa had raised before the lesson—how well is whole group instruction working? When Rachel asked Vanessa why this format appealed to her, she replied:

It feels so good to feel like I'm actually on time and on the ball. I don't think the centers that I did were as effective as what I'm doing now. I'm really pushing the kids a lot and they are learning a lot faster than they were last year . . . They are reading fast. We're zipping through these books quickly.

When Rachel asked, "How about [their] comprehension?" Vanessa acknowledged, "That's something I need to work on. Right now that's on the back burner because there are so many other aspects I want to teach . . . I'm assuming that comprehension is going well but that's not necessarily true."

Knowing that Vanessa was wedded to whole group instruction, Rachel suggested that she still needed "to look at what she was doing" and "modify" her instruction in light of her purposes for students' learning. After suggesting that Vanessa should also attend to comprehension, Rachel continued to move back and forth between accentuating the positive and naming potentially difficult issues in Vanessa's teaching. For example, Rachel agreed that while Vanessa could certainly accelerate the students' English reading, she worried that their increased fluency actually masked comprehension difficulties. To make the case, Sarah drew on evidence from her own work with Vanessa's children:

Rachel: They're becoming more fluent readers because of what you're doing, but I'm worried about the phenomenon of fluency rising without comprehension.

Vanessa: Right.

Rachel: The other day I read with several kids. When they came to parts they didn't know, they weren't concerned. They looked over them. The story had enough pictures and context that it didn't matter, but as they move into fourth grade literature that's going to hang them up a lot.

Vanessa: Mmm hmm. And this book [about Buddy] that we're reading right now . . . There's less pictures. There's more information, so that's a worry that I just don't know how to teach comprehension.

After Rachel framed the problem of promoting fluency at the expense of comprehension, Vanessa expressed uncertainty about how to teach comprehension. Moving back into a supportive mode, Rachel countered that Vanessa does know how to teach it and proceeded to point out several examples. Vanessa seemed to appreciate hearing the "beautiful" things she accomplished during her lesson:

Rachel: You do actually know quite a bit about it. Let me go over all the things that you know how to do because I think it's awesome how much you put into it.

Vanessa: This is good to hear.

Rachel: So the first seven minutes, you reviewed spelling words . . . Then you went on to proofreading . . . You went beyond the [teacher's guide] which was beautiful to see . . . What you're teaching them is how to make predictions about context . . . This is all about teaching comprehension.

After using her detailed observation notes to summarize the different parts of the lesson, Rachel suggested that they consider the issue of comprehension in relation to Vanessa's question about whether whole group was working.

It's possible to move a large group forward in reading comprehension, but what you're sacrificing with the large group on reading comprehension is you're not getting back how they're processing it. You're not getting back the sweet things they say, their insights, the questions that they're afraid to ask . . .

Rachel then explained that while Vanessa's "management is outstanding" and it appears that the students are with her, she is "missing the dangerous shortcuts that they take" when her students read. Rachel wrapped up the conversation by suggesting that Vanessa consider bringing back small groups for part of the day or week so that she could hear how students talked about their reading. Rachel also said that she would like to work with a small group of Vanessa's students so that she could explore comprehension strategies with second language learners herself.

Revisiting the Conference

Later that week, we talked with Vanessa about her conversation with Rachel. She maintained her initial assessment that the lesson had gone well, stating that while she would consider returning to "small groups half a day a week to incorporate more reading comprehension," the conversation with Rachel had helped her realize that she "want[ed] things to stay whole class." When we asked Vanessa what her reading lesson had been like the day after her conversation with Rachel, she described a whole class lesson that sounded a lot like the lesson that we and Rachel had observed where skills development and fluency took precedence over comprehension.

When we returned in the spring, Rachel explained to us that "it took quite a while to transition Vanessa into being willing to work with groups."

Even though Rachel worked with a small group of students every week in order to figure out for herself and model for Vanessa how to teach comprehension strategies to second language learners, several months passed before Vanessa began working with her own small group. As we observed Vanessa's teaching and Rachel's mentoring that spring, we saw that Rachel had extended her concerns about comprehension to the teaching of social studies.

Social Studies Lesson

In the 25-min small group lesson that we observed with Rachel, the students read and took notes on a section of a chapter in their social studies textbook dealing with the history of California. Once they finished the task, Vanessa planned to use the notes to teach students how to write a five-paragraph essay. The section of text called "Changes Come to California" discussed what happened to California when Mexico gained its independence from Spain. Vanessa suggested that the students use the section titles as the major headings in their note-taking outline. The students then read a paragraph at a time, stating the main idea of each paragraph in their own words. Finally, they recorded their agreed-upon ideas in their individual outlines.

One paragraph proved particularly difficult for students to understand and summarize. It stated that once Mexico gained control of the region, the rules they put in place were different from the ones Spain had enforced. The textbook stated, "Under Spanish law, the colonies were not allowed to trade with other countries, but Spain had trouble enforcing it [the law]." When students were unable to state the main idea of the passage, Rachel stepped in and asked, "I wonder if everyone knows what it means to trade with another country?" Vanessa replied, "Trading means when one country has something another country wants and vice versa. If Rachel has something I want and I have something Rachel wants, we can trade." She then pointed out that because Mexico was no longer under Spain's control, they were now free to trade with other countries. At the end of the lesson, Vanessa complimented students for doing "a great job."

Post Observation Conference

Before the lesson, Vanessa had asked Rachel to pay attention to whether or not the students were "getting it," saying, "I know the lower kids won't get it, but what about the medium and the medium highs? I don't know if I need to scaffold more." Their conversation followed a similar pattern to the one we observed in November. Rachel began by asking Vanessa what was going well. For the next 14 min, Vanessa shared recent frustrations including a "lack of connection" she felt to her students, a recent field trip that had gone awry, and a difficult conversation with a child's parent.

Once Vanessa finished venting, Rachel posed Vanessa's initial question back to her, namely how she felt the "medium and medium high students" had done during the lesson. Vanessa brightened, saying she was "pleasantly pleased and surprised" that they were "able to vocalize" their confusions about the social studies passage. Vanessa then admitted, "it was kind of nice that you were there to point out the trading thing because I wasn't focused enough to have been able to pick that out." After explaining her decision to step into Vanessa's lesson, Rachel provided her own answer to Vanessa's focal question:

> You asked me are they getting what you want. They definitely get the idea that they are forming an outline, that they're using the headings, the text features, that they're finding the main idea. So that in and of itself is a big step forward. Then there's building concepts. It's this hugely complex thing you have to do as an SEI teacher. They can read the word but do they have a clue of what trading means?

Rachel explained that the task Vanessa gave the children—reading and taking notes on the social studies textbook—required more than showing them how the textbook is organized or how to take notes. Vanessa also needed to build children's understanding of the underlying concepts in the text.[4] Vanessa agreed when Rachel claimed, "They can pick out the words, but they don't understand the concept."

Rachel then provided descriptive data about student involvement, stating, "You had seven out of eight students really engaged with what you were trying to do. That in and of itself is a huge developmental step in their reading." The rest of their conversation followed the familiar pattern. Rachel continued to raise concerns and offer praise and encouragement. She ended the conversation by outlining what Vanessa should do to help students read and understand the social studies textbook: " . . . move back and forth" between "analyzing the text, breaking down vocabulary, building meaning, and picking out main idea" as well as to constantly "check for student understanding."

Revisiting the Post Observation Conference
When, several days later, we spoke with Rachel about her conference with Vanessa, she explained that she had three goals for the conversation: (1) to

encourage Vanessa to keep working with the small group since Vanessa had the tendency to abandon instructional strategies when they proved difficult to implement; (2) to contradict Vanessa's belief that her students "don't get it" by helping Vanessa notice what her students were actually able to do; and (3) to provide Vanessa with several "concrete strategies" to use in future lessons. When asked how Vanessa might learn to act on the suggestions Rachel had offered (e.g. move back and forth between concept development, vocabulary development, and comprehension), Rachel seemed less certain:

> This is not something that I have mastered. Nobody has mastered how you bring along English language learners at a high conceptual level while teaching them the skill of accessing the material independently . . . If I had more time to work with her, I think I would come in and ask her if I could work with a small group on that and we could compare our two groups, saying, "How is it going?"

Speaking to Vanessa about her conversation with Rachel after the small group social studies lesson, we got some indication that she was just beginning to embrace the agenda that Rachel had been trying to help her work on all along. Vanessa wondered aloud, "How can I get the kids to kind of question things and wonder? How do I get them to decipher what the text is telling us rather than me telling them? I don't really know what the answer is."

Rachel, too, was beginning to see Vanessa in a new light. After two years of intensive work together, she had reframed her assessment of Vanessa's surface confidence and was beginning to see how far she was from being able to look at teaching through the eyes of her students. In an extended and open conversation with us, she acknowledged that Vanessa had "more bravado than I even admit to myself":

> Her understanding of what teaching reading is about is much more elemental than I even knew. It's like we're working backwards. She's taken two years to reveal to me how much she actually doesn't get for the amount that she appears to be confident in what she's doing . . . *She's not thinking in terms of what can they tell me about what they know? She's not in their heads and that hit me more strongly* (italics added).

After two intensive years of work, Rachel saw that Vanessa was not sufficiently invested in understanding children's thinking, something that Rachel believes is essential to good teaching. Perhaps, Rachel thought, Vanessa might now be "ready to dive into" that learning agenda. Unfortunately, her official stint as Vanessa's mentor was over. Rachel worried that "without continued coaching, [Vanessa] will get stuck."

Case Analysis

How can we account for Rachel's assessment that Vanessa seemed to move backwards in her development despite their two years of intensive work together? The more we thought about this question, the more we were led to consider the complex interplay of personal, contextual, and programmatic factors. Who Vanessa was as a student of teaching and what her school was like as a setting for teaching and learning to teach affected the character and quality of mentoring that Rachel was able to provide. That mentoring, in turn, was shaped by the induction program that selected, trained, and supported her.

While Vanessa appreciated the practical orientation of her alternative certification program, overall she found her teacher preparation "pretty irrelevant." Like most beginning teachers, Vanessa expected to learn teaching mostly through trial and error. As she said, "No one can prepare you for what your first year is like." Eager to collect ideas and strategies, she often experimented with things she saw other teachers doing. She also tended to drop things quickly and move on to something else when they "didn't work." Rachel faced the dual challenge of keeping Vanessa from prematurely abandoning promising practices while weaning her from less effective strategies.

Vanessa saw learning to teach as a finite, technical process. She believed that her learning needs would diminish over time. While Rachel readily admitted that, as an experienced teacher, she was still trying to figure out how to teach reading comprehension to students like Vanessa's, Vanessa stated: "I'm sure that the very first year you learn a lot and then every year that goes by you learn a little less." As a learner, Vanessa often resisted Rachel's agenda. In Rachel's words, Vanessa sometimes acted like she already "understood everything." For example, Vanessa was quick to declare that she had become bored with small group instruction because she "already knew how to do it," so she "needed to do something new."

Vanessa's technical orientation to teaching led her to expect direct answers from her mentor. Initially Vanessa assumed that Rachel would answer all her questions, as she explained to us: "I thought she could do it all, answer it all." Frustrated when answers to her "million and one questions" were not forthcoming, Vanessa concluded, "She wasn't somebody that I could expect to answer my questions" so she "started to go to other master teachers to find those answers," she explained. From Rachel she sought a sympathetic ear. "She's kept me sane and been great to just vent when things are frustrating . . . You want to hear that someone understands, gives you support, someone makes you feel better." Although the induction program explicitly encouraged mentors to go beyond "feel good support," Vanessa held this expectation for Rachel.

Vanessa's working conditions presented challenges. Despite its strong reputation, the school had experienced considerable turnover in administrators and teachers. The summer before Vanessa's first year, the principal and assistant principal had left and their exodus led to widespread teacher turnover. Besides two new administrators, Vanessa was one of 12 new teachers at the school. Since all the fourth grade teachers were either new to the school or new to that grade level, Vanessa had no experienced grade-level colleagues to rely on.

In addition, as both Vanessa and Rachel explained, there were "strong personality conflicts" and tensions between the Sheltered English Immersion (SEI) and English-only teachers on the 4th grade team. Team members rarely worked together or viewed one another as resources. Finally, Vanessa's teaching assignment created additional challenges. While the SEI program was designed for students fluent in their first language, Rachel and Vanessa found that many of her students lacked fluency in both their primary language and in English. Often Rachel felt like Vanessa's only support.

Sensitive to Vanessa's tendency to become "easily overwhelmed," Rachel tried to encourage and support her emotionally while also framing an agenda for her learning. At the end of Vanessa's second year of teaching, Rachel talked about the tension she felt between trying to keep Vanessa in teaching and risking her withdrawal by pushing too hard:

> To me it's a real victory that she's going to return next year to this fourth grade SEI class again. I put a lot of energy into keeping her coming back . . . If people make it too difficult for her, she's not going to stick around. In a way you don't want to coddle to that. On the other hand, I've never known how to come in and say, "You haven't mastered it. There are a lot of gaps in your program."

Rachel's attempts to build Vanessa up, something she seemed to need, made it hard for Rachel to address her vulnerabilities as a teacher.

Rachel used reflective conversations to help Vanessa consider aspects of student learning such as reading comprehension which she otherwise might not have considered. The time spent meeting Vanessa's emotional needs and pointing out what Vanessa needed to work on, however, left little time to actually work on it together. Vanessa may not have known how to identify the underlying concepts in the social studies text or how to help her students grasp the big ideas. Certainly her definition of trading indicated that she had a limited understanding of the term. Moreover Vanessa may have lacked concrete ways to check for student understanding or build students' vocabulary, all suggested by Rachel.

Rachel explained to Vanessa and to us that she herself did not always know how to support second language learners. She worked at extending her knowledge by teaching regularly in Vanessa's classroom. This provided Vanessa with a powerful model of a learning teacher attuned to students' "mind activity." Yet seeing this kind of teaching and learning how to do it oneself are very different activities. While Vanessa could observe Rachel teaching a small group of students, she did not have access to Rachel's planning or to her interactive decision making. We wondered what would have happened if Rachel and Vanessa had co-planned the next social studies lesson together, identifying the big ideas and figuring out how to scaffold students' learning. We saw this kind of "joint work" in Eileen's work with Anna and it suggested further possibilities in the practice of educative mentoring.

ANNA AND EILEEN: A CASE OF "EXCEPTIONAL GROWTH"

Anna was hired to teach second language learners in a 4th/5th grade multi-age classroom in a Title I elementary school that was also a professional development school (PDS) affiliated with the university coordinating the induction program. As a graduate of the teacher certification program at this university, Anna was already familiar with the school and its resources because she had completed a semester of student teaching there. Moreover, her student teaching supervisor, Eileen, who was the professional development coordinator at the school, was now Anna's advisor. A central focus in their work together was determining how to scaffold students' understanding in reading and writing.

Anna's First Year of Mentored Learning to Teach

Eileen's one-on-one mentoring of Anna took place against the backdrop of her ongoing work with Anna's grade level team. In addition to teaching demonstration lessons and debriefing Anna's teaching, Eileen focused her mentoring around what she and Anna called "curriculum development." Eileen met monthly with the 4th and 5th grade teachers to work on literacy instruction. First, she helped the team examine and prioritize the state language arts standards based on the specific needs of their students. Next they talked about "best practices" for teaching to the standards and considered what would count as meaningful evidence of student learning. Eileen also helped Anna and her team members develop curricular units which integrated quality literature and expository texts to teach social studies content.

In her first year of teaching, Anna's professional goals focused on increasing students' comprehension and analysis of what they read. After helping Anna establish structures for literacy instruction, Eileen and Anna turned to the question of how to support students' understanding. For example, Anna's grade level team was exploring the use of literature circles for reading instruction, and Anna believed in the importance of having students talk about books in rich, substantive ways. Once Anna had literature circles in place, she turned her attention to helping students "ask questions and hear each others' ideas":

> I could definitely lead the kids into talking, but it's one thing to sit around and talk and another thing to keep the big ideas in mind when they're talking. Eileen's modeling has really been crucial, being able to watch her facilitate a discussion. She's really helped me keep the big ideas in mind, to focus on what's crucial to know.

By the end of her first year, Eileen described Anna's instructional practice as "so congruent with current research and theory." She relied on Anna's "real keen sense of what she needs" to determine what they should work on together. In Anna's second year of teaching, Eileen continued to help Anna's grade level team develop curricular units, particularly writing units around different genres. This joint curricular work provided the foundation for their planning and refinement of individual lessons informed by ongoing analysis of student work.

Anna's Second Year of Mentored Learning to Teach

As a second year teacher, Anna had a new set of questions about how to scaffold students' learning. What is an appropriate amount of scaffolding? When is it too much? How specific must you be? These questions often came up in relation to teaching writing. She, Eileen and the other 4–5th grade team designed a writing unit on personal narrative which they planned to use as a bridge to teaching expository writing (e.g. a five-paragraph essay). In their grade level teamwork, they clarified the function of each part of a personal narrative: the introduction; beginning, middle and end of the story; and the conclusion. They also wanted to help students learn how organization, purposes, and voice in personal narrative differ from the organization, purposes, and voice used in expository writing.

To help Anna figure out how to scaffold students' learning to write personal narratives and expository essays, Eileen and Anna often planned new lessons based on learning needs that had surfaced in previous lessons. When Eileen observed and later discussed Anna's teaching, they generally divided their sessions into two parts: debrief the lesson, then plan ahead. We observed this pattern in the fall of Anna's second year when, with Eileen, we watched Anna work with students on developing introductions for their personal narratives.

Personal Narrative Lesson

In previous lessons, students had clarified the personal story they were going to write about through various prewriting exercises. In this lesson, Anna focused on drafting introductions. Trying to differentiate the introduction from the actual beginning of the story, Anna explained that the function of an introduction is to "let the reader in on what the story is about and why it's important." To help students get started, she offered two sentence starters—"I'll never forget . . ." and "It's important because . . ." Once students began working independently, Anna and Eileen circulated around the classroom, helping individual students with their introductions.

Post Observation Conference

When they got together to debrief the lesson, Eileen and Anna started by looking at students' writing. They were excited to find that some students had taken their individual coaching to heart and transformed their introduction. For example, Anna explained that one student had initially written, *"I will never forget going fishing with my dad. We went to Pinto Lake."* Anna told him that he was starting to tell the story before introducing it. She suggested that he revisit his pre-writing organizer where he had written why this story was important to him—his father had died shortly after the fishing trip. In response to their conversation, the student rewrote his introduction: *I'll never forget going fishing with my dad. It's important to me because it was the last time my brothers and I got to go fishing with him.*

Eileen told a similarly engaging story about her own success in eliciting a more compelling introduction. One student initially wrote:

> I will never forget the time my hair was on fire. I was about one year old when my hair was on fire. My mom and dad and brother were there when my hair was on fire. It was important to me because I could have died and everybody paid more attention to me than my brothers. I will never forget that time.

Coaching this student, Eileen suggested that she consider how to write her introduction "without telling them anything about the hair because that's dramatic and you don't want to let them in on that yet." The student's revised introduction began,

> Sitting by the fire I often think about the time I almost died. My whole family was around me and it scares all of us just to remember it.

Eileen suggested that Anna use these examples to illustrate the power of a strong introduction in the next day's lesson.

Looking through the other students' writing, however, Anna noticed that not everyone had hit the mark in their initial attempt. This led Anna to ask Eileen, "Should I designate tomorrow as more to do with the introduction?" In other words, should she postpone her original plan of having the students begin to write their actual story the next day and do more work on introductions or should she wait until the students complete their entire narrative before revisiting the introduction? Eileen responded directly, "No. You have too many people ready to go on to the beginning of their story." Anna then wondered what to do with those students who were not ready to move on. Eileen suggested that she first help students think about how to launch the beginning of their story, then pull the six or seven students aside who needed help with their introductions while the rest of the class began drafting their beginnings.

When we returned in the spring, we found that Eileen and Anna were engaged in the same kind of highly detailed, subject-specific work that included analyzing student writing, clarifying the content to be taught, figuring out what kind of support students needed, and refining specific lessons.

Writing Assessment Lesson

Along with Eileen, we observed another writing lesson that Anna taught in May. Anna, along with her grade level team, had developed a rubric for assessing students' personal narratives. To help students determine progress in their own writing, she passed out three writing samples so that they could visualize more concretely what it would look like for a piece of writing to exceed, meet or approach the standards embedded in the rubric. After collectively analyzing these samples, students used the rubric to assess their own previously written pieces.

Post Observation Conference

In this debriefing session, Eileen and Anna spent relatively little time discussing what had happened in the lesson. Mostly they concentrated on planning the first lesson in an expository writing unit that Anna intended to teach the following week. The excerpted conversation below illustrates a pattern that we noticed in their discourse. Anna, understandably focused on the next day's lesson, asks a specific logistical question. Eileen replies, often suggesting specific language that Anna might use in her teaching. This leads to refinement and revision, even to new ideas. Finally the interaction concludes with one of them summarizing what Anna will do. In this excerpt, they were trying to determine how Anna could launch the lesson. We use italics to indicate when Eileen adopts a "teacher voice," giving Anna explicit language to use the following day:

> *Anna:* During the overview, do I let them in on what an expository essay is?
> *Eileen:* Oh, yes. That's when you do the expository writing part. *We're going to be writing an essay as writers and historians. We've been collecting all this information. Now, how do historians write? Do they write the same way as we wrote in our personal narratives? No, they write in information. We're going to be doing something very different from the personal narrative. So voice, organization, purpose.*
> *Anna:* Maybe I should do it in a T-chart form on the overhead.
> *Eileen:* Yeah. *The purpose is different. In narrative, we're telling a story. In expository writing we're giving information. The voice is also different. In narrative we're talking about our personal selves. In expository writing we're going to have an expert's voice, and the organization is very different.*
> *Anna:* I see doing the T-chart. It's just that my fifth graders are going to have the schema around the word 'essay' but my fourth graders will not.
> *Eileen:* You could have your fifth graders talk to your fourth graders about what an essay is.

Anna: Yeah. Here's a question. My students have read social studies books but they've not necessarily read a 5-paragraph essay. Would it be helpful for them to read an essay before we even do any of this to get a sense of where we're going? Or do they need to actually create one before they can understand what one is? What comes first?

Eileen: I'm tempted to use essays that the fifth graders wrote in here last year.

Anna: Cool. I like that. They'll really see that it's an expert voice giving information.

Eileen: So the 5th graders are going to share significant essays they wrote last year with the 4th graders. Then you're going to talk about the purpose of an essay and how it's different from the personal narrative.

Anna's original question led Eileen to step into the teacher's role and think aloud about what Anna might say to launch the lesson. This also gave Eileen a chance to clarify the big ideas in the lesson (e.g. differences in purpose, voice, and organization between personal narrative and expository writing). As she imagined acting on Eileen's suggestions, Anna got an idea of how she could visually represent those differences using a T-chart. Anticipating what might be difficult for her students to understand, Anna then realized that the fifth graders would be familiar with the word 'essay,' but the fourth graders would not. This led Eileen to suggest that they show the fourth graders essays that the fifth graders had written the year before.

We were struck by Eileen's use of the "first person" (e.g. I'm tempted to use), a reflection of how much she was inside the content, the students' learning, and Anna's learning and how much she felt jointly responsible for the teaching. Once Eileen reiterated what the two had agreed on, they continued working through the concrete details of the upcoming lesson in much the same way, with Anna asking questions and Eileen giving direct suggestions. Their exchanges often led to new ideas and insights.

When we asked Eileen to describe Anna's learning near the end of her second year, Eileen encouraged us to examine the progress Anna had documented in her students' writing in order to understand how much Anna had learned. Eileen considered Anna to be an "exceptional" teacher who "because of her brilliance and determination as well as shared support" helped her students "make phenomenal progress" as readers and writers. Eileen further stated that Anna scaffolded not only children's learning but also her colleagues' as well, explaining that every teacher at the PDS is considered "both a teacher and a leader."

Case Analysis

In making sense of this case, we examine the connections between Anna's stance as a learner, the context in which she worked, and the character and quality of mentoring that Eileen provided her. As we found in the case of Rachel and Vanessa, the interaction of these factors seems to account for the exceptional growth that Anna made in her first two years of teaching.

Because Anna earned her Master's degree and teaching credential from the state university that coordinated the induction program she now participated in, she experienced continuity between the orientation of her teacher preparation and her induction experience. She had deliberately chosen a preservice program with a strong theoretical orientation because she saw herself as "a critical thinker" who wanted "to be surrounded by people who thought passionately about education, who have a vision." Previous work with Eileen who had supervised her student teaching created further continuity in Anna's learning. Because they had focused a lot on planning, Anna anticipated continued support and guidance with "curriculum development."[5]

The questions Anna raised as a first and second year teacher while co-planning with Eileen indicate her sophisticated understanding of teaching and her openness to learning. She explained, "I decided to teach because I love to learn. I'm not scared of how much I need to learn." Anna felt comfortable asking Eileen anything without fear of being judged. She believed that learning from practice first required "figuring out what you know" and "thinking about what you're doing," then finding a way to teach in line with your "philosophy."

At her school, Anna enjoyed what Eileen called a "broad system of support." Besides her mentor, Anna viewed her grade level teammates as "comrades, great critical thinkers" whom she relied on for support and guidance. In this sense, Anna benefited from Eileen's efforts to develop a school-wide professional culture. As a PDS, the school enjoyed many financial and human resources, a shared vision of teaching, and a shared focus on student achievement.

In terms of her mentoring practice, Eileen strove to ensure that whatever assistance she provided Anna directly benefited her students' learning. She explained, "We are engaged in trying to figure this out so that it really works for kids, and we share our students. I'm very invested in how the students are doing . . . We're working together to advance the academic achievement of kids." Eileen's mentoring consisted of modeling lessons for Anna, observing and debriefing Anna's own teaching, and co-planning curriculum with Anna. Anna identified Eileen's demonstration lessons as an important resource in learning how to facilitate discussions and keep students focused on "big ideas" embedded in a text. Anna seemed to have both the schema needed to make sense of Eileen's modeling and the intellectual capacity to transfer that knowledge into her own practice.

Eileen's mentoring included not only helping Anna learn from her teaching but also preparing for future instruction. This entailed two kinds of planning: (1) "big picture" planning of curricular units where Eileen and Anna deepened and clarified their knowledge of writing; and (2) lesson planning where Eileen reinforced Anna's content knowledge while helping her work through the particulars of enacting a lesson, including anticipating difficulties students might encounter and specific language she could use to introduce key definitions and give directions. Through their "joint work,"[6] Eileen and Anna were able to generate ideas that neither would have come up with on her own. Working together to plan units and lessons, Eileen drew on her extensive pedagogical knowledge, her desire to consolidate the content and skills they wanted students to learn, and her interest in figuring out the best way to teach them. In this form of mentoring, the mentor is both co-learner and expert.

DISCUSSION

These cases of mentored learning to teach provide vivid images of thoughtful mentors at work. They also shed light on the diverse learning needs of beginning teachers and on the way school cultures and structures enable and constrain educative mentoring. If we want to realize the benefits of mentoring as a vehicle for improving teaching and learning, we need to base induction programs and policies on dependable ideas about new teachers as learners, the nature of educative mentoring, and the role of schools in new teacher induction.

Beginning teachers still have a lot to learn if they are going to become effective teachers, especially in Title 1 schools serving low-income minority students. This is true for an accomplished beginner like Anna who is ready to work on a sophisticated agenda—how to lead discussions that are rich in ideas and how to scaffold the development of writing skills in her ESL fourth grade students. It is also true for Vanessa who is skilled in classroom management but does not know how to help her fourth/fifth graders read for meaning. It is surely true for the increasing numbers of teachers who enter classrooms with even less of a foundation to build on. The current generation of beginning teachers brings varied experiences and expectations to their work, but all need situated and sustained guidance and support as they tackle the challenge of learning to teach in a particular school context.

It is widely assumed that new teachers mostly need help with classroom management. Once that is addressed, they can learn the rest on their own. This represents a limited understanding of teaching and a limited view of learning to teach. Skill in classroom management is necessary but hardly sufficient for the kind of teaching that helps students learn to use their minds with power and pleasure. Independent, trial and error learning is no guarantee that new teachers will develop defensible teaching practices. We need induction and mentoring that respond to the varied and changing needs of beginning teachers and that increase the likelihood that what new teachers learn from experience reflects the best that we know. (Imagine the consequences for Vanessa's students if no mentor were around to point out the limits of whole class instruction and the dangers of sacrificing reading comprehension to fluency.) Until we face the fact that all beginning teachers are learning to teach, we will continue to define induction as short-term support rather than new teacher development.

The kind of mentoring that Rachel and Eileen practice does not fit the popular image of mentors as buddies or local guides. As teachers of teachers, both mentors expected to contribute to new teachers' learning and to influence the quality of their teaching. They demonstrated a sense of shared responsibility for student learning. They enabled new teachers to do with help what they were not ready to do on their own. While we noticed some differences in their mentoring practices, the similarities are more relevant to an understanding of educative mentoring.

If mentoring is to function as a form of individualized professional development, it must be guided by a vision of the kind of teaching to be developed. Both Eileen and Rachel worked from well-developed conceptions of good teaching. Besides the vision represented in the California teaching standards, they had subject-specific images of literate classrooms and balanced language arts programs. This enabled them to frame or recognize important issues in their conversations with new teachers, use observational data effectively, give sound advice, and assess new teachers' progress.

Equally important, both Eileen and Rachel were working at the edges of their own knowledge of teaching and the knowledge-base of the field, trying to figure out the best ways to develop powerful language skills in ESL students. Consequently, they were eager to work and learn alongside other teachers, including novices. This sent a powerful message about teachers as learners and teaching as an experimental practice.

Mentors need a flexible repertoire to help new teachers get inside the practical and intellectual demands of teaching. Rachel was more disposed to rely on "reflective conversations" to help Vanessa think about aspects of teaching that she may not have considered on her own. Eileen was more disposed to helping Anna learn what she wanted to know by actually doing the work together. Both Rachel and Eileen were skillful classroom observers and both used direct telling, asking, listening and modeling.

Research on the limits of one-on-one mentoring documents the following problems: mentors with no time to meet with new teachers; mentors in other schools, subjects, or grade levels than the new teacher assigned to them; mentors with little or no preparation for mentoring; or mentors with limited views of their roles and responsibilities (Feiman-Nemser & Parker, 1993; Norman, 2001; Smith & Ingersoll, 2003; Johnson et al., 2004). Whenever we hear claims about the value or limits of mentoring, we need to ask: what kind of mentoring are we talking about and what sorts of outcomes do we seek? If we want mentoring to improve the quality of classroom teaching, then we need mentors who are teachers of teaching and organizations that enable mentors to do their work.

Still, as we saw in the case of Vanessa, even serious and sustained mentoring is no magic bullet. What mentoring can accomplish is affected not only by the expectations and skill of the mentor, but also by the stance and expectations of the new teacher. If a new teacher is resistant or emotionally needy or slow to take seriously the legitimate concerns of the mentor, no matter how diplomatically presented, then the mentor may not be able to move the novice as far or as quickly as she would like. Finding a workable balance of support and stretch is an endemic challenge in educative mentoring. Even two years may not be long enough to help some new teachers establish good teaching habits.

An equally important factor is the school context where teaching and mentoring take place. Recent studies show that the professional culture in schools, "the blend of values, norms and modes of professional practice that develop among teachers," has a strong impact on new teachers and their work with mentors (Johnson et al., 2004, p. 140). Again the two cases are instructive. Anna worked in a school where she felt supported by her colleagues as well as her mentor. The formal mentoring that Eileen provided took place against the backdrop of a professional culture which valued collaboration among teachers at all experience levels. The following description of an "integrated professional culture" fits the Professional Development School (PDS) where Anna taught and Eileen mentored:

> In integrated professional cultures, mentoring is organized to benefit both the novice and the experienced teachers, and structures are in place that further facilitate teacher interaction and reinforce interdependence. Schools with integrated professional cultures are organizations that explicitly value teachers' professional growth and renewal (Johnson et al., 2004, p. 159).

On the other hand, Vanessa found herself in a school with a high proportion of inexperienced teachers (and new administrators). With no experienced teachers on the fourth grade team, she did not have regular and easy access to the "wisdom of practice." Nor did anyone in the administration do anything about the dysfunctional relationships among the fourth grade teachers. No wonder Rachel felt like Vanessa's sole source of support. One can only speculate about the trajectory of Vanessa's learning if she had started teaching in a school where new teachers cooperated and communicated with each other and with their experienced colleagues in order to improve school-wide instruction. Perhaps Rachel would not have been the only voice of conscience trying to keep Vanessa from letting even a single student fall through the cracks.

Without a web of professional support in her school, Vanessa was fortunate to have the services of a strong induction program jointly funded by the state and district to provide her with serious, school-based mentoring during her first two years of teaching.[7]

The cases presented here illustrate two structural models of mentoring—mentoring as part of a school-wide program of professional development and mentoring as part of a formal induction program. Arguing whether "inside" or "outside" mentoring is preferable misses the point. Until schools are organized to enable serious collaboration, interdependence, and learning on the part of all teachers, we need induction programs that take new teacher learning seriously. No matter what organization formally initiates such programs, induction and mentoring inevitably happen in schools. The more policy makers and educational leaders understand the formal and informal conditions in schools that enable new teachers to thrive, including the kind of educative mentoring that nurtures effective teaching over time, the better able they will be to advocate and build school-based systems of support and development for all teachers.

REFERENCES

California Department of Education. (1997). *California standards for the teaching profession.* California Department of Education.

Cohen, D., McLaughlin, M., & Talbert, J. (Eds.). (1993). *Teaching for understanding: Challenges for policy and practice.* San Francisco, CA: Jossey-Bass.

Dewey, J. (1904/1965). The relation of theory to practice in education. In R. D. Archambault (Ed.), *John Dewey on education.* Chicago: University of Chicago Press.

Erickson, F. (1986). Qualitative methods in research on teaching. In M. Wittrock (Ed.), *Handbook of research on teaching.* New York: Macmillan.

Evertson, C. M., & Smithey, M. W. (2000). Mentoring effects on proteges' classroom practice: An experimental field study. *Journal of Educational Research, 93*(5), 294–304.

Feiman-Nemser, S. (2000). *New teacher induction: Promising programs, policies and practices.* Final Report, National Partnership for Excellence and Accountability in Teaching.

Feiman-Nemser, S. (2003). From preparation to practice: Designing a continuum to strengthen and sustain teaching. *Teachers College Record, 103*(6), 1013–1055.

Feiman-Nemser, S., & Parker, M. (1993). Mentoring in context: A comparison of two US programs for beginning teachers. *International Journal of Educational Research,* 699–718.

Fideler, E., & Haselkorn, D. (1999). *Learning the ropes: Urban teacher induction practices in the United States.* Belmont, MA: Recruiting New Teachers, Inc.

Fuller, F. (1969). Concerns of teachers: A developmental conceptualization. *American Educational Research Journal, 6,* 207–226.

Fuller, F., & Brown, O. (1975). Becoming a teacher. In K. Ryan (Ed.), *Teacher education (74th Yearbook of the National Society for the Study of Education)* (pp. 25–52). Chicago: University of Chicago Press.

Gold, Y. (1996). Beginning teacher support: Attrition, mentoring, and induction. In J. Sikula, T. J. Buttery, & E. Guyton (Eds.), *Handbook of research on teacher education,* (2nd ed) (pp. 548–594). New York: Simon and Schuster Macmillan.

Hind, M. (2002). *Carnegie Challenge 2002: Teaching as a clinical profession: A new challenge for education.* New York: Carnegie Corporation of New York.

Huling-Austin, L. (1990). Teacher induction programs and internships. In W. R. Houston (Ed.), *The handbook of research on teacher education.* New York: Macmillan.

Ingersoll, R., & Smith, T. (2003). The wrong solution to the teacher shortage. *Educational Leadership, 60*(8), 30–33.

Johnson, S. M. & and the Project on the Next Generation of Teachers. (2004). *Finders and keepers: Helping new teachers survive and thrive in our schools.* San Francisco, CA: Jossey-Bass.

Kagan, D. (1992). Professional growth among preservice and beginning teachers. *Review of Educational Research, 62*(2), 129–169.

Little, J. (1990a). The mentor phenomenon and the social organization of teaching. In C. Cazden (Ed.), *Review of Research in Education.* Washington, DC: American Educational Research Association.

Little, J. (1990b). The persistence of privacy: Autonomy and initiative in teachers' professional relations. *Teachers College Record, 91*(4), 509–537.

Miles, M., & Huberman, A. (1994). *Qualitative data analysis: A sourcebook of new methods.* Beverly Hills, CA: Sage.

Norman, P. (2001). *Confronting the challenges of field-based teacher education: New roles and practices for university and school-based teacher educators.* Unpublished doctoral dissertation. East Lansing, MI: Michigan State University.

Schon, D. (1987). *Educating the reflective practitioner: Toward a new design for teaching and learning in the professions.* San Francisco, CA: Jossey-Bass.

Smith, T., & Ingersoll, R. (2003). Reducing teacher turnover: What are the components of effective induction? Paper presented at the Annual Meeting of the American Educational Research Association, Chicago.

Wang, J., & Odell, S. (2002). Mentored learning to teach according to standards-based reform: A critical review. *Review of Educational Research, 72*(3), 481–546.

Wells, G. (2002). A theoretical rationale for mentoring as a mode of teacher professional development. Paper presented at the Annual Meeting of the American Educational Research Association, New Orleans, LA.

Wildman, T., Niles, J., Magliaro, S., & McLaughlin, R. (1989). Teaching and learning to teach: The two roles of beginning teachers. *Elementary School Journal, 89*(4), 471–492.

The essays in this book are reprinted with permission from the sources below.

Chapter 1

Feiman-Nemser, Sharon. "Learning to Teach." In Shulman & Sykes, *Handbook of Teaching and Policy*, pp. 150–70. ©1983. Reproduced by permission of Pearson Education, Inc.

Chapter 2

Feiman-Nemser, Sharon. "Teacher Preparation: Structural and Conceptual Alternatives." From *HANDBK RES TEACHERS EDUC*, 0E. © 1990 Gale, a part of Cengage Learning, Inc. Reproduced by permission. www.cengage.com/permissions

Chapter 3

Feiman-Nemser, Sharon. "From Preparation to Practice: Designing a Continuum to Strengthen and Sustain Teaching." *Teachers College Record* 103, no. 6 (December 2001): 1013–1055.

Chapter 4

Feiman-Nemser, Sharon. "Multiple Meanings of New Teacher Induction." In *Past, Present and Future Research on Teacher Induction: An Anthology for Researchers, Policy Makers, and Practitioners*, edited by Jian Wang, Sandra J. Odell, and Renée T. Clift, 15–30. New York: Rowman and Littlefield: 2010.

Chapter 5

Feiman-Nemser, Sharon, and Margret Buchmann. "Pitfalls of Experience in Teacher Preparation." *Teachers College Record* 87, no. 1 (1985): 53–65.

Chapter 6

Feiman-Nemser, Sharon, and Margret Buchmann. "The First Year of Teacher Preparation: Transition to Pedagogical Thinking?" *Journal of Curriculum Studies* 18, no. 3 (1986): 239–56. Reprinted by permission of the publisher (Taylor & Francis Ltd, http://www.tandf.co.uk/journals).

Chapter 7

Feiman-Nemser, Sharon, and Margret Buchmann. Reprinted from *Teaching and Teacher Education* 3, no. 24, Sharon Feiman-Nemser and Margret Buchmann, "When Is Student Teaching Teacher Education?," 255–273, Copyright 1987, with permission from Elsevier.

Chapter 8

Feiman-Nemser, Sharon. "Linking Mentoring and Teacher Learning." *Velon* 19, no. 3 (June/July 1998): 5–13.

Chapter 9

Feiman-Nemser, Sharon. Reprinted with permission from S. Feiman-Nemser, "Helping Novices Learn to Teach: Lessons from an Exemplary Support Teacher" in the *Journal of Teacher Education*, Vol. 52, No. 1 (January/February 2001), pp. 17–30. Copyright 2001 by the American Association of Colleges for Teacher Education (AACTE); also reprinted with permission from S. Feiman-Nemser & C. Rosaen, "Guiding Teacher Learning: A Fresh Look at a Familiar Practice" in S. Feiman-Nemser & C. Rosaen (Eds.), *Guiding Teacher Learning: Insider Studies of Classroom Work With Prospective and Practicing Teachers*. Copyright 1997 by the American Association of Colleges for Teacher Education (AACTE).

Chapter 10

Norman, Patricia J., and Sharon Feiman-Nemser. Reprinted from *Teaching and Teacher Education* 21 (2005), Patricia J. Norman and Sharon Feiman-Nemser, "Mind Activity in Teaching and Mentoring," pp. 679–697, Copyright 2005, with permission from Elsevier.

Introduction

1. In the 1950s and 1960s, the Ford Foundation supported the establishment of Master of Arts in Teaching (MAT) programs in elite universities. The MAT combined graduate study in the teacher's discipline with an internship. By including disciplinary study, extending the amount of supervised experience, and limiting the number of education courses, MAT programs sought to attract liberal arts graduates, mainly for high school teaching, who were unlikely to attend a standard teacher education program. In this sense, they were more of a recruitment than a training strategy. Harvard actually established its MAT program before the Ford Foundation became involved.

2. New critics believed that structure and meaning are intimately connected. Named after John Crowe Ransom's 1941 book, *The New Criticism*, new criticism was the central mode of literary scholarship in American universities until the 1970s, when it was eclipsed by other theoretical approaches such as poststructuralism, deconstruction theory, and reader response theory. As an undergraduate and graduate student, I learned to read and understand poetry and fiction through the close reading of texts, and this orientation shaped my teaching as well.

3. The curriculum reforms of the 1960s emphasized the *structure of the disciplines*—giving students access to foundational concepts and modes of inquiry that characterize different domains of knowledge and allow knowledge to grow and change. Revisions of math and science curricula began in the 1950s because of dissatisfaction with what many perceived as the "intellectual flabbiness" of the schools (Silberman, 1970, p. 170). Most of the leaders were university scholars, some of whom sought to design "teacher-proof curricula." That made our experience as teachers engaged in discipline-based curriculum development all the more special.

4. See chapter 6, this volume.

5. Years later, when I encountered sociocultural theories of learning, I saw how they illuminated key aspects of this powerful learning experience. Supporting me in my "zone of proximal development" (Vygotsky, 1957), Jim and Darlene enabled me to do with help what I could not yet do on my own. They provided a "cognitive apprenticeship" (Collins, Brown, & Newman, 1989) in planning and teaching and inducted me into a "community of practice" (Lave & Wenger, 1991). Starting out as a legitimate but peripheral member of the community, I gradually became a more capable participant, and this helped shape my identity as a progressive educator.

6. To name some of the great teachers I had at Teachers College, Columbia University, in the late 1960s and early 1970s, I took courses from historian Lawrence Cremin; philosophers Maxine Greene, Philip Phenix, Jonas Soltis; curriculum theorist Dwayne Huebner; and teacher educator Margret Lindsey.

7. Over the years, I have had the privilege of working with philosophers Margret Buchmann, Robert Floden, Sophie Haroutunian-Gordon, Jon Levisohn, and Carol Wheeler, all of whom contributed greater clarity, precision, and depth to my thinking.

8. At a conference honoring Philip Jackson held in New York City on October 24–25, 2003, Linda Darling-Hammond quoted the same passage in her tribute to Jackson. In her essay, later published in *A Life in Classrooms: Philip W. Jackson and the Practice of Education* (Hansen, Driscoll, & Arcilla, 2007), Darling-Hammond describes reading Jackson through the eyes of a teacher just becoming a researcher, and how Jackson affirmed what she had experienced as a teacher, but not a student teacher, in her CBTE program in the 1970s (Darling-Hammond, 2007, pp. 17–18).

9. As Gage (1985) explains, a scientific basis for the art of teaching establishes "one or more relationships between things that teachers do and things that students learn (p. 15). Establishing such relationships depends on a progression from observational and descriptive studies, through correlational studies, to experiments that can establish dependable generalizations about how changing teaching practices causes desirable changes in student attitudes and achievement.

10. In 1974, Dunkin and Biddle published a five-hundred-page textbook for teachers summarizing all the studies to date that involved the systematic observation of classroom teaching. After a detailed review and assessment of the research, the authors concluded that the task of generating empirical knowledge about teaching is possible but had barely begun. "Most of the evidence is suggestive, not definitive, because crucial relationships must still be established, samples are limited, and/or findings have not been confirmed with experiments." But what we do have, they point out, are scores of variables for describing what goes on in classrooms. "The appearance of this research effort is one of the most significant developments in education during the twentieth century" (p. 418).

11. Kounin's findings are still taught to teachers in a contemporary program of professional development called "the skillful teacher" (Saphier, Haley-Speca, & Gower, 2008).

12. Flanders's law reflects the persistence of *teacher-centered instruction* over three-quarters of a century, which Cuban (1984) later documented in a study of "how teachers taught." Based on the examination of artifacts since 1900—including teacher accounts, newspaper articles, student recollections, photographs, formal studies, and school surveys—Cuban showed "a seemingly stubborn continuity in the character of instruction" (p. 21). In teacher-centered instruction, teacher talk exceeds student talk during instruction, whole-class teaching dominates, class time is determined by the teacher, and the classroom is usually arranged in rows facing a blackboard with a teacher's desk nearby (p. 3).

13. For a discussion of conceptual ambiguities and methodological problems associated with Flanders's work, see Dunkin and Biddle (1974, pp. 113–120).

14. During my last two years as a doctoral candidate, I worked as the coordinator and student-teaching supervisor for an urban in-residence teacher training program sponsored by the University of New York at Stonybrook. Stonybrook students spent a semester in the South Bronx, living together in apartments rented by the university, student teaching at James Monroe High School, and participating in various community service projects under the direction of a community coordinator. This was my

first experience in urban teacher education and a chance to try out ideas and practices I was learning about in my doctoral program.

15. These studies show that, by the end of student teaching, student teachers tend to adopt more authoritarian attitudes, replace concerns about pupils' learning with a need to get through the lesson, and use methods of instruction and discipline they initially considered unacceptable. For a summary of this research, see Peck and Tucker (1973, pp. 940–978).

16. One exception was the Teachers College model, which proposed broad categories of performance criteria organized around four major teacher roles (institution builder, interactive teacher, innovator, and scholar) but avoided the detailed breakdown into numerous behavioral criteria and modules (Joyce, 1968).

17. For a review of research on microteaching, see Peck and Tucker (1973, pp. 951–954).

18. For a rich history of the roots of open education in the U.S., see R. Dropkin and A. Tobier (Eds.). (1976). *Roots of open education in America*. New York: City College Workshop for Open Education.

19. The University of Chicago was on the quarter system. This meant that we could bring students to campus for the last two weeks of August and then have them observe in an elementary classroom during the month of September, before the fall quarter started in late September. This new structure added six weeks to the beginning of the program.

20. Joyce and Weil developed the *models of teaching* approach as part of the Teacher Innovator Program, one of the model competency-based programs funded by the U.S. Office of Education and developed at Teachers College, Columbia University, where Joyce served on the faculty. The models of teaching were the centerpiece of the Interactive Teacher component, which introduced students to a repertoire of models (Joyce, 1968). I had been intrigued by this variation on the CBTE theme, which prompted my short-lived but instructive experiment.

21. In subsequent years, we organized the Curriculum and Instruction Lab around helping students learn to lead *interpretive discussions of literature*, using the Great Books model of discussion leading. Students developed clusters of questions, which they used in leading discussions with their peers. Then they led discussions with small groups of pupils, which they audiotaped and analyzed. Sophie Haroutunian-Gordon, a doctoral student in the Department of Education at the time, led this work. Haroutunian-Gordon has made this the centerpiece of the Master of Science in Education program she directs at Northwestern University. See S. Haroutunian-Gordon (2009). *Learning to teach through discussion: The art of turning the soul*. New Haven, CT: Yale University Press.

22. Vivian Paley continued teaching kindergarten at the Laboratory School for thirty years and wrote many wonderful books about teaching. *White Teacher*, *Wally's Stories*, and *The Girl with the Brown Crayon* have been staples in my teacher education courses.

23. Unlike U.S. curriculum reforms in the 1960s, which often produced "teacher-proof" curricula, the Nuffield Foundation in England involved teachers in the production of mathematics curricula by including them on curriculum teams and inviting them to try out drafts of materials and provide feedback to the developers. Informal meetings were the basis for this work, and they became more widespread as developers tried to

help teachers understand the spirit as well as the content of the new curricula. Over time, these local groups became permanent teacher centers, supporting informal education in British primary schools. Joseph Featherstone wrote about the "revolution" in British primary schools that inspired American teachers' centers in the August 19, September 2, and September 5, 1967, issues of the *New Republic*.

24. Funded by the National Institute of Education and launched in 1975, the Teachers' Centers Exchange was a national network of approximately one hundred grassroots teachers' centers. The Exchange arranged meetings for teachers' center leaders and people interested in learning about centers, spotlighted and circulated information, maintained a national directory, and generally supported "give and take" about and among teachers' centers.

25. The name *advisors* signals a form of support that falls outside the existing supervisory structure and depends on voluntarism and trust.

26. With a small grant from the Study Commission on Undergraduate Education and the Education of Teachers and the help of doctoral students, I did a series of studies at the TCWC. I documented the center's history, philosophy, and organizational structure; instituted a system for tracking why people came to the center and what they did there; and conducted systematic observations of teachers' behavior and interaction during open hours (Feiman, 1975a; 1975b). I also reviewed the teacher center's literature, and proposed a typology for distinguishing three kinds of centers—behavioral, humanistic, and developmental—based on underlying beliefs, structures, and approaches to evaluation (Feiman, 1977). This led to more conceptual work on development as a metaphor for teacher learning (Feiman & Floden, 1980).

27. Public Law 94-482, October 12, 1976, Amendment, Part B: Teacher Training Programs, Sec. 532 – Teacher Centers.

28. For a discussion of the political, professional, and policy contexts during this period, see M. Cochran-Smith and K. Fries (2005).

29. The American Educational Research Association, the major professional/academic association for education researchers, signaled this by establishing a new division in 1984. Division K on Teaching and Teacher Education is now the largest division in an organization that numbers twenty-five thousand members.

30. The Holmes Group, an alliance of one hundred research universities, outlined its agenda in three publications: *Tomorrow's Teachers* (1986), *Tomorrow's Schools* (1990), and *Tomorrow's Schools of Education* (1995).

31. Committed to a vision of liberal/professional learning, we replaced the *early field experience* structure, in which students spent three hours a week in an elementary classroom and one hour in a discussion section, with a seminar organized around three core questions: (1) What is teaching? (2) What are schools for? (3) What do teachers need to know?

32. Both programs were part of a larger effort to reform undergraduate teacher education at MSU. The academic program emphasized theoretical and subject-matter knowledge. Many courses stressed teaching for understanding and conceptual change, and students had limited field experiences prior to student teaching. The decision-making program emphasized generic pedagogical knowledge and research-based decision making. Much of the program took place in an elementary school

where students spent time observing, aiding, and teaching. Chapters 6 and 7 grew out of the KULT project.

33. We identified three perspectives on mentoring. Some mentors functioned as *local guides*, helping novices fit into their school settings and backing off as soon as the novices seemed comfortable. Others functioned as *educational companions*, helping novices with immediate problems without losing sight of long-term professional learning goals. Still others functioned as *agents of cultural change*, fostering norms of collaboration and breaking down the traditional isolation among teachers. The case of Pete Frazer, chapter 9 this volume, grew out of this work.

34. Chapters 8 and 10 are based on my NCRTL research.

35. The phrase *teaching for understanding* was widely used to signal a "new" vision of good teaching that aimed to be responsive to students' thinking and offer serious encounters with subject matter. Core principles of this new vision of instruction included "(a) a conception of knowledge as constructed by the learner and therefore situated in the context of prior knowledge, skills, values and beliefs; (b) a conception of teacher as guide, as co-constructor of students' knowledge; (c) a conception of the classroom as a community of learners in which shared goals and standards, an atmosphere of mutual trust, and norms for behavior support students in taking risks and making the sustained effort entailed in serious learning." (D. Cohen, M. McLaughlin, & J. Talbert (Eds.). *Teaching for understanding: A Challenge for policy and practice*. San Francisco: Jossey-Bass, p. 169.

36. For a case of educative mentoring in China, see Wang and Paine, 2001.

37. In the elementary professional development school where we did this study, I had been collaborating with a second-grade teacher, Kathleen Beasley, on redefining the roles of cooperating teachers and university supervisors in teacher preparation, and on inducting other teachers into these new ways of thinking and working with interns. This local, collaborative research on mentoring as assisted performance (Feiman-Nemser & Beasley, 1997) complemented and contributed to my national and international research on mentoring.

Chapter 2

1. Feiman-Nemser, S. (1990). Teacher preparation: Structural and conceptual alternatives. In W. R. Houston (Ed.), *Handbook of Research on Teacher Education* (2nd ed., pp. 195–211). New York: Macmillan, 1996.

2. The author expresses appreciation to the following people for their helpful comments on an earlier draft of this paper: Margaret Buchmann, Robert Houston, Susan Melnick, Michelle B. Parker, Michael Sedlak, Alan Tom, Ken Zeichner, and Karen Zumwalt.

Chapter 3

This chapter was originally commissioned by the Strengthening and Sustaining Teaching Project (SST) which is coordinated by Bank Street College, the National Commission on Teaching and America's Future, the Teacher Union Reform Network and the National Network for Educational Renewal. The author wishes to thank Patricia Wasley for her thoughtful comments on an earlier draft, Sharon Dorsey for gathering materials and offering encouragement, Patricia Norman for helping with references and being a sounding board for ideas, and Jennifer Rosenberger for putting together the final manuscript. Funding for this paper was generously supported by the Philip Morris Corporation. The opinions expressed here are the author's.

1. Various labels have been attached to this kind of reform-minded teaching, including "teaching for understanding" (Cohen, McLaughlin, & Talbert, 1993; Holmes Group, 1990), "authentic pedagogy" (Newman & Associates, 1996), "adventurous teaching" (Cohen, 1988), "constructivist pedagogy" (Fosnot, 1996) and, more recently, "standard-based teaching" (National Commission on Teaching and America's Future, 1996).

2. Sources include recommendations from the Association of Teacher Educators (Brooks, 1987; Odell & Huling, 2000), findings from a study of clinical teacher education conducted by the Center for Research on Teacher Education at the University of Texas at Austin (Griffin, 1986), recommendations from a study of urban induction programs by Recruiting New Teachers (Fideler & Haselkorn, 1999), and the National Commission on Teaching and America's Future (1996), and Standards of Quality and Effectiveness for California's Beginning Teacher Support and Assessment Program (BTSA, 1997).

Chapter 5

An earlier version of this paper appeared under the same title in P. Tamir, ed., *Preservice and Inservice Education of Science Teachers* (Glenside, Pa.: International Science Service, 1984).

Chapter 6

This work is sponsored in part by the Institute for Research on Teaching, College of Education, Michigan State University. The Institute for Research on Teaching is funded primarily by the Program for Teaching and Instruction of the National Institute of Education, United States Department of Education. The opinions expressed in this publication do not necessarily reflect the position, policy, or endorsement of the National Institute of Education (Contract No. 400-81-0014).

An earlier version of this paper was presented as part of a symposium entitled "Teacher Thinking and Curriculum Change: New Perspectives," at the annual meeting of the American Educational Research Association, New Orleans, April 1984. The authors wish to acknowledge and thank Deborah Loewenberg Ball, who assisted in project management and data collection.

1. Hawkins, D. (1974) The Informed Vision: Essays on Learning and Human Nature (Agathon Press, New York).

2. Highet, G. (1966) *The Art of Teaching* (Alfred A. Knopf, New York), p. 280.

3. The study followed eight elementary education students through two years of undergraduate preparation, including student teaching. The students were chosen from candidates nominated by program co-ordinators and matched on the basis of survey data collected on all undergraduate teacher education students at Michigan State

University. Four are enrolled in the Academic Learning Program, and four in the Decision-Making Program. The two programs differ in structure, content and ideology. Each term and at the end of the year, students were interviewed about what they were learning and how that might help them in teaching and learning to teach. The interviews probed parallel aspects of the observed curriculum in relation to these issues.

4. All names in the two case studies are pseudonyms. Excerpts from the interviews are unedited except for the deletion of repetitions and "uh's." Occasionally we have highlighted key terms or phrases and structured long quotations into paragraphs. The numbers in parentheses after quotations from the interview data refer to pages in the interview transcripts.

5. A spiral curriculum allows for increasingly more sophisticated study of the same topic across grade levels.

6. Anyon, J. (1981) Social class and school knowledge. *Curriculum Inquiry, 11*, 1, pp. 3–42.

7. See for example Huberman, M. (1983) Recipes for busy kitchens: A Situational analysis of routine knowledge use in schools. *Knowledge: Creation, Diffusion, Utilization*, 4, pp. 478–510; Little, J. W. (1982) Norms of collegiality and experimentation: Workplace conditions of school success. *American Educational Research Journal*, 19, pp. 325–340; and Lortie, D. C. (1975) *Schoolteacher: A Sociological Study* (University of Chicago Press).

8. Buchmann, M. (1983) *Role over Person: Justifying Teacher Action and Decisions*. Research Series No. 135 (Michigan State University, Institute for Research on Teaching, East Lansing).

9. For a discussion of the underlying epistemology in both programs and their likely effects on students, see Feiman-Nemser, S. and Ball, D. Views of knowledge in preservice curriculum. Paper presented at the annual meeting of the American Educational Research Association, New Orleans, April, 1984.

10. See Buchmann, M., and Schwille, J. (1983) Education: The overcoming of experience. *American Journal of Education, 92*, pp. 30–51. Also available as Occasional Paper No. 63 (Michigan State University, Institute for Research on Teaching, East Lansing); and Feiman-Nemser, S. and Buchmann, M. (1983) Pitfalls of experience in teacher preparation. In P. Tamir (ed.) *Pre-service and In-service Education of Science Teachers* (International Science Services, Glenside, PA). Also available as Occasional Paper No. 65 (Michigan State University, Institute for Research on Teaching, East Lansing).

11. Goodlad, J. (1984) *A Place Called School* (McGraw-Hill, New York), p. 165.

12. Buchmann, M. (1984) The priority of knowledge and understanding in teaching. In L. Katz and J. Raths (eds.) *Advances in Teacher Education Vol. 1* (Ablex Press, Norwood, nj). Also available as Occasional Paper No. 61 (Michigan State University, Institute for Research on Teaching, East Lansing). See Buchmann and Schwille (1983); and Feiman-Nemser and Buchmann (1983) (see note 11). Goodlad, J. (1984) (see note 12).

13. Peters, R. S. (1977) *Education and the Education of Teachers* (Routledge and Kegan Paul, London). p. 151.

Chapter 7

This work is sponsored in part by the Institute for Research on Teaching, College of Education, Michigan State University. The Institute for Research on Teaching is funded primarily by the Office of Educational Research and Improvement, United States Department of Education. The opinions expressed in this publication do not necessarily reflect the position, policy, or endorsement of the Office or the Department (Contract No. 400-81-0014). A version of this paper was presented under the title "On What Is Learned in Student Teaching: Appraising the Experience" at the annual meeting of the American Educational Research Association, Chicago, April 1985.

1. The authors wish to gratefully acknowledge Deborah Loewenberg Ball for her helpful comments on earlier drafts.
2. Between 1982 and 1984, we followed six elementary education students through two years of undergraduate teacher education. The students were enrolled in two contrasting programs that are part of a major effort to reform the preservice curriculum. Each term we interviewed students about what they were learning in their courses and field experiences and how they thought that would help them in teaching and learning to teach. The interviews were grounded in systematic observations of core courses and field experiences in both programs. During student teaching, each student teacher was paired with one researcher who made weekly visits to observe and document the student teacher's activities. We also kept notes of informal conversations with the student teachers, the cooperating teachers, and university supervisors and conducted formal interviews before and after the experience.
3. The numbers refer to pages in the data set for each student. All the names are pseudonyms.
4. "I" indicates interview numbers.

Chapter 8

1. An earlier version of this paper was presented as a keynote address at the Flemish Educational Research Association meetings in Brussels, June, 1997. The research reported here was supported in part by the National Center for Research on Teacher Learning at Michigan State University. The NCRTL was funded by the Office of Educational Research and Improvement, U.S. Department of Education. The opinions expressed here do not necessarily reflect the position of OERI or the Department.
2. We also conceptualized the contexts of mentored learning to teach which include the mentoring relationship, the classroom and school, the larger policy arena, and broader social values. In the interest of space, I do not discuss that part of our conceptual framework in this paper.
3. For a more extended study of Nancy as a mentor and teacher, see Dembele (1997).

Chapter 9

1. All names of teachers and students in this article are pseudonyms. I want to acknowledge the contribution of Michelle Parker in gathering most of the data for this case study and express my appreciation to the support teachers and beginning teachers who participated so generously in the research.

2. The concept of educative mentoring grew out of an analysis of Teacher Education and Learning to Teach data from two beginning teacher programs. Based on a comparison of mentoring practice in these two sites, we identified three kinds of mentors: local guides, educational companions, and change agents (see Feiman-Nemser & Parker, 1993). We continued to refine the idea of educative mentoring in a cross-cultural study of reform-minded mentors in England, China, and the United States and through development work in a professional development school affiliated with Michigan State University (Feiman-Nemser & Beasley, 1998).

3. For a critique of Fuller (1969) and other developmental approaches to teacher education, see Feiman-Nemser and Floden (1981).

4. Lee Shulman (1983) explains the value of such a strategy: "It is often the goal . . . to pursue the possible, not only to support the probable or frequent. The well-crafted case instantiates the possible, not only documenting that it can be done, but also laying out at least one detailed example of how it was organized, developed and pursued." (p. 495)

Chapter 10

1. In the 1990–91 school year less than half of the beginning teachers responding to the NCES nationally representative Schools and Staffing Survey (SASS) said that they participated in an induction program or worked with a mentor. In the 2000–2001 school year, nearly 80% of beginning teachers said that they participated in an induction program or worked closely with a mentor (Smith and Ingersoll, 2003).

2. The case titles are taken from the mentors' language as they reflected on their two years of work with the beginning teacher.

3. Rachel was not the only person to express concern that Vanessa was not attending sufficiently to students' comprehension. After attending a workshop on reading instruction, Vanessa invited the workshop facilitator to observe her teach during reading centers. Like Rachel, the facilitator told Vanessa that she needed to give greater attention to how her students understood their reading.

4. Several days prior to Vanessa's lesson, Rachel had illustrated this point while teaching a demonstration lesson about a social studies passage that dealt with Mexico gaining its independence. Rachel had identified the concept of "independence" as particularly important to understanding the section of text the students would read, so she first conducted a 10-min mini-lesson on the term. After stating that independent means "being able to be on your own," Rachel asked the students if they were independent. Would their parents ever leave them? Are they independent as students? What about teachers and adults? Are they ever independent? Rachel then made an explicit tie to the text when she asked them what they thought it meant for a country to be independent. After some initial confusion about Rachel's opening, Vanessa later realized that Rachel had taken an "abstract concept" and made it accessible to kids, something Vanessa had "never thought about."

5. Anna's teaching context reflects the concept of "clinical residency programs" described in a recent Carnegie Challenge Report (Hinds, 2002). Clinical residency programs provide novices with critical support, including college faculty mentors who can aid novices in developing pedagogical and content knowledge. College fac-

ulty also embed their research in novice and K–12 students' learning, much the way Eileen does.

6. Little (1990b) introduced and defined the term "joint work" as "encounters among teachers that rest on shared responsibility for the work of teaching." We expand the notion of joint work to include mentor and novice sharing responsibility for and jointly engaging in the work of teaching, in this case planning.

7. The program also provided monthly seminars for new teachers planned and led by mentor teachers.

Sharon Feiman-Nemser is the Mandel Professor of Jewish Education at Brandeis University, with a joint appointment in the Near Eastern and Judaic Studies Department and the Education Program. She also directs the Mandel Center for Studies in Jewish Education, combining her expertise in teacher education with her deep interest in Jewish education. A coeditor of the third *Handbook of Research on Teacher Education* (2008), she has written extensively on teacher education, learning to teach, mentoring, and new teacher induction. Recent publications include *Transforming Teacher Education: Reflections from the Field* (2007), which she wrote with colleagues from Michigan State University, and *Teaching as a Moral Practice* (2010), which she coedited with colleagues on AACTE's Teacher Education as a Moral Community (TEAMC) committee.

Margret Buchmann was a professor and senior researcher at the Institute for Research on Teaching, College of Education, at Michigan State University, where she served on the faculty from 1982 to 1997. With degrees from Stanford University in philosophy of education, political science, and sociology, she published widely on topics ranging from relations of formal knowledge and experience to teaching and education, and presented her work in Europe as well as in the United States. Professor Buchmann served on the board of directors of the Institute for Research on Teaching, the John Dewey Society, and the Association for Philosophy of Education. She retired from academic life in 1997.

Patricia J. Norman is an associate professor in the education department at Trinity University in San Antonio, Texas. After earning her PhD at Michigan State University, where Sharon Feiman-Nemser served as her advisor, she came to Trinity to coordinate its Master of Arts in Teaching elementary teacher preparation program. As the clinical faculty member at one of Trinity's professional development schools, she works closely with graduate interns, their mentor teachers, and school faculty to create strong learning contexts for students, novices, and experienced teachers. Her research interests include field-based teacher education and mentor teacher development.